MACROMEDIA DREAMWEAVER MX MAGIC

By Angela C. Buraglia, Donna Casey, Josh Cavalier, Matthew David, Joyce J. Evans, Massimo Foti, Brad Halstead, Alwyn Joy, David C. Nicholls, Sean Nicholson, Linda Rathgeber, Daniel Short, Jason Cranford Teague, and Zac Van Note

With technical reviews by Chrissy Rey and Vernon Viehe

New Riders

201 West 103rd Street, Indianapolis, Indiana 46290

Dreamweaver MX Magic

International Standard Book Number: 0-7357-1179-8

Library of Congress Catalog Card Number: 2002107666

Printed in the United States of America

First Printing: August 2002

06 05 04 03 02 7 6 5 4 3 2

Interpretation of the printing code: The rightmost double-digit number is the year of the book's printing; the rightmost single-digit number is the number of the book's printing. For example, the printing code 02-1 shows that the first printing of the book occurred in 2002.

Trademarks

Warning and Disclaimer

Publisher
David Dwyer

Associate Publisher
Stephanie Wall

Production Manager
Gina Kanouse

Managing Editor
Kristy Knoop

Acquisitions Editors
Linda Anne Bump
Todd Zellers

Development Editor
Jennifer Eberhardt

Project Editor
Michael Thurston

Copy Editor
Kathy Murray

Product Marketing Manager
Tammy Detrich

Publicity Manager
Susan Nixon

Manufacturing Coordinator
Jim Conway

Cover Designer
Aren Howell

Interior Designer
Steve Gifford

Compositor
Scan Communications

Proofreader
Ben Lawson

Indexer
Larry Sweazy

CONTENTS AT A GLANCE

About the Authors

Angela C. Buraglia

After six years as an independent film makeup artist, Angela C. Buraglia realized she wanted a career that would allow her to start a family and stay home with her husband and child. In an effort to give back to the Macromedia Dreamweaver newsgroup community that helped and encouraged her in her new career, she founded DreamweaverFAQ.com. Although she intended only to be a web developer, life's path has led her to become that and more. In addition to her contribution to this book, Angela is the Lead Technical Editor for the *Dreamweaver MX Bible* (Wiley Publishing, formerly Hungry Minds) and Contributing Author to *ColdFusion MX Web Application Construction Kit* (Macromedia Press). Currently, she is also a Team Macromedia volunteer for Dreamweaver. Angela's future plans are to continue developing DreamweaverFAQ.com, to build and sell Dreamweaver extensions, to give presentations at conferences, and perhaps to become involved in new book projects. Long gone are the days of applying makeup; now Angela applies Behaviors and CSS to web sites—and most importantly—is home with her little boy.

Donna Casey

Donna is a designer, developer, and instructor with over eight years of experience working on web and CD-ROM based projects for corporations such as AirTouch Cellular, Macromedia, Palm Computing, Verizon Wireless, and Aeris.net. Donna is a painter/sculptor with a Fine Arts degree who brings real-world design and production expertise to teaching web design and development. Her web site (www.n8vision.com) was featured in the *Fireworks 3 Bible*. She has been a featured designer on Macromedia's web site as well as a speaker at Macromedia's EUCON (Paris) and WebBoston and CNETBuilder (New Orleans). As an experienced instructor, Donna also authored the Intermediate Dreamweaver 4 and Fireworks 4 Training CDs for Lynda.com and contributed to the *Fireworks F/X & Design* (Coriolis) book.

Josh Cavalier

Josh is the founder and director of Interactive Fun!, a digital media solutions and training firm. He has been in the print/multimedia/web design industry for over 10 years and has worked in various digital media fields including medical visualization, digital photography, and printing.

Prior to starting Interactive Fun!, Josh was Art Director for Handshaw, a computer-based training company. There he specialized in interface design, digital video, and print and audio production.

Josh has a BFA in Medical Illustration from the Rochester Institute of Technology. He has appeared in *People* magazine describing his method of historical digital photography. This method was used with a project for the Charlotte Museum of History to reconstruct the likeness of one of the city's founders, Hezekiah Alexander. Josh has been a featured speaker at leading industry conferences, including the National Association of Broadcasters (NAB 98 and 99), the Alternative Authorware Conference (1999, 2000, and 2001), and the North Carolina Information Highway Stakeholders Conference (2000).

Matthew David

Matthew's most recent publications include *Flash MX Magic, Inside Flash MX, Flash 5 Magic, Inside Dreamweaver 4, Flash 5: Visual FX, Web Publishing Bible*, and *The Dreamweaver Bible*.

Currently, Matthew is working on a *Flash MX Games* book and writes articles for Element K Journal's *Macromedia Solutions* magazine, *Inside Project*

Management, and *Multimedia: Solutions and Design* magazines. You also can see him popping up in many online magazines, such as Sitepoint.com, Windowatch.com, UDzone.com, and DevX.com.

Matthew is available as a freelance consultant. Examples of his work can be found at his web site (www.matthewdavid.ws) or you can email him directly at mdavid@email.com.

Joyce J. Evans

Joyce has over 10 years of experience in educational teaching, tutorial development, and web design. She has received Editors Choice Awards for her *Fireworks 4 f/x & Design* book and has authored numerous graphic design titles including *Dreamweaver MX Complete Course*. She also has contributed to several other books, such as *Fireworks Magic*, *Dreamweaver 4: The Complete Reference*, and the *Dreamweaver MX/Fireworks MX Savvy* book. Joyce actively writes reviews and articles for several graphic design magazines.

Massimo Foti

Massimo began using Dreamweaver on the very day the first beta was available, and he has used Dreamweaver ever since.

Massimo has been a prolific extension developer since the pioneering days of Dreamweaver 1. He is the creator of www.massimocorner.com and is a winner of the Macromedia Best Extension Developer award. His extensions are featured on the Macromedia Exchange for Dreamweaver and have been included in many books and magazines.

Massimo works at www.amila.ch developing database-driven web sites, using ColdFusion, PHP, and different kinds of databases.

Brad Halstead

Brad started out in the computer industry as a sales rep for a local company and moved up quickly to senior technician, where for several years he performed service contracts for companies such as IBM, PC Service Partners, Xerox, and Olivetti. In 1994, he became interested in web design and hasn't looked back since. Brad is very lucky and thankful for the support of his partner Brenda and children (Amanda, Aaron, and Megan) through his endeavors in this field.

Alwyn Joy

Alwyn currently heads the Animation and Web Technology Division of Whiz Networks Pvt., Ltd., a start-up company working on high-end animation and web applications. He strongly advocates the need for R&D using integration over multiple platforms and spends most of his time experimenting with new technology and understanding and expanding the possibilities. He currently is involved in creating content and providing solutions to India's biggest eLearning houses for various applications, including Dreamweaver, Flash, and 3ds max among others. When he isn't busy with all this, he enjoys making new friends on the net, coding games, and cooking. You can reach Alwyn at alwynjoy@yahoo.com.

David C. Nicholls

David is a web developer, physicist, writer, photographer, and a recognized authority on graphics compression software, antique golf clubs, and regional fern species. He is co-author of the book *Playing with Fire—Tapping the Power of Macromedia Firework 4* with Linda Rathgeber. He has contributed articles to numerous publications, including PC magazines, HiFi magazines,

Amateur Radio journals, computer instruction manuals, book reviews in newspaper literary columns, scientific journals, and government reports. David lives in Canberra, Australia with his wife, Trish, and assorted computers named Grunter, Darius, Perseus, and Wally. He can be reached at www.dcnicholls.com and www.home.aone.net.au/byzantium/.

Sean Nicholson

Sean is the Network Administrator and Web Developer for the Career Services Center at the University of Missouri (Kansas City). He and his development teams architect, develop, and manage foundation and backend execution for programs such as the CareerExec Employment Database (www.careerexec.com), UMKC Career Services Website (www.career.umkc.edu), and UMKC's Virtual Career Fair (www.umkc.edu/virtualfair). Sean also does private contract and consulting work on database and web development for organizations and individuals.

Sean's technical publications include *InsideUltraDev 4*, *Discover Excel 97*, and *Teach Yourself Outlook 98 in 24 Hours* and he has written several legal articles ranging in topics from Canadian water rights to the protection of historic artifacts lost at sea.

During his free time, Sean can be found traveling with his family, riding his motorcycle to biker events nationwide, or continuing development of his site at www.unitedbikers.com, with the hopes of building one of the largest motorcycle-related sites on the web.

Linda Rathgeber

Linda is a writer, web developer, and Macromedia Team member who coaches newcomers in the use of Macromedia's Dreamweaver and Fireworks programs. She's a former associate editor, and senior layout and graphic artist for the *Holistic Resource* magazine, and a contributing writer to such diverse publications as *Woman's World* and *Dream Quarterly International*. Since turning freelance, her graphic work has been featured by the independent film company King Pictures, in book ads for author Bill Stott, in the Fireworks 4 and Fireworks MX sample files, and on the companion CD-ROM's of Joseph Lowery's *Fireworks 3 & 4 Bibles*.

Recent writing credits include chapters of the *Dreamweaver 4 Magic* book, and with her favorite co-author David Nicholls, *Playing with Fire: Tapping the Power of Macromedia Fireworks 4*.

Linda lives in Sumter, SC with a monitor pet named Missy and a reliable but aging Dell PC. She can be reached at www.playingwithfire.com.

Daniel Short

Daniel never planned to be a web designer; it just happened. He started out in the Army tearing apart computers and eventually began putting together web sites. Dan is a devoted Macromedian (and Team Macromedia Volunteer) and uses almost the entire Macromedia Web Design Suite, including Fireworks and Macromedia Flash. He's been doing the web gig since the end of 1998 and has had great luck building his web design business through Web Shorts Site Design. Dan helps to maintain several HTML and Dreamweaver reference sites including www.dwfaq.com, for which he created the style changer and all ASP functionality, including the Snippets Exchange. He's also written articles for several resource sites, including AListApart.com, run by Jeffrey Zeldman, and Spider Food.net, run by J.K. Bowman. Daniel also is a contributing author for the dynamic chapters in the *Dreamweaver MX Bible* (Wiley).

Jason Cranford Teague

Jason Cranford Teague is an author, instructor, and designer who specializes in user interface design and multimedia. He has written on a variety of computer-related topics for the Apple Developers Center, Adobe, C|Net, Tripod, and *The Independent*, as well as several best-selling computer design books including *DHTML for the World Wide Web* and *Final Cut Pro 3 and The Art of Filmmaking*. Jason has taught classes and seminars in web-related topics around the U.S., Canada, and the U.K. In 1999, Jason started his own digital consulting service, webbedENVIRONMENTS, which specializes in interface design and video for the web. Check out the web site at www.webbedenvironments.com.

Zac Van Note

Zac earned a BFA degree in graphic design at New Mexico State University. In the years before college, he wrote, drew, and published comic books. In the years since college, he's worked as a graphic designer for two large jewelry wholesalers, creating catalogs, web sites, and hundreds of other marketing materials.

Since 1998, Zac has taught dozens of classes at the University of New Mexico and Santa Fe Community College, including Photoshop, QuarkXPress, Digital Prepress, and of course Dreamweaver. He was recently recognized with an Outstanding Instructor award at UNM. The site he created for his students, www.design-link.org, is a good reference for anyone interested in design and computer graphics.

Between working full-time, teaching, and a steady stream of freelance clients, Zac has somehow found time to have a family, which includes his wife Lori, daughter Samantha, and new son, Bryce. Because he's always busy with his family or working on other people's projects, he still hasn't completed his own company's site, www.stealthstudios.com, but stay tuned!

About the Tech Editors

Chrissy Rey

Chrissy is the Vice President of Education and a Senior Developer at digitalorganism®. She also is the founder and webmaster of FlashLite and founder of the Baltimore Macromedia Organization (BAMMO). A Maryland native, Chrissy graduated from the University of Maryland with a degree in Zoology (of all things). After a brief stint first as a zookeeper and then as an animal technician in a genetics lab, Chrissy discovered Flash and Generator. At digitalorganism, she uses her experience to lead internal, private, and public education efforts. She also leads digitalorganism's development efforts by capitalizing on her extensive array of knowledge.

Vernon Viehe

Vernon started his career in the computer industry in 1989 in Birmingham, Alabama, by contracting desktop publishing, consulting, and support. While in Birmingham, he served as the technical director of an electronic arts center for seven years. Vernon has worked at the San Francisco headquarters of Macromedia for the last several years, serving in various roles, including Dreamweaver Technical Support Lead, and most recently, as a Community Manager. Vernon has remained active in the Dreamweaver community by serving as consultant and tech editor for books and course materials featuring Dreamweaver and other Macromedia products.

Vernon lives in San Francisco with his orange tabby manx (Toonces) and shares his desk at Macromedia with a goldfish (Miss Fish).

A Message from New Riders

As the reader of this book, you are our most important critic and commentator. We value your opinion and want to know what we're doing right, what we could do better, in what areas you'd like to see us publish, and any other words of wisdom you're willing to pass our way.

As Associate Publisher for New Riders, I welcome your comments. You can fax, email, or write me directly to let me know what you did or didn't like about this book—as well as what we can do to make our books better. When you write, please be sure to include this book's title, ISBN, and author, as well as your name and phone or fax number. I will carefully review your comments and share them with the authors and editors who worked on the book.

Please note that I cannot help you with technical problems related to the topic of this book, and that due to the high volume of email I receive, I might not be able to reply to every message. Thanks.

Fax	317-581-4663
Email:	stephanie.wall@newriders.com
Mail:	Stephanie Wall Associate Publisher New Riders Publishing 201 West 103rd Street Indianapolis, IN 46290 USA

Visit Our Web Site: www.newriders.com

On our web site, you'll find information about our other books, the authors we partner with, book updates and file downloads, promotions, discussion boards for online interaction with other users and with technology experts, and a calendar of trade shows and other professional events with which we'll be involved. We hope to see you around.

Email Us from Our Web Site

Go to www.newriders.com and click on the Contact Us link if you . . .

- Have comments or questions about this book.
- Want to report errors that you have found in this book.
- Have a book proposal or are interested in writing for New Riders.
- Would like us to send you one of our author kits.
- Are an expert in a computer topic or technology and are interested in being a reviewer or technical editor.
- Want to find a distributor for our titles in your area.
- Are an educator/instructor who wants to preview New Riders books for classroom use. In the body/comments area, include your name, school, department, address, phone number, office days/hours, text currently in use, and enrollment in your department, along with your request for either desk/examination copies or additional information.

INTRODUCTION

Before we begin, let's take a moment and reflect on the "good old days" we spent building web pages. You remember, don't you? The days (and long nights) sitting with nothing more than a text editor and a sheet filled with HTML tags, trying to figure out how column spans would affect your page layout or why on Earth your nested tables weren't functioning properly? Ah, the good old days!

Fortunately, we can step back into the present and be happy that those days are pretty much gone for good! Today's web authoring applications offer a much more visual way of creating sites by combining the power of "WYSIWYG" (what you see is what you get) page layout with the easy-to-use button bars and dropdown menus found in most typical word processors.

Among the variety of web authoring tools on the market today, one application, Macromedia Dreamweaver, has consistently led the industry by combining ease-of-use and powerful functionality. With the new release of Dreamweaver MX, Macromedia again has set the standard by combining both Dreamweaver 4 and Dreamweaver UltraDev 4 into a single application and adding a variety of new features. From the design workflow between Dreamweaver MX and Fireworks MX to the ability to build dynamic sites on platforms including ASP, JSP, ColdFusion, and now PHP, Dreamweaver MX offers every web developer the ability to create powerful, interactive sites without spending endless nights writing code.

Who We Are

To demonstrate the types of web applications that can be developed using Dreamweaver MX, 14 authors from different development backgrounds combined their efforts to create the projects in this book. Each author brings a unique style and specialized experience to show you how to master one of Dreamweaver MX's features or implement a set of tools to add functionality to a site.

One of the biggest benefits of a book written in this manner is that you, the reader, get to experience a wide variety of approaches on how to use Dreamweaver MX. For instance, some authors might use the Page Layout view while others prefer the split Layout/Code view so they can monitor the code that is being created. In both cases, you get to experience the way each author uses Dreamweaver MX and eventually choose a style that fits your own needs.

Who You Are

Have you ever heard someone say, "Wouldn't it be great if we could add this to our web site?" Or maybe you've heard this: "We need to implement this feature ASAP." If these phrases (or the plethora of expressions out there just like them) are familiar to you, you're going to love this book.

Each project is designed to show you how to develop and implement a solution that easily can be modified for your web site. Throughout the projects, the authors include tips, hints, and warnings that help you speed up the development process and avoid potential setbacks.

If you already understand the basics of web design and are ready to expand your skills to include some of Dreamweaver MX's intermediate-to-advanced features, grab a cup of coffee, turn your computer on, and get ready to see just how quickly you can boost your skills.

What's in This Book

The projects in this book cover a wide range of topics that demonstrate how you can speed up the design process, add functionality to your pages, and even allow your site to communicate with a database. If you want to concentrate on the design and implementation process, you'll be interested in the projects that focus on the effective use of Dreamweaver MX templates, cascading style sheets, and project management techniques. Or maybe you are interested in making your site easier for your visitors to navigate. Projects demonstrating the use of crumb trails or adding search capabilities can assist you in that aspect. Other projects give you all the tools you need to take your site beyond its current static state by showing you how to connect to a database, add dynamic data, and even create password-protected pages.

The best thing about a project-oriented book like this is the fact that you can pick the project that interests you most and start there. If you are interested in cascading style sheets, jump back to Project 5, "Giving Your Pages Some Style." If usernames and passwords are your project for the day, just open Project 12, "Database-Driven Username and Password Validation," and you're on your way. Each project shows you how to use a feature or add functionality to a site without relying on the previous chapters.

Our Assumptions as We Wrote This Book

As we constructed the projects in this book, we assumed that you are comfortable with the basics of web design. If you don't already have an understanding of elements such as page layout, tables, forms, and basic formatting, it might be a good idea to build those skills before you start working through the projects covered here.

We assumed also that you are familiar with Dreamweaver or another web authoring application such as Adobe GoLive, NetObjects Fusion, or Microsoft FrontPage 2002. If you have used one of these other applications and are new to Dreamweaver MX, it would be a good idea to walk through the tour and tutorials included with Dreamweaver in order to familiarize yourself with the panels and menus.

The final assumption here is that you are seeking step-by-step instructions on how to master certain Dreamweaver MX features or implement a specific solution. Although each author provides as much detail as possible regarding the features used in each project, this book is not meant to discuss every individual aspect of Dreamweaver MX.

Conventions Used in This Book

Every computer book has its own style of presenting information. As you flip through this book, you'll notice that we have an interesting layout going on here. Because we know most of you are really into graphics, the project openers contain way-cool eye candy. The real meat of each project starts on the next page. Take a look:

In the left column, you'll find step-by-step instructions for completing the project, as well as succinct but extremely valuable explanations. The text beside the number contains the action you must perform. In many cases, the action text is followed by a paragraph that contains contextual information.

Note that if you want to perform the steps quickly and without any background info, you need read only the text next to the step numbers.

In the corresponding columns to the right, you'll find screen captions (and/or code) illustrating the steps. You'll also find Notes and Tips, which provide you with additional contextual information or customization techniques.

At the end of each project, you'll find unique customization information. Each *Magic* project is designed to be highly customizable; therefore, we provide many tips and examples of what you can do with the techniques you've learned so that you can apply them to your own work quickly and easily.

"The secret to creativity is knowing how to hide your sources."

—ALBERT EINSTEIN

DREAMWEAVER MX/ FIREWORKS MX WEB DESIGN WORKFLOW

Dreamweaver MX Web Workflow

In this project, you look at the close relationship between Macromedia Dreamweaver MX and Macromedia Fireworks MX in the web design process. Having a solid understanding of these techniques will save you hours in the prototype, development, and maintenance stages of a web site. We love teaching this in class—it gets the most "Ah-ha!"s.

Project 1

Dreamweaver MX/ Fireworks MX Web Design Workflow

by Josh Cavalier

This is the initial layout for the Doggie Diner web site. You can see that it needs some work.

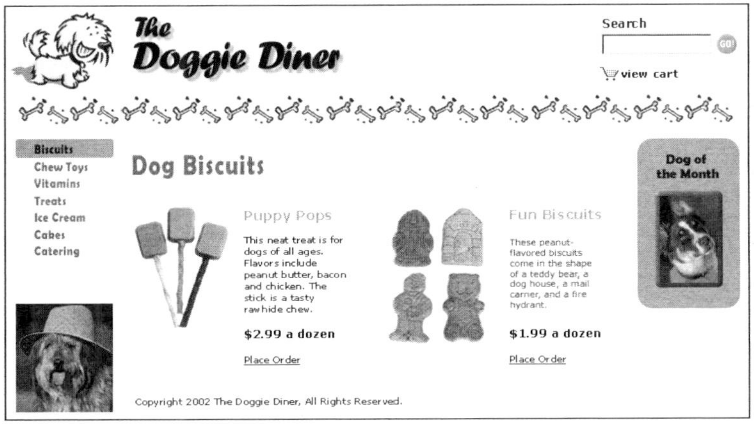

Here's the completed layout.

It Works Like This

Dreamweaver MX and Fireworks MX work together to allow design changes without affecting HTML or other important code structures like JavaScript or ColdFusion. This process is essential for making timely edits to your layout without disrupting work that has been completed in Dreamweaver MX.

For this project, you start with a simple layout of the Doggie Diner web site in Fireworks MX. You then import into Dreamweaver MX the HTML and images. Next you insert a few product descriptions from a text file and then return to Fireworks MX to change the location of the artwork and import new product pictures. After you finish the graphic changes, you'll jump back into Dreamweaver MX.

Preparing to Work

I'm sure you have already guessed that you'll need Fireworks MX for this project. If you need the software, you can install a free trial from the Software folder on the accompanying CD. After you have Fireworks MX in place, copy a project folder from the CD to your hard drive, and then define a new site in Dreamweaver MX.

1. Copy the project folder:
   - Browse to the Projects folder on the CD.
   - Copy the 01_integration folder to a convenient location on your hard drive. Rename the folder **project_one.**
2. Define a new Dreamweaver site using the **project_one** copy as your local root folder:
   - Open the Site menu and choose New Site.
3. Input your Local Info:
   - Type **project_one** as your Site Name.
   - Select the project_one folder on your hard drive.
   - Select the images folder in your project_one site as the Default Images Folder.
   - Click OK. Click OK to create the site cache if you are prompted to do so.

   You don't need to fill in additional site categories, such as Remote Info or Application Server, to complete this project successfully.

Note: If you are new to Dreamweaver MX and you are looking to fast-track your site setup, you may want to try the new Site Definition wizard. Select the Basics tab in the Site Definition dialog box to access this feature.

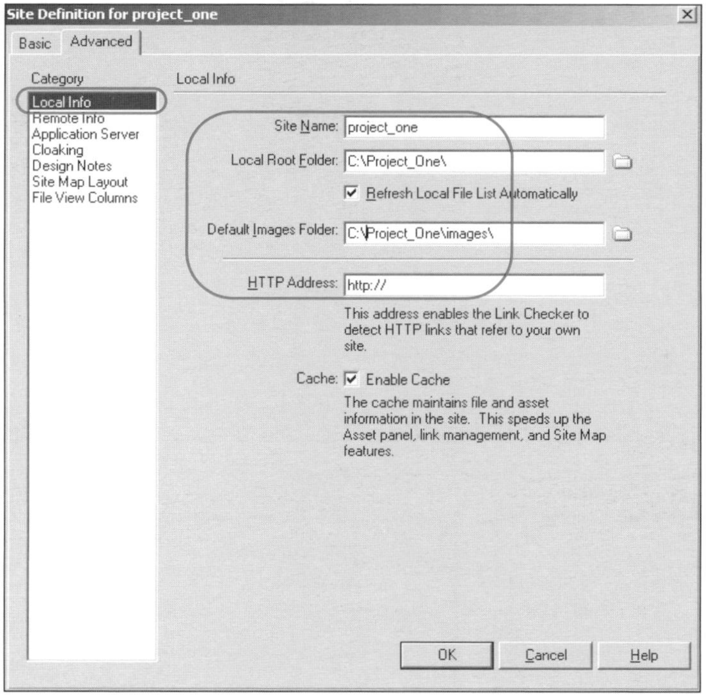

Enter your site information. Only the Local Info is needed for this project.

Setting External Editor Preference

To use Dreamweaver and Fireworks together effectively, you need to set a preference in Dreamweaver MX that selects Fireworks MX as the primary image editor. After you select this option, the ability to exchange code between tools (roundtrip HTML) becomes seamless.

1 Select the Edit menu.

2 Choose Preferences.

3 Set these options in the Preferences Dialog box:

- Choose File Types/Editors in the Category column.
- Click on .jpg .jpe .jpeg in the Extensions list on the left.
- Select Fireworks in the Editors list if it is not already selected.

  If Fireworks is not listed in the Editors list, click the plus (+) button, find the Fireworks application on your local drive, and click Open.
- Click the Make Primary button.
- Repeat the same steps for GIF and PNG file types.

Each time you edit any of these file types in Dreamweaver, Fireworks will launch and allow you to either edit the original PNG file or the exported GIF or JPEG.

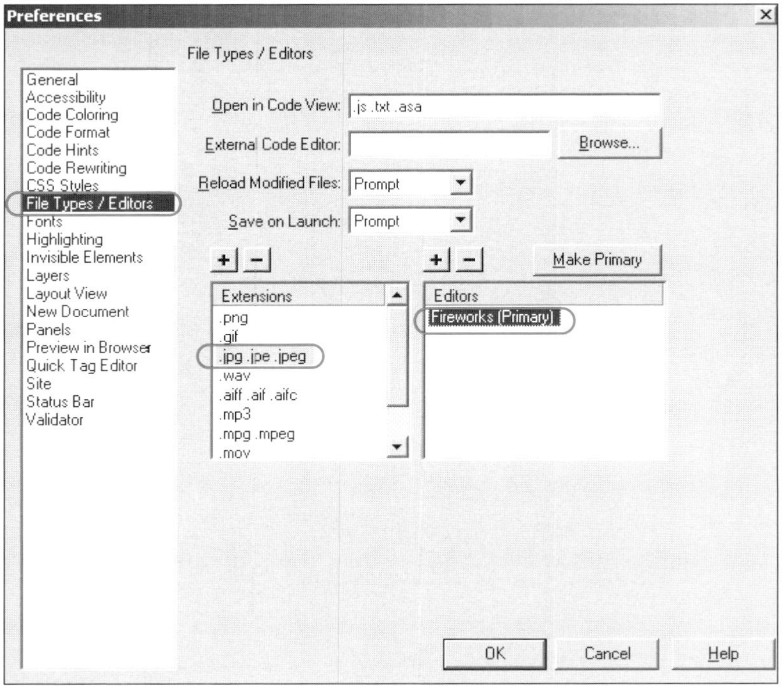

Setting these preferences allows you to use Fireworks MX as the primary graphics editor.

Setting Launch-and-Edit Preferences

You set preferences in Fireworks MX to handle source PNG files when you are editing artwork from Dreamweaver MX. Even though you will be working with a table in this project, it is still a good idea to set this up before using the applications together.

1 In Fireworks, select the Edit menu.

2 Choose Preferences.

3 Set these options in the Preferences Dialog box:

- Choose the Launch and Edit tab.
- Select these options:

  When Editing from External Application: Always Use Source PNG

  When Optimizing from External Application: Always Use Source PNG

- Click OK.

These settings will be used when your artwork originates from Fireworks PNG files. If you are using another graphics editor, or if no source PNG documents are available for some artwork, leave the default preferences in place (Ask When Launching).

Launch-and-Edit Options

When you attempt to edit or optimize a JPEG or GIF file from Dreamweaver MX, Fireworks looks for a Design Note path to the source PNG file. If the program can't find the original image, and that image is not part of a Fireworks table, it will handle the artwork in one of three ways:

- Always Use Source PNG: This option opens the Fireworks PNG file that is describe in the Design Note. Changes are made to both the PNG file and the associated JPEG or GIF image.
- Never Use Source PNG: This option opens Fireworks with the placed image, ignoring any source PNG file. Changes affect the placed image only.
- Ask When Launching: When you choose this option, you make the choice each time whether to use the source PNG file. Fireworks will display a message asking you to make a launch-and-edit decision. At this point, you also can choose a global launch-and-edit preference.

Exporting from Fireworks MX

Start by opening a Fireworks MX document and exporting both the HTML and graphic files. The layers and slices have already been completed, so all you need to do is get this layout into Dreamweaver. The Fireworks document 01_layout_start.png is in the assets folder of the working project site that you have defined.

Note: Click the Show slices and hotspots icon on the toolbar to reveal the existing slices. This shows you the table structure Fireworks will use when exporting.

1 Within Fireworks, open the file 01_layout_start.png in the assets folder of your project_one defined site.

2 Export Artwork and HTML to Dreamweaver:

- Click the Quick Export icon.
- Select Dreamweaver.
- Select Export HTML.

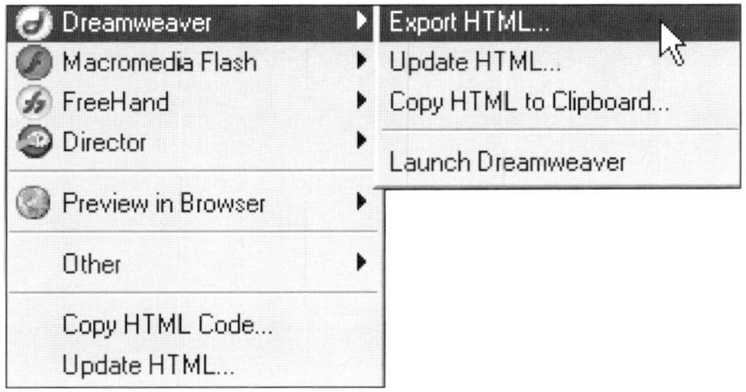

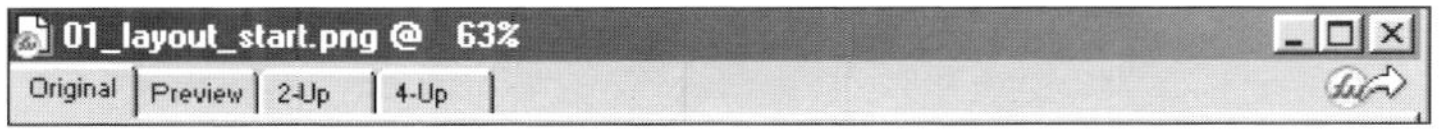

Select the Quick Export icon to view your output choices.

3 Fill in the Export dialog box:

- Save your HTML in the project_one folder.
- Enter the following options:

  File name: **start.htm**

  Save as type: **HTML and Images**

  HTML: **Export HTML File**

  Slices: **Export Slices**

  Include Area without Slices: **Checked**

  Put Images in Subfolder: **Checked**

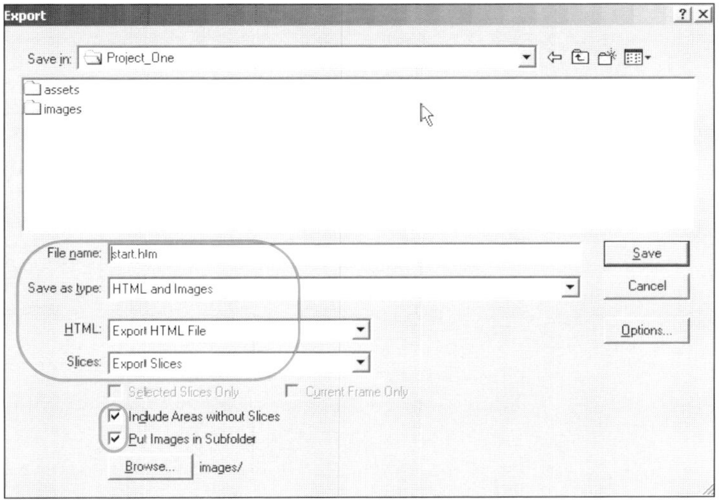

Fill in the options for the Export dialog box. Fireworks finds the images directory for you if one exists in the location you are saving the HTML file.

- Fireworks automatically finds the images directory for you. The images directory must exist in the same directory as your exported HTML file for this to work.
- Click the Save button.
- Save and close the file 01_layout_start.png.

Fireworks MX now exports an HTML file that you will import into Dreawmweaver MX. The default HTML export settings are set for Dreamweaver MX formatting, which means that you don't need to make any changes to the HTML format options. Also, the graphics are automatically being sliced, formatted, and placed into the images directory. Very efficient!

Note: You could change the optimization settings of graphics by selecting individual slices and making modifications within the Optimize panel. This allows you to export both JPEG and GIF images from the same layout. For instance, the Doggie Diner logo with flat color would be set as a GIF image, while the dog photo would be a JPEG.

Importing Fireworks MX HTML into Dreamweaver MX

During this process, you have the option to keep the original HTML or have Dreamweaver delete it and save a new document. In this exercise, you'll be deleting the original file, but it's really up to you how you want to handle this. A majority of the time, you will delete the Fireworks HTML to keep your files organized and limit the possible confusion between two similar-looking pages.

1 Open Dreamweaver MX and create a new file:

- Open the File menu and select New.

Note: XHTML is based on the XML language and is planned to eventually replace HTML. By implementing XHTML, you guarantee future compatibility of your documents in both web browsers and the latest Internet devices.

- Select the following:

  Category: **Basic Page**

  Basic Page: **HTML**

  Make Document XHTML Compliant: **Checked**

- Click the Create button.

2 Save the new file as index.htm in the root of your project_one defined site.

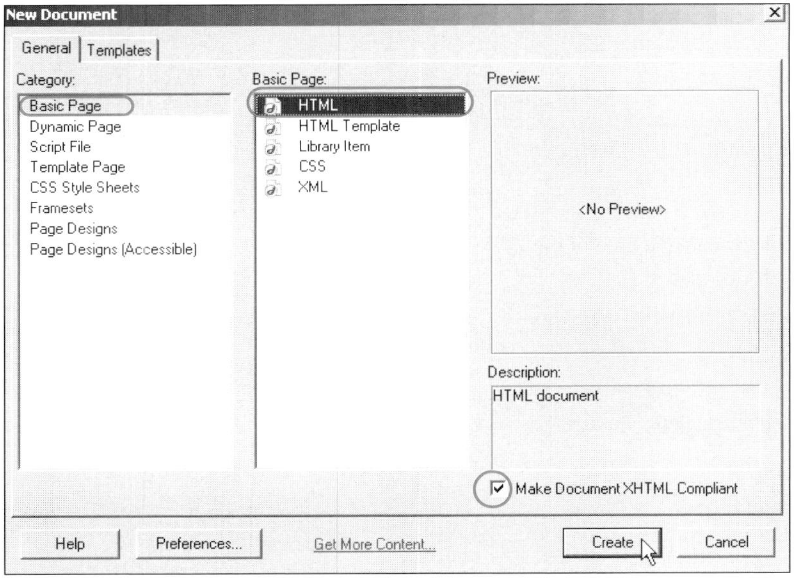

Set up a new HTML document in Dreamweaver MX.

3 Title your HTML file The Doggie Diner.

4 Import your Fireworks HTML file:

- Select the Fireworks HTML icon from the Common Object Panel.

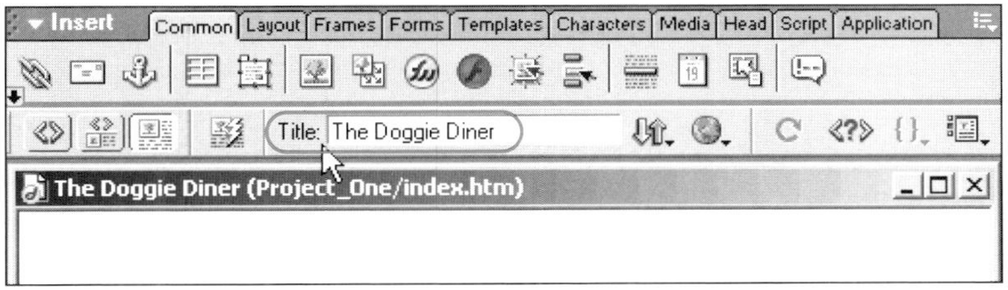

You can set your title by typing directly in the Title text field.

Tip: Another way to import is to select Insert>Interactive Images>Fireworks HTML.

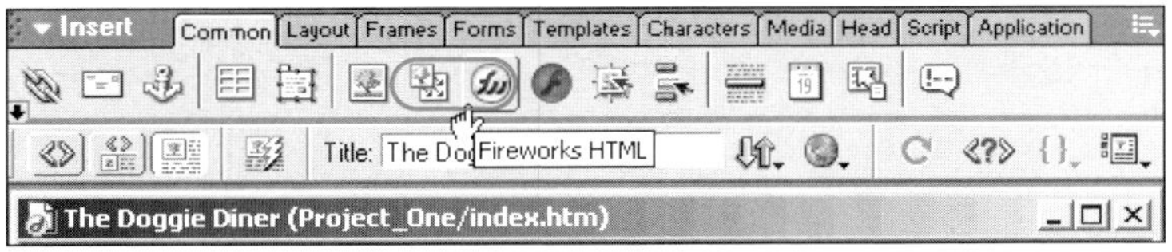

Click the Fireworks HTML icon. The Common Objects toolbar is in a new location in Dreamweaver MX.

- Click the Browse button to find start.htm in the root of your project_one site.
- Select start.htm; then click the Open button.
- Select the option to Delete file after insertion and click OK.

Your Fireworks layout now appears in the index.htm file. Select the Fireworks HTML table by clicking the outside edge with your cursor. This selection will be indicated by a thick black line. The Property inspector now shows a Fireworks table as the current selection and the source of the original PNG file.

Examine the structure of the table by clicking each of the individual graphics on the page. If you look at the Property inspector, you can see that Dreamweaver recognizes each of the images as being created by Fireworks. Graphic files from Fireworks will either be automatically named or will use the name of its associated slice. Take a look in the images directory located in the project_one site root to view all the exported images from Fireworks.

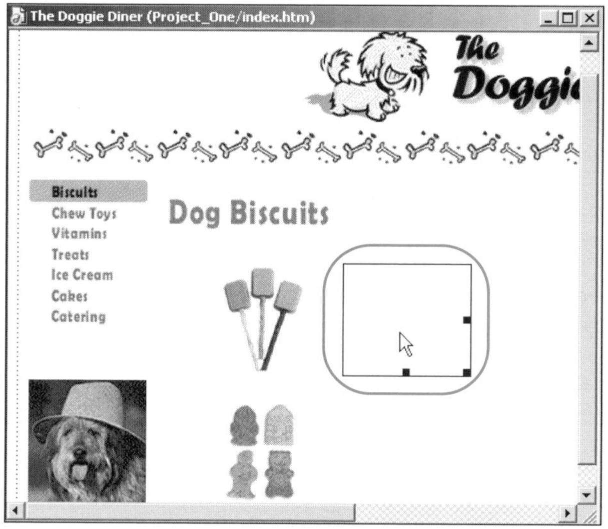

Select the different pieces of artwork in your table to see the underlying structure.

Adding Content to the Page

Once you have the Fireworks HTML table in Dreamweaver, you can remove individual graphics and replace them with HTML text, dynamic data content, or Flash animation.

In this example, you add text to your layout that describes the two biscuit products. This will be coming from a plain text (.txt) file.

1 Remove existing artwork and format table cells:

- Select the graphic Product_1_Text.gif.
- Remove the graphic by pressing the Delete key.
- In the Property inspector, set the Horizontal Alignment of the cell contents to Left and the Vertical Alignment to Top.
- Repeat the same steps for Product_2_Text.gif.

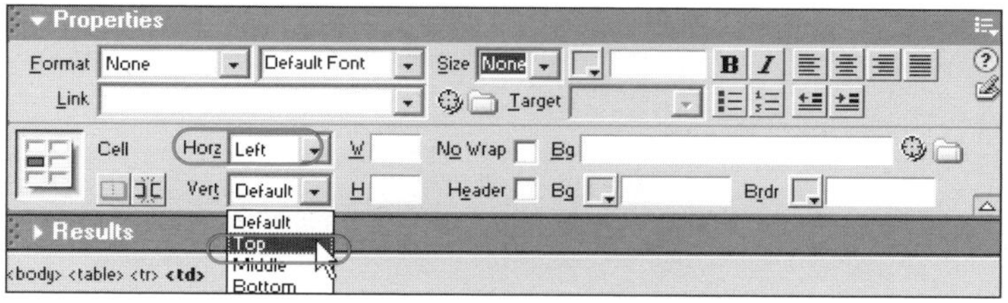

The Property inspector contains attributes for the selected table cell.

Note: You can find the name of a selected graphic by looking at the SRC attribute in the Property inspector.

2 Open the existing text document:

- Select the File menu.
- Open the text file 01_products.txt in the assets folder.

3 Copy and paste the description for Puppy Pops into the open table cell to the right of Product_1.gif.

4 Copy and paste the description for Fun Biscuits into the open table cell to the right of Product_2.gif.

Note: The Fireworks table will stretch vertically at this point. By the time you format the text and update your layout, things will look normal again.

5 Close the text file 01_products.txt.

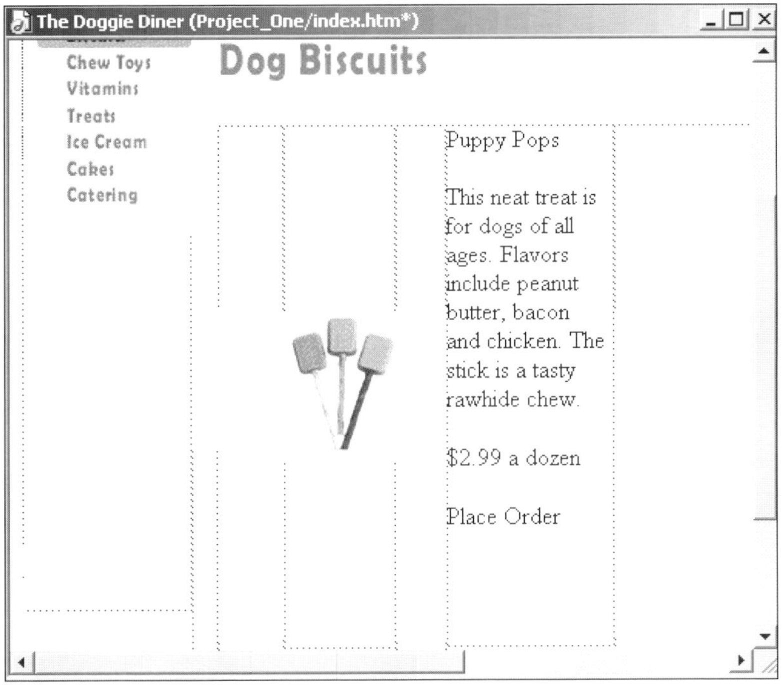

Pasting the text into the layout will stretch the table. This will be corrected later in Fireworks.

6 Format the Puppy Pops text:

- Select the text Puppy Pops in your index.htm file.
- Enter the following text attributes in the Property inspector:

Format: **Heading 4**

Font: **Verdana, Arial, Helvetica, sans-serif**

Text Color: **#C0A63D**

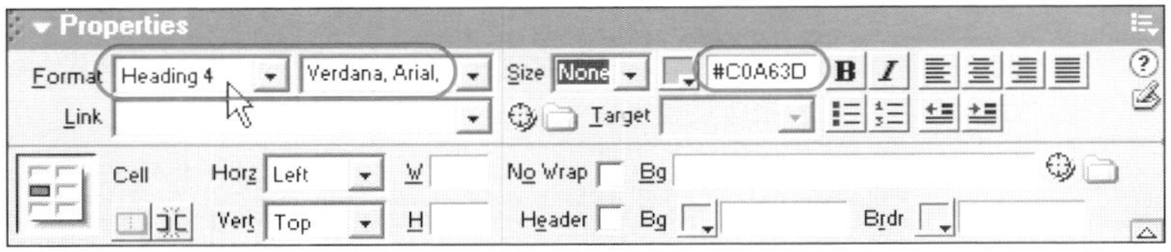

Input your text attributes in the Property inspector.

Tip: When you enter values in the Property inspector, you need to press Tab or Enter to finalize the change.

- Select the Puppy Pops product description and enter the following text attributes:

  Format: **Paragraph**

  Font: **Verdana, Arial, Helvetica, sans-serif**

  Size: **1**

- Select the Puppy Pops price and enter the following text attributes:

  Format: **Paragraph**

  Font: **Verdana, Arial, Helvetica, sans-serif**

  Size: **2**

  Text Style: **Bold**

- Select the Place Order text and enter the following text attributes:

  Format: **Paragraph**

  Font: **Verdana, Arial, Helvetica, sans-serif**

  Size: **2**

  Link: **order.htm**

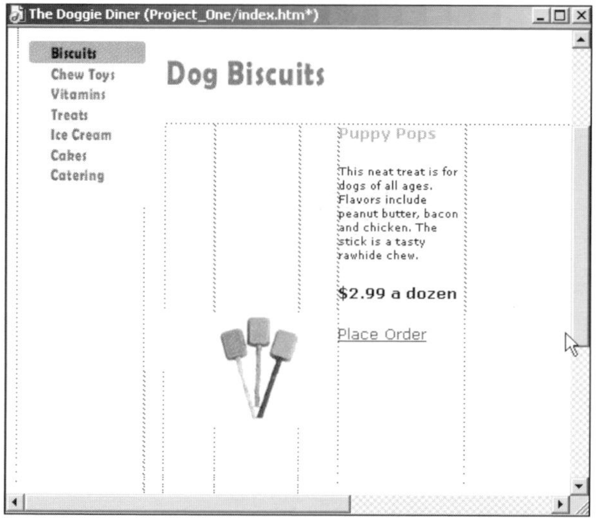

Your formatted text should look like this.

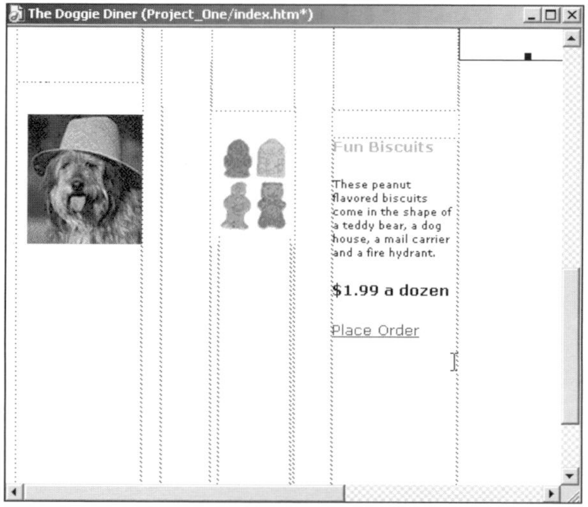

Here's the formatted text for the Fun Biscuits product.

7 Format the Fun Biscuits text:

- Select the text Fun Biscuits in your index.htm file and enter the following text attributes in the Property inspector:

  Format: **Heading 4**

  Font: **Verdana, Arial, Helvetica, sans-serif**

  Text Color: **#C0A63D**

- Select the Fun Biscuits product description and enter the following text attributes:

  Format: **Paragraph**

  Font: **Verdana, Arial, Helvetica, sans-serif**

  Size: **1**

- Select the Fun Biscuits price and enter the following text attributes:

  Format: **Paragraph**

  Font: **Verdana, Arial, Helvetica, sans-serif**

  Size: **2**

  Text Style: **Bold**

- Select the Place Order text and enter the following text attributes:

  Format: **Paragraph**

  Font: **Verdana, Arial, Helvetica, sans-serif**

  Size: **2**

  Link: **order.htm**

Your web design now has the Fireworks MX table and the new HTML content. This new content will remain intact as you bring your layout back into the Fireworks MX application for updates. Fireworks will leave your new HTML content alone, formatting and all, as you begin to make changes to the design in Fireworks MX.

Note: For simplicity of this project you are applying localized formatting of text. Even though this looks just fine, you should consider using Cascading Style Sheets when setting up global text and page formatting. It's fast becoming a standard for web page design.

Updating the Layout in Fireworks

During the web design process, it's inevitable that there will be changes to layout, text, images, etc. As you continue to add content to your layout in Dreamweaver, you have the ability to select your Fireworks table and return to the original PNG file for edits.

1 Be sure that your cursor is still in the text for Fun Biscuits. Select the Fireworks table by clicking the <table> tag in the tag selector.

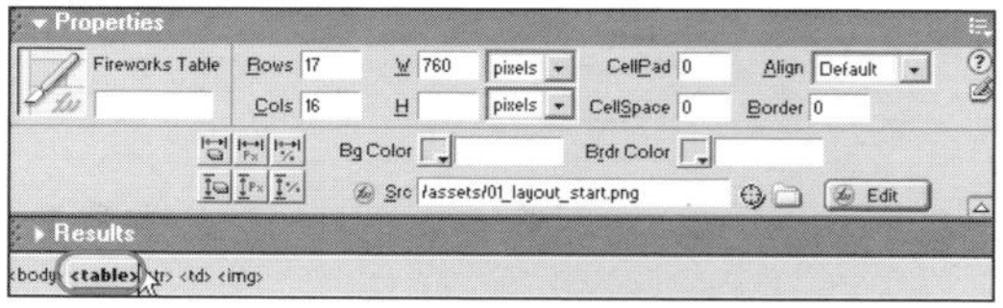

The tag selector is located at the far bottom left of the Dreamweaver MX interface. After the table is selected, click the Fireworks Edit button.

2 Click the Fireworks Edit button in the Property inspector.

Fireworks MX automatically opens 01_layout_start.png to begin layout edits. Notice that an indicator on the top left of the document window displays Editing from Dreamweaver. The product text slices now contain HTML code inside the slice area. This allows you to move the text without disrupting the integrity of the HTML code.

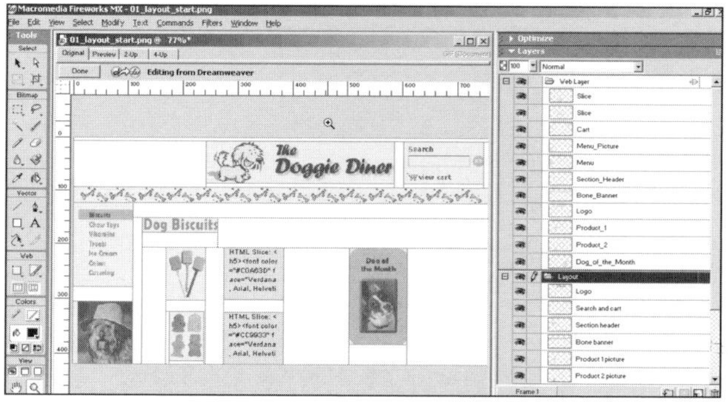

You can see the Editing from Dreamweaver icon in the top-left corner of the Fireworks Document window.

3 In Fireworks, open the file 01_layout_final.png. This is what you want the final layout to look like. The page might include fonts that are not installed on your computer. If a dialog box opens stating that fonts used on the page are not available, choose the Maintain Appearance option.

4 Switch back to the 01_layout_start.png file.

5 Move the Doggie Diner logo:

- Select both the Logo slice and the Logo artwork by holding the Shift key and selecting each item in the Layers panel.
- Change the X coordinate to 5 in the Property inspector.

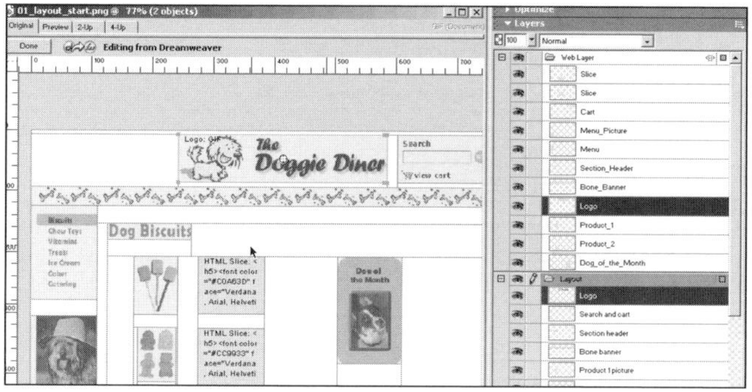

Select both the Logo slice and Logo layer before moving them.

> **Note:** A *slice* is a separate web object that defines a graphic's boundary, its optimization settings, JavaScript behaviors, and any link information. Slices reside in a special layer called the *Web Layer*.

6 Move the Dog of the Month graphic:

- Select both the Dog_of_the_Month slice and the Dog of the month artwork by pressing and holding the Shift key and selecting each Dog_of_the_month in the Layers panel.
- Enter the following attributes in the Property inspector:

  X: **646**

  Y: **138**

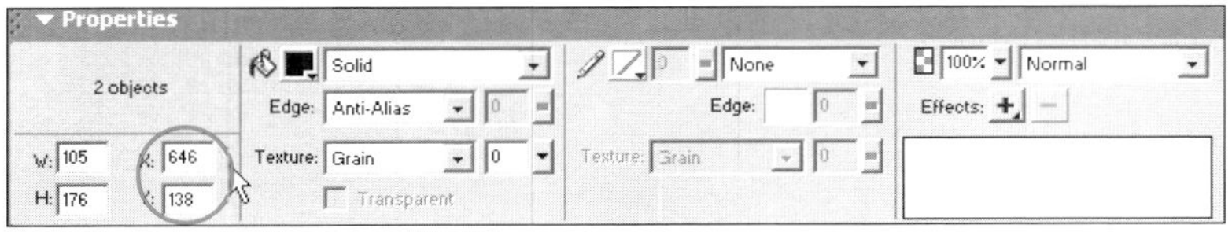

Use the Property inspector to change the X and Y position of your artwork.

7 Delete old product artwork:

- Select the following items in the Layers panel and delete them:

  Product_1 slice

  Product_2 slice

  Product 1 picture

  Product 2 picture

8 Import the Product 1 artwork and add a slice:

- Select the File menu.
- Import 01_product1.png located in the assets folder.
- Place the image anywhere on the page by clicking with the import cursor.
- Enter the following attributes in the Property inspector:

  X: **127**

  Y: **200**

- Right-click the Product 1 picture graphic.
- Select Insert Slice from the pop-up menu.
- Rename the new slice **Product_1** in the Layer panel.

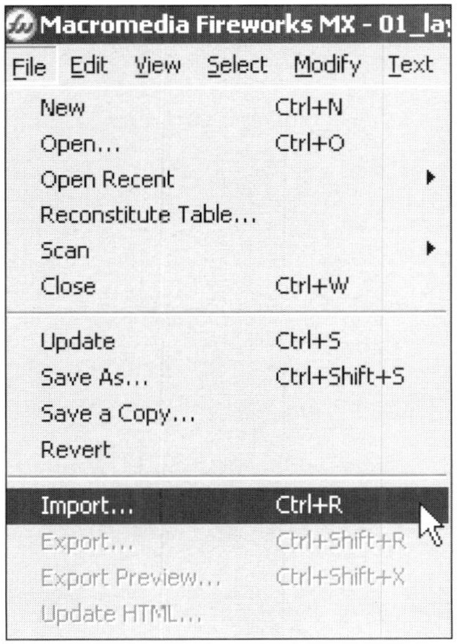

Choose File>Import to bring in the new product images.

9 Import the Product 2 artwork and add a slice:

- Select the File menu.
- Import 01_product2.png located in the assets folder.
- Place the image anywhere on the page by clicking with the import cursor.
- Enter the following attributes in the Property inspector:

  X: **391**

  Y: **207**
- Right-click the Product 2 picture graphic.
- Select Insert Slice from the pop-up menu.
- Rename the new slice **Product_2** in the Layer panel.

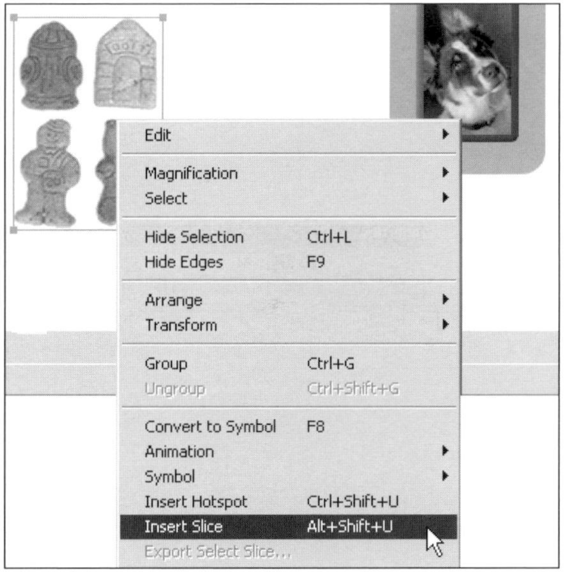

Right-click the Product 2 graphic to reveal the contextual menu.

10 Adjust the product description areas:

- Select the Product_1_Text slice.
- Enter these attributes in the Property inspector:

  W: **114**

  H: **194**

  X: **239**

  Y: **206**
- Select the Product_2_Text slice.
- Enter these attributes in the Property inspector:

  W: **114**

  H: **194**

  X: **511**

  Y: **206**

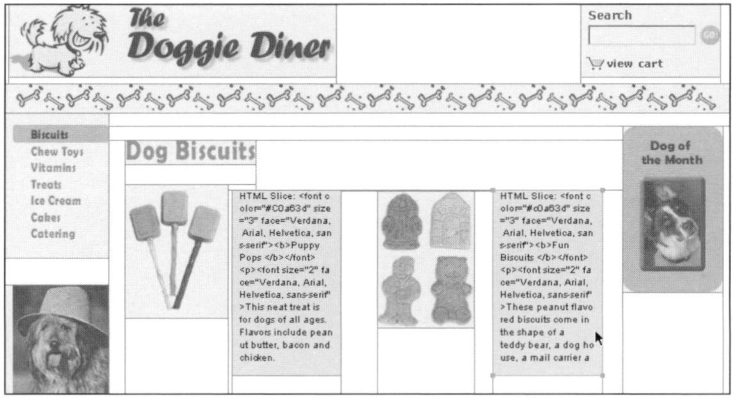

You can move the product descriptions around without affecting the Dreamweaver code. Way cool!

11 Add the copyright line:

- Click the Text tool in the tools palette.
- Enter the following text attributes in the Property inspector:

  Font: **Verdana**

  Font Size: **10**

  Anti-Alias: **No Anti-Alias**

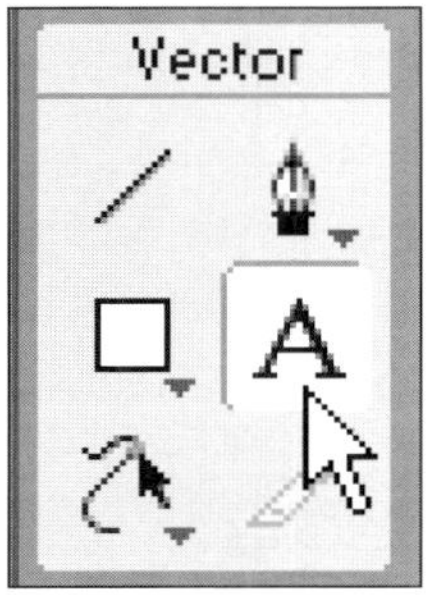

Select the Text tool to add the copyright text.

- Click anywhere on the layout and enter the following: **Copyright 2002 The Doggie Diner, All Rights Reserved.** (You'll move the text where you want it to appear.)
- If the text box is not already selected, use the Pointer tool to select it.

Click the Done button to return to Dreamweaver MX.

- Enter the following attributes in the Property inspector:

  X: **646**

  Y: **138**

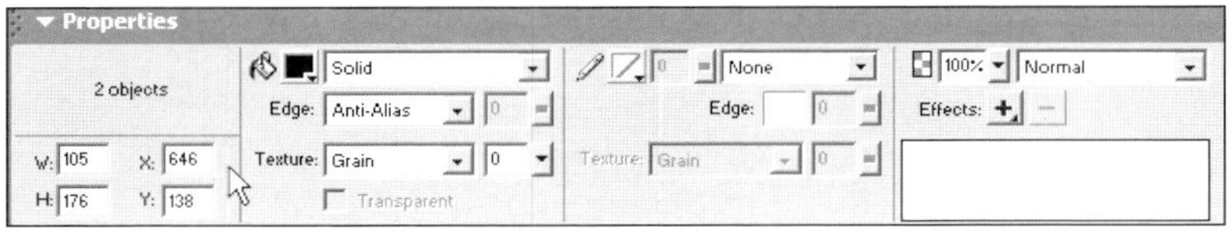

Use the Property inspector to change the X and Y position of your artwork.

When you jump from Dreamweaver MX to edit your table, all the features of Fireworks MX are available to you. This includes the repositioning, scaling, and importing of artwork. You can complete any graphic edits at this point without fear of disrupting the Dreamweaver MX code.

RETURNING TO DREAMWEAVER MX

Moving your new design back to Dreamweaver MX is extremely easy. The original layout file 01_layout_start.png is automatically closed when you switch back. All the new artwork is placed in the images directory, and Dreamweaver will show you the updated HTML content.

1. Click the Done button in the upper-left corner of the Fireworks document window. Fireworks moves you back to Dreamweaver MX.
2. Make sure that your layout looks correct in Dreamweaver.
3. Click the Fireworks Edit button in the Property inspector if you need to go back to Fireworks to make additional changes to the layout.
4. Click the Done button in Fireworks to return to Dreamweaver. The Fireworks PNG file is saved automatically, and you can preview your work in Dreamweaver by pressing the F12 key.

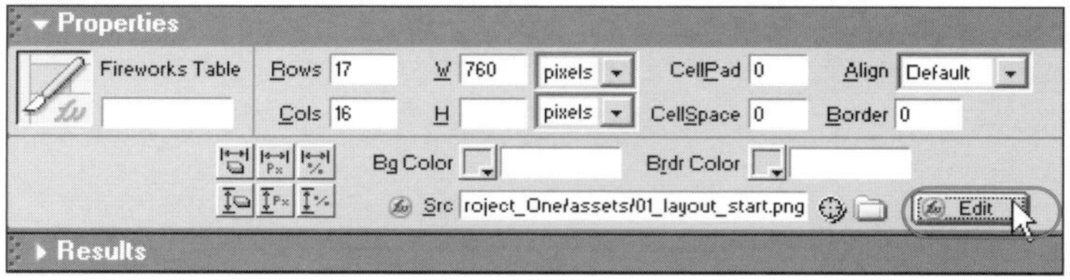

Click the Fireworks edit button to make further graphic changes.

The connection between Dreamweaver and Fireworks can save hours of development time by allowing web designers to make important design changes without sacrificing the integrity of the HTML code.

MODIFICATIONS

Using the connection between Fireworks and Dreamweaver for table layout is only the start. The real power happens when you use this technique with Dreamweaver templates. After you establish a base layout and bring it into Dreamweaver, you can create a template and apply it to numerous pages. Once you make edits in the table in Fireworks and bring it back into a Dreamweaver template, all pages based upon that template will update with the layout changes from Fireworks. Projects 2 and 3 describe templates in detail. As you go through those chapters, think about how Fireworks can be used to change a layout globally throughout your suite.

Dreamweaver MX and Fireworks MX in the Web Design Process

So you just pulled the wrapper off Dreamweaver MX and Fireworks MX, and it's time to get started on a web project. Which tool do you use first?

The illustration here shows the phases of a web project and highlights where Dreamweaver MX and Fireworks MX fit into the web design process. I have provided simple explanations for each phase so you can understand how this goes together and know where the software fits in the process.

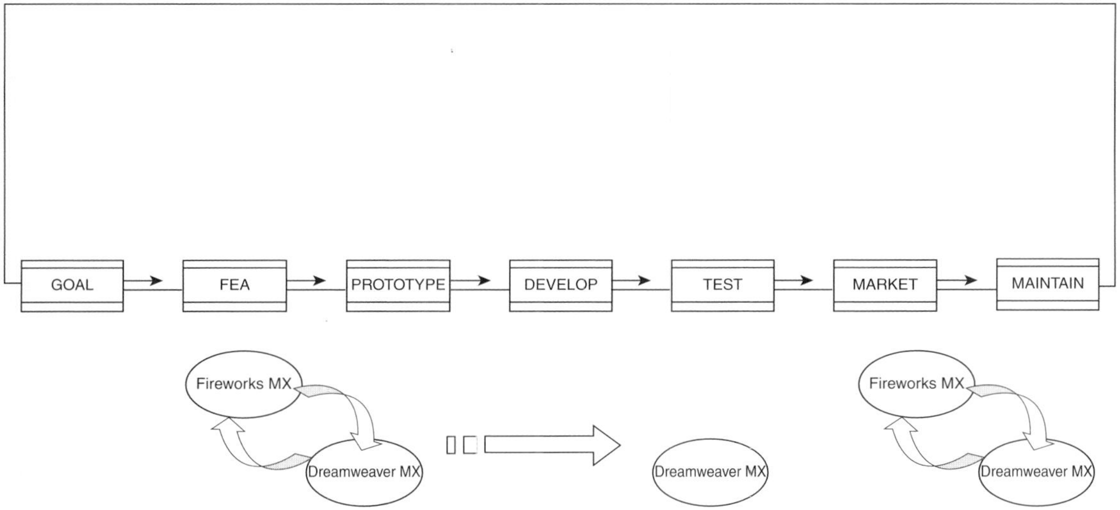

- **GOAL.** This is where the rubber meets the road. A clearly defined business, marketing, or personal goal is important to establish before any web design project begins. A defined goal will give direction throughout the entire project lifecycle.
- **FRONT END ANALYSIS (FEA).** Here you take a detailed look at all critical factors. Areas like audience, delivery system, marketing strategy, content gathering, human and financial resources, and branding all are researched. A detailed report and project plan are the outputs of this phase. Fireworks MX may be used for some initial comps during this phase.
- **PROTOTYPE.** Design, development, and content are all tested to see whether the goal will be achieved. Audience members give feedback during usability tests that either validate or discredit the design and information architecture of the web site. This is where the use of Fireworks and Dreamweaver come into play. Based on the feedback during the usability test, an entire prototype can take on a new look in Fireworks MX without destroying the Dreamweaver MX work.
- **DEVELOP.** All the content of the site is created in this stage. With text and database information being the focus of development, Dreamweaver MX takes a primary role, while Fireworks MX will be used for minor edits to the layout or individual graphic elements.
- **TEST.** Reporting is completed in Dreamweaver MX to check for broken and orphaned links, target browsers, and validate code structure.
- **MARKET.** Marketing of a web site through link exchanges, direct mail, email, and other forms of mass communication.
- **MAINTAIN.** Updates, corrections, additions, or even entire design changes are handled during this phase. Both Dreamweaver MX and Fireworks MX are used to keep the site fresh with content or make global graphic changes.

Fireworks Code in Dreamweaver

So how does Dreamweaver recognize the location of the original Fireworks PNG document? The secret lies in a comment tag prior to the Fireworks table.

```
<!-- fwtable fwsrc="01_layout_start.png" fwbase="index.gif"
fwstyle="Dreamweaver" fwdocid = "742308039" fwnested="0" -->
```

This tag is generated from Fireworks when HTML and images are exported.

If you look at the code, you can see three important attributes:

- fwsrc: Contains the name of the base Fireworks file that created the table.
- fwbase: The prefix name of slice images that are automatically named.
- fwstyle: Type of HTML formatting being used.

Notice that this code is contained within a developer's comment tag. Browsers will leave this code alone when interpreted. That's the beauty of the custom code used in both Dreamweaver and Fireworks.

Roundtrip HTML Exceptions

When moving code back and forth between Dreamweaver and Fireworks, you may run into a couple of problem situations:

- **Disjointed Rollovers.** Disjointed rollovers applied to image placeholders in Dreamweaver MX are not preserved when launched and edited in Fireworks MX. Most behaviors (JavaScript) will carry between applications, but this is one you need to look out for.
- **Table Destruction.** If a table in Dreamweaver is resized or changed in a dramatic way, Fireworks will not change the canvas or layout to reflect these updates. After you jump back to Fireworks for graphic edits and return to Dreamweaver, your table will return to the size described within the Fireworks document.

  A message appears warning you that changes you make in Fireworks will overwrite any edits you previously made to the table in Dreamweaver. Plan ahead if you need to make these types of edits!

OVERCOMING TEMPLATE ANXIETY

"Don't get your knickers in a knot. Nothing is solved and it makes you walk funny."

—KATHRYN CARPENTER

"Template!" There, We Said It . . .

If you're a frequent visitor to Macromedia's Dreamweaver forum, you know that no topic is more likely to provoke outbursts of frustration than templates. Yet templates are one of Dreamweaver's most powerful site-management tools.

In this chapter, you learn that, despite the uproar, templates are easy to create. By following a few simple rules, you can quickly construct templates that eliminate much of the grunt work of web design.

Project 2

Overcoming Template Anxiety

by Linda Rathgeber

The Sunrise Chamber of Commerce template design.

It Works Like This

Let's imagine that you are developing a web site for your local Chamber of Commerce. The contract calls for 80 pages of content, the look and feel of which must remain consistent throughout. To maintain consistency, you'll use some of the same components, such as headers and navigation elements, on every page. Manually inserting those components isn't difficult, but after six pages of it, the glamour of landing that nice contract has worn thin.

Dreamweaver templates enable you to "lock" a page layout into editable and non-editable regions. Every new page you generate from a template will be an exact duplicate of the original. You can create templates from blank or existing documents, including any flavor of dynamic document, such as ASP, ColdFusion, JSP, or PHP.

As the template designer, you are able to modify the locked regions of the template. Your modifications are then magically propagated to any pages you create from the template, site-wide. Content in the editable regions will remain undisturbed.

To demonstrate these concepts, we're going to create a template from a simple HTML document for our imaginary Chamber of Commerce.

Preparing to Work

Clean the mouse pad lint from the rollers in your mouse, take a deep breath, and smile. This is going to be a piece of cake! You'll need to copy the Projects/02_Templates folder from the accompanying CD-ROM to a convenient place on your hard drive, load Dreamweaver MX, and define a new site using your copied project folder as the local root folder.

1 Copy the projects folder.

- Browse to the Projects/02_templates folder on the CD-ROM.
- Copy the Sunrise folder to your hard drive.

2 Install the Corporate Mumbo Jumbo Generator extension or the Celestial Technical Babble Generator extension by double-clicking them to open the Extension Manager.

- Read the disclaimer and click the Accept button.
- When the installation is complete, click OK and then click File>Exit.

3 Load Dreamweaver and turn on Template highlighting.

- Choose Edit>Preferences.
- For Category, choose Highlighting.

Note: Remember that any time you want to see how your pages look, you can preview them in your browser from Dreamweaver. Choose File>Preview in your browser, or press the F12 key.

Note: If your Macintosh does not recognize the MXP (Extension) file format, open the Extension Manager and click the Install New Extension icon.

- Check the Editable Regions, Locked Regions, and Library items boxes.
- Click OK to accept the changes and close the dialog box.

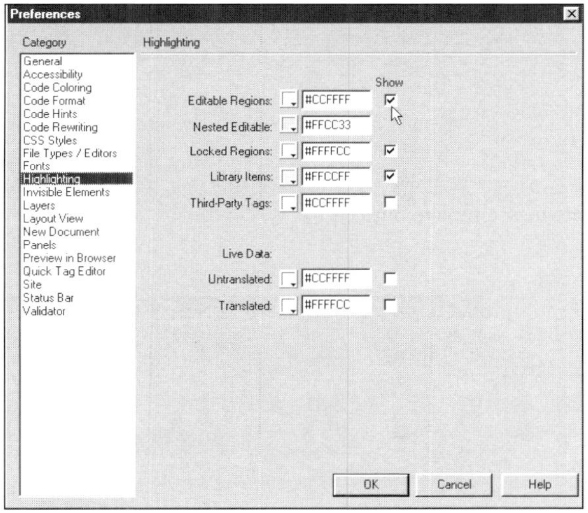

Turning on template highlighting in the Site Definition dialog box.

4 Define a new Dreamweaver site using the LessonFiles folder in the Sunrise directory as the local root folder.

5 You'll be adding material to the Design Notes at the end of the exercise, so although the Site Definition dialog box is still open, click Design Notes in the Category window and check the Maintain Design Notes and Upload Design Notes for Sharing boxes. Click OK to close the Site Definition box.

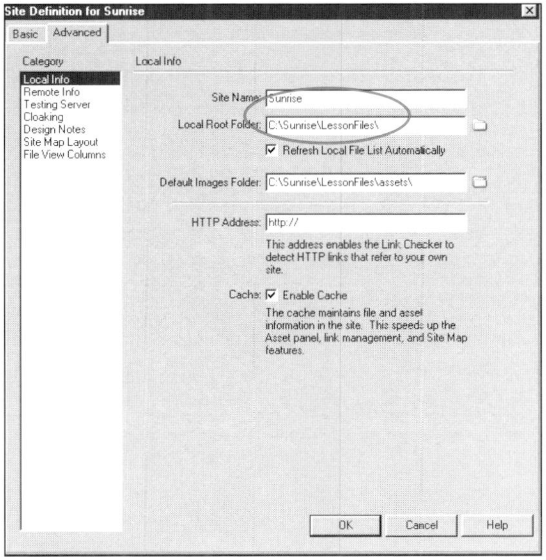

Defining a site in the Site Definition window.

Note: Dreamweaver links any template that you create with the location of the Template folder it creates in the local site root. Changing the name of the Templates folder, moving a template from the Templates folder, or moving the Templates folder to a location outside the site root will break the links.

Converting a Simple HTML Page into a Template

The Sunrise Chamber of Commerce page is composed of nested tables and includes a header graphic, an image gallery, and a navigation bar. In the following section, you explore Dreamweaver MX's new Insert bar and use the new template buttons to convert index.htm into the Sunrise site main template.

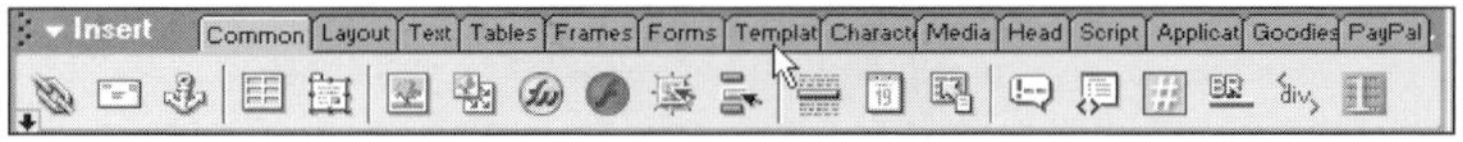

The new Insert bar.

1 Browse to the root folder of your new site. Locate the file named index.htm. Load index.htm in Dreamweaver.

Dreamweaver MX replaces the Objects panel in previous versions with a tabbed Insert bar located in a strip above the document window. Clicking the expander arrow in the left corner of the Insert bar's title bar enables you to access its features.

2 Open the Insert bar. Click the expander arrow of the Insert bar. Click the Templates tab.

3 Click the Make Template button to convert the index.htm document into a template. It doesn't get any easier than that!

The Save As Template dialog window opens.

4 Save the document as the site's template. For the site name, enter **Sunrise**. For Save As, type the word **Main**. Click the Save button. Dreamweaver then saves the file with a .dwt extension.

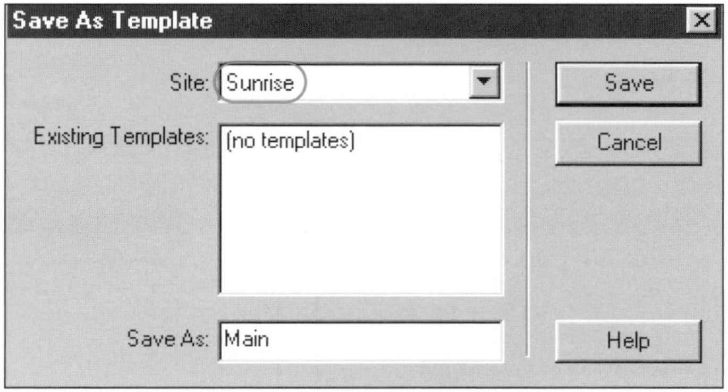

The Save As Template dialog box.

Note: You do not have to create a templates folder because Dreamweaver will do this for you automatically when you save the template document.

To locate your new template in Dreamweaver MX, expand the Files panel by clicking its expander arrow. Click the Assets tab, and then click the Templates icon. The Main template appears in the preview window at the top of the Assets panel. Information such as the template name, the Template's file size, and it's full path are listed in the menu below the preview window.

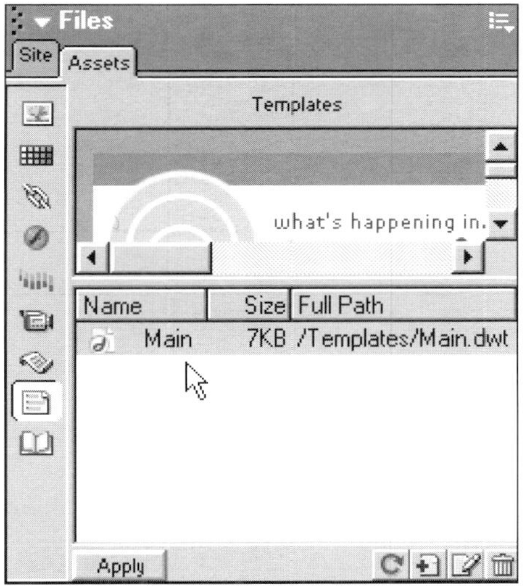

Preview the Main template in the Assets panel.

DEFINING THE TEMPLATE EDITABLE REGION

Editable regions are for content that will be unique and vary from page to page. Content added to editable regions does not propagate to template-based pages. By default, Dreamweaver locks most regions of a document that you save as a template. It's up to you to determine which regions of the document will remain editable.

The large table cell to the right of the navigation bar (highlighted by the hatched outline in the figure shown) serves as the main content area for each page generated from the Sunrise Chamber of Commerce template. The content for this table cell includes text and small graphic accents. The template user plans to make daily updates to the content on some of the site's pages and monthly updates to some of the other pages. You need to turn this large table cell into an editable region.

The main content area.

1 Mark the main content area as editable.

Place your cursor in the large table cell to the right of the navigation bar, and then, reading the tag selectors from left to right, click the last <td> selector on the selector bar at the bottom of the document window.

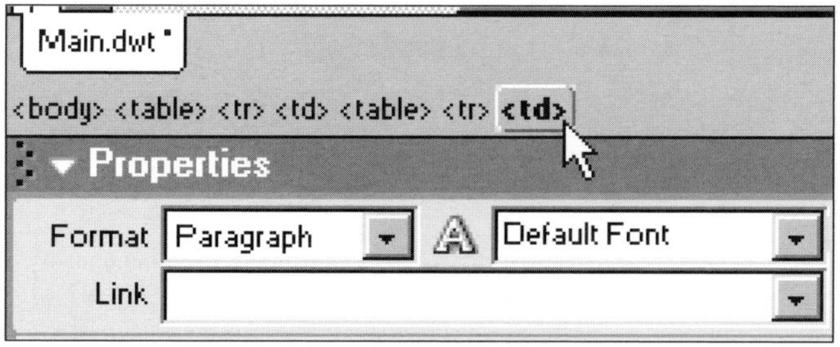

The Make Editable button.

Warning: Simply placing your cursor into the table cell that you want to convert into an editable region isn't enough. You must select the table cell itself. Doing otherwise will cause the first paragraph tags in the cell to be selected as the editable region, preventing you from adding other content to the cell.

Note: Editable regions can be defined in Code view by selecting tag pairs, such as <td> </td>. Editable regions can be defined in Layout view by using the tag selectors below the Document window, or by simply placing your cursor anywhere on the template document and choosing Insert>Template Objects>Editable region.

- Click the Template tab of the Insert bar.
- Click the Editable Region button on the Template tab of the Insert bar.

The New Editable Region dialog box will open.

2 Give the new editable region the name **EditMainContent** and choose File>Save.

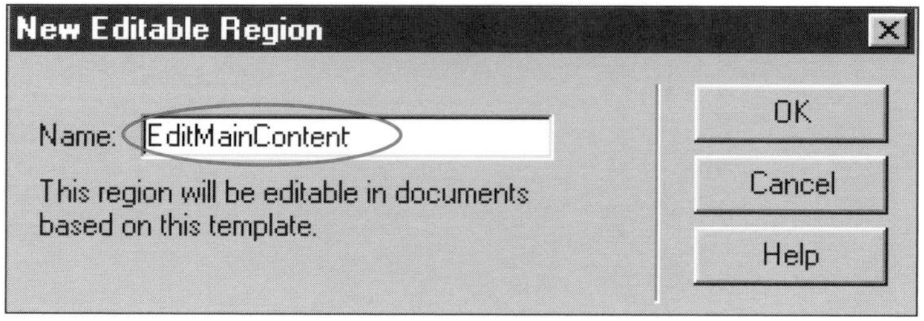

Naming the new editable region.

Dreamweaver will name the regions for you if you choose not to. Because Dreamweaver has no idea what you'll be using the area for, however, it numbers the editable regions in the order you created them. Numbers give you some information, but they don't offer much assistance in identifying editable regions when you, or an associate, are updating the page contents in Code view. Naming the editable regions in ways that clearly indicate what kind of content they contain is a trick you'll find useful, particularly when you learn to use some of the more advanced template features.

Adding a New Editable Region

Your contact person at the Sunrise Chamber of Commerce just called to ask whether it would be possible to make quarterly updates to the Image gallery graphic on the pages to reflect the changes of season. You've already signed off on the template for the site, but because your contract includes a "feature creep" clause, you agree to the additional work.

1 Reopen the Template for editing.

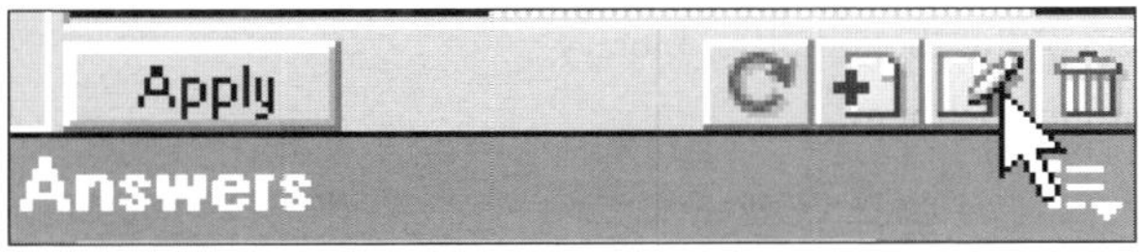

Click the Template edit button on the button bar at the bottom of the Assets panel.

- Open the Files panel group by clicking the expander arrow at the left corner of the Files panel title bar.
- Click the Assets tab. Click the Edit button on the button bar of the Assets panel.

2 Mark the Image Gallery area as editable.

- Click the Image Gallery graphic to select it.
- Click the <td> selector immediately to the left of the <img> tag on the Tag Selector bar.
- Choose Insert>Template Objects>Editable region.

The New Editable Region dialog box opens.

Note: The term *feature creep* refers to the way that clients, with uncanny regularity, request features not agreed upon in the original contract. They usually begin exhibiting this symptom about a third of the way through the development of the site.

3 In the New Editable Region dialog box, name the editable region **EditImageGallery**. Click OK.

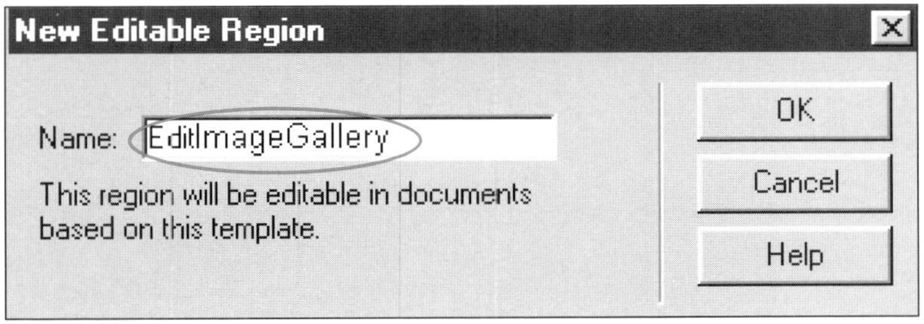

The New Editable Region dialog box.

4 Save your work by choosing File>Save and then File>Close.

Note: Are you a contextual menu junkie? You'll be happy to know that you can right-click (Ctrl-click for Mac users) in an area you'd like mark as editable and select New Editable Region from the context-sensitive menu.

Dreamweaver Library Items: A Template's Next of Kin

The most expedient way for you to handle the quarterly updates to the image gallery graphic is to use Dreamweaver Library Items. You can create Library Items from any element of a web page that resides within the body tags, such as text, images, tables, forms, navigation elements, and so on. Like their first cousin, the template, Library Items can be used to update all the pages of a site that include them.

1 Load Dreamweaver and open the Files panel. Click the Assets tab, and then click the Library icon. Next, click the New Library Item button on the button bar at the bottom of the Assets panel. When prompted to type a name, enter the name seasons_gallery and press Enter. Click the Edit button.

Creating a new Library Item.

2 Click the Assets panel Images button and locate the file fall_gallery.jpg. Drag the fall_gallery.jpg into the document window. If a dialog box appears stating that the selection might not look the same when copied to other documents because a style sheet is being used, click OK.

3 Choose File>Save and then File>Close. Dreamweaver creates a Library and saves the seasons_gallery Library Item in the new folder.

4 Open the Template by clicking the Template icon in the Assets panel, and then clicking the Edit button on the Asset panel's button bar.

5 Delete the fall_gallery.jpg from the EditImageGallery editable region by clicking it to select it, and then choosing Edit>Cut.

6 Drag the seasons_gallery Library Item from the Assets panel into the EditImageGallery editable region.

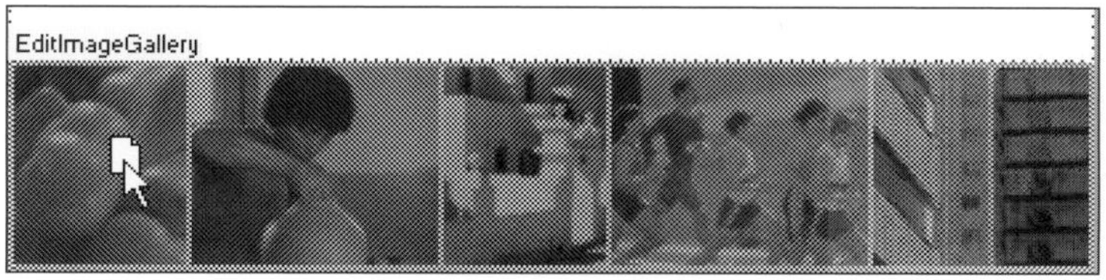

Dragging from the Assets panel to the editable region.

7 Choose File>Save and then File>Close.

Note: You also can create the Library Item directly in the template. To do this, click first the Template button and then the Edit Template button. Click the image gallery graphic to select it, and choose the Library button in the Assets panel. Finally, click the New Library Item button and name the Library Item Fall_gallery. Choose File>Save and then File>Close.

Updating Pages with Library Items

Just like their cousin, the template, Dreamweaver Library Items can be used to update pages site-wide. A Library Item is a kind of content wrapper. When you add a Library Item to a page, Dreamweaver inserts an HTML comment containing a reference to the actual content (fall_gallery.jpg), along with a reference to the container (seasons_gallery.lbi). Changes made to the content within the container will propagate site-wide.

1. Choose Window>Assets to open the Assets panel. Click the Library icon. If a dialog box appears asking you whether the other pages in the site should be updated, choose to update the files. If Dreamweaver provides you with a dialog box regarding inconsistent Region Names, click Cancel to close the box.
2. Select the seasons_gallery Library Item by clicking it.
3. Click the Edit button on the button bar at the bottom of the Assets panel, or double-click the Library Item itself. Dreamweaver opens the Library Item in the document window.
4. Delete the fall_gallery.jpg from the document window and choose Edit>Cut.
5. Click the images button in the Assets panel. Locate the summer_gallery.jpg, and then drag it from the Assets panel into the document window.

The summer gallery.

6 Choose File>Save. The Update Library Items dialog box opens with a list of each page the Library Item has been applied to. In this example, the only document you will see listed is the template. Click the Update button.

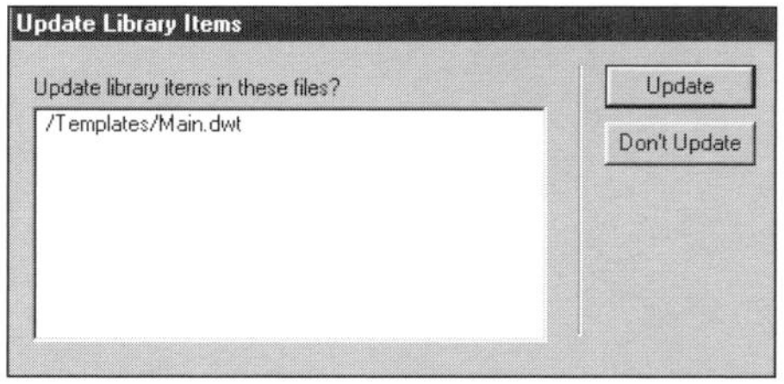

The Update Library Items dialog box.

When the document has been updated, the Update Pages dialog box opens with a wonderfully detailed report. The report lets you know which pages Dreamweaver attempted to update with the newly edited Library Item, which pages were successfully updated, and which pages were not updated. The report also tells you the amount of time the operation required.

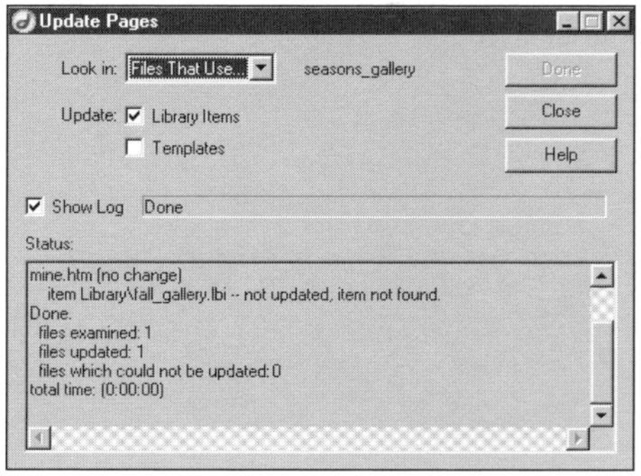

The Update Pages dialog box.

Note: Although the dimensions of the EditImageGallery editable region will automatically adjust to the size of your changed Library Item, replacing the image in the Library Item with an image of a different size can have unpredictable results! Test and test again!

Generating a New Page from the Template

The Create New File dialog boxes have been upgraded in Dreamweaver MX to a feature-rich, New Document dialog box that enables you to select, preview, and create many new document types. Consequently, creating a new document from a template in Dreamweaver couldn't be easier. To begin this section of the project, you'll spawn a child page from a template in the New Document dialog box.

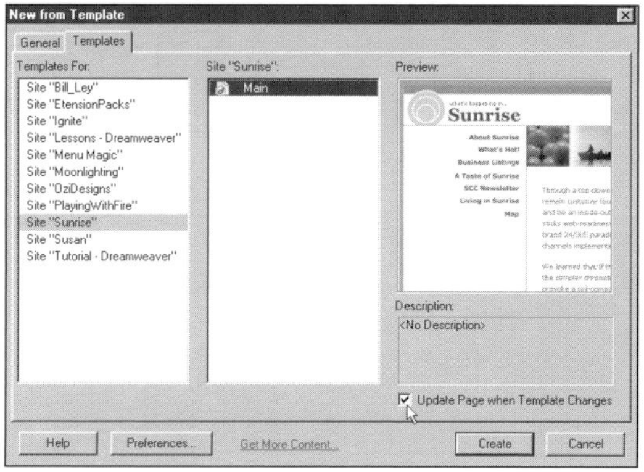

Selecting a template in the New Document dialog box.

1 Choose File>New, and then click the Templates tab.

2 In the Templates For: pane, choose Sunrise. Click the Update Page when Template Changes checkbox to enable it. Click the Create button. Dreamweaver now creates a page based on the Main template.

3 Dreamweaver MX opens with blank document by default. If you haven't changed this default, you can use the drag-and-drop method to create a child page from a template. To try this method, close Dreamweaver and reopen it.

Open the Files panel and click the Assets tab. Click the Template icon.

4 Click the Template name in the list below the Assets panel preview pane and drag the file toward the document window.

5 Drop the template onto the blank page.

When you open a page from the template, you'll see that the locked regions have been surrounded by a yellow highlight and labeled with the template name. Your cursor will change to a "no" sign when you attempt to place it in a locked region. The template editable regions have been highlighted in aqua and are labeled with the editable region name.

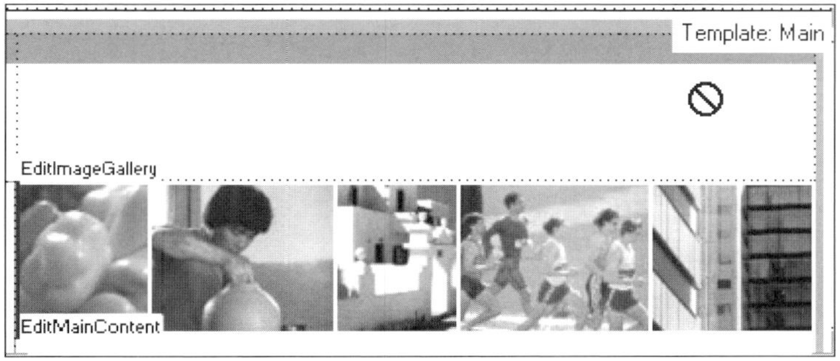

Editable and noneditable region markers.

Now let's test the EditMainContent editable region.

6 Highlight the text inside the EditMainContent editable region and delete it by choosing Edit>Cut from the menu bar. In the editable region, type **Secretary's Notes:** (including the colon).

The index.htm page you converted to the template has a style sheet attached to it. To see the list of styles, open the Design panel and click the CSS Styles tab. Highlight the text you just typed by clicking the <p> tag on the Tag Selector bar. In the Property inspector, change the format to Heading 1. You right-clickers can also change the format to the <H1> style in the right-click, contextual menu under the Paragraph Format submenu.

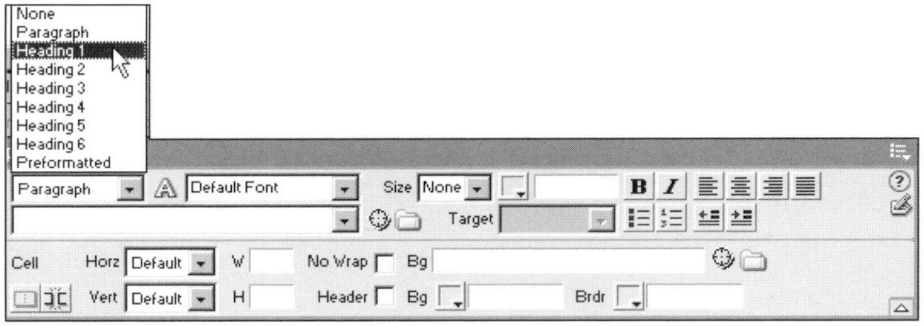

Changing the format to Heading 1 in the Property inspector.

7 Add some text.

- Press Enter to insert a paragraph break.
- Click the Goodies tab of the Insert menu, and then click the Corporate Mumbo Generator button. Shovel **300** characters.

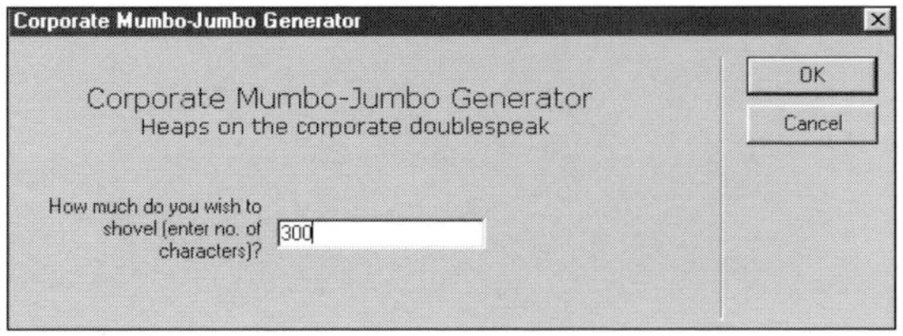

How much Mumbo Jumbo do you want to shovel?

8 Change the title. Dreamweaver MX automatically makes the <title> tags an editable region. Delete the text from the Title box of the document toolbar and add the title Welcome to Sunrise.

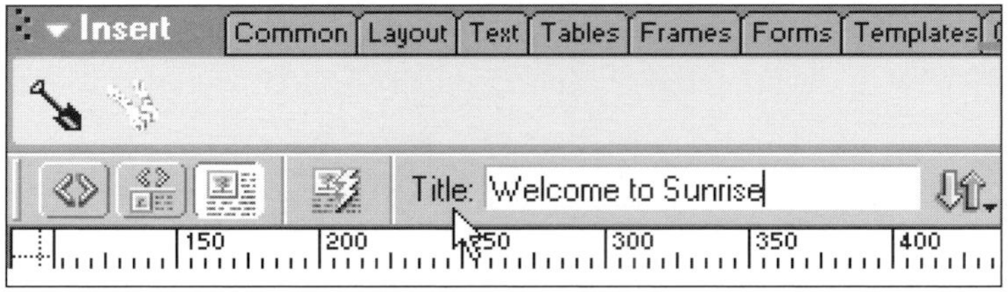

Adding the title in the Title box.

9 Save the page to the Sunrise site folder by choosing File>Save As, and name it **home.htm**. Save a second copy of the same page as **index.htm** (click yes, ignoring the overwrite warning).

10 Create seven more child pages by applying the same procedures you used to create the home and index pages. Change the phrase Secretary's notes to something new in each page and add document titles and file names as follows:

Title	Save As
About Sunrise	about.htm
What's Hot	hot.htm
Business Listings	listings.htm
A Taste of Sunrise	restaurants.htm
SCC Newsletter	newsletter.htm
Living in Sunrise	neighborhood.htm
Map of Sunrise	map.htm

In the next section, you learn how to update all those pages at once.

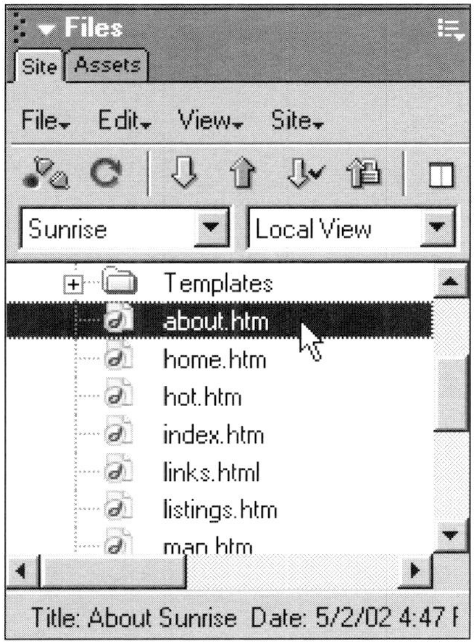

The list of HTML pages in the Site panel.

Note: Dreamweaver puts layer code at the top of the page. This code often falls within a noneditable region of a template. When this happens, any attempt to draw a layer inside an editable region pops up an alert. Making this change would require changing the code that is locked by a template or translator. To avoid this problem, open the template and create a special editable region at the bottom of the page. When you want to add a layer to a page spawned from the template, click in this bottom editable region first and then insert the layer.

Using the Template to Update the Site's Pages

One of the most powerful (and magical) features of Dreamweaver templates is their ability to propagate changes you make to the template locked regions to the locked regions of their child pages. To see this in action, add some links to the rollovers in the Sunrise site's main template's navigation bar.

1 Open the Template.

- Choose Window>Assets.
- Click the Template button.
- Click the Edit Template button.

2 Preview the navigation rollovers in your browser.

- Choose File>Preview in Browser.
- Mouse over the navigation bar.
- Close the browser.

3 Add the links to the rollovers.

- Click the About Sunrise image in the navigation bar and then click the Browse for File (folder) icon to the right of the Link box in the Property inspector. Select the about.htm file in the Select File dialog box. Click OK.
- Add the remaining links, as follows:

Image	**Link to**
What's Hot!	hot.htm
Business Listings	listings.htm
A Taste of Sunrise	restaurants.htm
SCC Newsletter	newsletter.htm
Living in Sunrise	neighborhood.htm
Map of Sunrise	map.htm

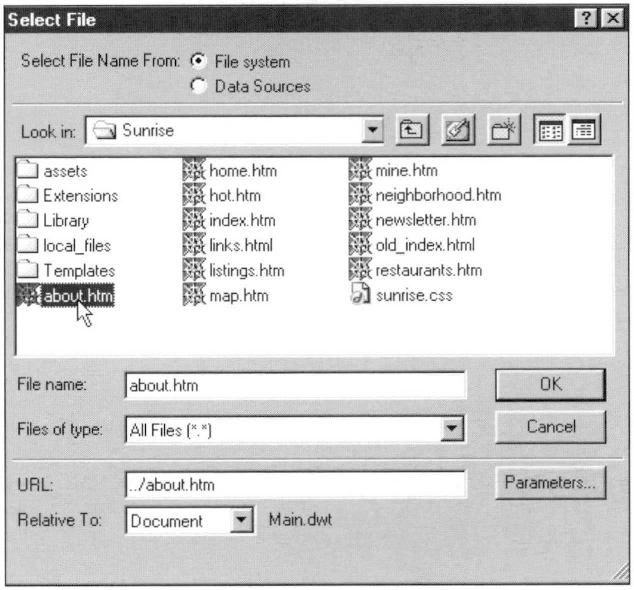

Adding links to the rollovers using the Select File dialog box.

4 Update the pages.

- Choose File>Save.
- In the Update Template Files dialog box, click the Update button.
- Choose File>Close.

Tip: If you're having problems getting a page to update after editing the template, open it in the document window to make it active, and use the Apply button in the Assets panel to reapply the template.

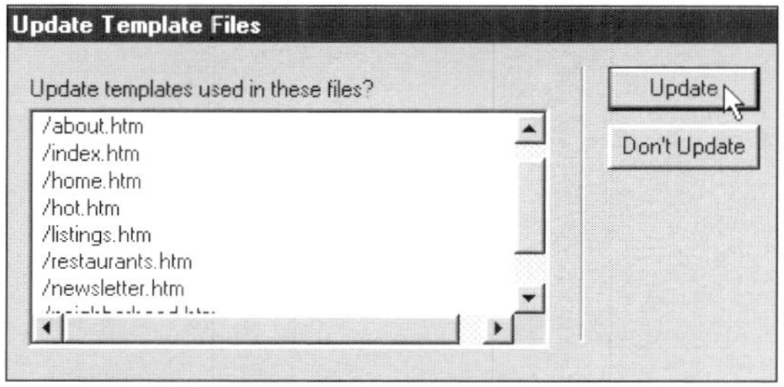

The Update Template Files dialog box showing the list of pages to be updated with the links.

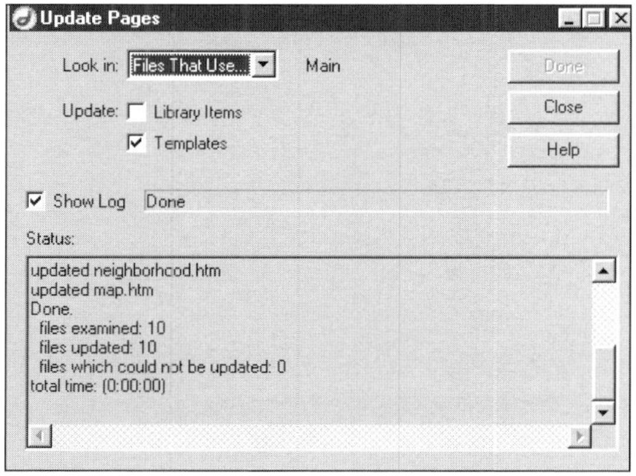

The Updated Pages log.

Inserting a Mini Editable Region in a Locked Area

Your Chamber clients are concerned that material submitted to them for use on the site isn't adequately protected unless there's an indication that it is protected by copyright. "That red bar at the bottom of the page would be an ideal place for it," says Madame Secretary. "Can you fix it so the copyright sign and date are locked in place, but the author's name can be changed when the content of the page is updated?" This one's a cinch because all that's necessary is to split the cell and make half of the split cell editable.

1 Open the template by clicking the Edit button on the button bar at the bottom of the Assets panel.

2 Place your cursor in the bottom (red) table row of the document, and then click the Split Cell button in the bottom left of the Property inspector.

3 In the Split Cell dialog box, click in the Columns radio button, enter 2 for Number of Columns, and then click OK.

Splitting table cells into columns.

4 Place your cursor in the left cell of the split row and click the Character tab of the Insert bar. Insert a copyright symbol and type the numbers 2002. If a pop-up warning appears stating that special characters might not be visible in some instances, click OK.

5 Highlight the copyright symbol and numbers and open the CSS panel. Click the Apply Styles radio button, and then click the copyright style. Enter a width of 50 pixels for the cell in the Property inspector.

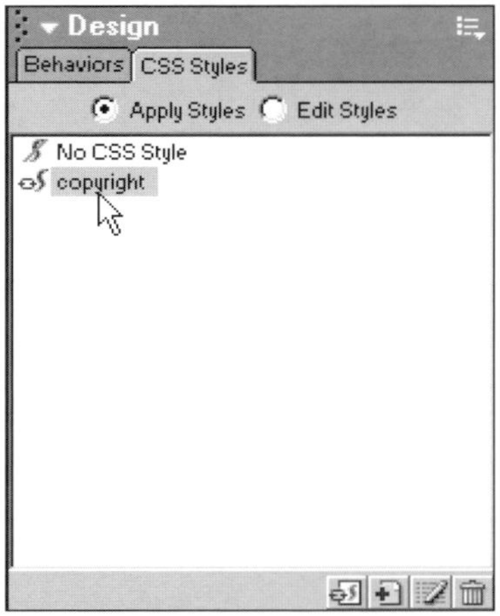

Applying a style to the copyright symbol and date in the CSS Styles panel.

6 Place your cursor inside the right cell of the split row, and then click the <td.copyright> tag for the cell on the Tag Selector bar at the bottom of the document window.

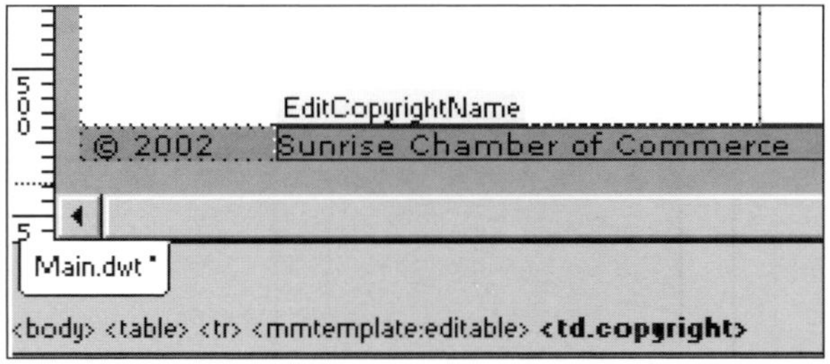

The EditCopyrightName editable region.

7 Choose Insert>Template Objects>Editable Region. Give the editable region the name **EditCopyright Name**. Type the words **Sunrise Chamber of Commerce** into the new editable region.

8 Choose File>Save As. In the Save As dialog box, select Main.dwt and click on Save.

Note: The only time the template affects the content in the editable region is the first time you open the page from the template. Because changing the default content of the mini-editable region in the template will not cause the content to be changed on any pages that have been created from the template, your customization will not be lost.

Modifications

In a final meeting with your Sunrise Chamber of Commerce client, you agree to add a Jump Menu hyperlinked to Chambers of Commerce from other cities. Although some of the template elements will be used on the page, the design of the form requires that most of the material in the main content region be removed. Opening a new document from a template and then breaking the document link to the template will speed up the creation of a customized page.

1 Create a new page from the template. Choose Modify>Templates>Detach from Template.

2 Delete all but three lines of the Mumbo Jumbo text from the main content area and press Enter.

3 Click the Forms tab on the Insert bar, and then click the Form button to insert a form field.

4 Click the Jump Menu button. The Insert Jump Menu dialog box opens. Enter the text **Select a Chamber of Commerce** and insert a Null link (#) in the box labeled When selected, go to. Click the Add button (+) at the top of the Insert Jump Menu dialog box.

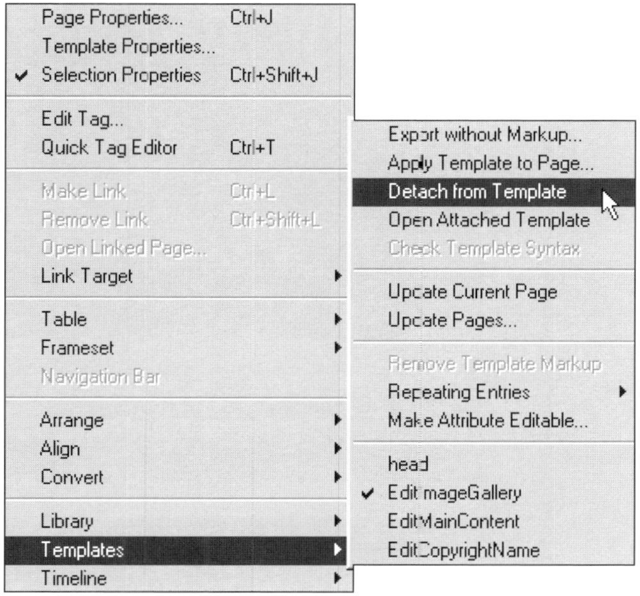

Breaking a page from a template.

5 Enter the name **Greater Austin Chamber of Commerce** in the box labeled Text. Enter the URL **http://www.austin-chamber.org/** in the URL box. Click the Add button (+). Enter the name **Novi Chamber of Commerce** in the text box of the Jump Menu dialog box and add the URL **http://www.novichamber.com/**.

6 Add as many names and links as you wish. Click OK to accept the changes and to close the Insert Jump Menu dialog box.

7 Enter a paragraph break afer the Jump box and insert 300 Mumbo Jumbo characters.

8 Choose File>Save As. Save the page as **links.html**. Open the page in your browser and test the jump menu links.

9 Reopen the hot.html page and add the text, **What's Hot in Other Cities!** to the bottom of the page. Highlight it with your cursor and click the Browse For File icon next to the Link box in the Property inspector. Select the links.html page in the Select File dialog box. Click OK and open the page in your browser to test the link. Save the page.

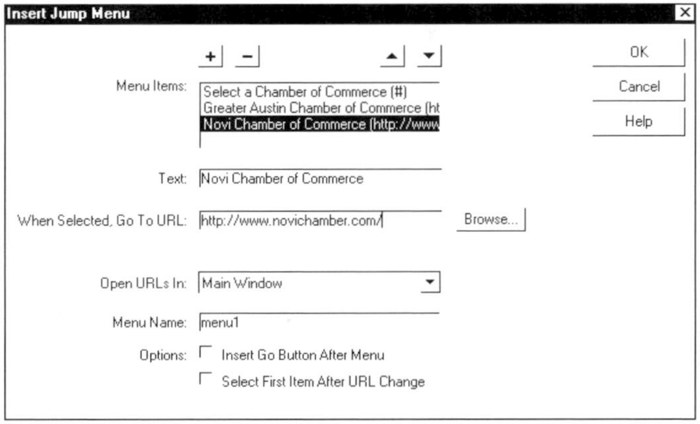

The Insert Jump Menu dialog box.

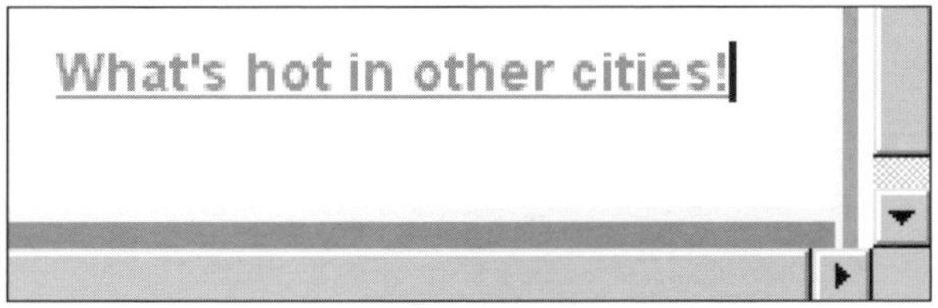

The hot link to the Links page.

Attaching Design Notes

Unfortunately, your web development partner wasn't able to attend that last meeting. It's Friday afternoon and you have a weekend of R & R planned in an exotic location, far, far away from computers. Shushila's desk is covered with disemboweled electronics and you dare not leave a note there. Design Notes to the rescue!

You can create Design Note files for each document or template in your site. When attached to a template, they aren't propagated to the child pages of the template. Whenever a file is copied, moved, renamed, or deleted, the associated Design Notes file is also copied, moved, renamed, or deleted.

To leave a note for your partner:

1 Choose File>Design notes.

The Design Notes dialog box opens.

2 Click the Calendar icon to add a date.

- Choose Beta for Status information.
- Type in your note: **Hi Shushila. What do you think of this Jump menu idea for the links page? It probably needs some more work. I'll bring back a coconut.**
- Click the Show When File is Opened checkbox.
- Click OK to save the notes.

Dreamweaver will create a special folder called notes in the same folder the document resides in and save the note to it as an MNO file. MNO files are XML files which contain meta-data about your site files. For instance, Dreamweaver uses MNO files to tell Fireworks which PNG to open for a given GIF or JPEG.

Had we set up a remote, the Design Note would be transferred when uploading the file to the remote site. To see the Design Note as Shushila will see it when she checks out the page, close the file and re-open it. You should see the Design Note pop open.

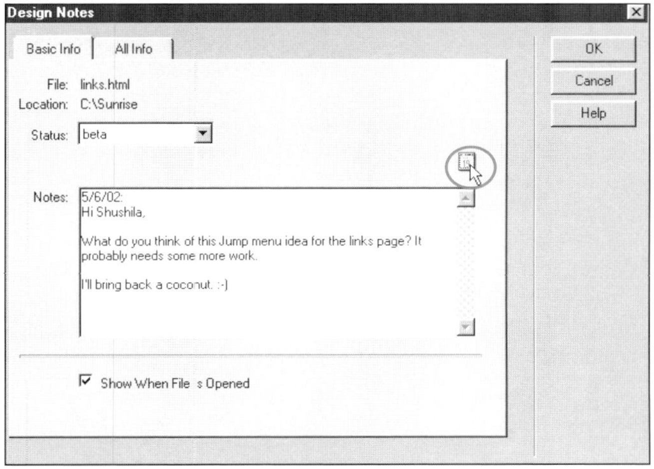

Design notes, and then some.

"Exploration is really the essence of the human spirit . . ."

—FRANK BORMAN

DREAM TEMPLATES

Exploring Dream Templates

Remember the days when you could have only editable and non-editable regions in your templates or when you tried adding a behavior or CSS to a template-based page and it failed? Headaches like these are all but gone with the release of Dreamweaver MX! Many new features have been implemented for templates. I recommend you go get your favorite non-alcoholic beverage, kiss your spouse and children goodnight, call into your boss's voicemail with your excuse for being late for work tomorrow, and strap into your computer chair because this project will get your creative juices flowing for sure.

Project 3

Dream Templates

by Brad Halstead

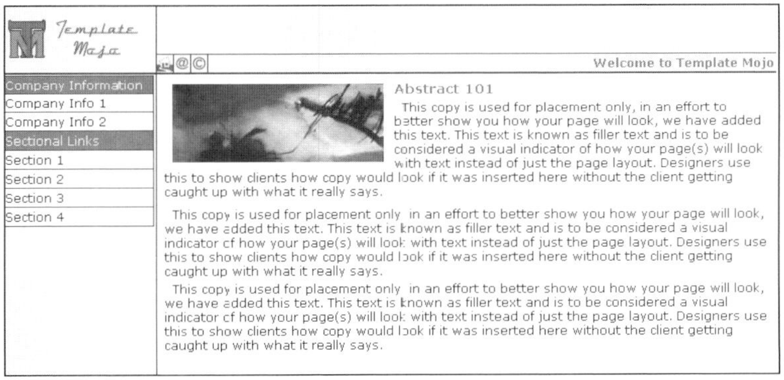

A Dreamweaver MX template in action.

It Works Like This

Dreamweaver MX templates are worth much more exploration and this project builds on Project 2, "Overcoming Template Anxiety," where you learned how to make a basic template. At the end of this project, you will have a highly customized and functional template set that can be used for site consistency, but also allows you the flexibility to have regions on some pages and not on others.

In this project, you learn many things, including how to add repeating regions (such as repeating tables and repeating rows and optional regions), inserting a MultipleIf expression, making a tag attribute editable, adding CSS to a template-based page, adding a behavior to a template-based page, checking template syntax, and working with methods of detaching template-based pages from a template.

Preparing to Work

Preparing for this project requires the same routine you have repeated with other projects. Copy the Projects\03_dream_templates folder on the accompanying CD to your hard drive, start Dreamweaver MX, and define a site using the folder you copied from the CD as the site root.

1 Start Dreamweaver MX and create a site using 03_dream_templates as the root folder. See the figure for a representation of the site settings.

2 Configure Dreamweaver MX to use Dreamweaver MX Workspace (choose Edit>Preferences> General>Change Workspace, select the Dreamweaver MX Workspace radio button, and click OK twice).

Note: I recommend that you use Document Split view to see the code that is being generated as you follow along in this project. (You will need to access Code and Design view in the project as you follow along.) This can be changed by selecting View>Code and Design.

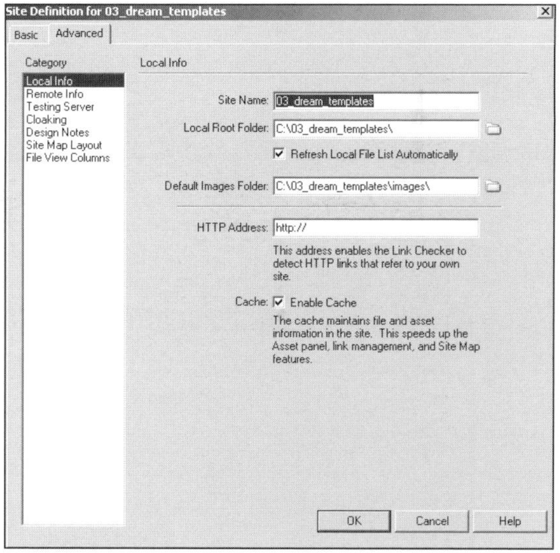

Project 3 Site Definition.

You may notice a lock icon beside the files in the Site panel; this means that the files are read-only. Before you can use these files, you need to remove the lock and make them editable. In the Site window, select the files and folders, right-click, and select Turn Off Read Only. Your local files are now editable!

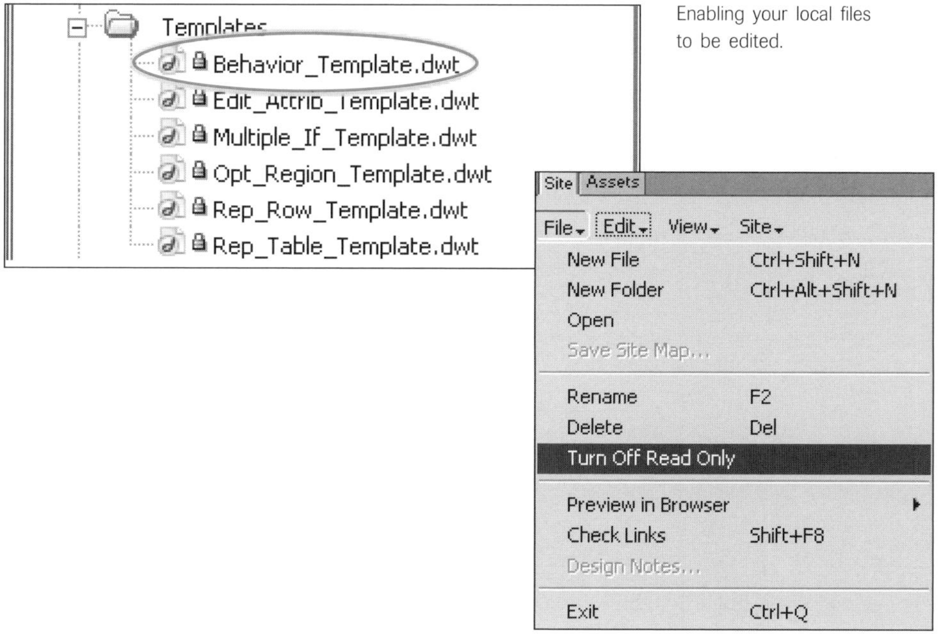

Enabling your local files to be edited.

For this project, I also have included an extension for you; it inserts the required Template comment to turn on/off code above or below HTML functionality as a Snippet. Updates can be found at http://www.prettylady2.net and support email is x10@prettylady2.net. I do plan on adding more template functionality to the Snippets as time permits.

3 Start Extension Manager (EM). Choose File>Install Extension.

4 Browse to the CDProjects/03_dream_templates/Extensions folder. Select dwm_03_Templates.mxp.

5 Agree to the license agreement and the extension will install.

Note: This extension creates a new folder called Templates in your Snippets panel and adds four Snippets. The Snippets include these:

- Ability to add a Template comment that enables/disables code above/below HTML (as specified in the help docs).
- Required base code for a MultipleIf conditional region, also as specified in the help docs.

We will be referencing some of these Snippets later in the project, so be sure to install this extension.

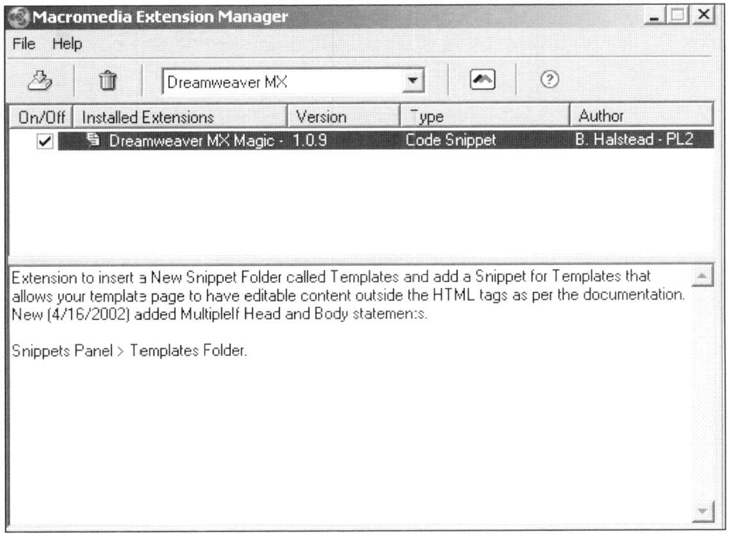

Extension Manager with the extension installed.

Repeating Regions—Rows

A repeating region can be used to allow the builder of the template-based page to add table rows or other types of repeating regions without having to edit the template. This allows for the template builder to have more control of the template while allowing the user of the template-based file the freedom to add content without messing up the structure of the template. In this project segment, you learn how to add, remove, and use a table row repeating region in your template and template-based page(s).

Tip: When naming regions, each region name *must* be unique.

1 Open the file named Rep_Row_Template.dwt in the Templates folder.

2 Position your cursor in the table cell that says Company Info 2. Using the Tag Selector, choose the right-most <tr> tag.

3 From the menu, choose Insert>Template Objects> Repeating Region.

4 Type **MenuRow1** in the New Repeating Region dialog box and click OK.

5 Select the content of the cell and from the menu, choose Insert>Template Objects>Editable Region.

6 In the Editable Region dialog box, type the name **MR1Content** and click OK.

7 Repeat Steps 1 through 6, selecting the Section 4 cell, using **MenuRow2** as the Repeating Region name and **MR2Content** for the Editable Region name. Save the template.

8 You should be prompted to Update Template Files that are based on this template. Choose Update. Close the update report dialog and continue on to Step 9.

9 Close the template file.

10 Open the root file named Repeat_Row.htm. This file is based on the template you worked with in Steps 1 through 9, Rep_Row_Template.dwt.

11 Notice that there is a new GUI where you added editable rows. Position the cursor in the MR1Content cell that is named, select the cell contents, and type **Additional1** (or use your own text).

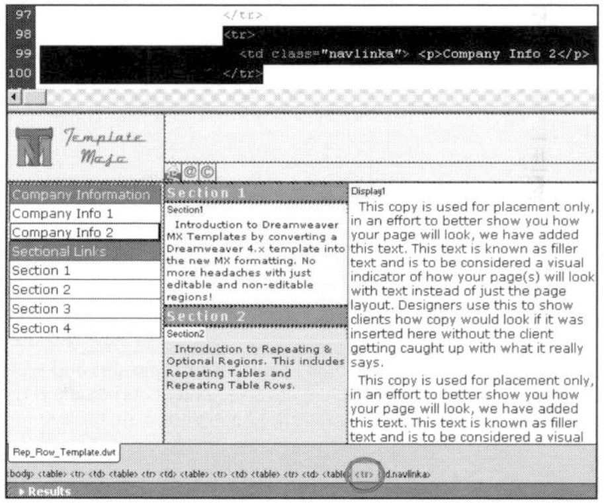

Tag Selector.

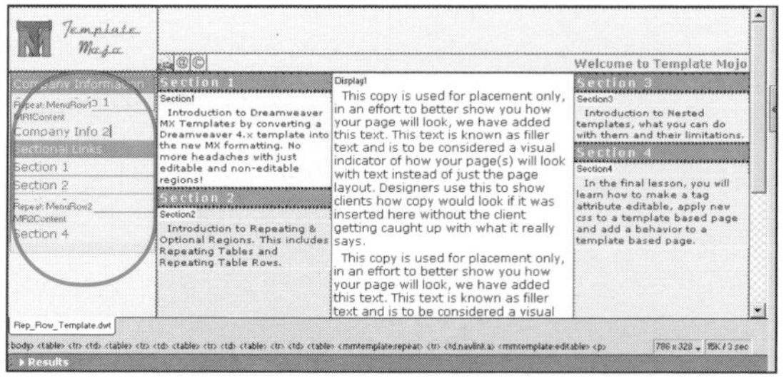

Template with editable repeating rows.

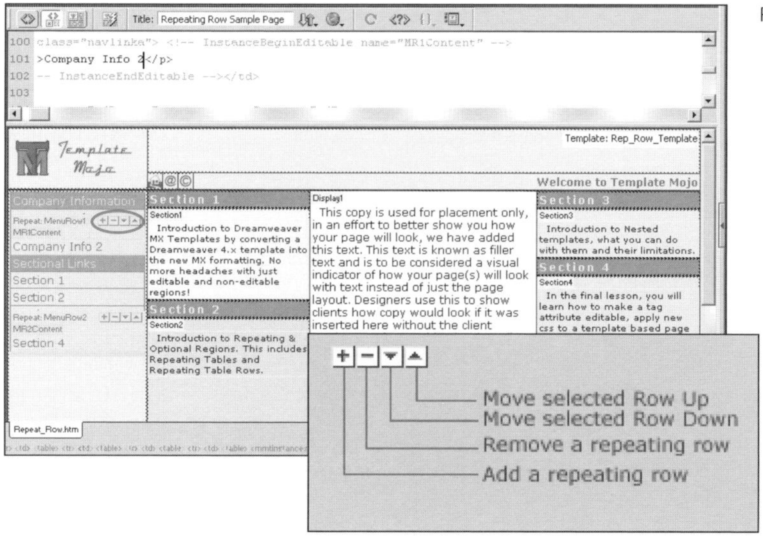

Repeating row is shown.

Warning: If you are too vigorous with your mouse selection, you may inadvertently overwrite the <p> tags for the content in the repeating region cells. If you do that, the menu will not display properly. To correct the problem, you may have to select the content and set it as a paragraph for proper cross-browser rendering. To do this, open the Property inspector, click the Format drop-down menu and choose Paragraph. This caution applies to Steps 11, 12, and 13.

12 Click the GUI + button to add another row; then select the content of this row and replace it with Additional2 or use your own content.

13 Repeat Steps 11 and 12 for the MR2Content repeating row using Additional3 and Additional4 as your entered text.

You may have to select the content and set it as a paragraph for proper cross-browser rendering. To do this, open the Property inspector, click the Format drop-down menu and choose Paragraph.

14 Save the document, preview in a browser to see that your edits are viewable, and then close the document when you are satisfied with your additions. You have successfully added a repeating region, made it editable, and controlled it from the template-based page.

15 So now you decide that you don't want the repeating editable regions anymore, and now they have to be deleted. Open the template Rep_Row_Template.dwt.

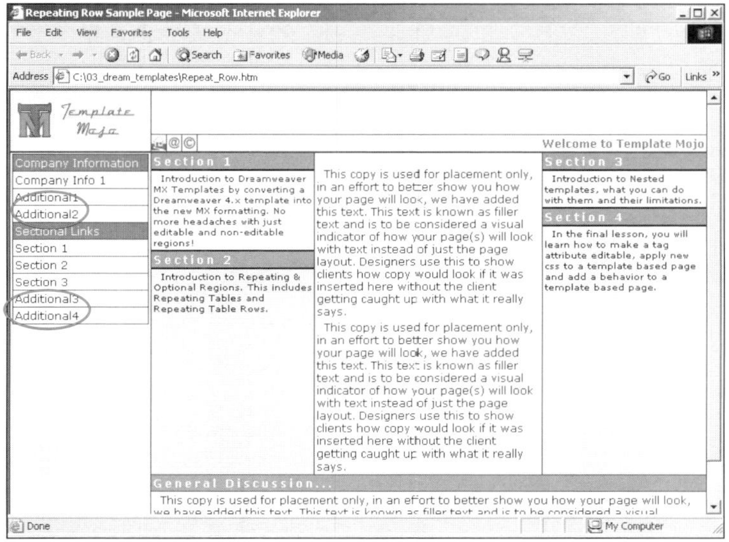

Browser view of the project with Steps 1 through 14 completed.

16 To remove an inserted editable region, select the editable region you want to remove by clicking inside the editable region. Then select the <mmtemplate:editable> tag using the Tag Selector. Use the Modify>Templates>Remove Template Markup menu item to remove the selected editable region. At this point, remove the MR1 Content editable region.

17 To remove an inserted repeating region, select the repeating region you want to remove by clicking inside the repeating region, and then select the <mmtemplate:repeat> tag using the Tag Selector. Use the same menu item (Remove Template Markup) to delete the repeating region. At this point, remove the MenuRow 1 repeat region.

18 Repeat Steps 16 and 17 to remove the other editable and repeating regions you added to the page.

19 Save the document, update the pages associated to this template, and close the template. You will be prompted to relocate found content in the Inconsistent Region Names dialog. Select the MenuRow1 and choose nowhere from the drop-down list. Repeat this for MenuRow2. This action makes sure that they are completely deleted from the template-based page. Close the template file.

20 Open Repeat_Row.htm again to verify that the repeating row and editable region are removed from the page. Close the file when verified.

With this segment, you have learned how to add a repeating row, make it editable, and modify a template-based page to use the repeating editable region. You then decided that you wanted a change and deleted the editable region and the repeating region.

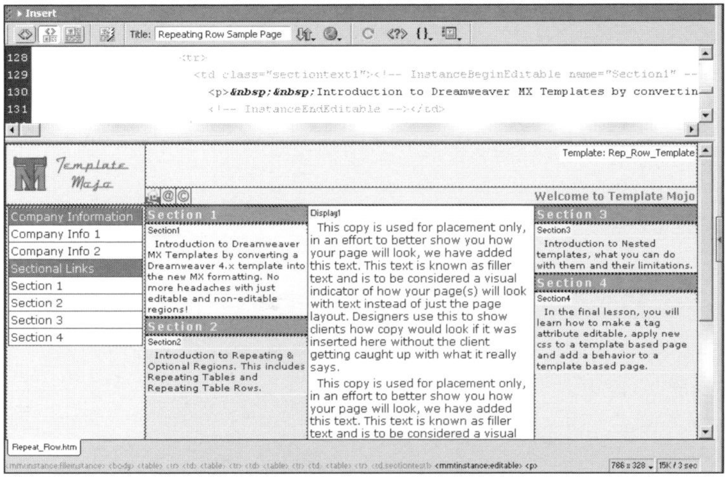

The repeating row is removed.

Repeating Tables

Although this segment is similar to the previous one, there are important differences. A repeating table has a complete row that is marked as repeating and each cell in that row is an editable region. Another difference is that instead of using the <tr> tag as your selector, you use a friendly user interface (UI) to perform the insertion of the Repeating Table object.

Tip: Region names cannot contain spaces or any special characters; you can use only alpha-numeric characters.

1 Open the file named Rep_Table_Template.dwt in the Templates folder.

2 Position the cursor in the large center cell with a white background (to the right of the menu system).

3 From the menu, choose Insert>Template Objects>Repeating Table. Fill in the following properties in the Repeating Table dialog box and then click OK:

Rows: **2**

Cell Padding: **5**

Columns: **3**

Cell Spacing: **0**

Width: **75 Percent**

Border: **1**

Starting Row: **2**

Ending Row: **2**

Region Name: **DataTable1**

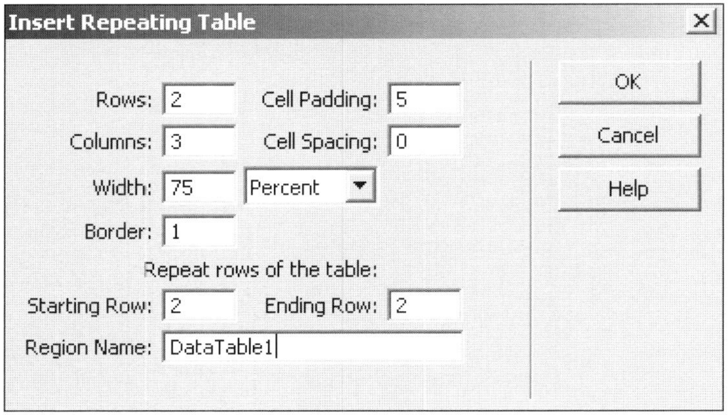

The Insert Repeating Table dialog box.

4 In Code view, change the top row <td> tag pairs to <th> to make them table headers instead of standard table cells.

This includes code lines 122 through 124, where you change the cells from <td> </td> to <th> </th>. You do this to make the row your table heading row. You also may decide you want column 1 to be the headings. Changing from <td> to <th> centers the content and makes it bold by default.

5 Now back to Design view. In row 1 (which is now table headers), type the following in the cells, beginning on the left and moving to the right: **Item No.**, **Item Name**, and **Item Description**.

To do this, position the cursor in the appropriate cell and type the text; then move the cursor to the next desired cell and repeat.

6 Click the region header labeled EditRegion3 in the Design window (this is your editable region label), open the Property inspector panel (the name should say Editable Region), and change the contents of the Name field to **ItemNo**.

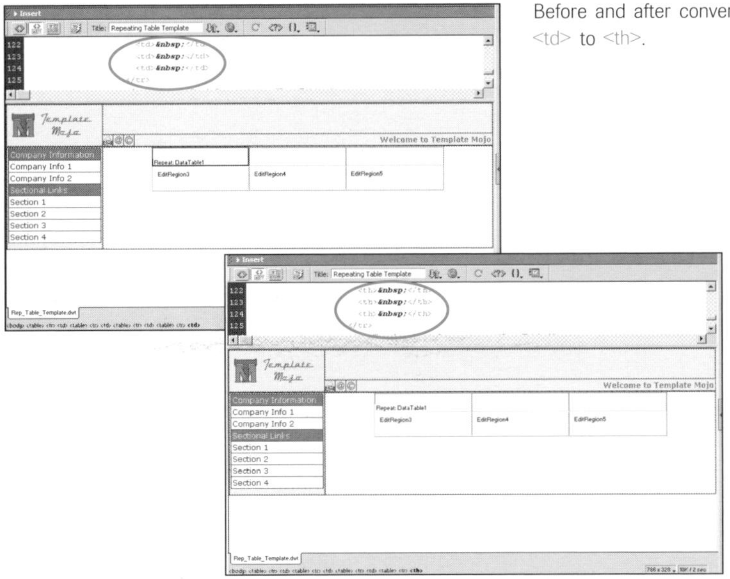

Before and after converting <td> to <th>.

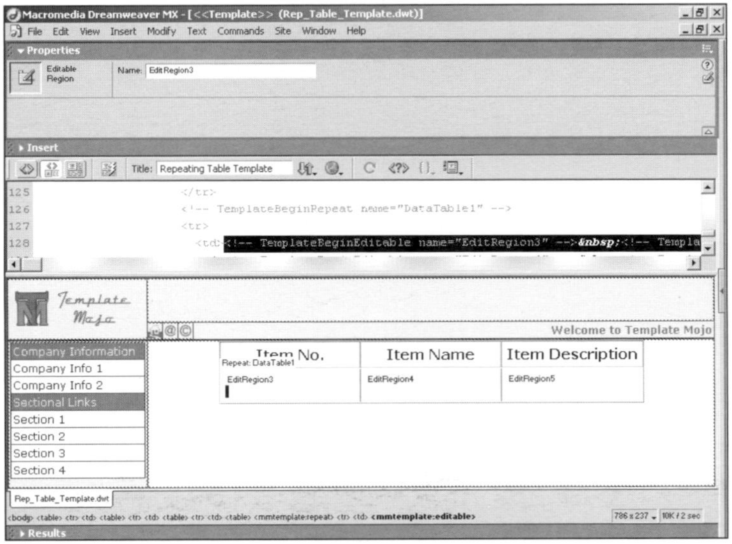

Working with Editable Region Properties.

Note: You can display the template region Property inspector three different ways when you are editing a template (not a template-based file):

- Using the Tag Selector, select <mmtemplate:regiontype>.
- Select the <!-- TemplateEndRepeat --> comment in Code view. (This is the closing comment for the region. Note that this method does not work for most region opening comments!)
- Carefully select the region header in Design view. (Note that you have to be very careful in selecting when you use this method because you could easily select the parent region by mistake.)

I recommend using the first method because it is the most reliable.

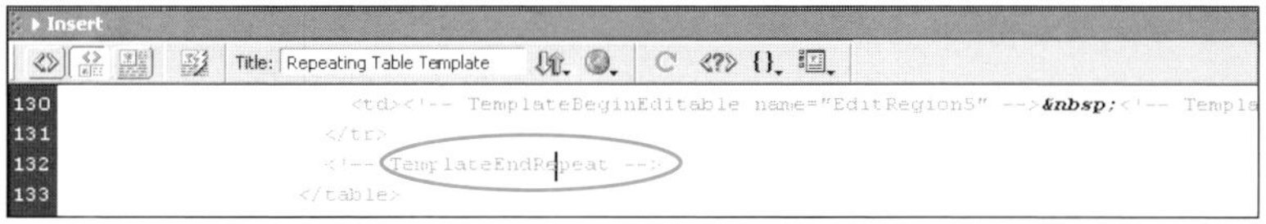

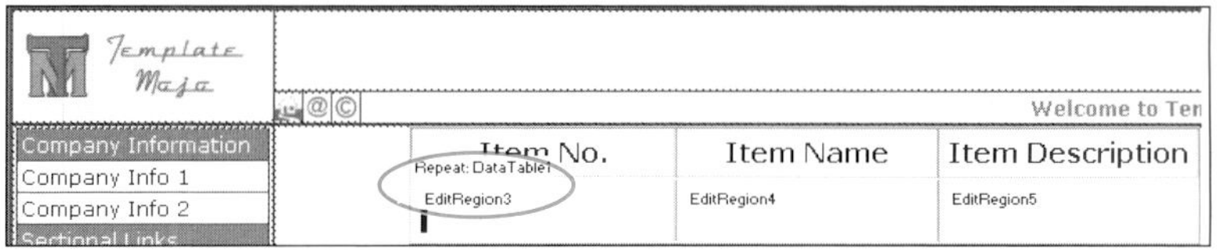

7 Repeat to the right, naming the remaining two fields **ItemName** and **ItemDesc**.

8 Save the template. (If you are prompted to update the template files that are based on this template, choose Update. Close the Update Report dialog box.) Close the template.

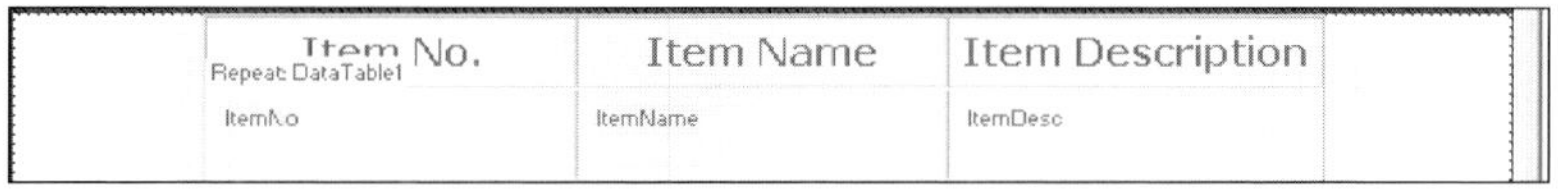

The completed repeating table template.

9 Open the root file named Repeat_Table.htm. Notice that the row contains an editable region in each cell and that it looks identical to the repeating region row discussed in the previous segment.

Position the cursor in row 2, column 1 (this should be the first editable region named ItemNo) and type **03**, then press the Tab key and type **Ring** in the editable region named ItemName. Press Tab again and type **1 karat Diamond Cluster** in the editable region named ItemDesc. Save the page and preview it in a browser.

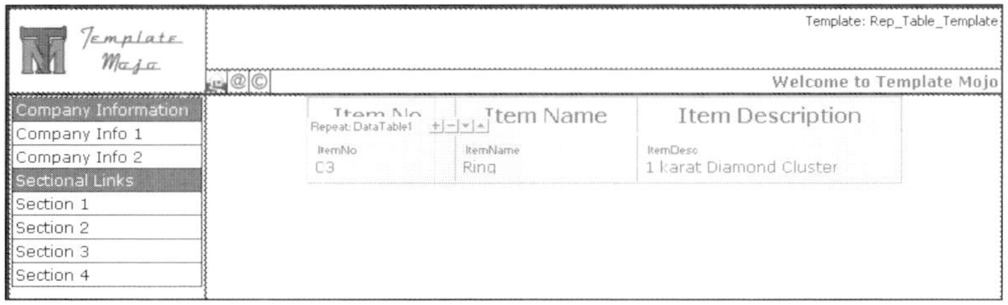

The repeating table document.

10 Click the + button in the repeating table GUI three times to add three more rows to the table. Starting in the third row, insert the data displayed in the list to the right:

Note: You can use the Tab key to move from field to field and then to the next row just like a normal table. You cannot, however, add another repeating table row by using the Tab key because an error message will be displayed.

When you've finished entering the data, save the page and preview it in a browser. Your item list should be 03, 01, 04, and 02 as you look from top to bottom in the Item No. column. Notice that the items are out of order! We'll fix that in the next few steps. Close your browser session and go back to Dreamweaver.

11 Position your cursor in the Item No. 03 row and click the down-arrow of the Repeating Object GUI once. This repositions the currently selected row down one position each time it is clicked. The order should now be 01, 03, 04, and 02.

12 Now position your cursor in the Item No. 02 row and click the up-arrow of the Repeating Object GUI twice. This moves this row up two positions. The order should now be 01, 02, 03, and 04. Save the page and close it.

You're probably wondering what the difference is between these last two objectives. With a repeating table, you can define more than one row and use an interface to control which row is the repeating row with an interface; it also makes every cell in the defined row editable. A repeating region, on the

Item No	Item Name	Item Description
01	Watch	Analog
04	Bracelet	Gold
02	Necklace	Silver

Repeating table content.

Item No.	Item Name	Item Description
01	Watch	Analog
02	Necklace	Silver
03	Ring	1 Karat Diamond Cluster
04	Bracelet	Gold

The completed repeating table.

Tip: If you know your Optional Region is going to be editable as well, use Insert>Template Objects>Editable Optional Region.

other hand, is selectable, which means that if you were to select the entire row, you could make only the last two cells editable and leave the leftmost cell non-editable so that cell remains the same down the table. (This is perfect for working with bullets, for example.) Repeating regions don't have to be a row; they can be an image or just about any tag. (Lists provide a good example for a repeating region.)

Inserting Optional Regions

In this section, you learn how to insert an optional region in your template, set it as viewable or hidden, and control it in your template-based page.

1. Open the file named Opt_Region_Template.dwt in the Templates folder.

2. Select the abstract art image in the large center cell with a white background. Select Insert>Template Objects>Optional Region.

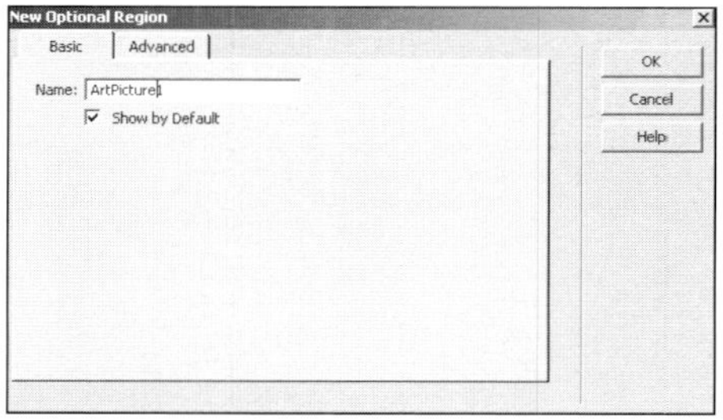

The New Optional Region dialog box.

3. In the Optional Region GUI, give the region a name of **ArtPicture1** and place a checkmark in the Show by Default field if it is not already checked. (The Advanced tab is not used at this time.) Click the OK button.

4. In Code view, scroll to just above the closing head tag </head> and you should see the following code added to your document (line 38 in the top figure).

   If you select the image and view the code, you will see the code shown in lines 124-126 of the figure on the bottom. (I have modified the document for the purpose of the screenshot, so your view may be different than the code around line 122 in Code view.)

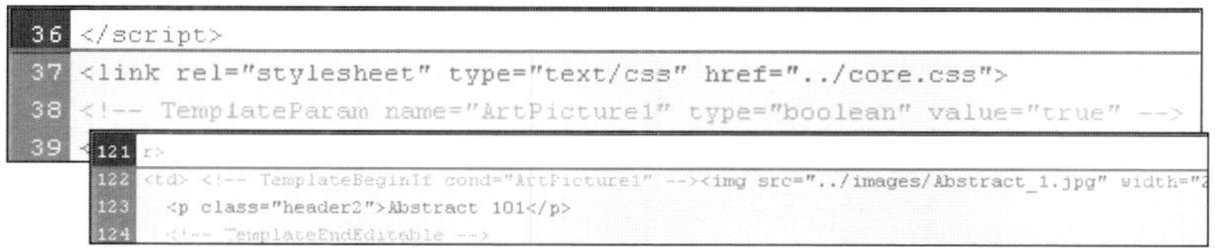

The Optional Region head code.

The Optional Region body code.

Note: The body code and the head statement are related and one cannot exist without the other. Well, that is not entirely true—as of this writing, you can move the body code around the image and the head statement remains. This occurs because the parameter may be used by another expression and currently Dreamweaver has no way of detecting that.

5 Save the template. (If you are prompted to update the template files that are based on this template, choose Update. Then close the Update Report dialog box.) Close the template.

6 Open the root document Opt_Region.htm. Notice that the editable regions are there. Select Modify>Template Properties.

7 In the UI, select ArtPicture1. By unchecking the Show ArtPicture1 checkbox, the image will not be shown. Notice that the source template provides only the initial state of the image, and the htm page itself controls the other state of the image—in this case, off. Remove the checkmark from the Show ArtPicture1 checkbox, save your document, and preview it in a browser.

8 Repeat Step 7, this time placing a checkmark in the Show ArtPicture1 checkbox; then save the document and preview in a browser. When you are satisfied with the results, close the document in Dreamweaver.

You have just successfully created and used an optional region. Congratulations!

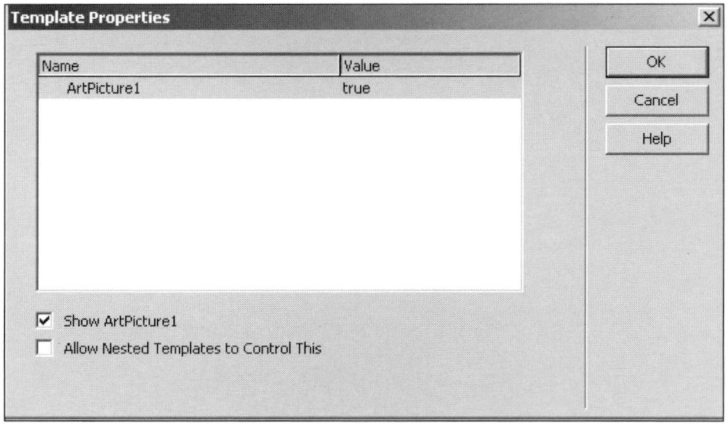

The Template Properties dialog box for the optional region.

INSERTING A *MultipleIf* CONDITIONAL STATEMENT

So, you want to have a specific image shown on certain pages—or not at all! To do this, you use an optional region and convert it to a MultipleIf conditional statement.

> **Tip:** MultipleIf conditional regions must be entered by hand, but you can use the Advanced tab of the Optional Region dialog box to generate your conditions. If you installed the extension for this project, your Snippets>Templates folder will display the head and body regions as usable Snippets.

1. Open the file named Multiple_If_Template.dwt in the Templates folder.

2. In Code view, insert the highlighted line of code shown just above the closing head tag. You can use the Snippet in the Snippet Template folder called MultipleIf Expression and then modify it to match the highlighted code on the right, or you can open MI_Head.txt and copy and paste it into the head region of the template file.

```
<link rel="stylesheet" type="text/css" href="../core.css">
<!-- TemplateParam name="ArtPicture1" type="number" value="1" -->
</head>
```

3. Select the abstract art image in Design view and go to Code view. Notice that the code for the image is highlighted. Press the Delete key to delete the image reference in the template file.

4. Press the Ctrl+` keyboard shortcut (Cmd+` for Mac) to go to the Code window of the Split view. (Your cursor should be positioned beside the <td> tag, where the image was located.) Type the highlighted code listed at the right. Alternatively, if you don't want to type all the code, you can open MI_Body1.txt and use the copy and paste operations to insert the code into the template file.

```
<td>
<!-- Define the appropriate image to display -->
<!-- TemplateBeginMultipleIf -->
<!-- TemplateBeginIfClause cond="ArtPicture1 == 1" --><imgsrc="../images/Abstract_1.jpg"
➥width="210" height="80"hspace="10" vspace="5" border="0" align="left"><!--TemplateEndIfClause -->
<!-- TemplateBeginIfClause cond="ArtPicture1 == 2" --><imgsrc="../images/Abstract_2.jpg"
➥width="210" height="80"hspace="10" vspace="5" border="0" align="left"><!--TemplateEndIfClause -->
<!-- TemplateEndMultipleIf -->
<!-- TemplateBeginEditable name="Header" -->
```

The code you just entered says this: "Provide the end user of the template-based file with the choice of two images. If image 1 is set, display image 1 and hide image 2. If image 2 is set, display image 2 and hide image 1."

What you've done here is manually enter a conditional region. In this instance, all the images are defined in the template; the end page allows you to choose which image to show. This is an excellent way to define a specific image for, say, a support department and a sales department not yet using the exact same layout.

Note: Notice that both images are shown in the template. This is the best presentation because you are editing the template file and you need to see the options available while editing. This won't be the case in the template-based page, though, as you will see below.

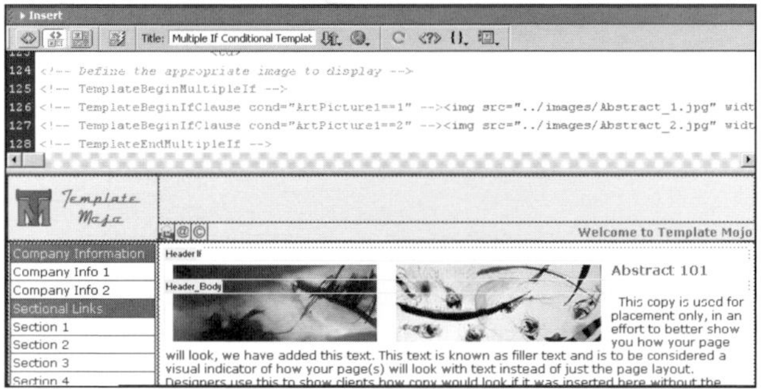

The MultipleIf optional region for the template.

5 Save the template. (Choose Update if you are prompted to update the template files that are based on this template; then close the dialog box.) Close the template.

6 Open the root document Multiple_If.htm. Notice that the editable regions are there, but wait and select Modify>Template Properties.

7 In the UI, select ArtPicture1, change the value from 1 to 2.

Because you have a choice of two images, placing a value of 3 or higher there will work, but no image will be displayed when you view the page online or in a local browser! Try it, insert any number other than 1 or 2 and see what happens!

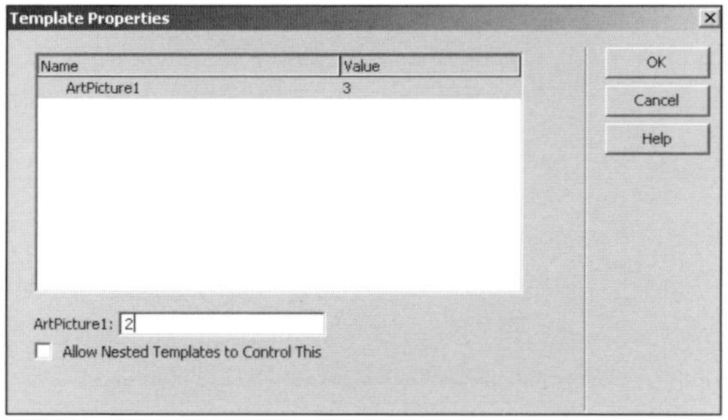

The Template Properties dialog box for MultipleIf.

8 You can correct this by opening the template file (Multiple_if_template.dwt) and manually adding another conditional test using the following line (outlined to the right) just before the closing <!-- TemplateEndMultipleIf --> statement. Add the highlighted code at right. If you don't want to type all the code, open the file named MI_Body2.txt and use copy and paste to place the code into your template file.

```
<!-- TemplateBeginIfClause cond="ArtPicture1 != 1 &
➥ArtPicture1 != 2" --><p>Your parameter selection for
➥ArtPicture1 is out of range!<br>Please use a 1 or a
➥2.</p><!-- TemplateEndIfClause -->
<!-- TemplateEndMultipleIf -->
```

Tip: Here's what I did to generate the conditional statement: I selected a clean area on the document, selected Insert>Template Objects>Optional Region, clicked the Advanced tab, selected Enter Expression, and typed ArtPicture1 !=1 & ArtPicture1 != 2. I then modified the following generated line:

```
<!-- TemplateBeginIf cond="ArtPicture1 !='1' & ArtPicture1 !=
'2'" -->
<!-- TemplateEndIf -->
```

to look like:

```
<!-- TemplateBeginIfClause cond="ArtPicture1 != 1 & ArtPicture1
!= 2" --><p>Your parameter selection for ArtPicture1 is out of
range!<br>Please use a 1 or a 2.</p><!--
➥TemplateEndIfClause -->
```

Finally, I pasted the code into the appropriate place in the MultipleIf code segment.

What this does is tell Dreamweaver to display a text message in the template-based file if neither option 1 nor option 2 is selected. If you used more images or objects, reflect this in the conditional test. What you have done here is add a conditional statement that checks the template-based page template property of ArtImage1. If this property is not set to a 1 or a 2, the inserted message is displayed. If the value is a 1 or a 2, the appropriate image appears.

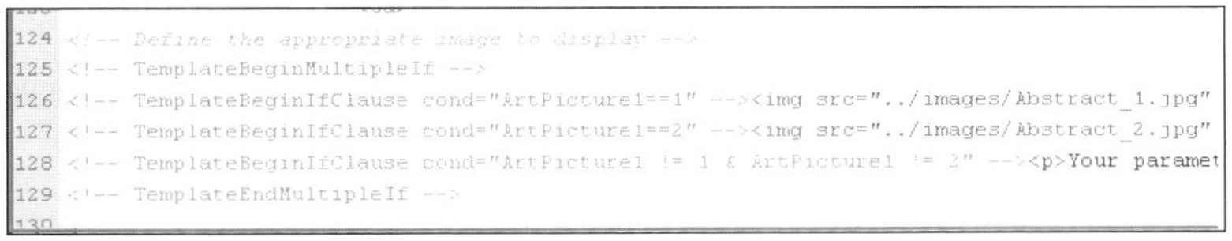
<!-- Define the appropriate image to display -->
<!-- TemplateBeginMultipleIf -->
<!-- TemplateBeginIfClause cond="ArtPicture1==1" --><img src="../images/Abstract_1.jpg"
<!-- TemplateBeginIfClause cond="ArtPicture1==2" --><img src="../images/Abstract_2.jpg"
<!-- TemplateBeginIfClause cond="ArtPicture1 != 1 & ArtPicture1 != 2" --><p>Your paramet
<!-- TemplateEndMultipleIf -->

The template with the MultipleIf condition.

9 Save the template (choose Update if prompted). Close the Update Report dialog box. Close the template.

10 Open the root document Multiple_If.htm and modify the Template Properties, trying various values from 1 through 5, saving the page and previewing in a browser each time.

11 Click OK, save the document, and preview the page in a browser.

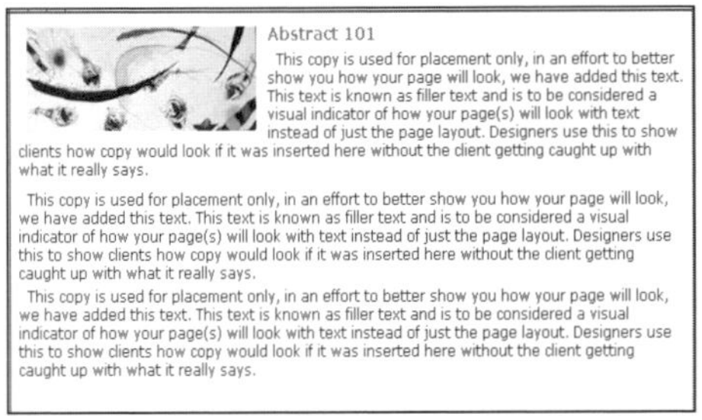

MultipleIf conditional using ArtPicture1=2.

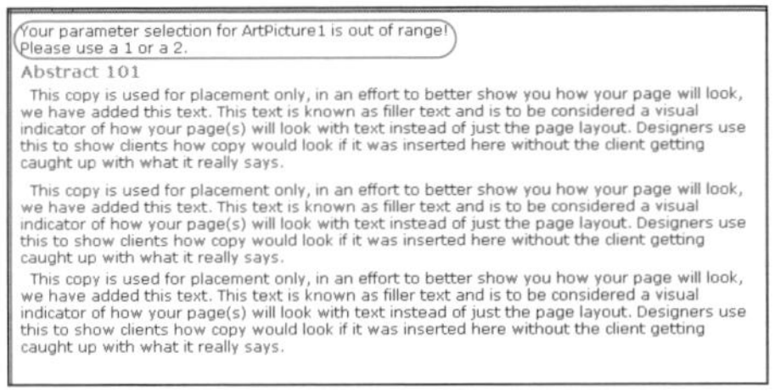

MultipleIf conditional using ArtPicture1=3.

12 Close any open documents and continue to the next segment.

Here, you can see that the template allows you to define template parameters to, in this instance, control which image shows on which page. The template allows you only to define the choice of images and the page itself. End users can use Template Properties to define the desired image without messing up the layout by editing the template itself.

Note: *Always* use Modify>Template Properties to modify the desired MultipleIf element; otherwise, elements could be selected or displayed incorrectly.

Editable Tag Attributes

You want to allow the page-building personnel to have some creative input into the design without risking corruption of the template? Great, let's add some editable tag attributes to the mix to get control over the <img> tag's alt attribute content.

1 Open the file named Edit_Attrib_Template.dwt in the Templates folder.

2 Select the abstract art image and choose Modify>Templates>Make Attribute Editable. The Editable Tag Attributes dialog box opens.

The Attribute field populates with a drop-down of found attributes for the selected tag. If an attribute is not available in the list, and you know it is specific for the tag, click Add and type the attribute name.

3 Click the Add button and in the dialog, type **ALT** and click OK. Notice that the Make Attribute Editable checkbox was automatically checked by this action!

4 In the Label field, type **Alt1**. In the Type drop-down, choose text, and in the Default field, type **Alternate Text** and then click OK.

5 In Code view, you see that the image tag now has an alt attribute and it is defined with @@(Alt1)@@. If you also look in the head section just before the </head> tag, you will see that the following code has been added:

```
<!-- TemplateParam name="Alt1" type="text"
➥value="alternate text" -->
```

Oh look, another parameter type!

6 Save the template (choose Update if you're prompted to do so; then close the dialog box). Close the template.

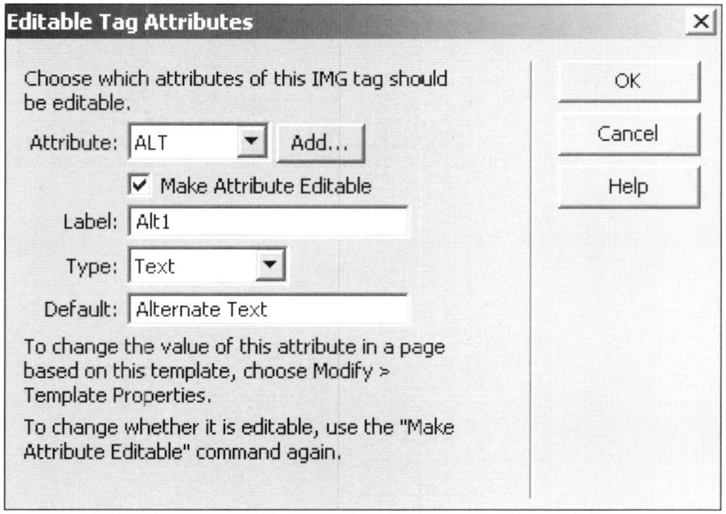

The Editable Tag Attribute dialog box.

7 Open the root document Edit_Attrib.htm. Notice that the editable regions are there and select Modify>Template Properties.

8 In the UI, select **Alt1**, and change the value to **Abstract Art**. Click OK, save the document, and preview in a browser.

9 Repeat Steps 2 through 8, this time selecting other attributes of the image tag to make them editable. Define their defaults and experiment! Save the document and preview it in a browser. Close the document when you are satisfied with the results.

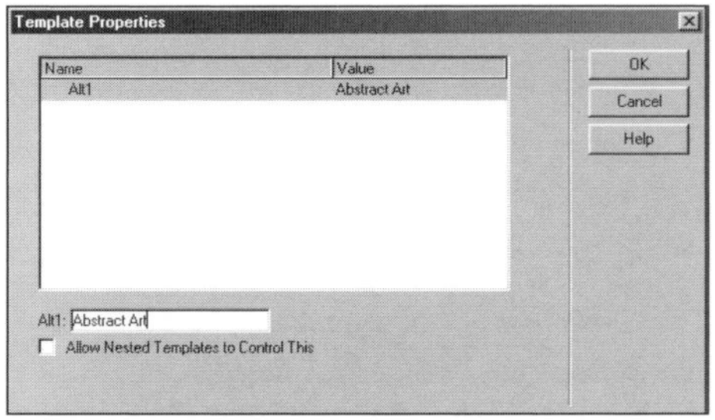

The Template Properties dialog box with the editable tag attribute.

This is a great way to add a customizable link in your document to allow a template page author to insert links. Experiment with this; try making it a repeating region and see what you can do with it.

Adding CSS to a Template-Based Page

In the days of Dreamweaver 4, you could not add or edit a style block of a page that was based on a template (without hand-coding a workaround, that is). Well, that feature is built into Dreamweaver MX now, and you will learn and use that method here.

1 Open the file named Edit_Attrib.htm in the root folder.

Note: You cannot add CSS to a non-editable region of a page. To add CSS to a non-editable region, it must be done in the template itself.

Tip: You can add an editable tag attribute in the template to make the desired tag accept user-added CSS!

2 Open the CSS Styles panel, and click the Edit Styles radio button. Choose the New CSS Style button from the bottom of the panel and choose the Make Custom Style (Class) radio button. Type .testpara in the Name field, and lastly, in the Define In Option, click the This Document Only radio button and click OK.

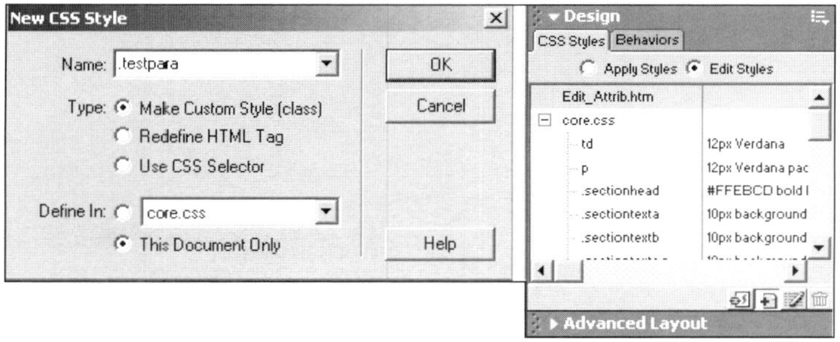

The New Style button in the CSS Styles panel and New CSS Style dialog box.

3 Under Category, choose Type, and choose the following settings:

Font: **Times New Roman, Times, serif** (Your font choices may vary depending on the platform, OS, and fonts installed on your machine.)

Size: **14 Pixels**

Style: **Italic**

Color: **#008080**

Click Apply and OK to close the CSS Editor.

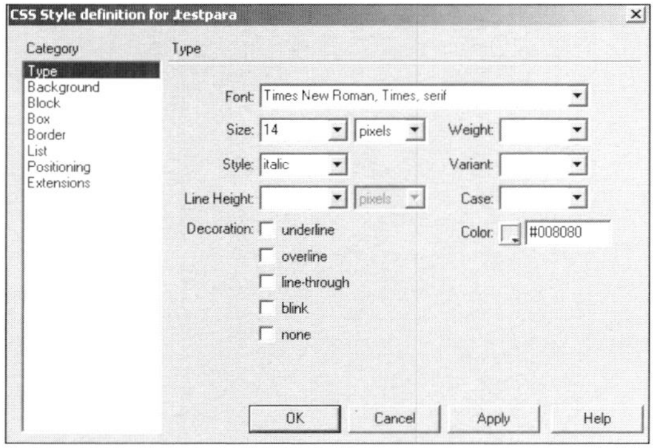

Style Editor.

4 Now view your document in Code view and look at the page, specifically, at an editable region named head in the head block of the document, where you will see the class added inside a new style block. Dreamweaver MX automatically adds this editable region to templates and template-based documents for just this reason as well as adding behaviors.

```
<!-- InstanceBeginEditable name="head" -->
<style type="text/css">
<!--
.testpara {
   font-family: "Times New Roman", Times, serif;
   font-size: 14px;
   font-style: italic;
   color: #008080;
}
-->
</style>
<!-- InstanceEndEditable -->
```

5 Using Design view, position your cursor in the first paragraph of the Body_Content editable region and select the <p.Contenttext> tag using the Tag Selector.

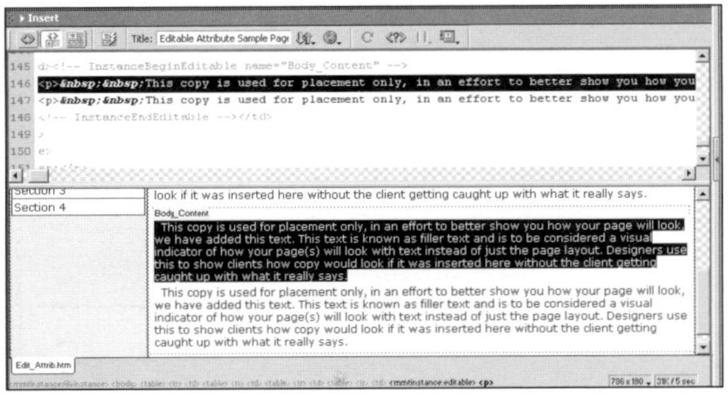

Paragraph that will be styled.

6 Select Text>CSS Styles>testpara. and your document view will be refreshed with the selected style.

7 Save the document, and preview it in a browser. Close the file when you are satisfied with your changes.

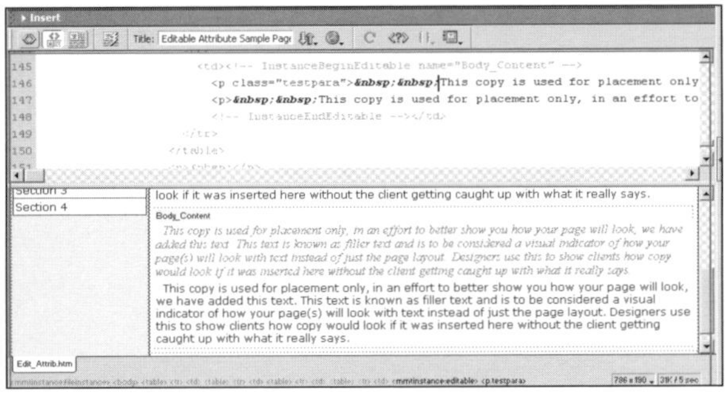

The paragraph tag after the CSS addition.

Adding a Behavior to a Template-Based Page

With the advent of editable tag attributes, you can add behaviors to the body tag with ease, as long as the JavaScript already exists on the page and you know what the function name and parameters are. (It pays here to apply your behavior to a non-template-based page and use copy and paste to insert the required code in the Template Properties dialog box.)

1 Open the file named Behavior_Template.dwt in the Templates folder.

Note: A few notes about behaviors:

- You can add behaviors to any body-area editable region without issue.
- If you want to add a behavior to a non-editable region, the appropriate tag must have an editable tag attribute. (See the section, "Editable Tag Attributes.")
- If the behavior JavaScript block does not exist on the page when you add the behavior, the JavaScript will go in the same editable region (called head) as the page added CSS as in the previous segment.

2 Select the body tag and make it editable as you have done previously. For the editable attribute, choose onLoad. (If you don't see onLoad in the drop-down list, click the Add button, type **onLoad**, and click OK.) Label the tag **LoadIt** and leave the remainder of the dialog fields at their defaults; then click OK.

This does not assign a value to the onLoad event, but rather assigns a parameter that you can use from the Template-based page to the onLoad event.

Save the template, updating the files if prompted. Close the template.

3 Open the file in the root folder named Behavior.htm.

4 Select Modify>Template Properties, choose LoadIt from the dialog box, and in the text field, type **MM_showHideLayers('LyrCopyr','','show')**. Click OK.

5 Save the document, preview it in a browser to see the copyright message layer shown onLoad at the top of the page. Close the document when you are satisfied with the changes.

You can select just about any element and apply a behavior to it, but it has to be in an editable region or an editable attribute in the desired element.

```
37  <link rel="stylesheet" type="text/css" href="../core.css">
38  <!-- TemplateParam name="LoadIt" type="text" value="" -->
39  </head>
40
41  <body leftmargin="0" topmargin="0" marginwidth="0" marginheight="0" onLoad="@@(LoadIt)@@">
42  <div id="LyrCopyr" style="position:absolute; width:500px; z-index:1; left: 155px; top: 7px;
```

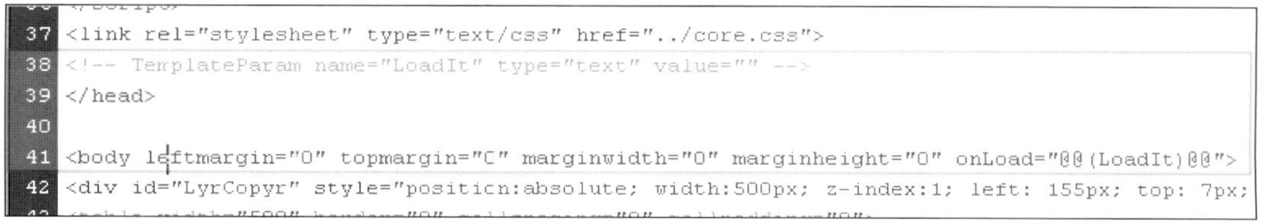

Code view showing the modified body tag.

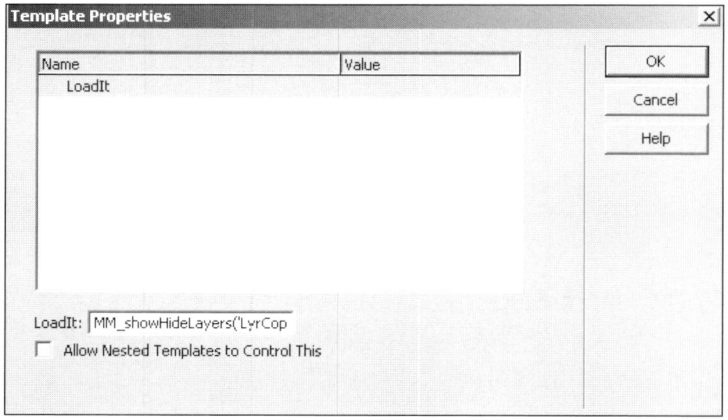

The Template Properties dialog box.

CHECKING TEMPLATE SYNTAX

You now have the capability of manually checking your template syntax prior to saving the template or Dreamweaver will do it for you automatically when you save a template. If any errors are detected in your template syntax, they are reported to you in a dialog box showing the error description, line number, and the location of error.

1 To check your template syntax manually, choose Modify>Templates> Check Template Syntax.

2 To automatically check your syntax, save the template file.

3 If any errors are detected, the syntax checker dialog box appears. When you are manually using the Check Template Syntax functions, if everything is OK, the OK dialog appears. Note that when you "automatically" save your template, you will not see the OK dialog box if everything is fine.

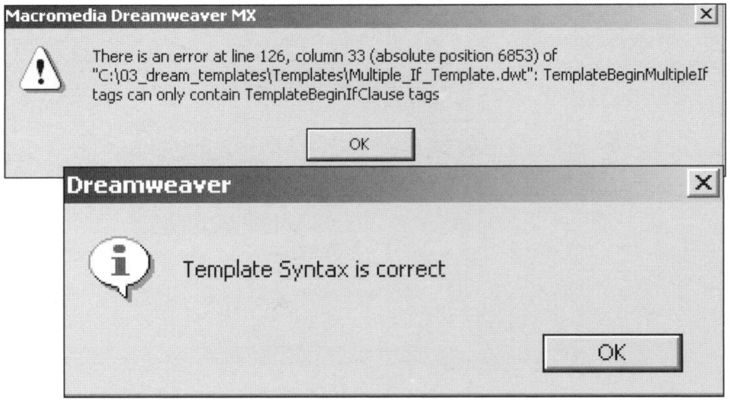

A Check Template Syntax warning.

A dialog box telling you that the Check Template Syntax is OK.

Detaching Your Template-Based Pages

Remember in Dreamweaver 4 when you had to detach the page from the template to add a custom behavior to the body tag? That functionality is still there, but you have a new way to do it without completely messing up your template-based page. This segment of the project deals with methods of detaching your pages from a template.

You really have no reason to detach your pages from a template anymore due to functionality reasons (such as adding a behavior to the body tag); however, you might have other reason to detach your pages. These reasons include, but are not limited to the following:

- To reduce the amount of code in your page, thereby reducing bandwidth usage.
- To make troubleshooting your page(s) easier for outsiders who might not have your template.
- To camouflage the fact that you used a template to build the site.
- To make a unique change to one instance of the template, that you do not want applied in other instances in the same template.

Method A: Clean Up HTML

1 Open the file name methoda.htm in the root site folder.

2 From the menu, choose Commands>Clean Up HTML. The Clean Up HTML/XHTML dialog box appears.

3 Place a checkmark in Remove>Dreamweaver Special Markup. When you do this, a warning message appears telling you that library items, templates, and tracing images will no longer be updated. Click OK.

4 The Clean up summary report lets you know how many tags were affected on the page. Click OK.

5 Dreamweaver refreshes the page in your original view. The page is 100 percent editable—no more locked regions.

6 Save the resulting page as methoda_done.htm and close the document.

When to use this method: Use this method when you are working on a single page that is based on a template, if you want a level of control to delete all template markup and do a code check at the same time.

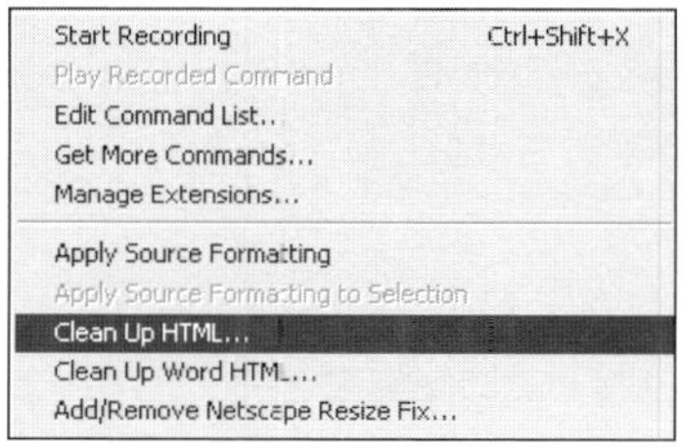

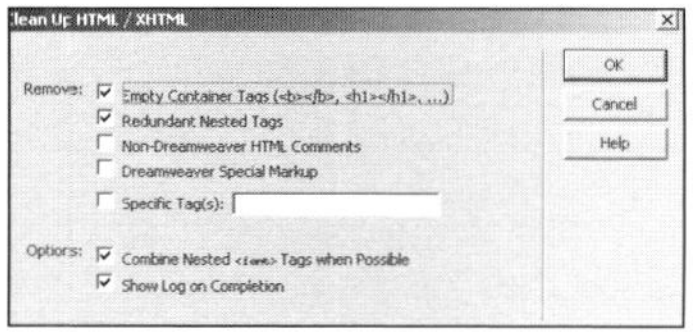

Choosing the Clean Up HTML command.

The Clean Up HTML/XHTML dialog box.

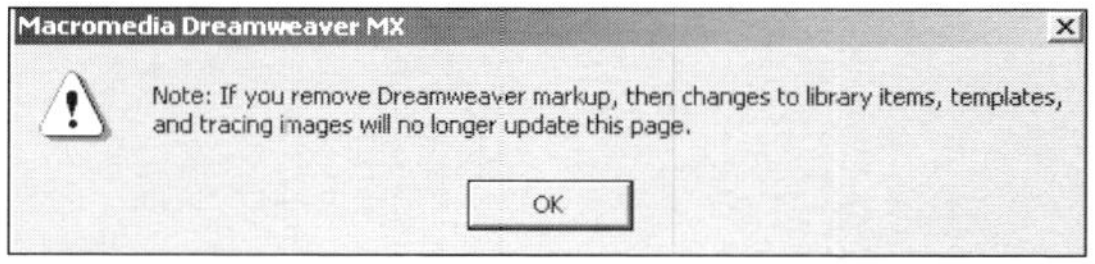

The warning message explaining what the operation will do.

The Clean up summary report.

Method B: Detach from Template

1 Open the file name methodb.htm in the root site folder.

2 From the menu, choose Modify>Templates>Detach from Template.

3 Save the resulting page as methodb_done.htm and close the document.

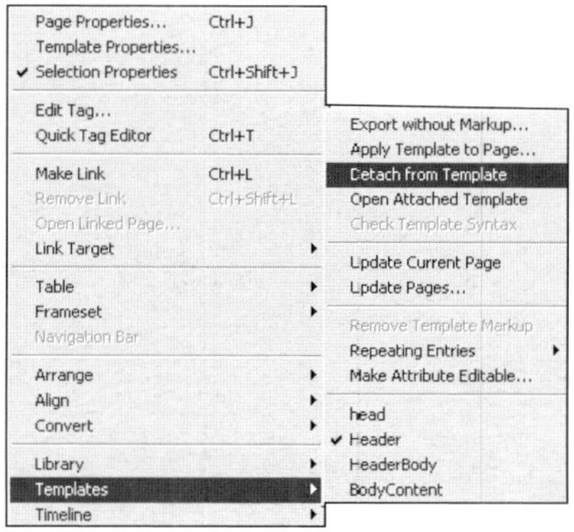

Choosing the Detach from Template command.

When to use this method: Use this method most for single-page detachment. The reason for this is that there are no dialog boxes to complete and no warning prompts—it's instantaneous.

Method C: Export Without Markup

1 Using your file manager application, create a new folder on your local hard drive and label it **methodc**. (*Do not create this folder in the site structure or errors will occur!*) Close your file management application and start Dreamweaver if necessary.

2 You can open any document or not open any at all for this procedure. It's your choice—either way, the result is the same. For the purpose of this demonstration, open methodc.htm from the site root.

3 From the menu, choose Modify>Templates>Export without Markup.

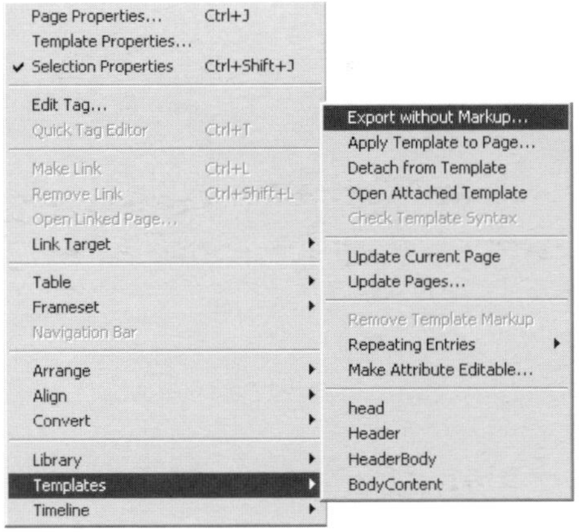

Selecting the Export without Markup command.

4 The Export Site Without Template Markup dialog box appears.

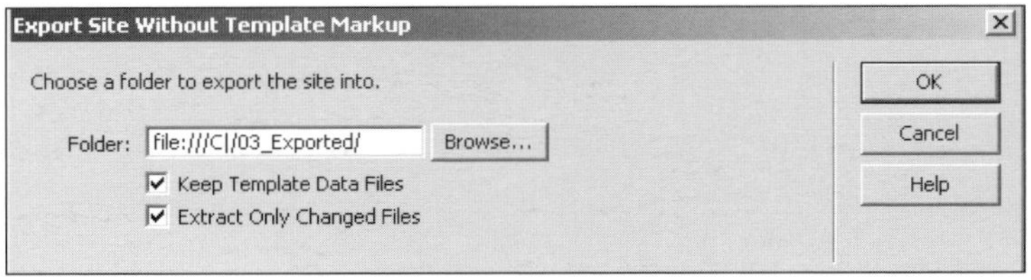

The Export Site Without Template Markup dialog box.

5 Using the Browse button, navigate to the methodc folder, open it, and click the Select button in the Extract Template XML dialog box.

6 *Optional:* Enable Keep Template Data Files by placing a check in the checkbox, if it is empty. This exports the template data to an .xml file, which makes it easier in the future to apply the removed template to the page again. It also helps Dreamweaver decide if the page needs updating when the Extract Only Changed Files is enabled. If you decide to disable this, no .xml files will be generated and it will be difficult to recreate or apply the template to the pages again, and Dreamweaver won't know the change status as discussed in the following steps.

7 *Optional:* Enable Extract Only Changed Files by placing a check in the checkbox, if it is empty. (This exports the files that have changed since your last export or the entire site if no export has been previously performed.)

8 Click OK. Dreamweaver's processing dialog may show up with the cursor in the busy state and after a little bit the dialog goes away. At this point, your entire site is exported with no visual clue even if you had a document open at the time.

9 Close the document if you had one open.

10 Using your file management application, navigate to the folder methodc and have a look. Now there is an additional .xml file for each template-based page. These .xml files are used by Dreamweaver and Dreamweaver alone and do not require publishing to the web site on the server. You could delete them if you like, but the reasons for keeping them are detailed above if you decided to create them in the first place.

11 Close your file management application.

When to use this method: Use this method when you want to be able to delete all template markup on the entire site or only on changed files since last export, and you don't want to affect your local site files.

Cautionary Note: Unless you are careful with the options, you could export newer files that you don't want updated, so choose your options carefully. All template-based pages will have their template code removed using this method, excluding the templates themselves.

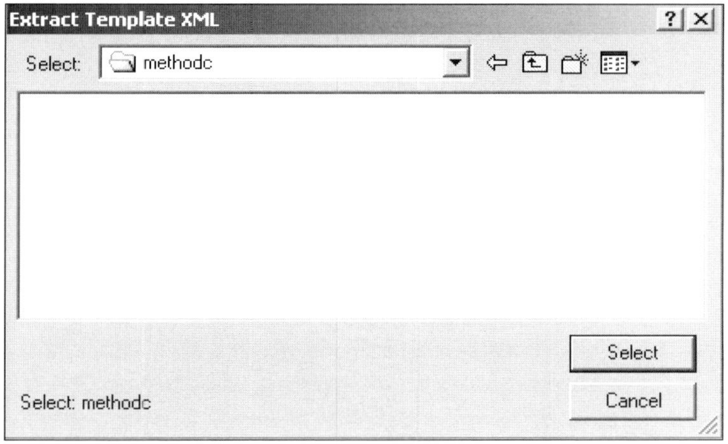

The Extract Template XML dialog box.

Here you have learned various ways to detach a file or a group of files from the template with which they were created. Exercise caution using any of the methods; it is easy to overwrite good pages with bad and lose the template update capability in a site.

Play with the various methods you have learned and decide for yourself when you should use which method for your own needs and situation.

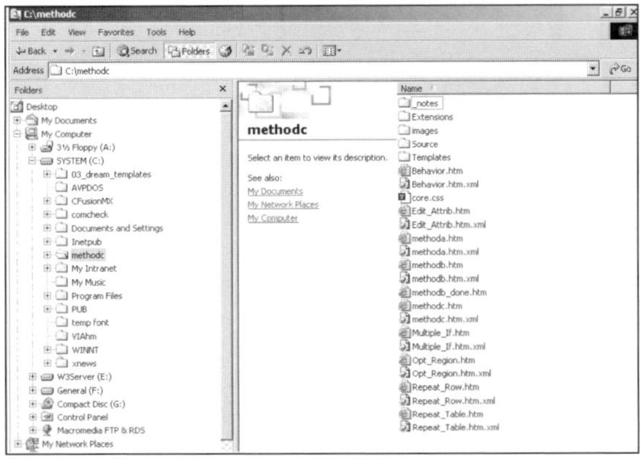

File management application view of the exported site.

Modifications

You can go in many different directions with this template set, which contains two basic templates. One template could be used for the index page, a news area start page, or just about any sectional starting page. The other is useful for the remainder of the site. For instance, you could make a nice PC service web site out of this template or perhaps a web design site. All you need to do is modify the provided template to your requirements, but try adding CSS styles to the repeating and optional regions to further customize it. Any element of the template set can be customized by combining what you have learned throughout this project into one template that controls your whole site.

Not only can you modify the templates, but you now have the knowledge from Projects 2 and 3 to create a completely new template that matches your site design requirement. But wait, there's more... check out the help files (press F1 when Dreamweaver is active) and do a search for the different regions of a template because you can do much more with templates than you've seen here. To give you a teaser, think about having the capability of programmatically telling a table row to alternate colors. And we didn't even get a chance to touch on the completely new Nested Templates.

I'm sure that after you read Projects 2 and 3, the help files that you will be making your own templates with will be far superior region conditional statements than the ones we have explored here. Don't be afraid to experiment!

Enjoy...

Tip: If you have a dynamic site that was created with a server-side language such as ASP, PHP, and so on, you are required to use the following code Snippet in the Template file:

```
<!-- TemplateInfo codeOutsideHTMLIsLocked="true" -->
```

This code must be typed, or you can use the extension to add the Snippet to your Snippet panel. The reason for this is that server-side technologies often add code above the opening <html> tag, and adding this line ensures this server-side code will be transferred to the template-based page(s).

If your template-based page contains no server-side code, you don't need to add this line. Also note that you can still add server-side code to template-based files without issue.

Tip: Use the MultipleIf Template Snippets to save yourself some typing when using these conditional regions.

"The power of the web is in its universality. Access by everyone regardless of disability is an essential aspect."

—TIM BERNERS-LEE

ACCESSIBILITY: SEEING AS OTHERS SEE, OR OTHERWISE

Designing Accessible Web Pages

Everyone has heard of accessibility and the need to design accessible web sites, but not too many of us are confident in doing it. This project explores the new accessibility tools in Dreamweaver MX. In this project, you learn how to design for accessibility, comply with Section 508 and other accessibility legislation, and test and retrofit your existing web pages to meet accessibility guidelines. The good news is that Dreamweaver makes it easy, once you know how!

Project 4

Accessibility: Seeing as Others See, or Otherwise

by David Nicholls

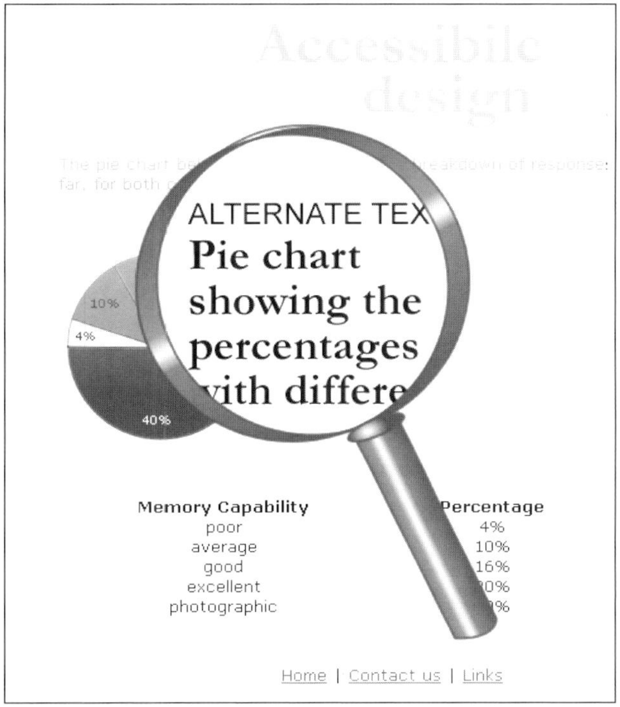

It Works Like This

The major part of this project leads you through building a web page with several standard components which are fully compliant with U.S. Government accessibility requirements and W3C guidelines. In this project, you become familiar with the accessibility tools built into Dreamweaver, understand what they mean, and see how to use them. Then you take a brief look at how to update an existing web page for accessibility. Finally, you learn about other testing tools available and find some of the more useful and readable online sources of accessibility information.

What Is Accessibility and Why Is It Important?

Before we go any further, let's review what accessibility is all about. The quote from Tim Berners-Lee at the start of this chapter gives you a simple and clear definition: Accessibility is about giving people with disabilities the same access to information on the web that people without disabilities have. Because the web still is primarily a visual medium, accessibility means giving people with visual disabilities the means to access the same or equivalent information others can view, by alternative means if necessary.

Apart from the egalitarian and democratic rationale for accessibility, today we also have legal imperatives. In the U.S., Australia, and other countries, legislation or regulations have been put in place requiring government web sites to be accessible to persons with visual disabilities. These rules take into account the way information is delivered over the web (using HTML and other technologies) and the means by which the visually challenged user accesses web pages (for example, screen readers).

The motivation for this is twofold. First, governments are delivering services to citizens via the web and they want all citizens to have access to these services. Second, we live in an increasingly litigious world, and already cases have developed in which people have sued organizations because they could not obtain a service that was provided only via the web. A case in point occurred during the last summer Olympics, in which the Olympic Organizing Committee was taken to court because visually impaired persons could not book tickets for Olympic events using the official web site.

An accessible web site is one whose information is available to all users; one that can be navigated; one that can be explored using methods other than the mouse (by keyboard, for example); and one that can be clearly and easily understood.

Note: Accessible web sites and usable web sites have many factors in common, and frequently a fully accessible site also is readily usable.

So it behooves web site builders to take accessibility requirements into account when building sites for both commercial and government clients, for ethical reasons as well as self-interest.

Note: One common form of visual disability, affecting as much as five percent of the population, is colorblindness. The way in which you use color on your site can make a big difference in how intelligible the images are to colorblind people. The illustration available on the CD-ROM shows a simulation of one particular type of colorblindness (deuteranope) when unsuitable colors are used.

Red-green colorblindness—technically called *deutanopia* and *protanopia*—can make certain colors indistinguishable. If you use colors to convey information, be sure that you avoid red-green problems. See http://webexhibits.org/causesofcolor/2.html for more information.

The simulation was made with a plug-in (for Fireworks, Photoshop, and so on) available from Vischeck (www.vischeck.com). To see the full-color image, check the CD-ROM. As you will see, the two-color image is frustrating—you can't see the color information because of the printing process—the effect is a bit like the problems a colorblind person can experience on some web sites.

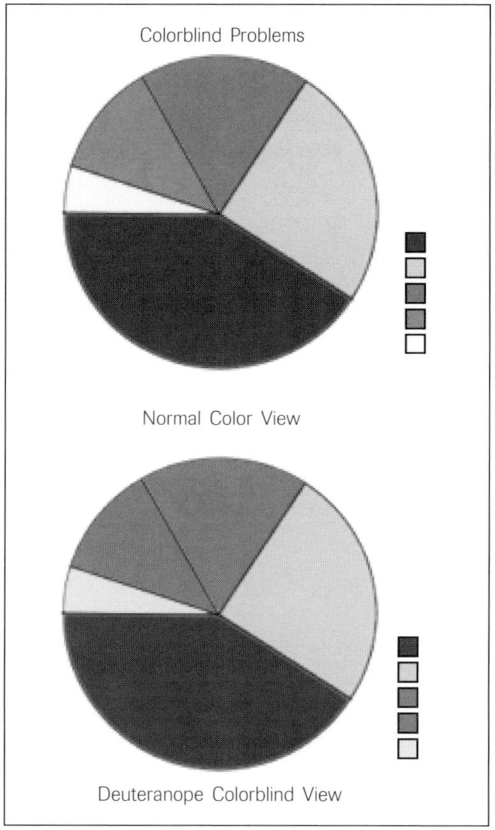

What the wrong color choice can look like if you're colorblind. In this version, you can't see much difference. That's a problem colorblind people have all the time.

Note: Because this is a two-color book, we are unable to show the images in full color. We have included copies of the original, full-color images in the 04_accessibility/color_images folder on the accompanying CD, however, in case you want to view them.

How Do You Decide What Makes Web Pages Accessible?

The answer to this is simple: In the U.S., a federal regulation known as Section 508 details the accessibility requirements. Elsewhere, the W3C Web Content Accessibility Guidelines are used. The two standards are very similar, and it is likely that other regulations and legislation will be enacted around the world in the future.

How Do You Build Accessible Web Pages?

One way to build accessible web pages is to become completely familiar with the regulations and guidelines and to check all HTML and related code line by line. This method is unreliable and extremely tedious, however.

A far easier way is to use Dreamweaver MX with Accessibility Preferences active and take advantage of its built-in prompting tools. Although accessible HTML code cannot be completely automated—on some occasions, a decision must be made as to whether a particular tag element is required—you can avoid mistakes more easily if you are using an authoring system that reminds you each time an accessibility question arises.

Finally, you can use several means of testing and validating HTML pages to confirm they meet accessibility requirements. Later in this chapter you learn more about this.

Preparing to Work

To set up the project, all you need to do is transfer the working files from the CD-ROM to your hard drive and define a new site in Dreamweaver.

1 Open the CD-ROM and navigate to the Projects/04_accessibility folder. Copy the folder elephants to your hard drive.

2 Open Dreamweaver MX and create a new site called **Elephants** using the Site Definition box.

- Browse to set the Local Root folder (C:\elephants\, or wherever you have located the elephants folder).
- For the Default Images folder, browse to set the assets subfolder. This is the folder where all the images, style sheet, and auxiliary text files are located.
- For the purposes of this exercise, leave the HTTP Address unchanged and the Cache check box checked. Click OK.

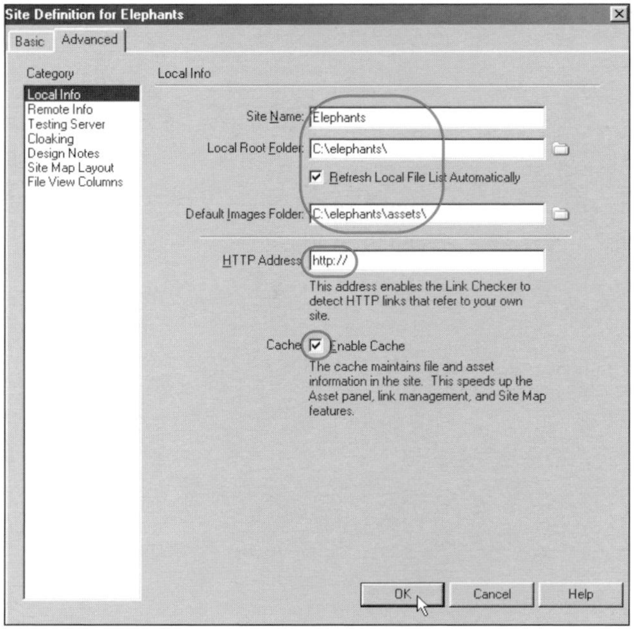

Creating a new site from the menu.

3 Set the Accessibility Preferences.

- From the Menu bar, choose Edit>Preferences and select the Accessibility category.
- Check all the Show Attributes boxes and click OK.

Setting these preferences causes Dreamweaver to prompt you every time you enter an HTML element for which accessibility tag components are desirable or necessary.

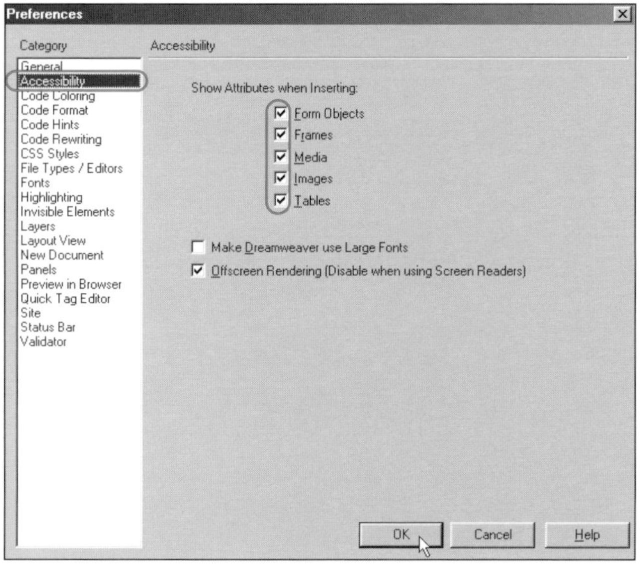

Setting the Accessibility Preferences from the menu.

Setting Up the Page Layout with a Table

OK, we're ready to start. Grab a cup of coffee and we'll get down to business. You're going to use Dreamweaver to build a simple web page from scratch, using some of the more important HTML components where accessibility is an issue.

Note: In the project files on the CD-ROM, I've used lowercase tags, but you can use either upper- or lowercase. Lowercase tags are better for XHTML compatibility.

1 Open the file index.html in the Elephants site in Dreamweaver. The initial file is a blank page with only the HTML type declaration included.

Tip: If you were only going to add a title to the page header, it would be easier to use the Title box in the Document toolbar, but because you also want to modify the <HTML> tag, it's quicker to do both in the Code View window.

2 Click in the Code View window and add the title **Elephant Survey** for the page in the TITLE tags. Then set the language of the page—in this case, English—by adding LANG="EN" to the HTML tag so that it reads <HTML LANG="EN">. Return to Design view by clicking in the Design View window.

Note: The LANG attribute in the HTML tag alerts screen readers and helps automate translation.

3 Next you need to create a table to set the page layout and fill it with the elements that need to be handled properly to ensure accessibility. Click the Insert Table icon to start the process, and in the Insert Table dialog box, create a table with the following settings:

Rows: **3**

Columns: **3**

Cell Padding: **0**

Cell Spacing: **0**

Width: **80%**

Border: **0**

Click OK.

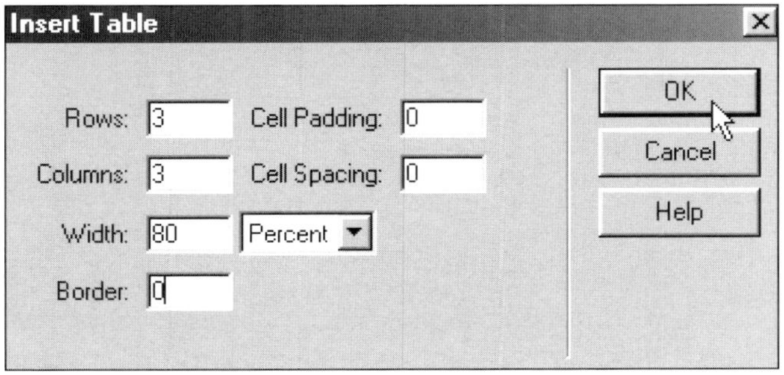

Setting up the table.

4 Immediately after you have accepted these values, the Accessibility Options for Tables dialog box opens to alert you to set values. In this case, because you are using the table for layout purposes, enter only a Summary indicating this and leave the other entries blank. You'll use the other settings later on, so all you need to do right now is type **Page Layout Table** in the Summary field.

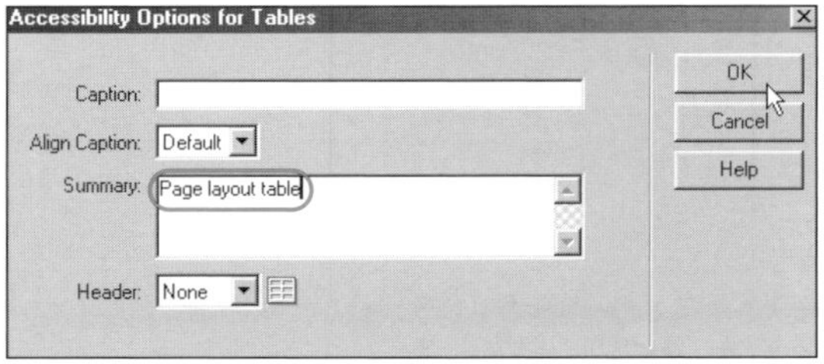

Setting the table's accessibility options.

After you accept these settings by clicking OK, the table is inserted into the page.

5 Take this opportunity to center the table on the page. Select the <table> tag in the Tag Selector bar under the Design View window, and in the Property inspector, choose the Center option from the Align drop-down list.

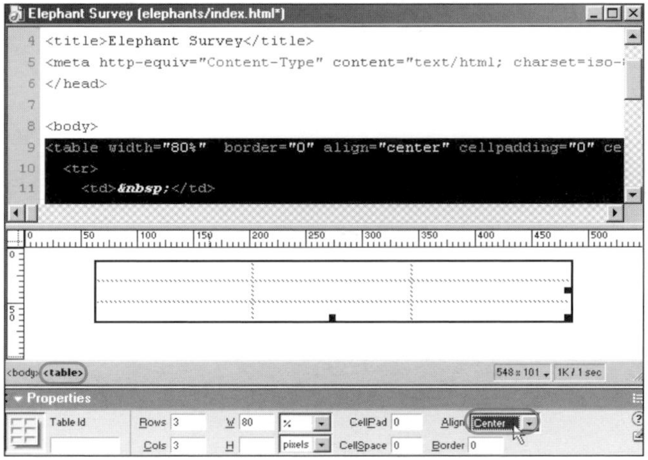

How the empty table appears in Design view.

6 Click in the top-left cell in the Design View window: You are going to add a transparent spacer GIF here.

7 Click the Image icon in the Common tab of the Insert toolbar (or choose Insert>Image) and then navigate to the assets folder and select the file transparentPixel.gif.

Click OK, and the Image Tag Accessibility Attributes dialog box opens.

8 This is one of the most important accessibility qualifiers: Every image should have alternate (ALT) text, and if the text is complex, the image needs Long Description (LONGDESC) text as well. In this case, you need to set only the ALT text. In the Alternate Text box, enter a space. Because the spacer GIF has no information content, you need to indicate this by entering null information—either a space or nothing—for the ALT text.

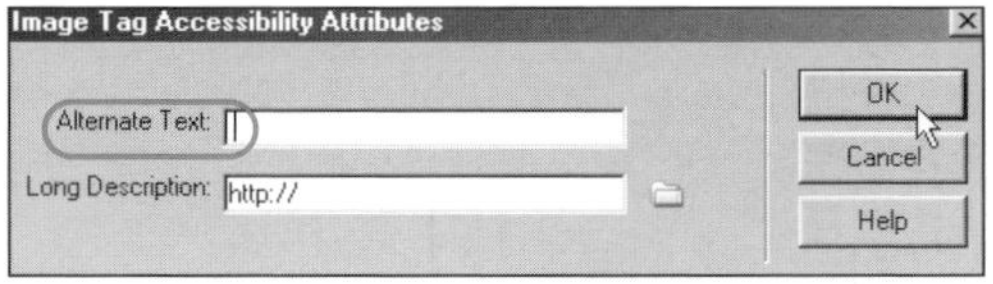

A key step—setting the alternate text.

Note: Downloadable screen readers are available, but they take a lot of experience to use properly, so if you have normal vision, using a service like WAVE is a much better way to understand what a screen reader will encounter. See details at the end of this chapter.

Note: If you leave the ALT text blank in the attributes window, Dreamweaver adds no ALT element in the IMAGE tag, so be sure to insert a blank space in the window. If you are entering the ALT text directly into the tag in the Code View window, you can insert either ALT="" or ALT=" ".

9 This GIF is a 1×1 pixel image but you want to space the column out to 100 pixels, which means you need to tell Dreamweaver to draw the image 100 pixels wide. Select the image (click the <IMG> tag in the Tag Selector bar beneath the Design View window), and enter 100 for the Width value in the Property inspector.

Note: When you change the dimensions of an image, Dreamweaver alerts you when the size differs from the true image size by displaying in the Property inspector the width or height in bold type. Changing the dimensions of an image is generally not a good idea because resizing in the browser often displays the image with "jaggies," but in this case, the image is transparent and is used only as a spacer, so it is quite acceptable.

10 Create the same spacing element in the top-right table cell by clicking in the top-right cell in the Design View window and repeating Steps 6 though 9.

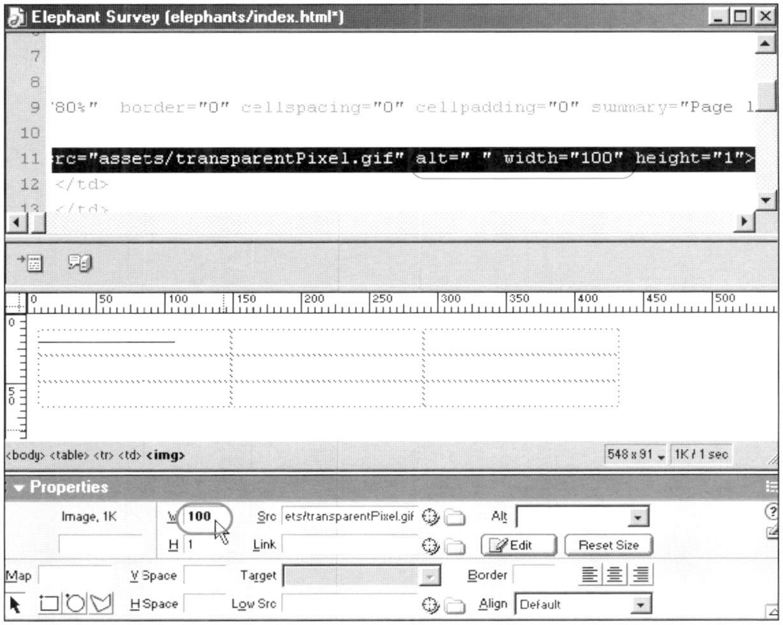

Widening the spacer GIF.

11 To complete the top row, you need to insert a banner image in the center cell. In the Design View window, click in the center-top cell and insert the image file elephant_banner.gif found in the assets folder. The Image Tag Accessibility Attributes dialog box opens again. This time, enter **Elephant memory survey banner image**. Leave the Long Description empty because the image does not require a detailed explanation.

Click OK and save your work.

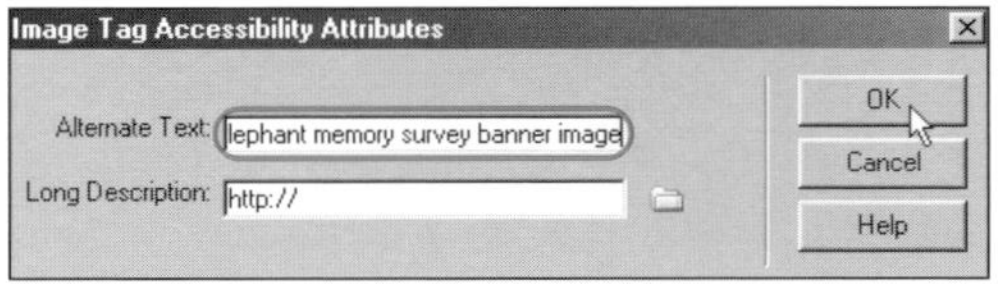

Setting the banner image accessibility attributes.

So now that you know what it means to make images accessible, you are ready to add a form and explore the accessibility requirements particular to this aspect of an HTML page. You might want to get more coffee, or perhaps a cup of Darjeeling tea, before we set out for the next stage.

Tip: All graphical elements in a web page require alternate text to indicate to screen readers what the graphic means. Spacer GIFs should be accompanied by a blank ALT value (either nothing or a space). Decorative images with no important information content should have an ALT value that explains what the image is for and repeats any text included in the image. Complex diagrams such as pie charts and graphs require more detailed explanations and for this you need the long description or LONGDESC attribute in the IMAGE tag. The long description is an HTML file containing a sentence or two that describes the information content in the image. If the image is too complex for a verbal description like this, it is important to repeat the information in tabular form.

Adding an Accessible Form to the Page

In this example, you'll add form elements that are typical of a simple online submission form: two radio buttons, a select list, and a submit button.

1 In the Design View window, click the center table cell in the second row and type the heading title Survey Form. Use the Property inspector to set the Format to H1. Press Enter and insert the following text (don't worry, it's just filler nonsense!):

This form is intended to provide data for a survey of the memory capabilities of elephants. If you are an elephant and wish to participate in this survey, please fill out the form below.

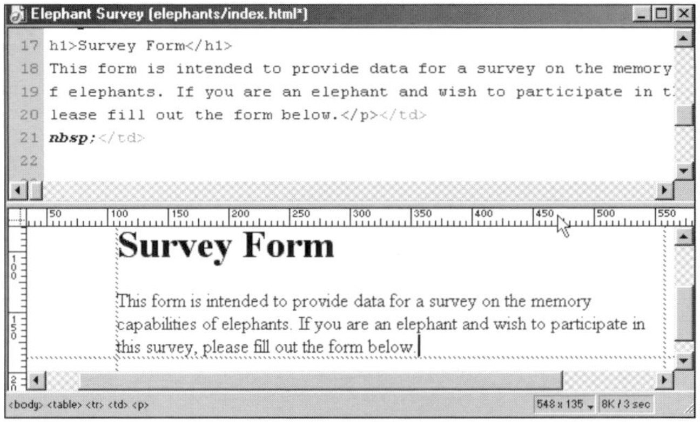

Entering the heading and introductory text.

Press Enter and type the following text:

Please indicate whether you are an African or Indian Elephant.

Press Enter once more.

2 Next, insert a blank form by clicking the Form button (in the Forms tab of the Insert Panel menu bar) or by choosing Insert>Form.

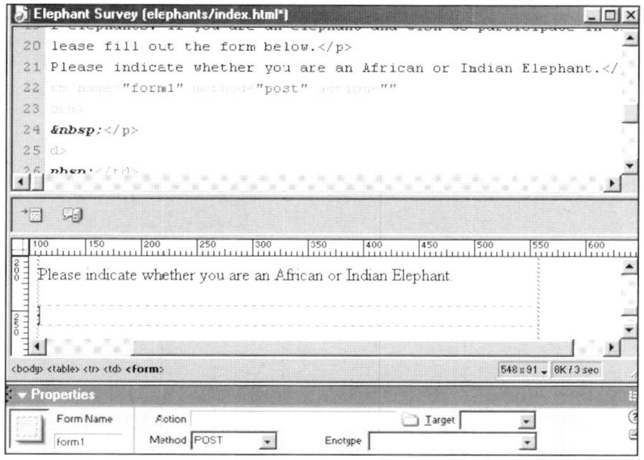

Inserting the Form element.

3 Next you want to create two radio buttons users will click to identify the elephant type as African or Indian. With the cursor still located within the Form marker (the red dashed box) in the Design View window, insert a new radio button via the Forms tab or choosing Insert>Form Objects>Radio Button. Immediately the Input Tag Accessibility Attributes dialog box opens. You can set five options in this dialog box:

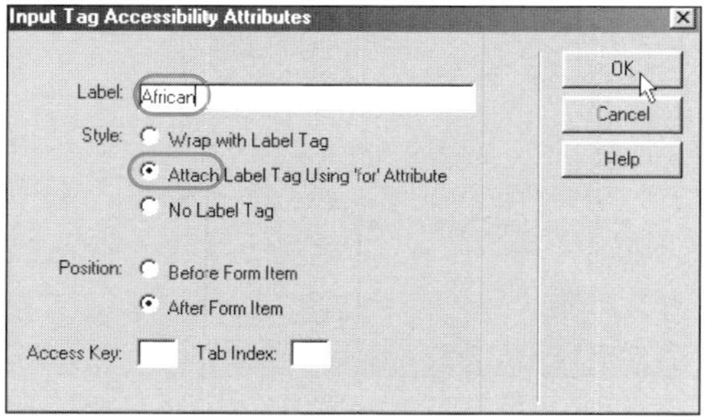

Input Tag Accessibility Attributes dialog box with values set.

- **Label:** This is the text to be shown next to the radio button. Insert **African**.
- **Style:** Select the Attach Label Tag Using 'for' Attribute option because it seems to be more acceptable to some of the testing systems. When you select the Attach label option, the clickable area of the radio button is expanded to include the name, making it easier for users to click. This doesn't work in all browsers—Netscape 4 is an example. You can use No Label if you want to enter text for the radio button separately—but beware; this choice will likely fail accessibility testing suites. We'll use the second option, Attach Label Tag Using 'for' Attribute, as our choice.
- **Position:** This option is a matter of personal choice. We'll use the After option because it's neater on the page in a conventional browser.

- **Access Key:** This option specifies a special keystroke combination (Alt+A, and so on) that can activate the button. If you inform users, for example, that a particular Access Key combination takes them to a particular point in the form, they can use this repeatedly to avoid having to navigate through the page to find the right place. Unless the page is going to be one of many with a special set of access keys, you normally will not need to set this option. Leave this setting empty.
- **Tab Index:** This option determines the order in which active elements in the page (links, checkboxes, radio buttons, and so on) are accessed when a user is navigating the web page using the Tab key. The default sequence is to start at the top and progress through the page code in sequence. You may wish to take the user straight to a starting point, in which case you would set the Tab Index for that element to 1. In this simple page, there's no purpose to be served by setting an Index value. Leave this entry blank.

Click OK to accept the values.

Note: With a normal, logically laid out page, you should not need to set the Tab Index option, but there may be circumstances in which you need to be specific. The Tab Index values, when set, should be sequential numbers.

4 You also need to name the radio button and its Checked Value in the Property inspector: Select the radio button in the Design View window and enter **type** in the RadioButton name box and **African** in the Checked Value box, leaving the Initial State button Unchecked.

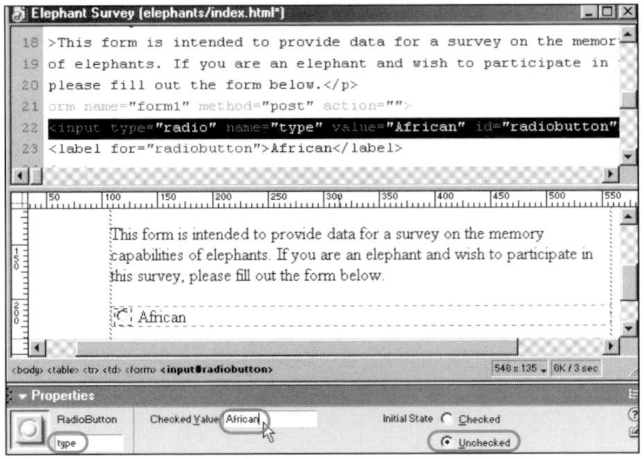

Name the radio button and its Checked Value and Initial State.

5 Now you want a second radio button to accept Indian as an elephant type. Click in the Design View window after *African* and press Enter; then repeat Steps 3 through 4, but use *Indian* instead of *African* for the accessibility label, and check the Indian button as the default. (If you leave both buttons unchecked, there could be some ambiguity as to what is intended when the buttons are read in non-graphic browsers, and some accessibility tests might fail.)

Save your work.

6 Next, you need to add a selection list. First, position the cursor after the second elephant type name (Indian, in the Design View window), press Enter, press Enter, and insert the following text:

Please rank your memory from the following list:

Then press Enter again.

7 Insert a List/Menu using either the Forms menu bar (in the second row if you have a small screen) or by choosing Insert>Form Objects>List/Menu.

8 In this case, label the list item **Memory quality**, select the style as Attach Label Tag Using 'for' Attribute, and leave the position at the default, Before Form Item. Click OK.

Tip: Placing the radio button label before or after the button normally is clear when read in screen readers. An exception can occur when both buttons are on the same line, in which case you should place the button ahead of the text. If you don't do this, users may have trouble identifying the set value for the button.

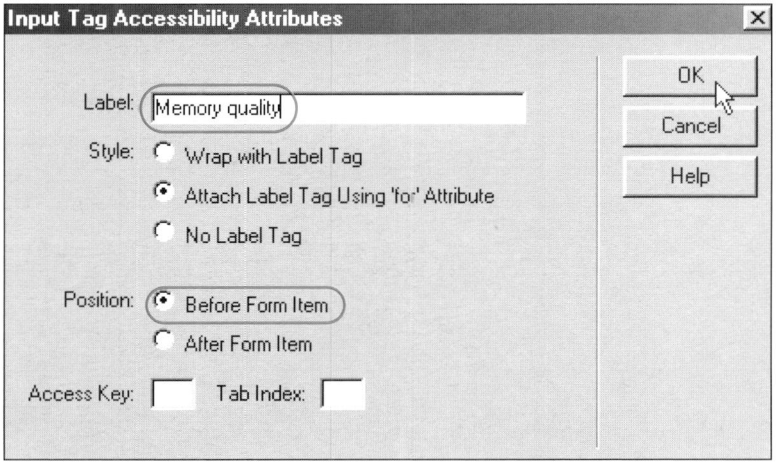

Setting up the list value accessibility attributes.

9 Select the list box in the Design View window.

Click the List Values button in the Property inspector. Add the following values by typing them into the Item Label column and clicking the plus sign: **poor**; **average**; **good**; **excellent**; **photographic**. Click OK.

Set good as the initially selected value.

Set the Type button to List with height 1.

Leave Allow multiple unchecked.

Note: Because this isn't a real form, you don't need to worry about the Method or Action for the form.

10 Position the cursor in the Design View window after the select list box, press Enter, and add the following text:

Thanks. Please press the Send button to send your response.

11 Press Enter again and then insert the final form element, the Send button, by clicking the Button icon on the Insert panel Forms tab or by choosing Insert>Form Objects>Button from the menu bar. In the Accessibility dialog box, set Label to **Press once to send**.

Set Style to Attach Label Tag Using 'for' Attribute.

Set position to Before Form Item. Click OK.

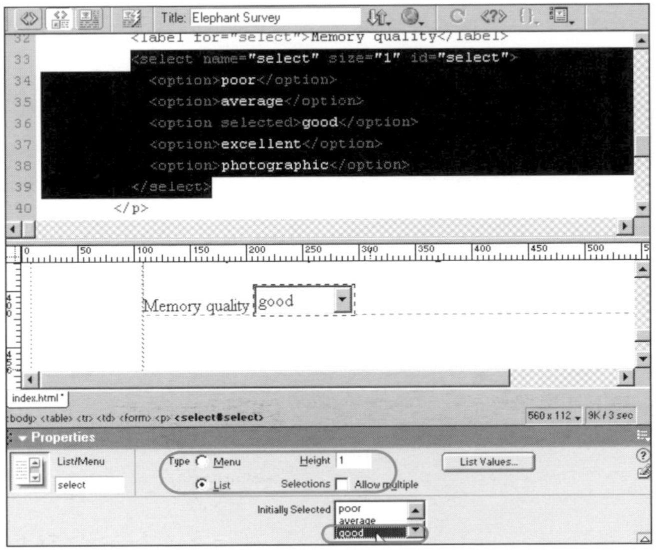

Setting up the List Value options and default values.

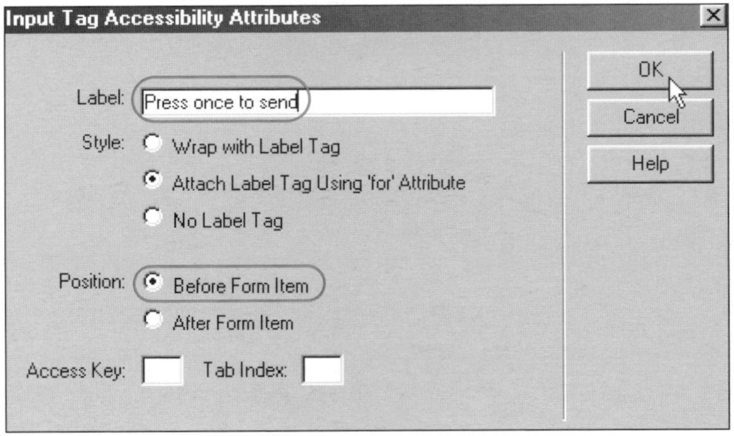

Setting up the Send button's accessibility attributes.

12 Finally, select the button in the Design View window and in the Property inspector, change the label of the button from Submit to Send. And that's the form section, finished! Save your work.

If you preview the work in a browser, you should see something like the figure shown here. Take a break!

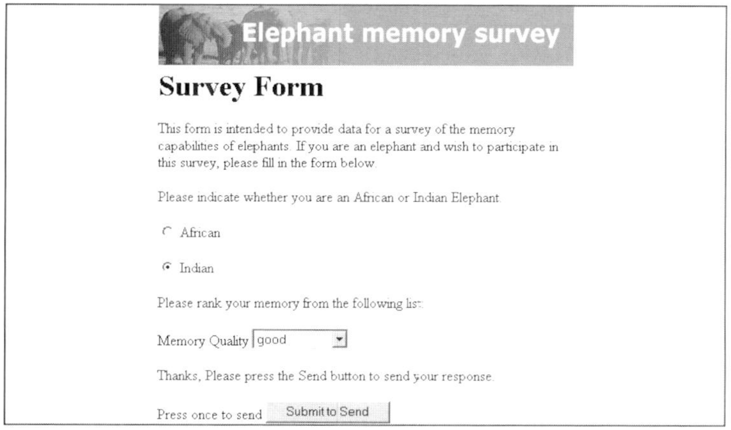

What the form looks like at this point.

Note: If your form is in more than one part—such as a search page with a simple and an advanced search—you can separate the two parts of the form using the FIELDSET and LEGEND tags. FIELDSET wraps around the section of code you want to associate, and LEGEND provides the title for the FIELDSET box. These put a nice clean box around the connected parts of the form for conventional browsers (though not in Netscape 4) and help keep things separate for screen readers. See for example, www.ausaud.gov.au/search/search.cfm.

Tip: It's best not to use graphic images in place of the standard SUBMIT and RESET buttons in forms. Screen readers work better with the standard HTML elements, and you don't need to bother with ALT tags.

Making Complex Graphic Elements Accessible

In many web pages, making complex graphics accessible is quite easy, provided you understand what needs to be done. There are two lines of attack: You can use the Long Description text to describe the contents, or, if that fails due to complexity, such as might occur with a graph or pie chart, you can use a table presenting the same data. In this part, you'll try both methods.

To get things started, make sure your cursor is located below the Form by clicking outside it (check the Tag Selector bar to see where you are).

1 Add a horizontal rule to space the two sections of the page by choosing Insert>Horizontal Rule or by clicking the Horizontal Rule button under the Common tab on the Insert bar. Place your cursor below the horizontal rule.

2 First, you need to enter some text to introduce the pie chart graphic. Enter the following text:

The pie chart below shows the statistical breakdown of responses received so far, for both categories of elephant.

Press Enter to start a new paragraph. Into this, you'll add the pie chart graphic: As before, use the Image icon in the Common tab of the Insert toolbar (or choose Insert>Image) to insert the image file piechart.gif. You may recognize the image from earlier in this chapter, where the colorblind example was mentioned. When you've chosen the file to insert, the Accessibility dialog box opens again. This time you'll add both Alternate Text (ALT) and a Long Description (LONGDESC) reference.

Note: The LONGDESC text actually says: "Pie chart showing the percentages of elephants with photographic memory (40%), excellent memory (30%), good memory (16%), average memory (10%) and poor memory (4%)." Although this text explains things reasonably clearly, a tabular presentation may be a better way to provide this information.

The LONGDESC text is available to screen reader browsers but doesn't appear in normal browsers unless they support this tag.

Tip: You also can add a TITLE element to the IMG tag. Some screen readers—recent versions of JAWS, for example—read this if available, and you can provide a longer description. It's sort of a half-way house between ALT and LONGDESC. Curiously, Netscape 6.2 doesn't show ALT text (which is a bug) but it does show TITLE text in a pop-up box. Internet Explorer 5 and later will show the TITLE if there's no ALT. However, most accessibility testing suites—including Dreamweaver MX's built-in one—get upset if there's no ALT tag for an image.

3 As the Alternate Text, enter **Memory statistics pie chart analysis**.

4 For this graph, you'll use the text contained in the file longdesc.html in the assets folder. Use the folder icon in the Accessibility dialog box to browse to that folder and select the file. Click OK and save your work.

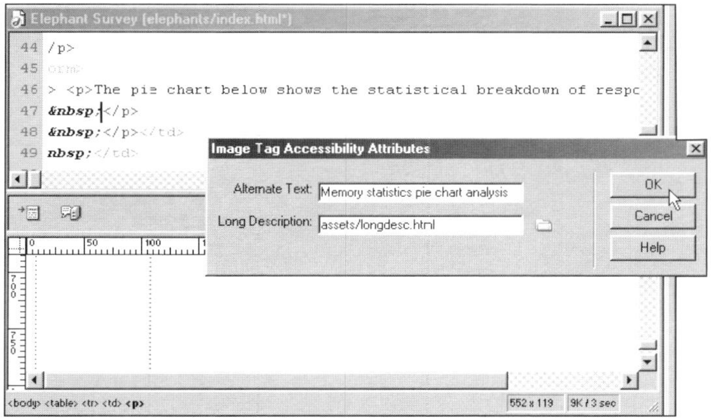

Setting accessibility attributes for the pie chart graphic. This time you also use the LONGDESC attribute.

Note: If you used piechart2.gif instead of piechart.gif, it would look quite acceptable to people with normal color vision, but to people with deuteranope colorblindness, it would look as though you had instead inserted piechart3.gif. You can try inserting these two files in the HTML code and previewing the page in a browser to see the final effect. It's a salutary lesson in how not to choose colors that convey important information.

5 To present the same content in tabular form, you can insert a table to contain the pie chart data. Click in the Design View window to the right of the pie charts and press Enter.

Again you can insert this table by clicking the Table button on the Insert panel Common tab and entering the following settings:

Rows: **6**

Columns: **2**

Cell Padding: **0**

Cell Spacing: **0**

Width: **80%**

Border: **0**

Five of the rows are for the memory categories and their values, and the first row is for the headers. When you have accepted the table setting, the Accessibility Options for Tables dialog box opens. Insert the values you see shown in this figure.

6 Set the Header value to Row so that the first row provides the titles for the two columns. Click OK.

7 Now in the Design View window, click in the top left of the two-column table and insert the title **Memory Capability** and then in the right header cell, enter **Percentage**. These titles appear in bold text, indicating that they are headers, not data values. Next, transcribe the values from the pie chart into the data cells below the headers. Finally, select all the data cells and center them using the Property inspector.

8 Click the Show Design View button to view the page. If you started your table with the poor value, the table should appear like the one shown in the figure. Return to Code and Design views after you've had a look. Save the file and preview it in the browser of your choice.

9 This isn't the most beautiful piece of HTML, so let's dress it up by using a style sheet to set font sizes and faces.

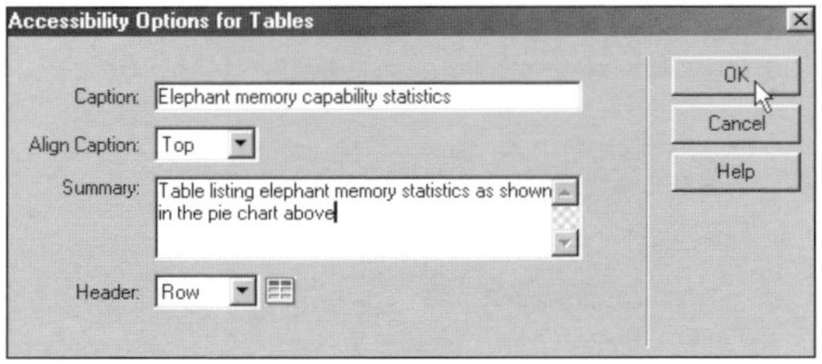

Accessibility attributes for the data table.

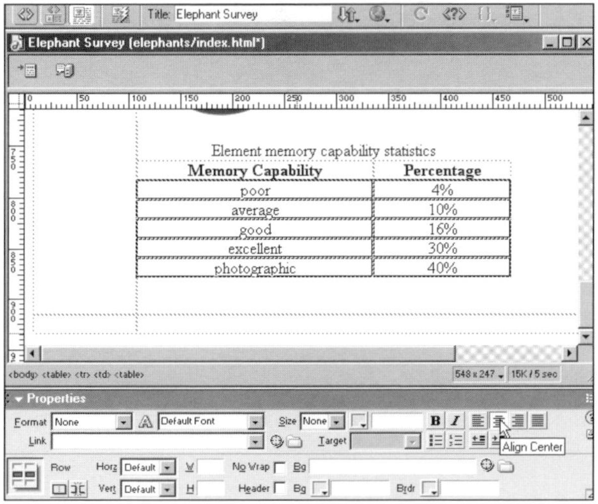

The completed table. Note the important accessibility element for the data table, the column headers, set in the <TH> tags.

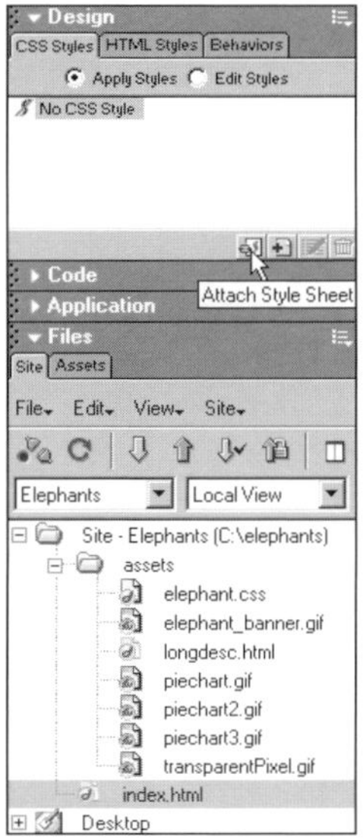

Adding an external style sheet.

To do this, choose Window>CSS Styles. The Design panel opens. Select the Apply Styles button, click the Attach Style Sheet icon beneath the CSS Styles window, leave the Add As button set to Link, and browse to the file assets/elephant.css. Finally, click OK. This is not the most elegant style sheet but it improves the look a bit, and the style sheet does not affect the accessibility. More to the point, if you view the page with the style sheets turned off, the page is fully functional. Preview the page in a browser to see the effect.

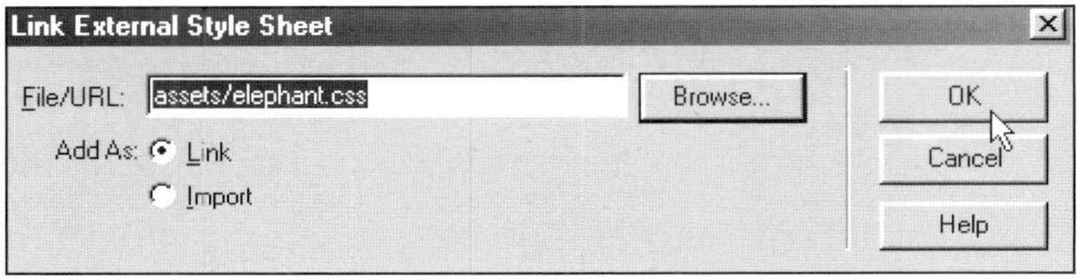

Linking an external style sheet. Note that for accessibility purposes, the page should be fully functional without the style sheet.

Adding Simple Navigation

You still have one more matter to consider; namely, a navigation bar. In this section, you insert a plain text bar in the bottom center table cell.

1 Enter the words **Home**, **Contact us**, and **Links** (for example); and then separate each word with a space, the bar (|) character, and another space. Select each phrase (do not select the bar character) and in the Property inspector, insert a dummy link using the pound sign (#). (The dummy link serves as a placeholder until you have a real page to link to.) Center the cell using the Property inspector Align Center tool.

  This may not seem significant, but you should separate navigation links by a non-space character so that screen readers do not run the links together.

Note: If you use a graphic element to separate the links, be sure to use a simple, non-empty, and non-space character as the ALT text. The bar character (|) is suitable, although it may confuse testing suites.

Ideally, use text as navigation links rather than graphics if you want to make the links as easy as possible for visually challenged users to access.

Add the TITLE tag to the link if you want to add a bit of explanatory text to each link. Not all browsers show this (it works in Internet Explorer 5 and later and Netscape 6), but it is available to the more recent screen readers.

Tip: You can add the TITLE attribute to the link tag quickly using the Quick Tag Editor at the right end of the Property inspector. Select the first Home link using the Tag Selector bar in the Design View window, click the Quick Tag Editor icon, and add the text **title="Go to Home Page"**. Add similar explanatory text for the other two links (for example, **How to contact us by email, mail or phone** and **Some other interesting elephant pages**). If you hover the mouse over the links when previewing in Internet Explorer 5 or later, you'll see the extra explanatory text appear in the pop-up box.

2 Save the file and preview it in different browsers to see what it looks like. And that finishes the main exercise! Now you can take a well-earned break.

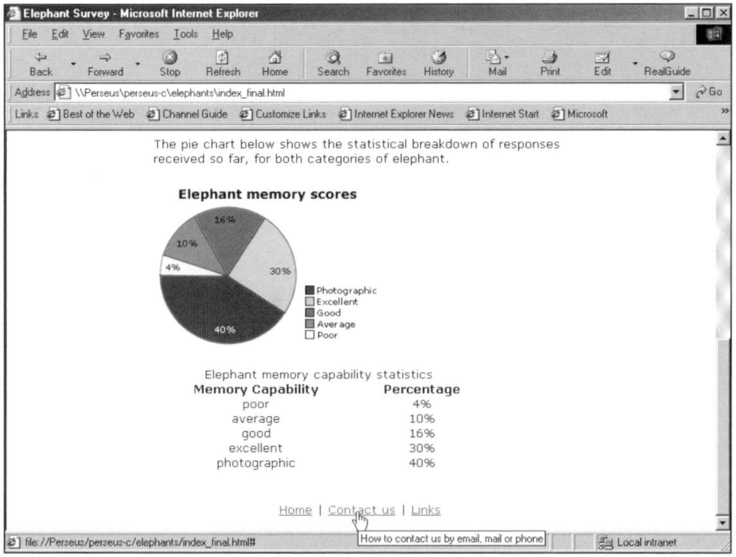

The TITLE text pop-up in Internet Explorer 5.

By now, you should be getting quite familiar with the Dreamweaver Accessibility dialog boxes. You learned to set up the Accessibility Preferences and found out how they prompt you to enter the necessary accessibility information. You also looked at a few real-world examples where these changes can make a big difference to visually challenged people who are accessing information on web pages.

Next, you take a look at existing pages. This is a world unto itself. Dreamweaver MX includes a number of tools to help you test pages: Dreamweaver extensions, external testing applications, and online tools. The next section starts with the built-in tools and extensions.

Testing an Existing Page

Although creating new pages that are accessible to the visually impaired is reasonably straightforward once you know the tools, you will most likely need to check and correct existing pages far more often than you create new ones, especially if you are managing a large web site. Web site testing can be a confusing process because of the sheer level of detail you manage.

In this exercise, you'll use Dreamweaver MX's page-checking capabilities. After that, you'll look at other tools available for Dreamweaver, plus external tools and online tests. Let's start with the page you just created. If you wish, you can use the pre-built version of this page, called index_final.html, on the CD-ROM.

1 Open the page to be tested in Dreamweaver and invoke the Accessibility test by choosing File>Check Page>Check Accessibility.

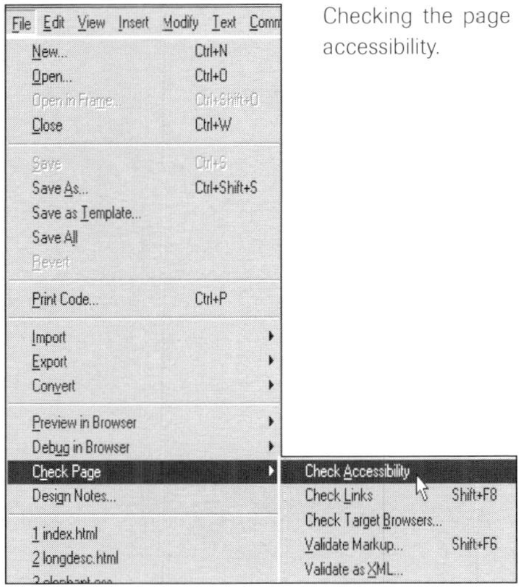

Checking the page accessibility.

2 The results of the check are saved as an XML file in a new sub-folder in the site /_notes with filename Results.xml. The content of this file is displayed in the Results window at the bottom of the main window.

3 The figure shows this display. The result gives an analysis of the page according to W3C and Section 508 rules and guidelines. Don't take this report as gospel. It's intended as a guide only, and your understanding of the real meaning of the accessibility requirements, in the context of the page tested, is vital to deciding whether a change needs to be made.

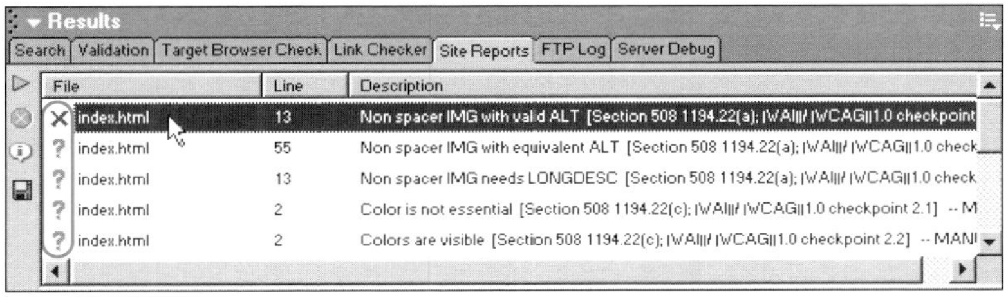

The Results window showing the outcome of the accessibility check.

If you inspect the report, you'll notice that some of the items are prefixed with a question mark and others with a red cross. A question mark means you should look at the code and decide from its context whether you need to make a change. It indicates that a possible accessibility problem could be present but the software cannot decide because the problem is context-dependent.

The red cross indicates a definite accessibility problem. In this case, I took advantage of a minor bug in Dreamweaver MX to illustrate what a problem line looks like. In fact, no error exists (see the Tip). I've included it here to illustrate what you will see in a typical page if it does contain an error.

4 The results for this page, as you'd hope, indicate that it meets accessibility criteria. If you look at the results, you'll see that the header banner image attracts the comment Non spacer image may need a LONGDESC attribute. You'll recall that when you inserted the header image, the ALT attribute was all that was required. The Attributes Checker has now drawn it to our attention just in case the image did need a LONGDESC description.

5 All the other messages relate to one aspect or other of the W3C guidelines or Section 508 regulations. Each line contains a reference to the specific guideline or regulation, and you can refer to the source documents for clarification.

Tip: The Accessibility Checker is designed to analyze ALT text to see whether you've used "generic" wording that does not describe the image properly. If you used, say, *Banner Image* as the ALT text, that phrase would not meet the strict requirements for accessibility. ALT text should repeat the text contained in an image or describe it in a useful way, such as *Picture of a rose*, *View of front panel*, and so on. Common sense is the final arbiter. The red cross in this analysis arises from the accessibility checker being a bit too conscientious!

Note: An interesting alternative to the built-in Accessibility Checker is the 508 Accessibility Suite extension, available from the Macromedia extensions site, and included on the CD-ROM. This extension doesn't add anything new to the built-in tools but it has a slightly more extended interface and could be useful if you are running Dreamweaver MX on a small screen. In addition, the extension allows you to check a whole site in one go (which may not be so useful because it unleashes a blizzard of information!). The extension also is a very good way to add accessibility tools to Dreamweaver 4.

Tip: Extensions are a valuable part of Dreamweaver. They are available on the Macromedia web site and other Dreamweaver-oriented sites. They extend Dreamweaver's base functionality in many useful ways. You install them by choosing Commands>Manage Extensions. This opens the Macromedia Extension Manager, which is installed with Dreamweaver. From that point, it's simply a matter of selecting the right application (Dreamweaver MX, in this case), clicking the Install Extension button, and navigating to the folder in which you want to install the extension.

Writing Valid Code

When you use Dreamweaver to create web pages, you can be sure that the code is going to be sound. However, it's a good idea to set the Centering preferences: Do this by choosing Edit>Preferences>Code Format and then set Centering to use the DIV rather than the CENTER tag. I prefer to set tag attributes such as <TD ALIGN="CENTER">, but this isn't an option in Dreamweaver, so using the DIV tag is a reasonable choice instead of the older CENTER tag, which usually gets remarked when you validate a page.

When you've completed a page, in addition to testing for accessibility, you need to validate it as well. You can do this using Dreamweaver's built-in validator. Choose File>Check Page>Validate Markup, as you see in the figure. The validation results appear in the Results window at the bottom of the screen.

You also can validate using the W3C online validator. You learn more about this in the section "HTML Validator," later in this chapter.

Finishing Thoughts

That concludes the exercises in this chapter. They should start you on the continuing road to building accessible web sites. But you can't expect to drive a Formula 1 racing car before you've learned how to steer! Dreamweaver MX's tools are a good way to start the learning process, and a useful part of any workflow.

Because the accessibility coding tools in Dreamweaver MX are primarily designed to build pages accessible to the visually challenged, we focused on those tools in this chapter. The program itself has a number of aids for Dreamweaver users who have both visual and/or motor impairment. These additional aids are described in the manual.

Coding a page for people with motor impairment doesn't present significant changes to what we've discussed. However, setting the Tab Access attributes for links and form elements is a good idea if your page contains many links. This allows people who cannot use a mouse to navigate easily by pressing Tab.

Other Section 508/WAI requirements to keep in mind that we've not touched on here are the need to provide alternate descriptions for animations—Flash

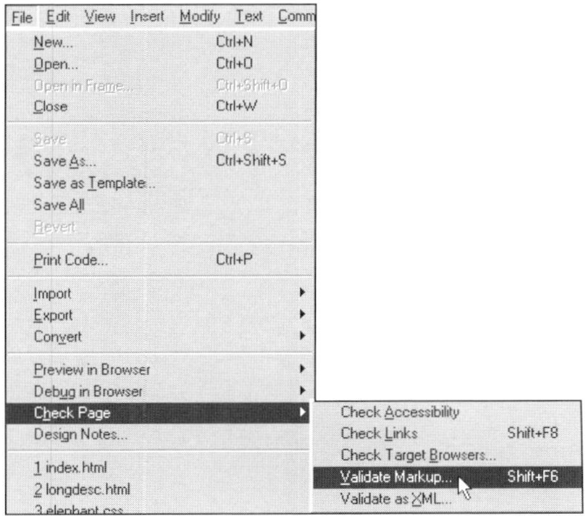

Validate your page code using Dreamweaver's built-in validator.

movies, animated GIFs, and so on—and also transcripts of audio information for the hearing impaired.

Designing accessible web pages is a field that continues to emerge, as people's understanding of what constitutes accessibility grows and browser capabilities develop (both conventional browsers and those used by the visually challenged). In this chapter, we've covered only the starting points and illustrated the tools you need to begin. As you practice using accessibility tools and validating your web pages, you'll learn from the feedback you get how to build accessibility compliance into your workflow. This is the real secret to the art of accessibility: continuous learning.

Additional Tools for Dreamweaver

If you need thorough checking for usability and accessibility in the web sites you design or manage, you should consider purchasing the industrial-strength checking program from UsableNet (the people who provided the built-in tools for Dreamweaver MX).

LIFT for Macromedia Dreamweaver is a very powerful tool set, and tests other aspects of usability beyond accessibility. The utility generates extensive reports and should not be used until you are comfortable with the accessibility rules, regulations, and built-in Dreamweaver tools. When you are ready to tackle it, it's very powerful indeed (see www.usablenet.com).

Testing Your Web Pages Online

A comprehensive list of testing tools is available on the W3C web site at www.w3.org/WAI/ER/existingtools.html. Notable among these are Bobby, Wave, and LIFT.

Bobby

Probably the best known accessibility testing tool, Bobby checks pages automatically and alerts the user to the need for manual checking where necessary. The tool also analyzes web pages for browser compatibility. Bobby is available as a free online test at www.cast.org/bobby/ and as a downloadable Java application. Bobby currently tests to the WAI 1.0 Guidelines and U.S. Section 508. It provides detailed reports on all aspects of the web page and gives explanations and suggestions on how to fix problems. If your web page meets the WAI and/or Section 508 requirements, you're entitled to add the Bobby compliance badges to the page.

Wave

Wave is an initiative of the Pennsylvania Temple University Institute on Disabilities. It provides online testing at www.temple.edu/inst_disabilities/piat/wave/. Wave's main role is to provide a visual display of how your web page appears and in what sequence the various elements are accessed by non-visual browsers. You can use Wave as a very quick way to spot images with missing ALT attributes!

LIFT

UsableNet provides free online testing for a single page. When you pay an annual subscription fee, the full LIFT online service allows you to test a complete web site multiple times. The service is extensively configurable and the reports provided by LIFT are very detailed. They cover many aspects of accessibility and usability. LIFT is available at www.usablenet.com.

> **Tip:** As a first step, when you're ready to test your own web site, try Bobby first and then take a look at Wave. When you have gained confidence, try the LIFT free trial.

HTML Validation

Finally, it's a very good idea to validate your HTML code. There are a number of validation application programs available, but if you want to get the results "from the horse's mouth," use the W3C validation service at http://validator.w3.org/ (note, the URL suffix is w3.org, not w3c.org!). If you pass the W3C test, you have another badge you can add to your page! There's also a CSS style sheet validator available at the same URL.

What if I'm Still Using Dreamweaver 4?

If you're still using Dreamweaver 4, you'll want to get the 508 Accessibility Suite extension from UsableNet, which is available from the Macromedia Dreamweaver extensions page (http://dynamic.macromedia.com/bin/MM/exchange/ main.jsp?product=dreamweaver). A copy of this file is also provided on the CD-ROM.

This extension gives you most of the functionality for testing pages that is now built into Dreamweaver. Its much more powerful stable-mate, the LIFT extension for Dreamweaver (available from UsableNet), also works well with Dreamweaver 4. If you're not upgrading to MX just yet, use these plug-ins to add industrial strength accessibility testing to Dreamweaver 4.

Building Colorblind–Proof Graphics

The first part of this chapter addressed the problems of colorblind users and the risks in choosing colors you intend to use as a key to providing information. If you are colorblind, you are already aware of these pitfalls, but if not, it's hard to know whether your graphics are up to the mark. You need to know about Vischeck, a very useful plug-in for Fireworks, Photoshop, and other graphics programs that accept standard Photoshop plug-ins, available free from www.vischeck.com. This program accepts bitmap graphics and transforms their colors to simulate the way they would appear to people with three different types of colorblindness. The files piechart2.gif and piechart3.gif in the elephants site illustrate the before and after results of processing an image with Vischeck. The figure opposite shows the Vischeck interface as seen in Macromedia Fireworks 4. A copy of the plug-in is available in this project's folder on the CD-ROM (Windows only). The Vischeck site also provides a Java applet and a remarkably effective online test for whole web pages.

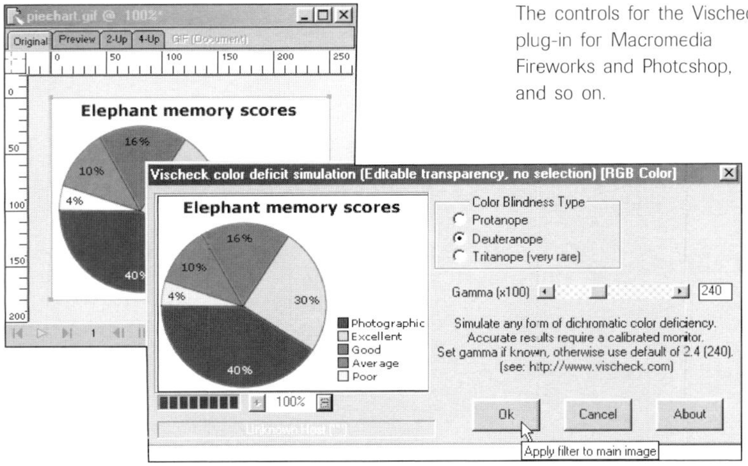

The controls for the Vischeck plug-in for Macromedia Fireworks and Photoshop, and so on.

Sources of Information for Further Reading

If you need to master accessibility concepts, you need to do plenty of reading on the subject—it's the only sure way to become familiar with the accessibility regulations and guidelines that form the basis of government web site requirements. A great deal of the accessibility information on the web is hard to read. The Section 508 government site and the W3C site are comprehensive, but heavy going. Here is a selective list of web sites that are worth exploring.

The ***Using Dreamweaver*** manual chapter on Accessibility and the Help file are valuable resources for information on Dreamweaver tools.

W3C Web Accessibility Initiative (WAI), at www.w3.org/WAI/, is a huge site with all sorts of goodies tucked away in it.

The **Section 508** government site at www.section508.gov/ and the U.S. Government Access Board site at www.access-board.gov/ are the places to go when you need the full details—large sites and a lot to digest!

Jim Thatcher provides a very instructive and succinct comparison of Section 508 and the W3C Web Content Accessibility checkpoints for readers interested in getting down to analytical detail. See www.jimthatcher.com/sidebyside.htm, and also check out the tutorial pages starting at www.jimthatcher.com/webcourse1.htm.

UsableNet at www.usablenet.com and in particular its suggested readings page at www.usablenet.com/accessibility_usability/readings.html are valuable resources.

The **Web-Savvy Top Ten Accessible Web Authoring Practices** page at www.websavvy-access.org/resources/top_ten.shtml is a comprehensive list of key accessibility techniques, with clear illustrations and explanations of accessible code.

Designing More Usable Web Sites at www.trace.wisc. edu/world/web/index.html is another useful compendium.

Sarah Horton and the **Web Teaching Group** at Dartmouth College have yet another valuable resource at www.dartmouth.edu/~webteach/articles/access.html. See in particular the first link at the bottom of that page on Accessible Design Guidelines, a downloadable 22-page document with more useful accessibility information.

And finally the page **How do things look to Colorblind People** at webexhibits.org/causesofcolor/ 2.html is well worth a visit.

Modifications

The best way to get familiar with the concepts and tools we've explored in this chapter is to build a web page for your own purposes, using Dreamweaver set up the way we've done here. Make sure the accessibility tools are turned on and see how the page turns out.

Next, open an existing page and test its accessibility—this will help you become more familiar with the sort of problems you might encounter. Run Bobby over the page as well—you may need to work quite hard at first to get Bobby's stamp of approval. And remember to look at the items Bobby and the internal Dreamweaver accessibility tests indicate as requiring manual examination; you can build a page that tests satisfactorily but still has accessibility problems.

Remember that although some accessibility testing can be automated, in the end it's you, the web designer, who must rely on your own common sense—and the basic principles you've learned—to design accessible web sites.

"Experience is what you get when you didn't get what you wanted."

—A WISE SAYING ATTRIBUTED TO WHITE-WATER KAYAKERS AND WEB DEVELOPERS

GIVING YOUR PAGES SOME STYLE

Using CSS

Do your pages suffer from a lack of style? For page presentation and site consistency, CSS (Cascading Style Sheets) is the way to go—and it's never been easier than with Dreamweaver MX. Using a fluid layout, this project will show you just how easy it can be to create and use selectors, classes, and contextual rules to put a bit of style into your designs!

Project 5

Giving Your Pages Some Style

by Donna Casey and Joyce J. Evans

It Works Like This

With today's sophisticated designs and complex page layouts, the last thing you need is more font tags to manage. Well, font no more! Cascading Style Sheets give you pixel-perfect control and make managing your pages, well, manageable. While you build the fluid layout of this project page, you'll create embedded and external styles that declare rules for selectors, custom classes, pseudo-classes, and contextual selectors; you then apply the styles to page elements using Dreamweaver MX's spiffy new CSS Style panel and the ever-useful Tag Selector.

Of course, in the process you'll encounter the vagaries of browser support (so what else is new?). Throughout this chapter, tips, notes, and explanations help you build solutions and learn workarounds for the most common issues. Then, when a single style rule just *won't work,* you'll use the @import directive with an alternate style sheet to determine which rule settings to apply based upon the visitor's browser.

Preparing to Work

To prepare for this project, you need to copy the Projects/05_style_sheets folder to your hard drive, and then start up Dreamweaver and define a site based on the project_start folder. Preview the finished project page before you begin to get familiar with where you'll go in this chapter (project_final/index.htm).

1 Copy the Projects/05_style_sheets folder on the Magic CD to a convenient location on your hard drive.

2 Define a site in Dreamweaver.

- Choose Site>New Site.
- Name the site **Mary's Garden**
- For the Local Root Folder, navigate to the Projects\05_style_sheets\project_start folder, select it, and click Done.
- Click OK to create the site cache.

3 Add a stylesheets folder and index page.

- Select the site-root folder and right-click (Ctrl-click on Mac) to add a new folder named **stylesheets**.
- Right-click the site-root folder again and add a new file named **index.htm**.

4 Set the home page.

- Right-click (Ctrl-click on Mac) on the index.htm page and choose Set as Home Page from the context menu.
- Double-click index.htm to open the page.

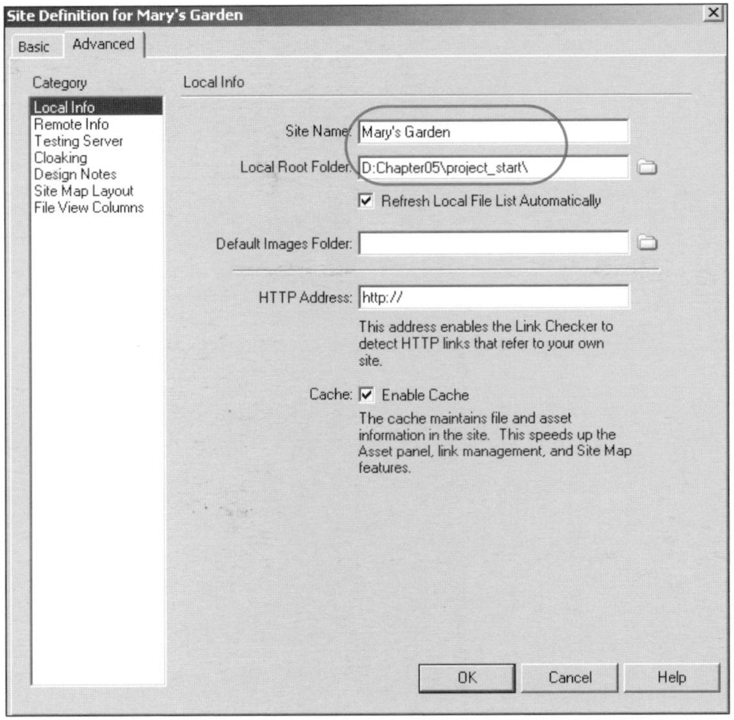

Name the site and locate the root folder as part of defining the site.

CREATE A FLUID PAGE LAYOUT

In this section, you build the fluid table layout, add a few absolutely positioned layers to achieve an otherwise difficult design, and then drop in some page content. After all, you'll need some elements to style, right?

Note: A copy of this file is saved on the CD as endofpagelayout.htm if you'd rather skip this portion.

1 First, get rid of the default page margin offsets.

- Choose Modify>Page Properties (or right-click and select Page Properties from context menu).
- Set Top Margin, Left Margin, Margin Height, and Margin Width to zero. Click OK.

2 Build the top table.

- Insert a table to position the menu (Insert>Table).

  Rows: **1**

  Columns: **1**

  Width: **98%**

  Border: **0**

  Cell Padding: **0**

  Cell Spacing: **0**

- Click inside the single cell of the table and align to Right and Bottom using the Cell Align menus (Horz, Vert) in the Property inspector.

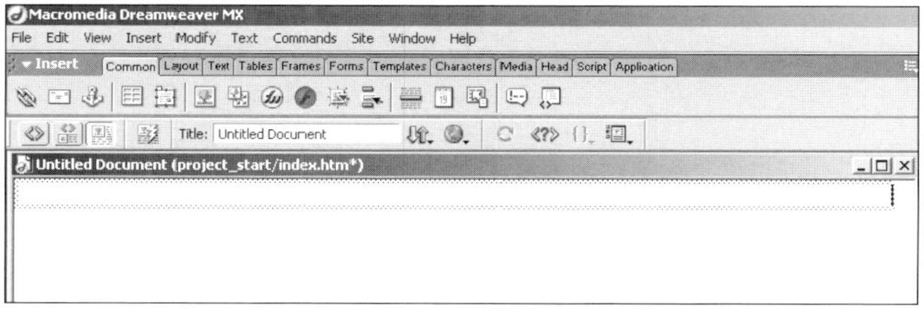

The single cell table added and aligned using the Cell Align menus.

3 Add the navigation images.

The navigation images and corner image added to the first table.

- Open the Assets panel. Select the spacer.gif image and click the Insert button.
- Set the spacer's width and height. In the Property inspector, change the Width to 375 and Height to 15.
- Press the right-arrow key to place the cursor in the cell and off the spacer image, and add a line break after the spacer by pressing Shift-Enter/Return.
- Add another spacer. Set the spacer Width to 50px and its Height to 25px.
- Next you add the navigation images. The images will be placed right behind the last spacer you added. You do not need to deselect the spacer image; Dreamweaver will automatically insert the next image behind the selected one. Insert the main navigation elements, in the following order:

  btnshop.gif

  btnhow.gif

  btnabout.gif

  btnright.gif

- Don't forget to save your page!

4 Add the second (main content) table.

- Place your cursor outside the first table and insert a table with these settings:

  Rows: **1**

  Columns: **2**

  Width: **98%**

  Border: **0**

  Cell Padding: **0**

  Cell Spacing: **0**

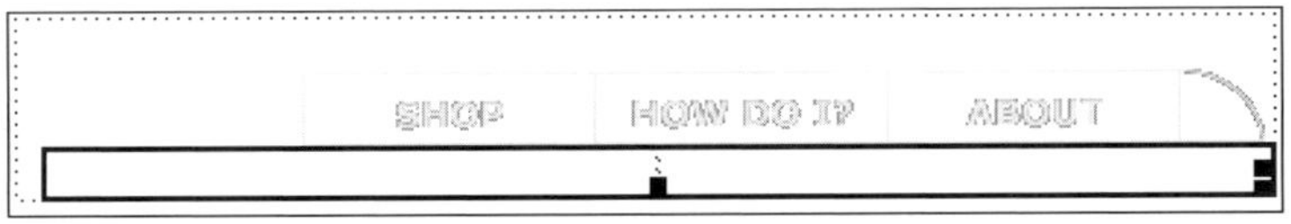

The second table added.

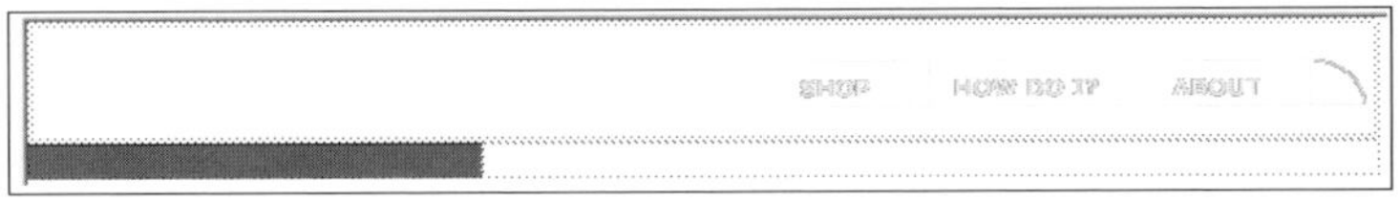

The second table with the first column width set, a spacer added, and a background color. The left column is now fluid.

Note: If you have trouble getting outside a table, try this: Place your cursor in the table and select the <table> tag using the Tag Selector. Then use your right-arrow key to move out of and after the table code. To move out of and before the table code, use the left-arrow key.

Note: Never add a line break or paragraph return between tables. Tables, by default, stack just like paragraphs. A break or return will result in unwanted space.

- Place your cursor in the table and select the <tr> tag in the Tag Selector. In the Property inspector, set the Vert cell alignment to Top.
- Click in the left column, set the first column width to **240px**, using the W field in the Property inspector.
- Set the BG color to **#464D3A** for the first column only.
- Add a spacer in this cell (to prevent the cell from collapsing); then set its Width to **240px** and its Height to **10px** using the same method described earlier in this project.
- Click in the right column and set the BG color to **#FFFFFF** using the Property inspector.
- With your cursor still in the second column, set

Warning: Never, never, never, *ever* drag on table borders to resize a table or adjust its row height or column width. Dragging causes all cells to be sized and can later hinder more than it helped!

Tip: Don't drag and drop spacers! If you use the Asset panel and the Insert button to insert a spacer, it will be auto-selected in the Property inspector, making it easy to change the H and W values.

the <td> width to 100%, manually adding the percent sign in the Cell Width field in the Property inspector. Set the Horz and Vert alignment to Left, Top.

Tip: This is the secret to the hybrid, or fluid, table. A relative (%) table that contains a fixed-width column *must* contain at least one column whose width takes up the slack. Setting its width to 100% tells the browser to use up all the remaining width of the table. To prevent the fixed-width column from collapsing, place "real" content (an visible image or spacer gif) into the column. The content should be as wide as the desired column width.

5 Add the main content to the second column.

- Use the Site Files to locate and open main_content.htm.
- In Design view, place your cursor in the page and select Edit>Select All and then Edit>Copy.
- Return to the project page and paste into the second table's second column.

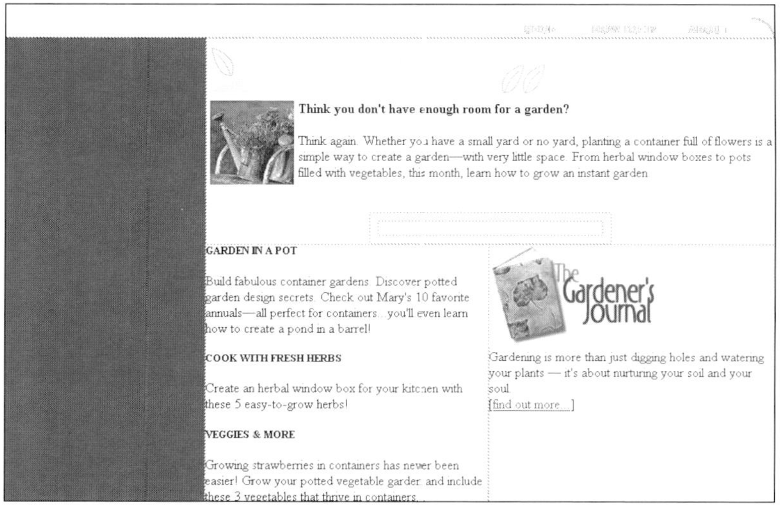

Content is pasted into the 100% fluid column.

6 Build the footer table.

- Place your cursor outside the second table (or simply select the second table) and insert a new table with these settings:

  Rows: **1**

  Columns: **2**

  Width: **98%**

  Border: **0**

  Cell Padding: **0**

  Cell Spacing: **0**

Note: By adding an additional table for the footer, you keep your design modular and easy to upgrade. These tables are very simple, which allows them to load and display faster in the user's browser.

Tip: To create a null link, select the desired text, and then type **javascript:;** into the link field. To make the next null link, select the next bit of text and press Ctrl-Y (PC) or Cmd-Y (Mac) to repeat the step. You could also use Link History.

- Using the same steps described earlier, set the left column Width to **240px**. Add a spacer and set its Width to **240px** and Height to **25px**.
- Set the right column width to **100%**, just as you did with the main content table. Set the Cell Horz to Center.
- Select the table row tag <tr> using the Tag Selector and set its BGcolor to **#660099**.
- Type the following text into the right cell:

  home | shop | how do I? | about

  Add a line break. Then add **Copyright 2002. All rights reserved.**
- Make each of the home, shop, how do I?, and about items into null links.

7 Add a layer to hold the flower image.

- Use the Draw Layer tool to draw a layer in the top-left corner of the document; then select it by clicking the layer's handle.
- In the Property inspector, set the layer L to **0px**, T to **0px**, W to **240px**, and leave H blank. Name the layer **lyrFlower** and set its visibility to visible.
- Place your cursor in the layer and add flower.jpg using the Assets panel.

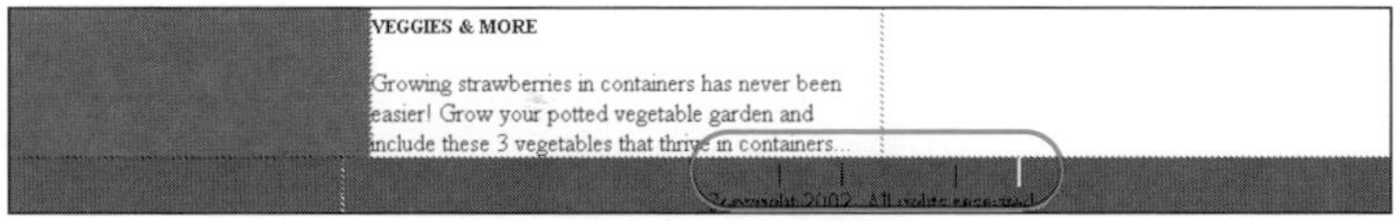

The footer text added and the null links set.

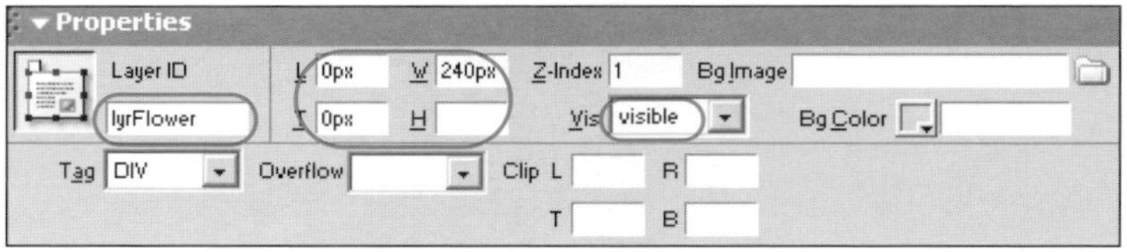

The Property inspector showing the Layer settings used.

Note: Be sure to place your cursor inside the layer before inserting the image. You can use the Layers panel (Window>Others>Layers) and select the layer there. The black handles indicate the selected layer. Click inside the layer and then insert the image.

8 Draw another layer to hold the logo.

- Name the layer lyrLogo and set its visibility to visible.
- Set L to 0px, T to 0px, W to 240px, and leave H blank in the Property inspector.
- Use the Asset panel to insert logo.gif into the layer.
- This graphic contains transparency and the flower image layer, and has a Z-index of 1. It is below and will show through the logo graphic.

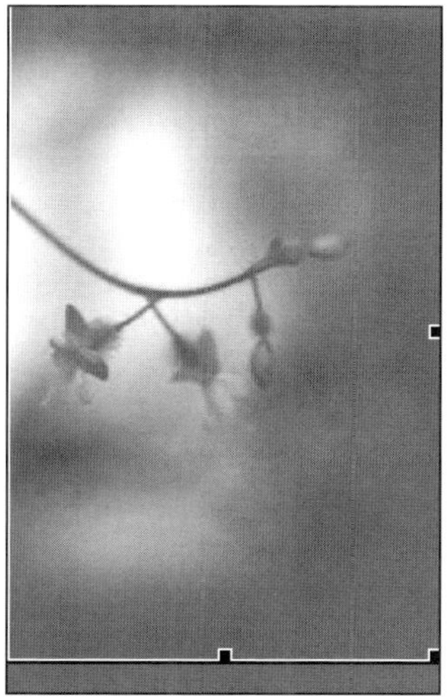

The flower is inserted into the layer.

The logo layer is added above the flower layer. The logo is transparent, showing the flower layer below.

9 As you did previously, draw another layer to hold the rest of the sidebar content.

- Name the layer lyrSidebar and make it visible. Enter the following settings for this layer: Set L to 0px, T to 50px, W to 240px, and leave H blank and make it visible.
- Use the site files to locate and open sidebar_content.htm. Select all the page content and copy it in Design view.
- Return to the project page; then use the Layer panel to select lyrSidebar, insert the cursor in lyrSidebar, and paste.

10 Save your page. Now you're ready to start stylin'.

A copy of the file up to this point is in the file named index_1.htm in the project_final folder.

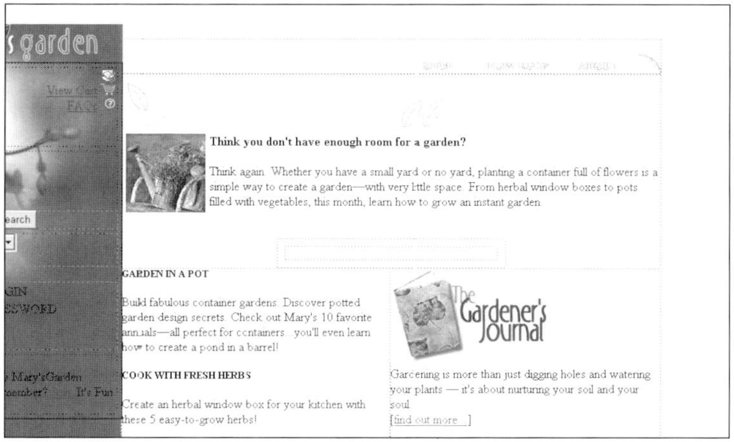

One layer is used for the flower, another layer for the logo, and yet another layer for the remaining sidebar content.

Warning: Select the layer *first*. Clicking in what appears to be the layer is not the same as selecting it. Use the Layers panel and make sure in the Tag Selector that the correct layer <div> is selected!

Redefine HTML Tag to Set Your Main Style Declarations

Now the styling fun begins! In this section, you create an external, linked style sheet where you'll define most of your style rules or *declarations*, using Redefine HTML Tag to set the properties and attributes of selectors like <body>, <p>, and <td>. To overcome a Netscape 4x problem, you'll embed additional declarations, using the cascade principle to your advantage.

You'll start with the most basic page element: the <body> tag. You could set these properties using Modify>Page Properties, right? But remember your goal: You are using CSS to remove the presentation of the page from the HTML and putting it into styles, which give you more control and are far easier to update!

1 Set the body style declarations.

- Click the expander arrow of the Design panel group and click the CSS Styles panel tab to make it the active panel.
- Select Edit Style mode to build styles.
- Click the Add (+) button at the bottom of the CSS Styles panel. Choose Redefine HTML Tag.
- Choose the body tag from the pull-down Tag menu or type **body**.
- Select New Style Sheet in the Define In drop-down and click OK.

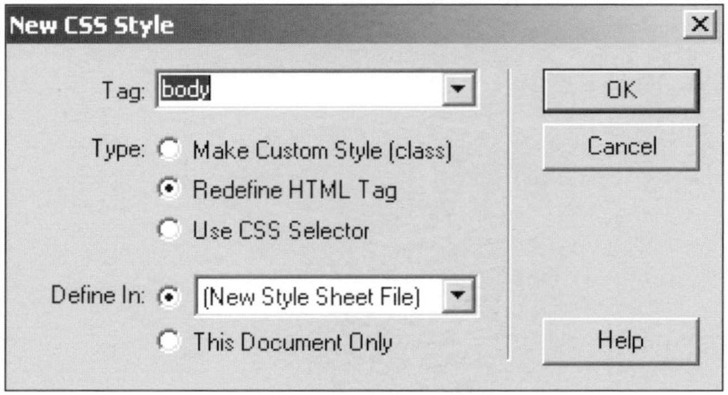

The settings used for the new CSS style.

Note: An HTML tag is a *selector*, but this label lets you know that you will change the *default* properties for the specific HTML tag you select.

2 The Save As dialog box will open. Navigate to your stylesheets folder and name the style sheet **gardenstyle.css**, set the Relative to Document, and Save.

The CSS Style Definition for body in gardenstyle.css dialog box will open.

3 Set the style properties and attributes to create your declaration.

- In the Type category (Text properties) set the following attributes:

  Font (Family): **Verdana, Arial, Helvetica, sans-serif**

  Size: **11px**

  Color: **#333333** (a dark charcoal gray)

- Leave the other settings at default.
- In the Background category (Background properties), set the following attributes:

  Color: **#845AAD** (purple)

  Click the Browse button for Background Image, navigate to the backgrounds folder in your site, select leafbg_anim.gif, and click OK.

- Leave the other values at default and click OK.

4 Save your page and preview in both Internet Explorer and Netscape 4x if you have it (Netscape 6 works fine). Wait for the animated background image to run.

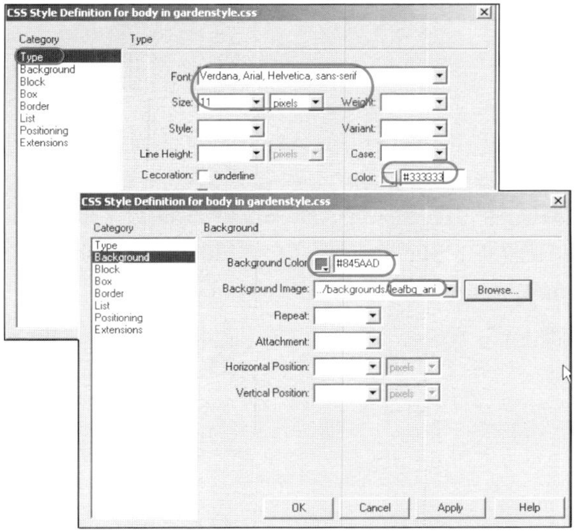

Setting the style properties and attributes.

Animated Background Images

The background image is an animation—yes, that's right, you can use animation in backgrounds, but keep it subtle, okay? In Internet Explorer, the background tile appears just as it would if you'd set it with HTML. But what happens in Netscape 4x? The image never shows up! The CSS specification states that background-image (URL) should be relative to where the style rule is defined. Internet Explorer gets this right. But Netscape 4x looks for the URL relative to where the style is used—and that's a big difference! To get around the Netscape 4x issue, you have several options, some easier than others. You can:

- Use an absolute URL (http://www.mydomain.com/backgrounds/image.gif), which is difficult if you are not sure where the site will be located and also is not visible locally.
- Place your style sheets and pages in the same folder or set up a folder structure that will work from both the stylesheets folder and an HTMLpages folder. The path from stylesheets to backgrounds is the same as from HTMLpage to background (backgrounds/leafbg_anim2.gif).
- Add an additional declaration for body in the head of the page, setting only the URL attribute. This last option seems the easiest, and it will be your course of action in Step 5.

5 Set an embedded <body> style to fix the Netscape 4x problem.

- Add a new style.
- Select or type **body**, choose Redefine HTML Tag, and select This Document Only to embed the declaration in the head of the page. Click OK.
- When the Style Definition dialog box opens, click the Background category and choose Browse to locate the leaf_anim.gif image. The path to the image is now relative to the document, which will make Netscape 4x happy.
- Click OK and Save.
- Preview in both browsers.

You may have noticed that in both browsers, the text of the page is rendering oddly; in Netscape 4x, it appears to ignore the style settings altogether, while in Internet Explorer, the font-family is used but the size may be ignored. Remember that the text of the page is in a table cell. If the text were simply placed in the page, you would see the same results in both

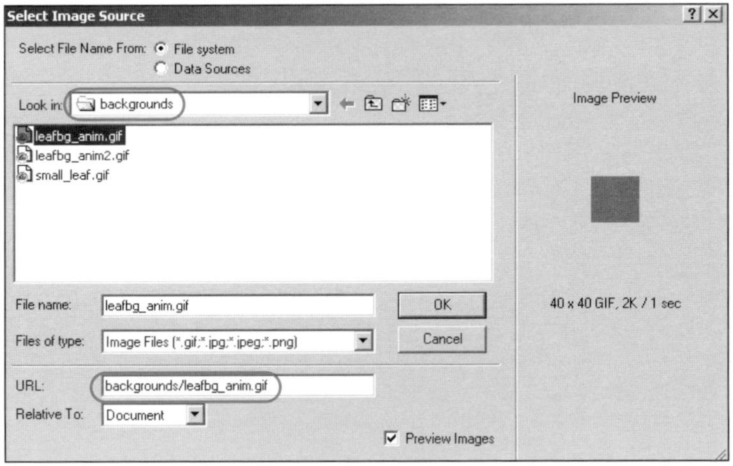

The Background category showing the path change when making a style that is For This Document Only, which is a work-around for Netscape browsers.

Note: Netscape 4x can now find the image and Internet Explorer continues to work just fine. You don't have to add all the same declarations because Netscape will get these from the linked sheet. They are not in conflict, as is the URL. For URL, a conflict occurs and cascade takes over. If the same style is defined in both internal and external style sheets, the definition closest to the affected tag wins. In this case, it's the internal style sheet definition.

browsers. Technically, all these values should be inherited by the table and its cells, but sadly this isn't always rendered correctly by browsers. To get around this problem, you'll group the <td> and <p> selectors and re-declare the same Text properties you used for the body. You won't add any Background properties.

6 Group the <td> and <p> selectors and set their Text properties.

- Select the style sheet (gardenstyle.css) in the CSS Styles panel and click the New CSS Style icon.
- Choose Use CSS Selector. You are still redefining a selector, just like you did with <body>, but Dreamweaver only lets you group selectors in the CSS Selectors option field.
- Type **td, p** and click OK.
- Set the same Text properties as used in the <body> style.

  Font (Family): **Verdana, Arial, Helvetica, sans-serif**

  Size: **11px**

  Color: **#333333** (a dark charcoal gray)

- Click OK.

7 Save your page and preview in both browsers.

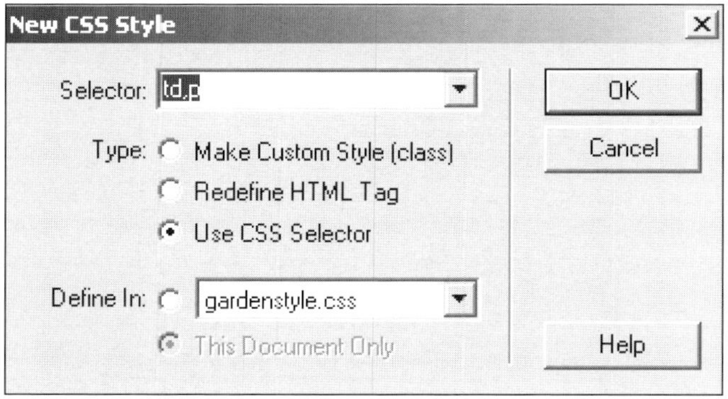

The settings used to group the td and p selectors.

Style Declarations

Style declarations can be defined in a *linked, external* style sheet or *embedded* in the head of the document. Some style rules apply automatically (redefined tags), while others require specific application (classes). Still others apply only in context of another class or selector. *Cascade* (the general principle that applies whenever there is a conflict of rules) and *inheritance* (the way page elements are affected by their containing element) are the major factors in the way a page renders. In this project, you take advantage of both to make the page render correctly in the major browsers.

Custom Classes

To take this design to the next level, you define some custom classes and apply them to different selectors in your page. So far, you have not had to apply anything; the styles just applied themselves because you changed what it meant to be the body, cell, or paragraph in this page.

A *custom class* is a different method of declaring a style rule. You can apply a class to any element. How the properties and attributes affect a selector depends on the element you choose—in some cases, it is possible to set inappropriate properties and values. In this section, you define some classes that you will apply to specific table cells and paragraphs.

> **Note:** Although you might think padding would be appropriate as we start out with Step 1, there are two reasons to work with margin instead: Padding will not work in all browsers (that's Netscape 4x *again*), and you cannot set a negative value for padding, but you can for a margin.

1 Create the .mypara class style

You've already defined the <p> tag so that all paragraphs use a specific font-family, size, and color. In this step, you use the class to create a style that will be applied specifically to the main content paragraphs to add some additional white space around them. Also, class names always start with a period and cannot start with a number or contain spaces or special characters—not even an underscore!

- Click the New Style (+) button.
- Choose Make Custom Style (class) and select the linked style sheet (gardenstyle.css). Name the style .mypara and click OK.
- Select the Box category (property) and uncheck the Same for All checkbox in the Margin values (not Padding).
- Set the following margin values:

  Top: **0px**

  Right: **10px**

  Bottom:(blank, or default)

  Left: **10px**
- Click OK and return to the document.
- Later you will use a negative value to correct a presentation difference between Netscape 4x and W3C compliant browsers.

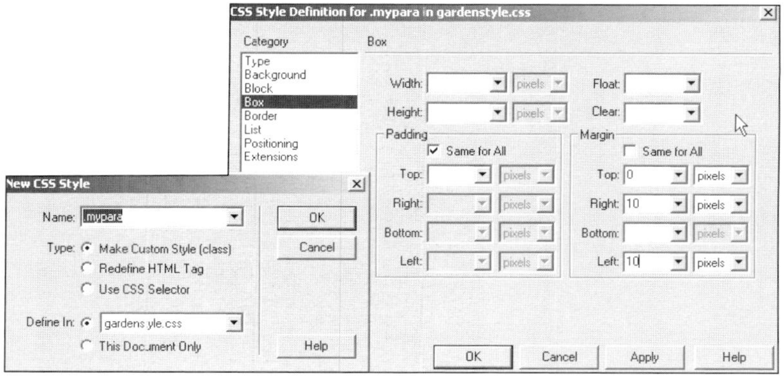

The New CSS Style dialog box and the Box category showing the settings used for the margin.

2 Apply the .mypara to the first main paragraph.

Place your cursor in the text of the first paragraph in the main content area, below the Grow an Instant Garden image. The first line is set to the <h4> heading style. Be sure to place your cursor in the paragraph below the first line.

- In the CSS Styles panel, click the radio button to select Apply Styles. Select .mypara from the styles listed.

  The Apply Styles and Edit Styles modes are new to Dreamweaver MX. They eliminate the Auto Apply option, which often caused more trouble than it saved. With the new modes, you can safely double-click any style in Edit Styles without accidentally applying it.

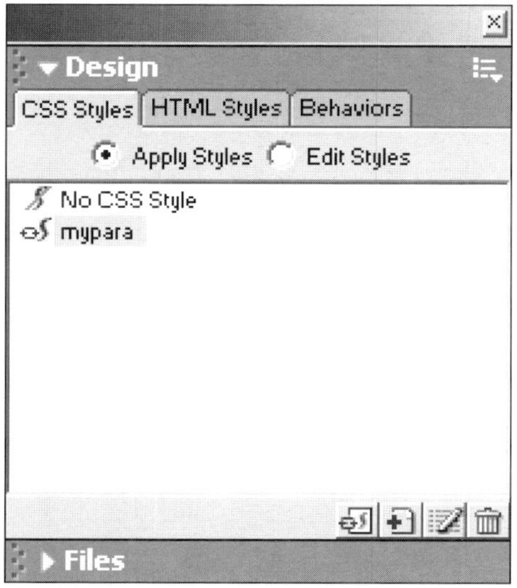

New options in the CSS Styles panel.

- Or, you can stay in Edit Style mode and simply select an element with the Tag Selector and right-click or (Ctrl-click for Mac) to choose Set Class.

3 Apply the .mypara class to the paragraphs in the lower content.

Some of the paragraphs are preceded by <h5> headings. Style only the <p> tags.

- Place the cursor in the paragraph below the heading GARDEN IN A POT.
- Select the paragraph tag in the Tag Selector, right-click (Ctrl-click for Mac), and choose Set Class>.mypara.
- Repeat for the remaining paragraphs.

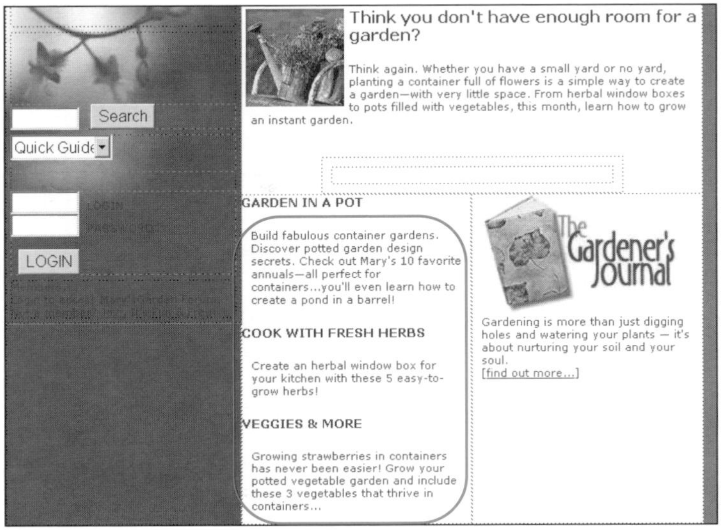

The custom class of .mypara is added to every paragraph, not the headers.

4 Redefine the grouped selectors <h4> and <h5>.

You can refer to Step 6 in the previous section about grouping selectors and using CSS Selectors to refresh your memory for this step.

- Add a new style (be sure the Edit radio button is selected). Select Use CSS Selector, gardenstyles.css, type **h4**, **h5**, and click OK.
- In the Style Definition dialog box, set the Text properties as follows:

  Size: **11px**

  Color: **#660099**

- Set the Box properties, Margin (uncheck Same for All).

  Bottom: **0px**

  Left: **10px**

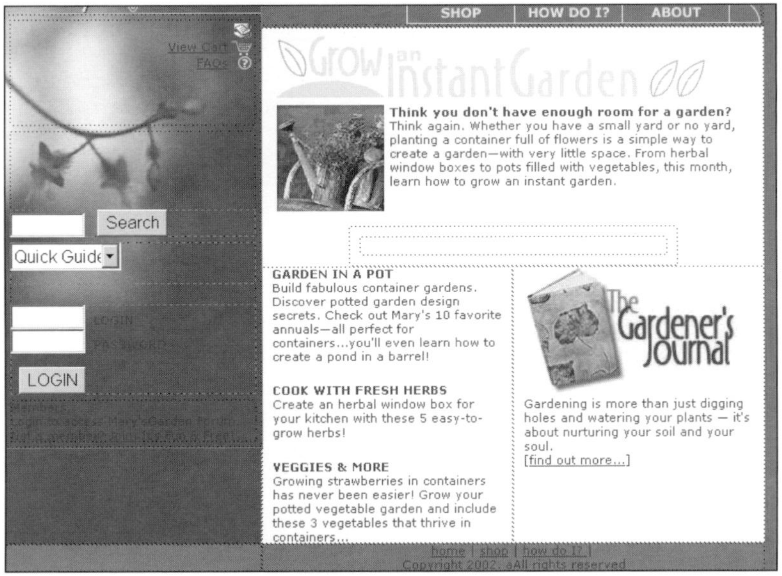

The <h4> and <h5> selectors are redefined. Notice the change in the title headings in the main content.

- OK the style rules. You don't have to apply anything. The page contains <h4> and <h5> tags, so the new rules are automatically applied.

5 Create the .leadpara style.

- Add the new style.
- Choose Make Custom Style and select your linked sheet.
- Name the class style **.leadpara**.
- In the Line-Height field, type **200** and select % from the menu.

For an in-depth discussion of all the ramifications of line-height, we recommend reading Eric Meyer's book, *Cascading Style Sheets: The Definitive Guide* (O'Reilly), or visiting the W3C site.

- Set the Box properties in the Margin area to show Top: **0px** and Left: **-10px** (uncheck Same for All).
- Click OK to save the style.

Select the text of the first main paragraph. This is not the same thing as selecting the <p> tag. You already have a style applied to the <p> tag of this paragraph.

- Press Ctrl-T (or Cmd-T on the Mac) to fire up the Quick Tag Editor.
- Type **span** to wrap the tag around the selection (the opening and closing span tags are added before and after the text selection).
- Press Enter or Return to disengage the Tag Editor.
- Right-click (Ctrl-click for Macs) on the <span> tag in the Tag Selector, and set the class to .leadpara.

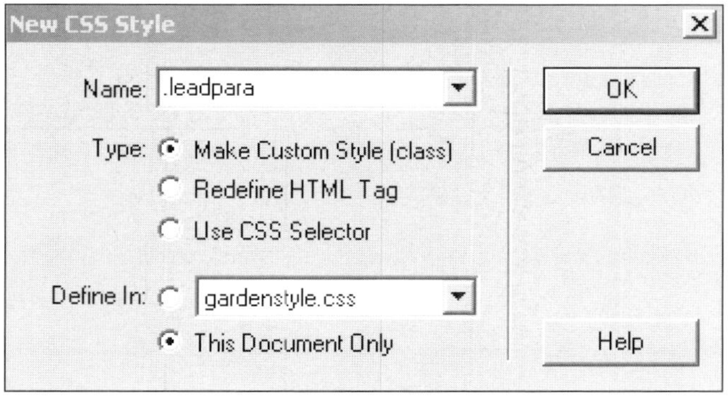

The settings used for the custom class .leadpara.

Note: All elements have line-height. *Line-height* is the CSS equivalent of *leading*, a term used by printers when printing was still done using lead type. The term refers to the lead strip printers placed between lines. Line-height determines the space between lines of text and also affects the box of every element in a very complex way. Take great care using line-height because some browsers (such as Netscape 4x) have issues when line-height and images in the block element and pixel lengths all collide during printing.

Apply Style wouldn't work correctly in this case. It would simply replace .mypara with .leadpara, which isn't the same thing at all! Although this is still a .mypara-styled paragraph, new attributes are added and in some cases, will override others. More explanation on this later in the chapter.

6 Save and preview in both browsers.

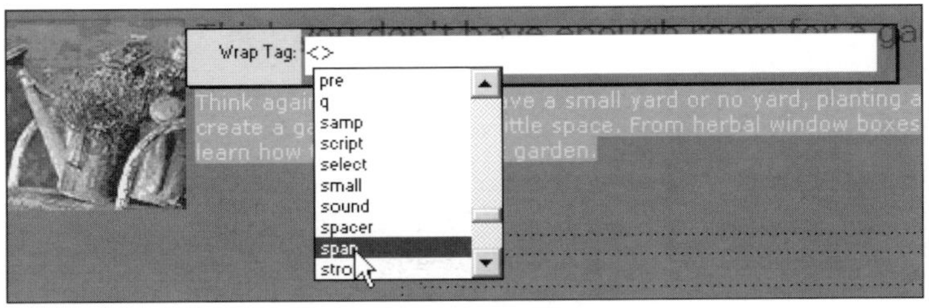

The Tag Selector where the Wrap Tag>span is being added to the paragraph text only.

Styling Your Links with Pseudo-Classes

Of course you can control the presentation of any anchor element with an <HREF> attribute. With CSS, that's a given. But the anchor tag has a subset of selectors as well. They are as follows:

a:link

a:visited

a:hover

a:active

You're probably familiar with three of the four from their use in the HTML process of formatting the <body> tag. In this section, you'll use the CSS Selector option to set up all pseudo-selectors.

1 Create your default a:link style.

- Add a new style.
- Choose Use CSS Selector and select the linked style sheet.
- In the Selector field, choose or type **a:link**; then click OK.
- Set the Text Color to **#660099** (don't worry that the color is the same as the background; it'll change).

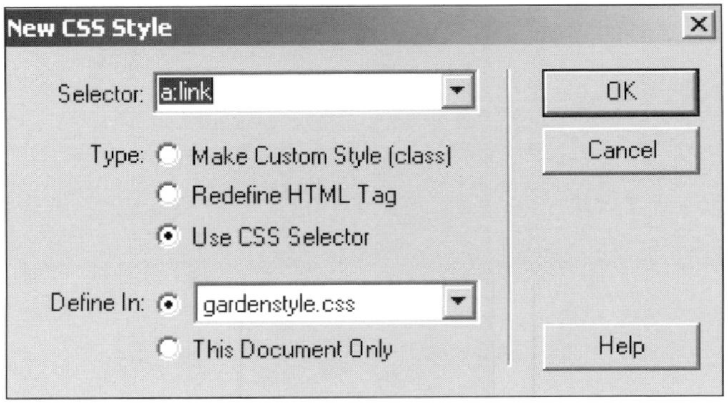

Settings used for the a:link.

- Don't feel obligated to set every attribute—let inheritance take its course. You don't know where a link might show up and this style is applied automatically to all links, unless other contextual styles are created.
- Click OK.

Note: You must define link styles in a specific order: link, visited, hover, active. In the case of active, support is buggy or non-existent in Netscape 4x; active is red no matter what. You can choose not to set an active style, which is what we'll do here.

2 Create the a:visited style.

- If you are still in Apply Style mode in the CSS Styles panel, switch to Edit Style mode, and then highlight the a:link style in the list.
- From the panel options (the small list-like arrow button in the top-right corner of the panel), select Duplicate. Be sure to set Define In to the external style sheet. Choose a:visited from the drop-down list.
- OK the style.

Tip: This method of duplicating a style makes it easier to determine where the style is defined. In this case, you want your style in the same location as the one you chose to duplicate. When you find yourself using more than one style sheet and adding new styles, you may simply want to repeat a style into a different sheet, especially where you plan to provide different settings for specific browsers. You will do this later on in this chapter.

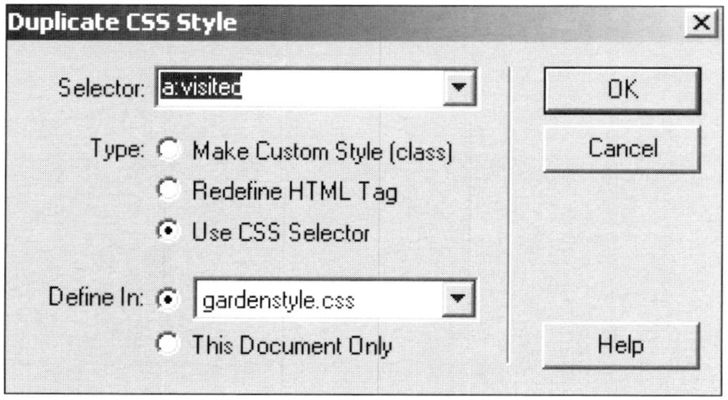

Settings used for a:visited.

3 Duplicate the a:visited style to create the a:hover style. Click Edit to set the hover style's color to #006600 or choose your own color value.

4 Save and preview your page.

News You Can Use

Convention is a useful thing. Take advantage of it and be very careful where you choose to ignore it! For example, Netscape 4x browsers completely ignore hover. If your design relies on hover to tell a user that a link is present, you may want to rethink your style if you are targeting that browser. If, for example, you remove the conventional underline decoration and rely on the color change to alert users that they are hovering over a link, you run the risk of this not working on pages viewed in Netscape 4x. Inline links are hard to find when color is their only attribute.

Later in this project, you'll remove the underline from footer links and have them underline on hover. Visitors understand that footer-style links are links because of where they are—even without underlines.

Conversely, don't create text styles with underlines when they are not links. Underline *means* link and you risk confusing and even irritating visitors after they click a few underlined words and find they are not links.

Other stylizations can be problematic, too. Be careful about setting your links to bold on hover. Links that bold on hover can completely re-flow paragraph text when they occur inline.

Contextual Selectors

Element selectors (basic HTML tags) and class selectors (.class) can be designed to occur only in context. Contextual selectors use rules that apply whenever the specific selector occurs within a container using a class style. The application is automatic; it is the container's class—setting the context that causes the style to be applied.

In this section, you set up some classes just to have them as a context. Yes, that's right, a class can contain no specific properties or attribute values! This is quite a useful method for determining specific page regions that will automatically use the correct styles. After all, if you can avoid setting every instance of a style, it makes you more efficient and lessens your workload! (And it also makes updating your pages easier later on.)

1 In the external style sheet (gardenstyle.css), create custom classes to use for context, using the names and attributes listed here:

- Add a new style.
- Select Make Custom Style (class), and name it .icons. In Define In:, choose gardenstyle.css, and click OK.
- In the Type category, enter the following settings:

  Weight: **bold**

  Color: #**99FF66**

- Click OK.
- Add another new style
- Choose Make Custom Style (class) and name it .footer. Choose Define In: gardenstyle.css, and click OK.
- In the Type category, enter:

  Color: **#FFFFFF**

- Click OK.

2 Apply the .icon class to the cells of the table in #lyrSidebar.

- First, select lyrSidebar from the Layers panel.
- Place your cursor in the first table cell, press Shift, and then click in the last cell.
- In Apply Style mode in the CSS Styles panel, click the .icons style to set the class to the selected table cells.

3 Apply the .footer class to the right cell of the bottom footer table.

In Apply Style mode in the CSS Styles panel, click the .footer style to set the class to the right column of the footer table.

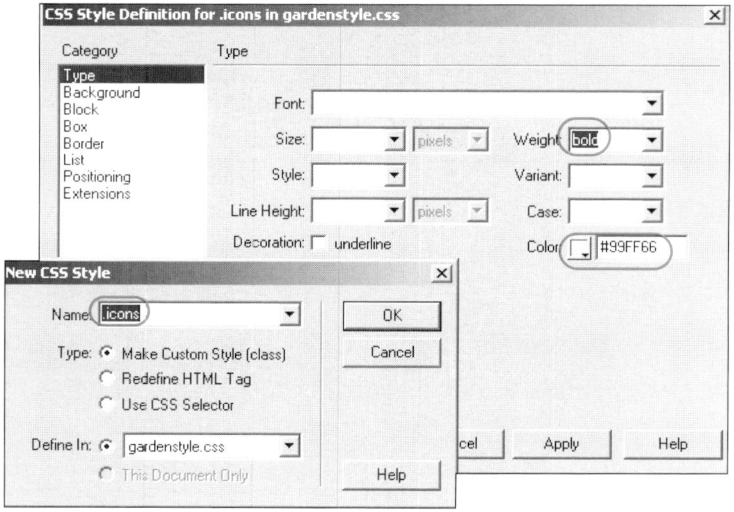

The settings for the .icons custom class and the text attributes.

The contextual icon selector is added to the icons.

4 Create the contextual pseudo-class .footer stylex a:link, a:visited, and a:hover.

- Add a new style.
- Choose Use CSS Selectors and Define In: garden-style.css style sheet.
- Type **.footer a:link** into the Selector field.
- Set the following Text properties:

  Color: **#FFFFFF**.

  Decoration: **None**.

- Click OK.
- Repeat Step 4 to create .footer a:visited, setting the following Text properties:

  Color: **#FFFFFF**

  Text Decoration: **None**.

- Click OK.
- Repeat the steps to create .footer a:hover.

  Color: **#FFFFFF**.

  Decoration: **Underline**.

- Click OK.

5 Create .icon pseudo-classes, defining a:link, a:visited, and a:hover.

Note: When you are creating link styles, order is important. Follow the link, visited, hover, active rule when defining these styles. The same is true when creating contextual link styles.

- Add a new style.
- Choose Use CSS Selectors and Define In gardenstyle.css style sheet.

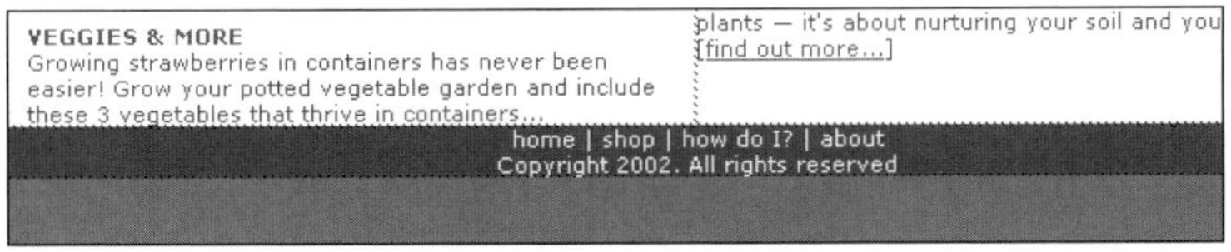

The .footer pseudc-class is added to the footer.

Note: Underline is the default decoration of links. If you choose to use None instead of Underline for link and visited, and you want the Underline decoration to return on hover, you must explicitly select the Underline value.

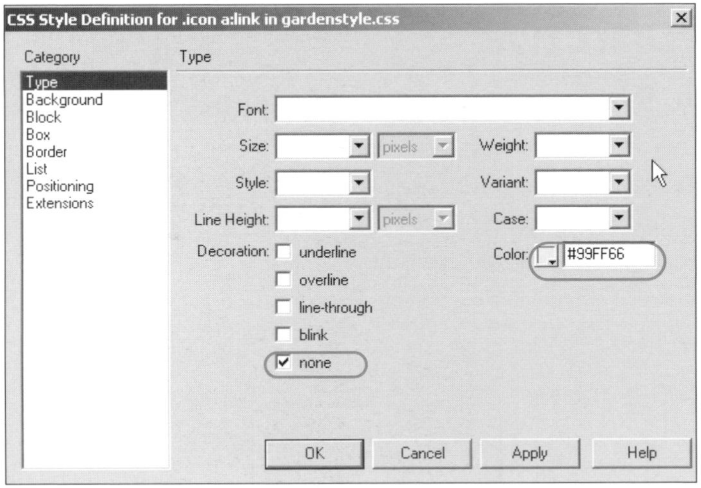

The Type settings, including None for the Decoration.

- Type in the Selector field: **.icons a:link**
- Click OK.
- Set the following attributes:

  Color: **#99FF66**

  Decoration: **None**
- Click OK.
- Duplicate the .icons a:link style. Type the following text: **.icons a:visited.**
- Click OK.
- Duplicate the new .icon a:visited style.
- Type the following text: **.icon a:hover.**
- Click OK.
- With the newest style still selected, click the Edit button. This re-opens the Style Definition dialog.
- Set these properties:

  Text Color: **#FFFFFF**

  Background Color: **#660099**

6 Save your page and preview in both browsers. The hover, of course, will not work in Netscape 4x.

Tip: If you want to experiment, try setting a Text decoration of Overline and Underline.

Using the @Import Directive to Bypass Netscape 4x

Until Netscape 4x is a thing of the past, your job is made more difficult because you want consistent page presentation. Although hover and certain spacing issues are minor issues, other style options are buggy and harder to work around. Styles applied to form objects are a perfect example. Although largely ignored by non-W3C compliant browsers, early browsers choke completely, and even crash! That *hardly* fits the graceful degradation billing for CSS.

What *is* graceful is that when a style is missing, it is ignored. You'll use that concept to go ahead and fearlessly style your form objects and address some Netscape 4x-only issues with top and bottom margins.

The @Import directive is a different method of attaching a style sheet to your page. Ignored completely by Netscape 4x and earlier browsers, you can use this method and tap into the power of cascade to provide additional styles and settings strictly for the browsers that do recognize it.

1 Duplicate the linked style sheet.

- Double-click to open the gardenstyle.css sheet from the Site Files panel.
- Save as **gardenstyle_compliant.css** into the stylesheets folder.
- Close the file.

2 Import the new style sheet.

- Choose Text CSS Styles>Attach Style Sheet. Browse to the new style sheet. Select gardenstyle_compliant.css, and click OK.
- Set Import in the Link External Style Sheet dialog box, and click OK.
- Switch to Split view.
- Choose View>Head Content. Select the embedded styles icon. (*Note:* On a PC, this looks like an S, but on a Mac, it has a boomerang shape.)
- Check to see that the embedded styles icon appears *after* the linked style sheet. This is very important! If the icon is in the wrong place, you can drag the Link icon in Head view to place it before the embedded styles icon.

3 Add a custom class for the form buttons and text fields in the second style sheet only.

- In the CSS Styles panel, select the gardenstyle_compliant.css imported sheet.
- Add a new style.
- Choose Make Custom Class and name the style **.formbtn**.

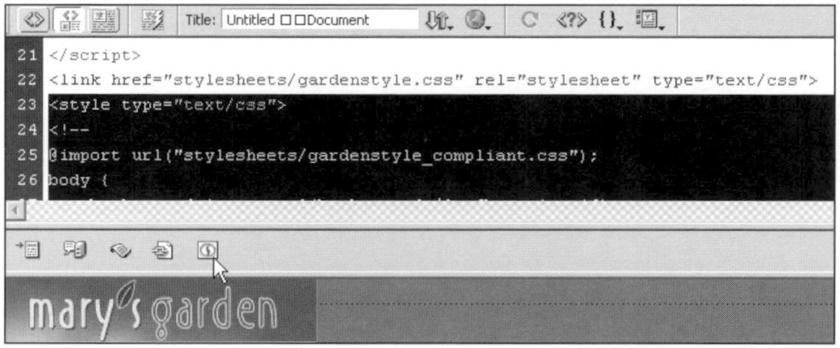

The head content is visible, and the Embedded Styles icon is selected, showing the code in the Code and Design view.

- In the Style Definition dialog box, set the Text Properties for formbtn to:

  Size: **10px**

  Weight: **bold**

  Color: #**660099**

- Click to the Background category and set the Background Color to **#99FF66**.
- Click to Box category and set Width to **90px**.
- Click to the Border category and set the Border properties as follows (leave Same for All checked):

  Style: **Solid**

  Width: **1px**

  Color: **#003366**

- Set the Extensions Properties of formbtn to Cursor: **hand**. Click OK.

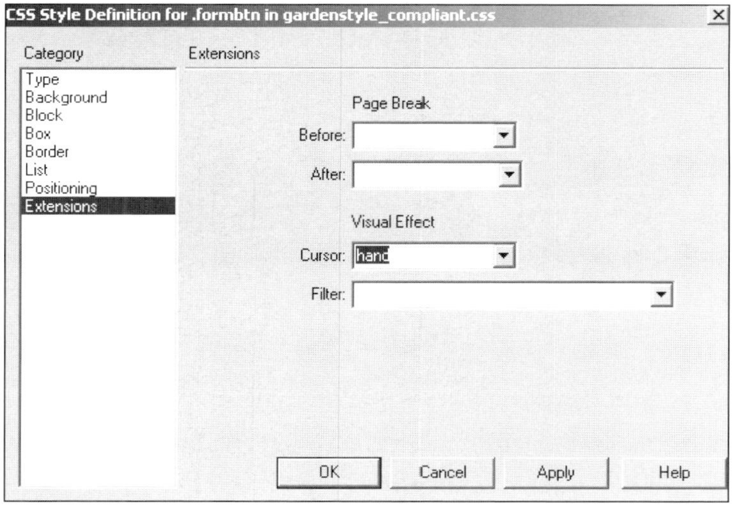

Entering a value in the Extensions category.

4 Apply the style to the Search and Login buttons.

- Select the Search button.
- Right-click (Ctrl-click for Mac) on the <input> tag and set the class to .formbtn.
- Repeat for the Login button.

The form buttons as seen in Netscape 6 after the new .formbtn style is applied to the Search and Login buttons.

5 Duplicate the .formbtn style to create the .formmenu style and apply it to the Jump menu.

- Select the gardenstyle_compliant style sheet in the CSS Styles panel.
- Click the Edit Styles button.
- Highlight .formbtn and Duplicate.
- Name it **.formmenu**.
- Click OK.
- Edit, changing the following settings as you see here:

  Text Weight: **Normal**

  Box Width: **180px**

  Extensions Cursor: (delete any, set to blank)

- Click OK.
- Select the Jump menu, click the <select> tag, and set the Class to .formmenu.

The form buttons as seen in Netscape 4.7. The style is ignored so the form buttons render nicely.

6 Duplicate the .formmenu style to create the formfield style and apply it to the Text Fields.

- Select the gardenstyle_compliant style sheet in the CSS Styles panel.
- Click the Edit Styles button.
- Highlight .formmenu and Duplicate.
- Name it **.formfield**.
- Set Box Width to blank.
- Click OK.

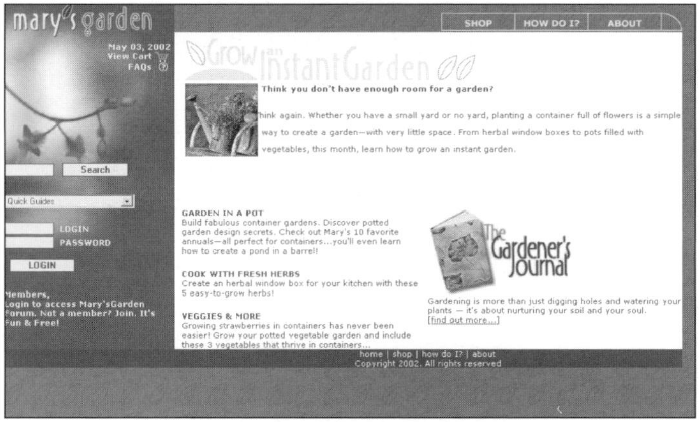

The sidebar as rendered in Internet Explorer 5.5.

- Apply the .formfield style to the text fields (to the left of the Search, Login, and Password fields).

Note: Sometimes applying styles to form buttons disables the default hand cursor. Specifically setting it alleviates this issue.

Test in both Netscape and Internet Explorer. The page works as it should. Internet Explorer shows green fields and purple text, while Netscape ignores the custom styles of the form elements.

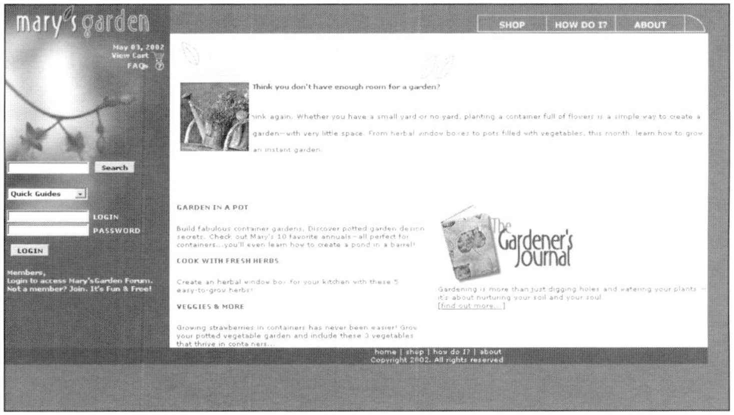

The sidebar as rendered in Netscape 4.7.

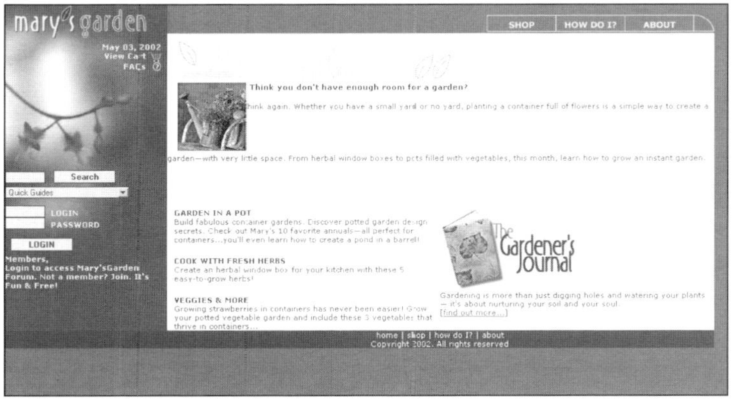

The sidebar as rendered in Netscape 6.2.

Vertical Adjacent Margins and Netscape 4x

The sheer number of non-compliance bugs and quirky behavior in Netscape 4x prohibits us from listing them all, but a major issue deals with how Top and Bottom Margin is handled. The specification states that vertical adjacent margins should collapse in favor of the largest value. That means that given a heading with a setting of Margin-Bottom: 0px and a paragraph with Margin-Top: 0px, you should not have extra space between the lines. But Netscape 4x ignores the setting values and auto-applies the default settings. You need a negative margin setting to overcome this behavior. But any negative value is rendered correctly in all the compliant browsers, resulting in an overlapping mess! This is where @Import can make your day.

1 Edit the .mypara setting in the original linked style sheet (gardenstyle.css).

- Double-click the .mypara style in Edit Style mode in the CSS Styles panel.
- Flip to Box properties and set the Margin-Bottom to **-11px**.
- OK the style change.
- Save and preview in both browsers.

Note: If you really want to see what could happen, alter the .mypara style in the other imported sheet and preview it in Internet Explorer or Netscape 6x. You find that the block elements crash together in a mess!

- Change the Bottom-Margin back to **0px** and save the page again.

These are the CSS Styles you've added in this project.

MODIFICATIONS

Modifications are what CSS is all about, so telling you to experiment with your styles belabors the obvious. But here is another style technique you can try in the project. This one sets an X-axis tiling effect for a background in a table cell.

1 Create and embed the new style into the page.

- Highlight the document (index.htm) in the CSS Styles panel.
- Add a new style by clicking the New Style icon.
- In the dialog box, be sure that you are adding to This Document Only!
- Make the new style a custom class, naming it .callout.

Because the text size and other properties will be inherited from the <td> and <p> style you set early on, you can skip setting any Text properties, unless you want to make the text different.

- Set the Background property's background image to background\small_leaf.gif.

Note: No-Repeat is useful, too. When setting a background image with HTML, many designers have been forced to add tons of extra width or height to an image to prevent tiling. No more! If you have a design that uses a single image, just set the Repeat attribute to No-Repeat.

- Set the Repeat attribute to Repeat-X.

Note: X tiles horizontally, while Y tiles vertically. Of course, the default is to repeat both directions, but you don't have to set this explicitly to make it happen; this occurs by default. Keep in mind that support for attachment and positioning of the background image is, at best, buggy in most browsers. And don't forget the Netscape 4x URL issue whenever you use the Background property.

STYLE SHEETS

In the Site Files window, you can double-click your style sheet to view the code in Dreamweaver MX. This is very cool because you can easily organize and insert comments (developer notes) for your styles. Open and review the final project's style sheets to see what we mean.

To insert a CSS single-line style comment, write your text note, and then select the text. From the Code Dock, Snippets panel, open the Comments snippets, select Comment, CSS-JS single-line, and press the Insert button at the bottom of the Snippets panel. Voila! Your comments are wrapped with the correct style of comment for CSS.

One other note: We write comments in all uppercase because our code is, by preference, all lowercase. That makes a comment extremely noticeable.

- Flip to Border Properties and set the following values (leave Same for All checked):

  Style: **Solid**

  Width: **1px**

  Color: **#669900**

- OK the style and return to your page.

2 Apply the style to the cell.

- Locate the empty, single cell table below the first part of the main content, but above the two-column section (just above GARDEN IN A POT).
- Place your cursor in the cell and apply the new .callout style by selecting the <td> style and right-clicking (Ctrl-click for Mac) to choose Set Class>.callout.
- Set the cell Horz to Center.

3 Add the following content in the cell:

- Add a line break by pressing Shift-Enter/Return.
- Type **Look What's New in Mary's Garden!**

You may need to adjust the table width to fit the pattern created by the graphic.

4 Save and preview the page.

A copy of the modified file is saved as index_modified.htm.

The final page in Internet Explorer 5.5 after the modification has been made.

"The only people for me are the mad ones, the ones who are mad to live, mad to talk, mad to be saved, desirous of everything at the same time, the ones who never yawn or say a commonplace thing, but burn, burn, burn."

—JACK KEROUAC

BUILDING AN ONLINE PORTFOLIO

Showcasing Your Work for a Wider Audience

Unlike a simple résumé, which presents your life in text, a portfolio can show, rather than tell, the kinds of work you have done and what type of work you are capable of doing. How you present that work is almost as important as the work itself in creating a positive impression with the viewer.

Although the web lacks the tactile experience a person gets flipping through a physical portfolio, an online portfolio does not have to be a static or linear experience, either. By using Dreamweaver's Navigation Bar tool and frames to create a virtual portfolio, you can offer viewers the same versatility they have flipping through paper pages.

Project 6

Building an Online Portfolio

by Jason Cranford Teague

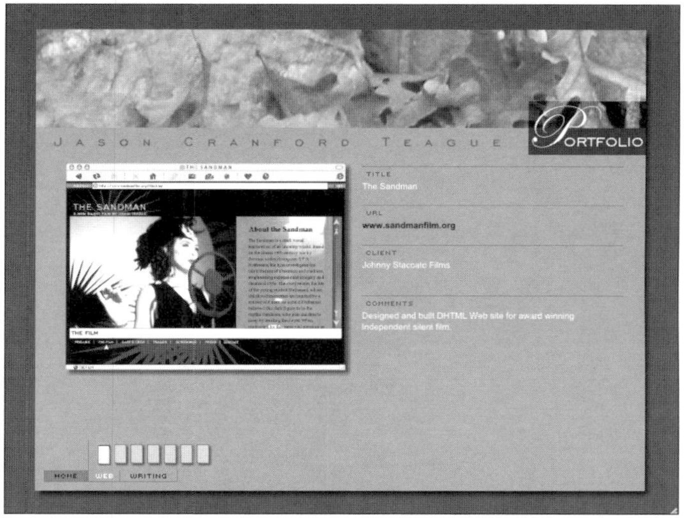

It Works Like This

The traditional portfolio is a ringed binder, often resembling a briefcase with a zippered edge, that holds sheets of plastic or paper used to store and present works of art, illustrations, or other visuals. Although the portfolio can work in some respects like a resume, a good portfolio shows, rather than tells, what you can do and provides a much more powerful message to potential employers or clients. If you do any type of work that produces something that can be shown, a portfolio can help you explain to a wider audience what you do and how you do it.

Note: Illustrators, for example, commonly use portfolios to show off the work they have produced in recent years. They present carefully selected pieces, the top illustrations that best reflect their expertise, presented one on a page. These pieces often include a short explanation of the piece, describing the client it was produced for, the project, the client's role in the project, and challenges in the project that were overcome. The viewer can then flip back and forth through the portfolio, comparing different pieces, and developing an opinion about the illustrator's capabilities.

With a physical portfolio, you either have to reproduce multiple copies to be sent out to the (hopefully) numerous interested parties—which gets expensive—or shuttle your precious few copies around from place to place. The web allows you to create a virtual portfolio that can be viewed by any number of people at anytime.

For my portfolio—I am a web designer and author—I set up a design to show off works I have produced in both of these separate arenas. For the web pages, I wanted to present a screen capture of one of the pages in the site, describe the client and my role in the project, and then provide a link to the live web site. For my books, I wanted to show the cover image, list the title and publisher, detail anything special about the book, and then include a link to a page on which the viewer can purchase the book online. In addition, I wanted to include a brief introduction to my work on the home page, a full copy of my résumé, and the various ways I can be contacted.

The design of my portfolio is confined within a central gray rectangle with fixed dimensions and a drop shadow to help set it off. Users select different options from a menu at the bottom-left corner of the interface. When users select either the Web, Writing, or Resume options, they see a submenu of page icons immediately above the main menu. The visitors can then click on individual pages in the submenu to flip through examples in the portfolio or pages in the résumé.

In this project, I show you how to create an online portfolio that allows the viewer to flip through virtual pages in a portfolio organized into two topics: web and writing. One key Dreamweaver feature you use to create the portfolio is the Navigation Bar tool, which presents an easy-to-use interface for setting up complex menus. In addition, in this project, you will be learning one of my favorite frame tricks: how to set up a drop shadow around a central frameset. You also learn how to set up a simple template page that allows you to quickly add new pages to the portfolio.

Planning and Designing the Interface

To design my portfolio, and to create my layout, backgrounds, buttons, animations and other graphics, I used Photoshop 7. However, everything I did in Photoshop and ImageReady, can also be done using Macromedia Fireworks—more or less. But this book is about Dreamweaver, not Photoshop or Fireworks, so let me quickly describe what I did and explain how I prepared the graphics for use in the Dreamweaver.

Tip: Although you may want to create some variety in the design between sections—maybe by using different titles or image sizes—keep the overall design as consistent as possible from page to page by creating a design versatile enough to accommodate any content you may throw at it.

Note: If you are interested in seeing the design before it has been webified, you can check out the finished file (PortfolioComp.png) in the Resources folder on this book's CD. (Dreamweaver users should choose the PNG version and Photoshop users can choose the PSD version.) If you are not interested in the visual design aspects of the site, skip the next two sections and dive right into "Setting Up the Site."

I started a new document using the standard 800×600 pixel screen size as the size for the canvas. I wanted to keep the colors as simple as possible so that the actual full-color portfolio images stand out. Therefore, I used gray background colors: a dark gray background with a lighter gray rectangular "stage" where the portfolio pages will be presented. I added a drop shadow to the light gray stage area to give it the appearance of floating on the screen, setting it off from the background.

The background and header. The central gray square will be used to present the portfolio material. When selecting colors, remember that lighter colors (especially in backgrounds) draw the viewer's eye when contrasted with darker colors.

Next, I added the header elements. It is important to make the right impression on viewers, and, for a portfolio, the right impression is often a strong impression. In this example, I took a photograph I had of a stone wall with autumn leaves and pumped up the color saturation, giving it a strong vibrant appearance. I then masked the image so that it occupied only the top of the stage area, which created a strong visual element to attract the viewer's eye and make an immediate impression upon loading. I then added my name using a very elegant font, Engraver's Gothic, stretching the text slightly and adding extra kerning between each letter. Finally, I added a "Portfolio" label so that viewers will instantly know the context of the page they are viewing.

Tip: Always show your designs around to friends, family, work mates, or anyone else who will give you feedback. For my design, I showed it to several people and received a range of comments, some of which convinced me to make changes to the final design.

Now for the important part: adding navigation menu and submenus. Keeping the menus as simple as possible is important while still allowing for maximum navigation flexibility. I add a textual menu for the main options (Home, Web, and Writer). Two of the areas—Web and Writer—will have submenus that are also created using the Macromedia Navigation Bar builder. In order to relate the menu option to its submenu, I added a line connecting them.

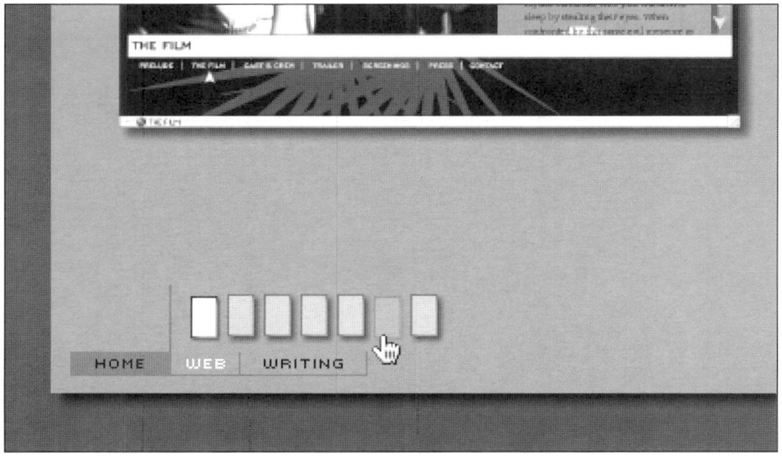

The menu and submenu.

Both the main menu and submenus can use up to four graphics for each option. These graphics represent different states (Up, Over, Down, and Over While Down) that the menu option can have. You learn more about these states when we start building the menu in Dreamweaver.

Finally, I added representative content to the design. This is not actual content used in the site but is "Greeked" to indicate what type of content goes where. Depending on your needs, you will want to reserve an area in the design to display graphics representing your work and an area to include a brief description of the work. Here I have added two columns: one on the left for the portfolio image and then one on the right to hold information that describes what the image represents.

Note: Design the menu states to optimize the contrast between different states, but don't make them too jarring or distracting.

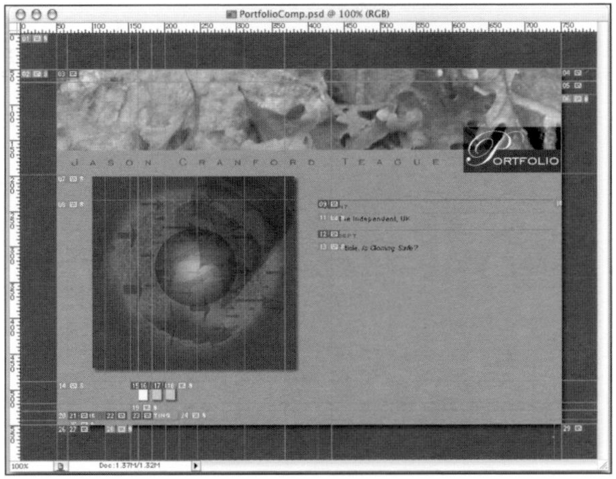

The final comp with "Greek" content in the design.

Note: The term *greek* is used to refer to content that is simply used to show placement. Another term for this is *FPO* (For Placement Only).

The Interface Chrome

Next, you will need to create the graphics that are used to create headers, buttons, and visual effects (such as the drop shadow). The following list briefly describes the graphics I created for this project, but I have included copies of all of these graphics on the CD in this project's Portfolio/images folder for you to use.

Note: Both Photoshop and Fireworks have the capability to slice interfaces created in them. This is a special method of selecting particular areas to be used when building the interface.

Note: The individual pieces used to create a graphic interface are referred to as the *Chrome*.

- **Header:** The header will be placed into a frame at the top of the central rectangle and includes the graphic, name, and portfolio title. I decided to cut this as one big piece and use JPEG to compress it.

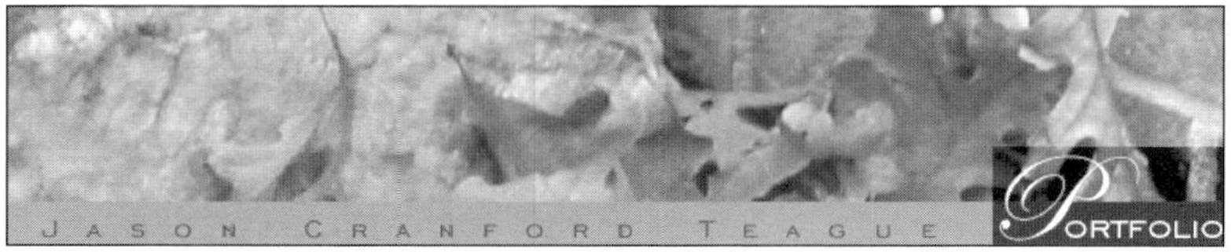

Interface Chrome: The header (header.jpg).

- **Menu Options**: Each individual menu option (in both Up and Down states) need to be cut. Save each menu graphic as m_*sectionName*.gif and m_*sectionName*_on.gif depending on the state.

Interface Chrome: The Writing menu option in Up and Down states (m_writing.gif and m_writing_on.gif).

- **Submenu Options:** For the submenu, you will be reusing one icon (with three different states) to represent each page.

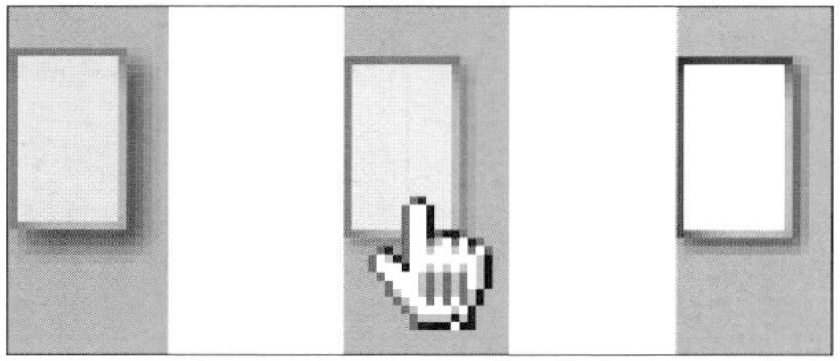

Interface Chrome: Submenu options showing the Up, Down, and Over states (page_up.gif, page_over.gif, and page_down.gif). The Over state will animate, slowly fading between 100% and 15% opacity.

- **Titles**: Each title used to describe the portfolio item being displayed (client, project name, Role in Project, and so on) needs to be cut separately. Save each title as st_*titleName.gif*.

Interface Chrome: An example of the Client title (st_client.gif).

- **Drop Shadow**: To add the drop shadow around the central frame, I created three background images and two "caps" used to round off the edges of the shadow.

Interface Chrome: Drop shadow pieces. There are background pieces for the right (bg_right.gif), bottom right corner (bg_corner_br.gif), and bottom sides (bg_right.gif) as well as two cap pieces to round off the shadows in the top-right and bottom-left corners (bg_capstone_bl.gif and bg_capstone_tl.gif).

- **Portfolio Images**: For each page in the portfolio, I created a variety of screen shots of web sites and images my book covers. To help find these images more quickly, I created a folder called portfolioImages within the images folder, and named each image depending on its section in the site, either *web*_imageName.jpeg or *write*_imageName.jpeg.

A Portfolio Image. I added a drop shadow underneath it to set it off from the rest of the page.

Setting up the Site

Now, it is time to get to work in Dreamweaver putting the pieces together. Rather than creating a new site from scratch, I show you how to import a barebones version of the web site I created, which already includes all the images mentioned in the previous section and an HTML file with the basic frame structure to create the interface.

Note: A completed version of the site is available in the PortfolioCompleted folder so that you can see the finished results.

To begin, as you should begin most Dreamweaver projects, you need to define your web site's file structure. These are the folders in which you will be placing your various HTML files. You can, of course, set them up as you go along, but I find it more useful to have them in place beforehand to avoid confusion.

1. Copy the folder 06_portfolio folder from the CD provided with this book to your hard drive. Open Dreamweaver and choose Site>New Site.

2 In the Edit Site dialog that opens, click the Advanced tab, type **Portfolio** as the Site Name and then click the folder icon next to Local Root Folder field. Browse to find the folder Portfolio in the folder 06_portfolio. Select the folder and click Select (click Choose on the Mac).

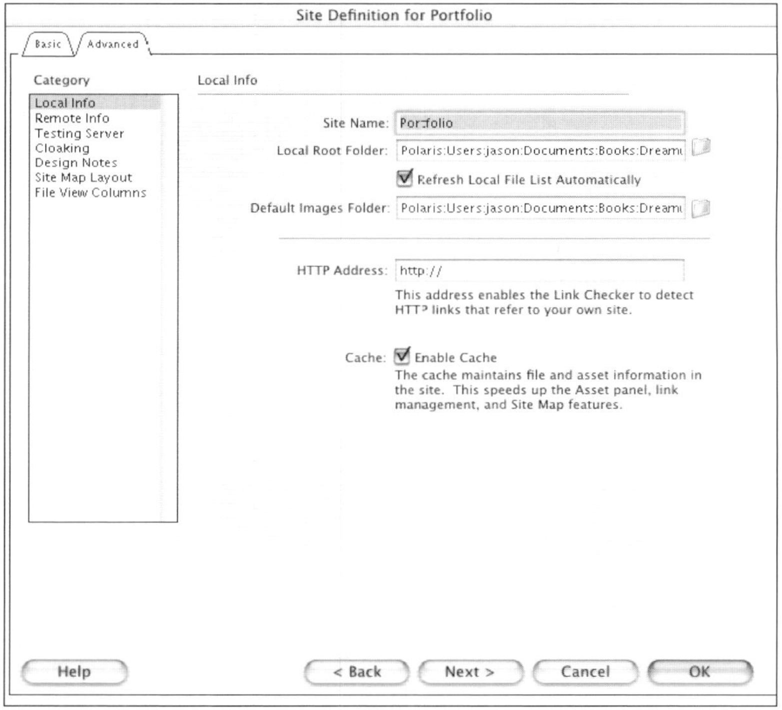

Use the Site Definition dialog to set the site name and root folder.

Next, click the folder icon next to the Default Images field, browse to the images folder inside the Portfolio folder and click Select (Choose, on the Mac).

Make sure that the Refresh Local File List Automatically and Enable Cache options are checked and click OK. Dreamweaver now identifies this and all of its content as a site and will include it in the list of available sites in the Site Window.

Note: You can, of course, incorporate your portfolio into your current web site, but it is a lot easier to treat the portfolio as a separate project and create a new site for it (even if you upload it into an existing web site).

Currently the site includes only the images folder (all of the graphics you will be using in this project.) and index.html (the frameset for the interface). Now we need to set up the rest of the folders. See Project 3, "Dream Templates," for details on how to remove the read-only attribute from the files.

3 In the Site window (if you don't see it, choose Window>Site to add a checkmark beside the menu option), Ctrl-right-click the Site-Portfolio icon and select New Folder from the contextual menu. Type **border** to name this folder. The border folder will contain the HTML files used to create the dark gray border around the portfolio.

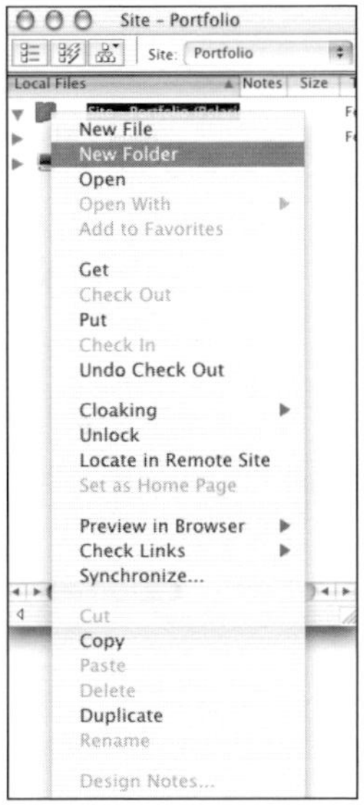

Start a new folder in the site.

4 Repeat this step to create the following folders:

css: Contains all CSS documents used in the site.

home: Creates a folder to hold your home page.

Create additional folders to hold the pages of the different sections of your portfolio.

web

writing

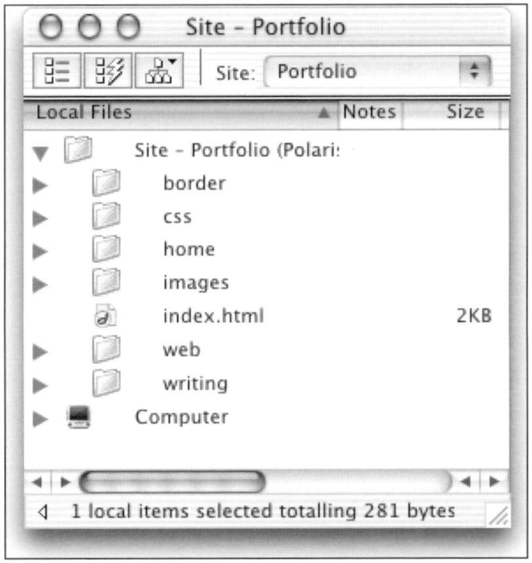

Site structure for the portfolio web site.

Note: As you are working, Dreamweaver may add additional folders to your file structure: Library to store Library Items, and Templates for templates that you create for this site.

Setting Up the Basic Interface

Obviously, the way in which you set up the design for your portfolio will dictate how you need to set up the basic interface. This section shows you how to work with the basic frame structure used in this design and shows you how to place a drop shadow around a central frameset. First, you need to set up two placeholder HTML pages and the general CSS to be used in the site.

Note: Some designers simply do not like frames. For this project, however, frames make a lot of sense because they allow you to create an interface that is easy to change and add to. Although I will be using nine separate frames to create the entire interface (including five frames to create a drop shadow around the central content area), there are only three frames that are required to create this interface: content, menu, and submenu.

1 Start a new HTML page and save it as **content.html** in the Portfolio folder.

2 Open the CSS Styles palette (Window>CSS Styles) and click the New CSS Style button.

Choose Redefine HTML Tag, type **body** in the Tag field, choose Define In: (New Style Sheet), and click OK. In the Save Style Sheet File As dialog, name the new CSS file **content.css** and save it in the site's css folder.

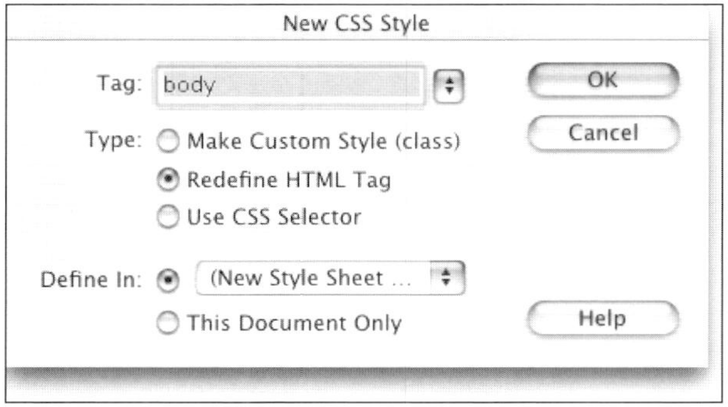

To start a new external style sheet, select the tag you want to redefine.

3 In the CSS Style Definition dialog, set the following:

- In Type, set the Font to Arial, Size to **10px**, and the Color to **#ffffff** (white).
- In Background, set the Background Color to **#889095**.
- In the Box category, set the Margin and Padding on all four sides to **0** pixels. A quick way to do this is to set one of the sides to **0** and then click Same for All.

Close the CSS dialog by clicking OK, save the changes to the HTML file (File>Save), and close the document (File>Close).

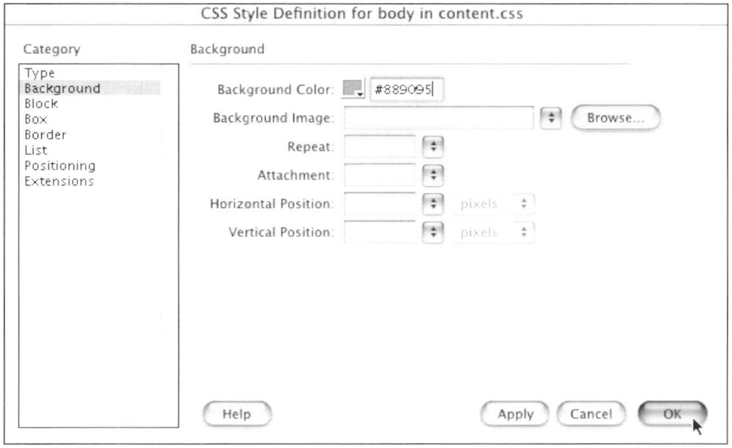

The CSS Style Definition Dialog with the gray background set.

4 Repeat Steps 1 through 3 to create another HTML file called **border.html**, with a style sheet **border.css** with the same settings except for the background color, which should be #333333.

5 Open the file index.html and switch to Design mode to view the frames. If you set up content.html and border.html correctly, you will see a gray rectangle with a dark gray border. You may need to open the Dreamweaver document window wide to see the border.

Note: You will also want to add other styles to this style sheet for fonts, links, and headers.

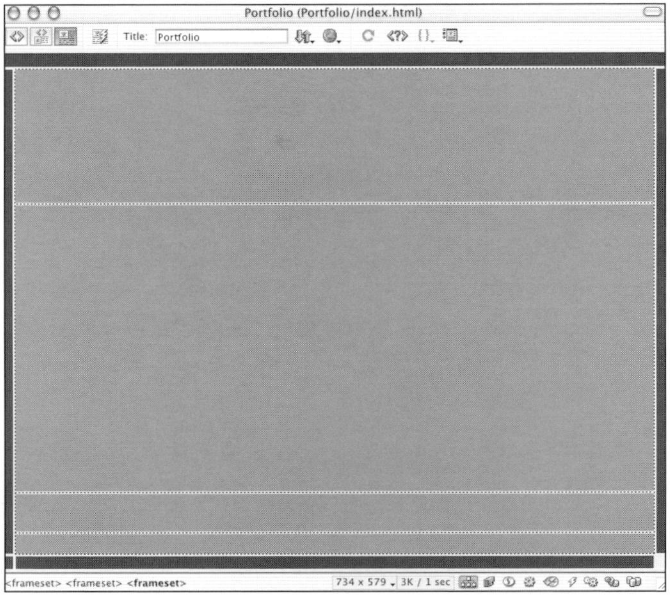

index.html in Dreamweaver's Design view showing the placeholders.

Tip: To view the frame borders in Design view, select View>Visual Aids>Frame Borders. Light gray borders appear to help you see where one frame ends and the next begins.

This frameset contains 10 frames in order to accommodate all the content and create a border around the fixed area.

Currently, the frames contain the placeholder documents set up earlier in this section, but you will be changing most of them. The frames are:

topFrame, bottomLeft, and leftFrame: The source for these frames is set to border.html. These frames will remain blank.

bottomMiddle, rightMiddle, and bottomRight: The source is set to border.html for now. Eventually each of these frames will be customized to hold the drop shadow.

header: The source is set to content.html for now. Later, this frame will hold header.html.

content: The source is set to content.html for now. Later, this frame will display the various portfolio pages.

submenu: The source is set to content.html for now. Later, this frame will be used to display the submenus for each section with links (targeting the content frame) to the pages in that section.

menu: The source is set to content.html for now. Later, this frame will be used to display menu.html, the site's main menu with links that target the submenu frame.

Content: Provide description here (this frame has been omitted).

6 Open content.html and resave it as **header.html** in the Portfolio folder.

7 Click the New CSS Style button in the CSS panel. In the New CSS Style dialog box, choose Redefine HTML tag, type **body** for the tag, choose This Document Only, and click OK.

In the CSS dialog box, select Background, click Browse, and select the file header.jpg in the images folder. Set repeating to no-repeat. Click OK to close the CSS dialog.

Save the changes to this file and close it.

8 Switch back to index.html and set header.html to be the source for the header frame. Do this by opening the Frames Panel (Window>Others>Frames) and clicking in the frame labeled header. Then, in the Properties panel, type **header.html** in the Src field. The header should now appear in the frameset.

Note: If you navigate to the desired file using the Browse button, the proper relativity is maintained through the site and you are guaranteed not to have typos and support questions.

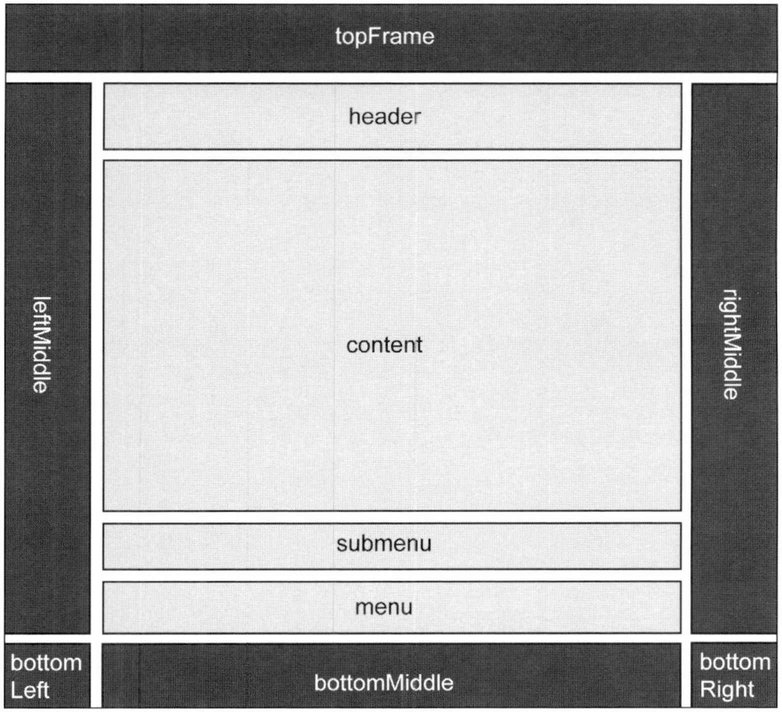

Frame structure for this project.

The Frames panel with the header frame selected. Each frame in the document is represented here. Click in the frame to make changes to it in the Properties panel.

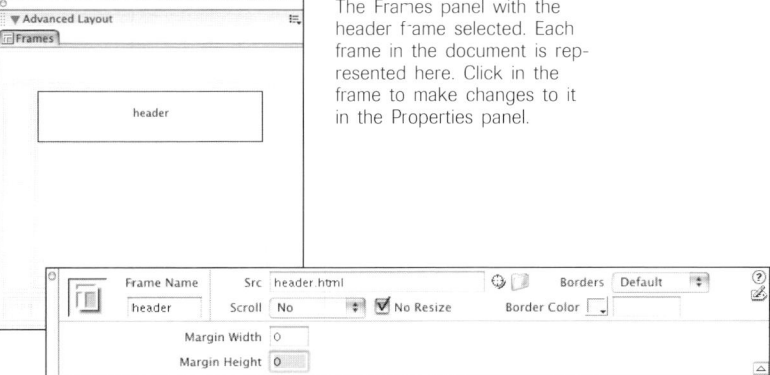

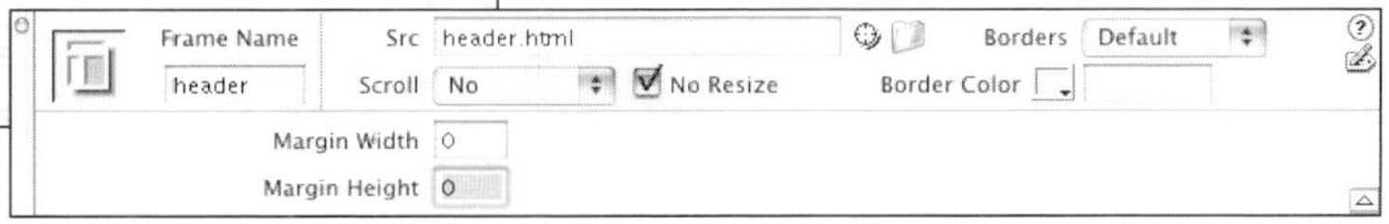

The Properties panel with the frame source set to header.html.

Setting Up the Drop Shadow

Drop shadows provide a time-honored way to add depth and texture to an image or interface. They are commonly used in web design. For this design, I wanted to add a drop shadow around an entire frameset, which can get a bit tricky. The basic structure is already in place, now you just need to add the right background graphics in three of the frames to create the drop shadow effect.

1 Open border.html and immediately resave it as **borderRight.html** in the border folder. This file will form the right side of the drop shadow.

2 Click the New CSS Style button in the CSS panel. In the New CSS Style dialog box, choose Redefine HTML tag, type **body** for the tag, choose This Document Only, and click OK.

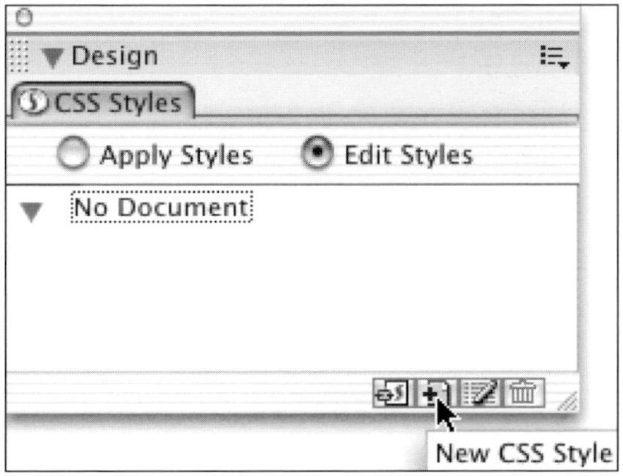

The New CSS Style button in the CSS Panel.

3 In the CSS Style definition dialog box, click Background, click the Browse button next to the Background Image field, and then choose the file bg_right.gif in the images folder. Set the Repeat attribute to repeat-y, which causes the drop shadow to repeat only down the side of the page rather than tiling. Click OK to close the CSS Style definition dialog box.

4 Add to the page the graphic bg_capstone_tr.gif from the images folder. This image serves as a "capstone" to the drop shadow at the extreme top of the frame, rounding it off.

Save the changes to this file and close it.

5 Switch back to index.html and set borderRight.html to be the source for the header frame. If you can't find the correct frame, switch to the Code view and look for the line that starts with **frame src="content.html" name="rightMiddle"** and change the source attribute to **src="border/borderRight.html"**. Do this by opening the Frames Panel (Window>Others>Frames) and clicking the frame labeled header. Using the Property inspector, set the frame src to borderRight.html. The right border frame should now show the drop shadow.

6 Repeat Steps 1 through 5, saving the file as **borderBottom.html**. Use the file bg_bottom.gif as the background image, set Repeat to repeat-x, add the graphic bg_capstone_bl.gif. Save the file and close it, and set it as the source for the bottomMiddle frame.

7 To finish the drop shadow, open the file border.html and immediately resave it as **borderBR.html** in the border folder. This file will form the right bottom corner of the drop shadow.

8 Click the New CSS Style button in the CSS panel. In the New CSS Style dialog box, choose Redefine HTML tag, type **body** for the tag, choose This Document Only, and click OK.

In the CSS dialog, select Background, click Browse, and select the file bg_corner_br.gif in the image folder. Set Repeat to no-repeat. Click OK to close the CSS dialog.

Save the changes to this file and close it.

9 Switch back to index.html and set the file bg_corner_right.gif to be the source for the bottomRight frame.

The shadow should now surround the center area.

The drop shadow around the central frameset.

Creating the Main Menu

Most web sites use some form of menu to help visitors navigate between different sections. Recognizing what a common feature this is, Dreamweaver includes a simple system for creating navigation bars that rely on graphic links with up to four different rollovers to show the state of the menu option:

- **Up:** This is the off state for the link and should let the visitor know that this is a link and can be clicked.
- **Over:** This is the on state for the menu option and should let the visitor know that the link is ready to be clicked. You can communicate this through color changes, shifting size, shifting position, or adding additional markers (such as a pointer). The idea is that there should be an obvious change between the up and over states.
- **Down:** This is the current state for the menu option and should be clearly contrasted with the up state. Generally, Down will be used to indicate that this is the currently selected menu option (that is, the current page).
- **Over While Down:** This is the on state used for an element currently in the down state. Because the element is already down, indicating that it is selected, this is a special case. You need to communicate to the visitor that this link is already active or simply leave it looking the same as the down mode to indicate that clicking it will not change anything.

1. Open the page index.html, click in the menu frame to open the content.html document. Immediately resave the file using File>Save Frame As, and name it **menu.html** in the Portfolio folder.

2 Click the Navigation Bar button in the Insert panel or select Insert>Interactive Images>Navigation Bar. This selection opens the Insert Navigation Bar dialog box.

3 When the Insert Navigation Bar dialog opens, it creates a blank menu option by default, called unnamed1, for you to modify. Type in the element name—in this case, **home**—and type **Home** for the alternate text.

Tip: You should use alternate text for every image on your page—even spacers and other seemingly unimportant design elements—in order to create a universally accessible web site.

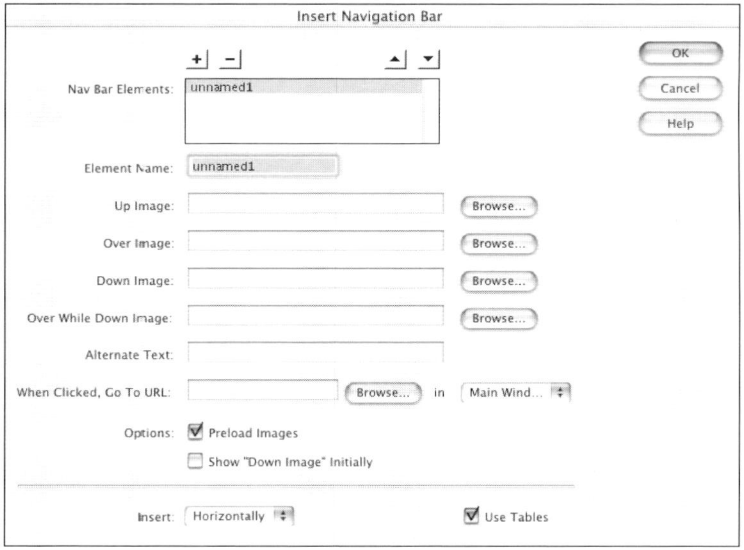

An empty Insert Navigation Bar dialog box ready to be filled in.

Specify the images to be used for the four different states. You can either type the path directly (if you happen to know it off the top of your head) or select the Browse button to locate it in the site's images folder. Although you can specify a different graphic for each state, try to keep the menu simple. For this example you will use only two different graphics for the main menu:

- m_home.gif for the up state.
- m_home_on.gif for the Over, Down, and Over While Down states.

Enter the URL for the submenu this menu option links to (home/submenu.html, this time around) and specify that the link should target the submenu frame.

Note: If you leave the URL field blank, Dreamweaver will automatically insert a # character. If you are working with a frames document, all the frames will appear in the targeting list. If you decide to leave the links blank, you may want to change them to javascript:; instead. Clicking a link with the # character will cause the browser to jump to the top of the page rather than do nothing.

Decide whether you want the graphics for this element to be preloaded. This is generally recommended because it will prevent a potentially unattractive pause as the image loads for the first time during a rollover.

Choose whether this element should initially be in the Down state. Because the Down state will generally be used to indicate the current page, this allows you to set the initial page for the menu. Select this option if you are setting up the menu option for the Home page (the first page loaded); otherwise, leave it unchecked.

This completes Step 3, but do not exit the dialog box.

The element that has been set to show the Down state initially will have an asterisk (*) beside its name in the Nav Bar Elements list.

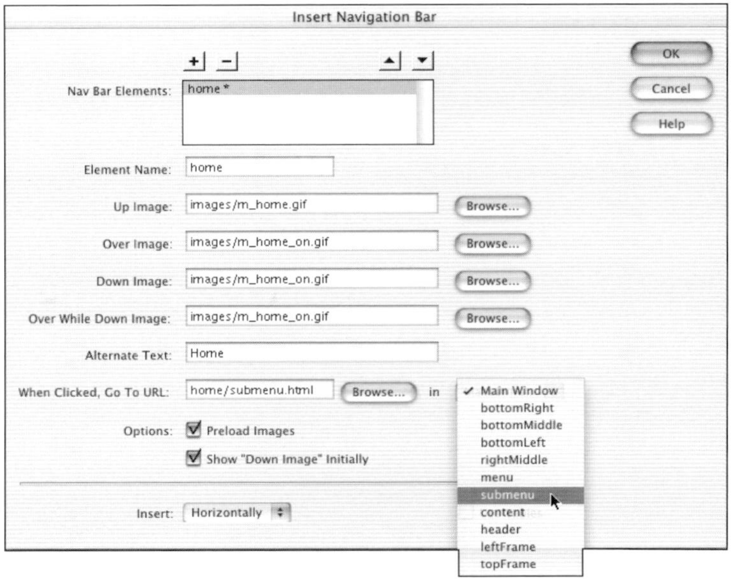

Select submenu to set the target for these links.

4 Click the + sign and repeat Step 3 to add the rest of the menu options:

- **Web**: Link to web/submenu.html same target frame?
- **Writing**: Link to writing/submenu.html same target frame?

Note: You can adjust the menu options up or down in the menu hierarchy or delete an element entirely by selecting it in the Nav Bar Elements list and then using the up and down arrows or the – sign to delete it.

5 Choose whether you want the navigation bar to run horizontally across the page or vertically down the page and whether you want to use tables to create the layout. For this design, a horizontal non-table design will suffice.

6 Once you have added all of the Navigation Bar Elements, click OK and the new navigation bar will be displayed in Design view.

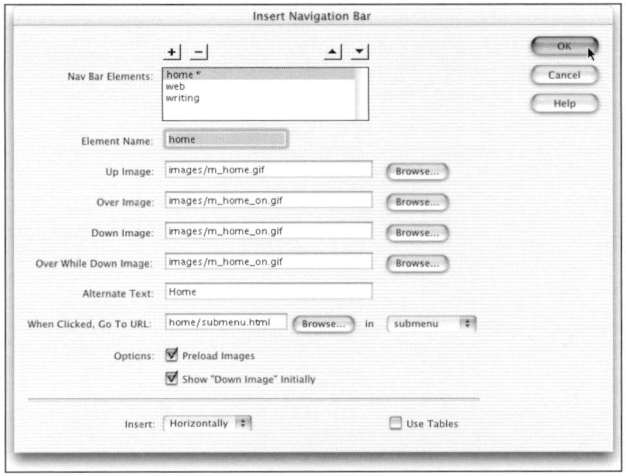

The settings for the finished navigation bar.

7 Because we set the margins and padding in the content.css file to 0 pixels, the menu is pushed against the left edge of the frame. To change this, click the New CSS Style button in the CSS panel. In the New CSS Style dialog box, choose Redefine HTML tag, type **body** for the tag, choose This Document Only, and click OK. Then, in the Box category, change the left margin (and only the left margin) to 10 pixels. Click OK and save the changes to this file.

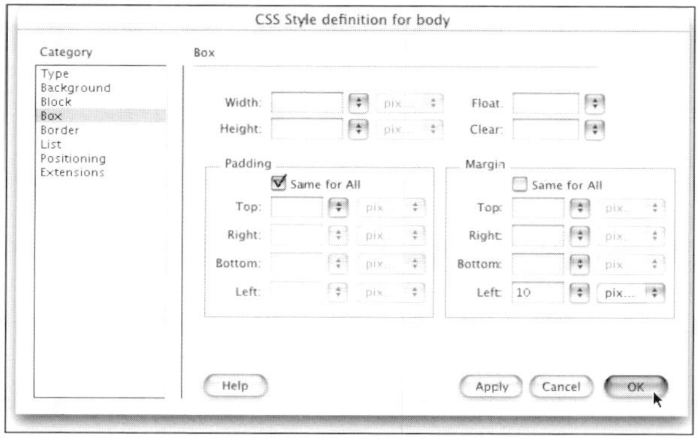

Set the left margin to move the menu 10 pixels from the edge of the frame.

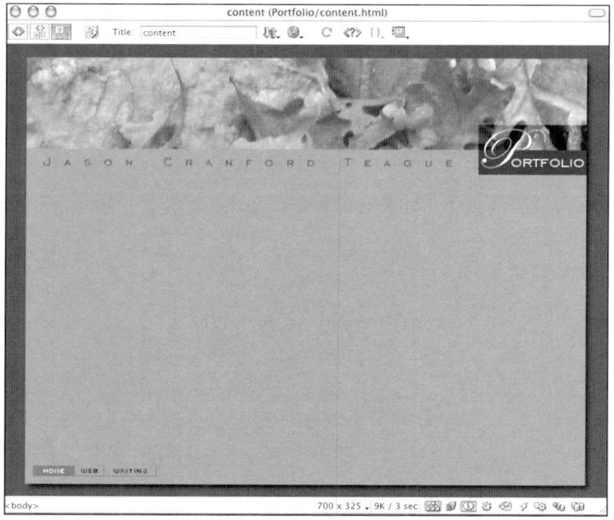

Select the content frame and link to index.html.

Setting Up the Submenus

Now that the menus are set up, you are ready to set the submenus. You will be creating a submenu for each section where there will be multiple pages. However, the submenu can be set up in such a way that it will apply only to the folder it is in. To do this, you link each submenu option to local files called page1.html, page2.html, page3.html, and so on.

1 Open the page index.html in the Portfolio menu, and click in the submenu frame to open the content.html document. Immediately resave the file as **submenu.html** in the home folder (File>Save Frame As).

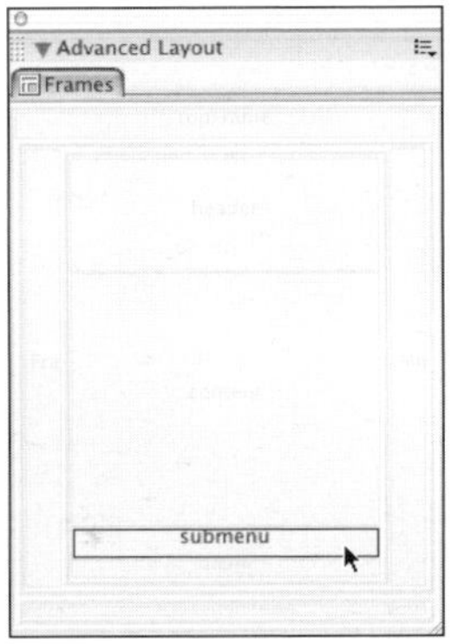

Select the submenu frame in the Frames panel.

Because it is hard to distinguish between certain frames in Design view because they have the same background color, remember that you can use the Frames panel to select a frame quickly (Window>Others>Frames).

2 Before you add a submenu to this file, you need to set up a special case without the menu for the home page. The home page will not have any submenu options, but it will need to load the home page into the content frame.

Select Go To URL in the Behaviors panel.

To have the submenu page automatically load the first content page of its section when loaded, we are going to add a behavior to the page. Make sure that you have the submenu frame selected (check the Frames panel if you are not sure); open the Behaviors panel (Window>Behaviors). Select the Add Behaviors drop down (the +), and choose Go To URL.

In the Go To URL dialog box, select frame "content" and then enter **index.html** in the URL field. Click OK. Check the Behaviors panel to make sure the event is onLoad (if it isn't, click the event and select onLoad) and save this document (File>Save Frame).

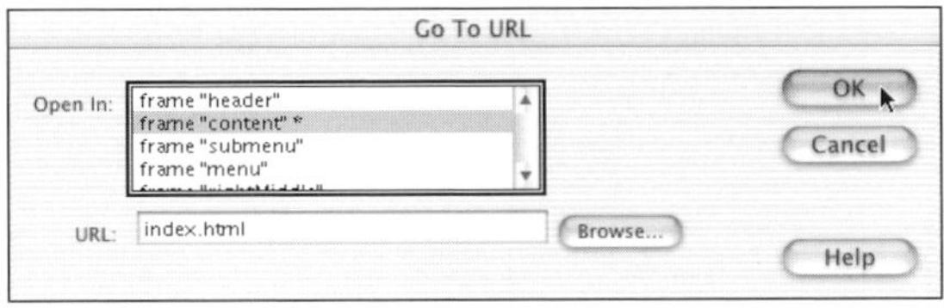

Select frame "content" and type **index.html**.

Now, when this page loads, it will load the page index.html in its local folder—the home folder, in this case (we'll set up that file a little later).

3 Now it's time to add the navigation bar to the submenu. But first, save this file again, into the web folder. With your cursor in the submenu frame, choose File>Save Frame As. Browse to the web folder and click Save.

4 Each submenu starts spaced over from the left of the page to align with the menu option beneath. In order to create this space, add the spacer GIF (located in the images file) to the submenu file and set the width to 61 pixels in the Property inspector. This will push the first submenu over to align with the Web menu option. You probably will need to adjust this after you add the rest of the graphics. Next to the spacer, add the graphic rule_here.gif, also in the images file, to connect the submenu to the menu.

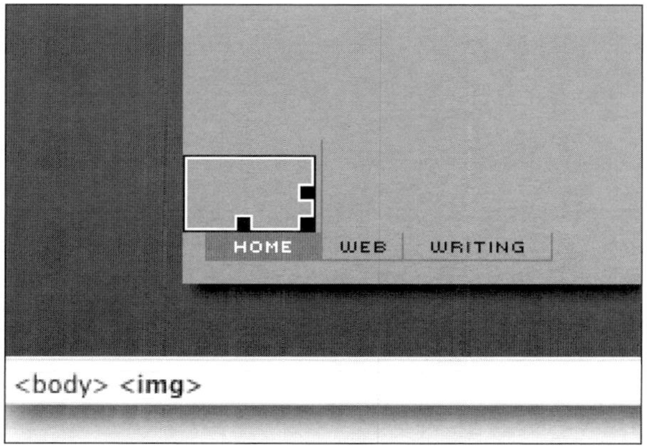

Adjust the spacer GIF so that the line connects with the menu option beneath.

Note: The spacer GIF is simply a single-pixel transparent graphic.

You are now ready to use the Navigation Bar dialog box to create the submenu.

Tip: Programs such as Free Ruler (www.pascal.com/software/freeruler) are indispensable tools for web designers when they need to precisely place objects within an interface.

5 Choose Insert>Interactive Images>Navigation Bar.

6 Start your new submenu by entering Page 7 for the element name and alternate text. You are going to add pages in reverse order, so that newer pages can always be at the beginning of the list when added.

7 Define the images for the rollover states. Unlike the main menu in which each menu option used different graphics, each link in the submenu will use the same graphics to represent each page in the section and the various states:

Up Image: **images/page_up.gif**

Over Image: **images/page_over.gif**

Down image: **images/page_down.gif**

Over While Down image: **images/page_down.gif** (same image as the Down state)

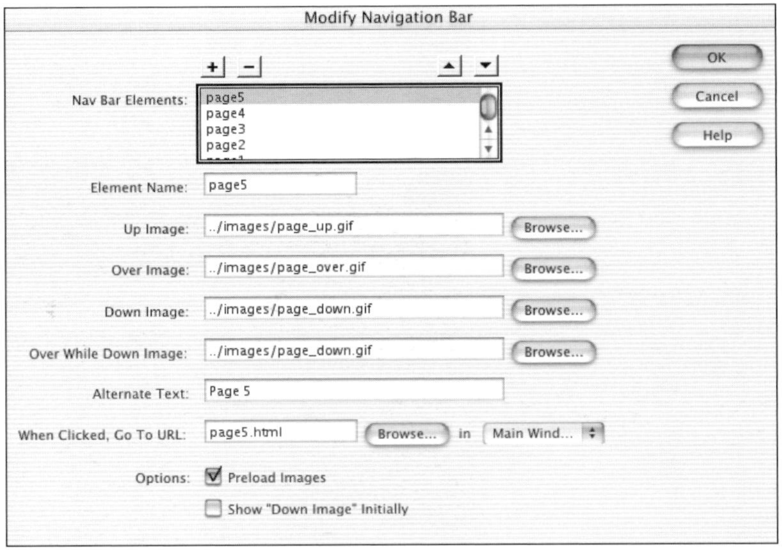

Add seven pages to the submenu.

Tip: Reusing the same graphic for the links in the submenu pages simplifies graphic production and speeds download. Obviously, it is easier to produce and download three graphics rather than three times the number of pages in the section. However, another approach that adds organization is to create graphics corresponding to the page number.

8 Set the link to **page7.html** and set the page to load in the content frame. This option in the submenu is finished.

9 Click the + sign and repeat Steps 6 through 8 to add seven different pages, using the same rollover states but decreasing the page number by 1 each time.

Click OK to finish the submenu. Save this document (File>Save Frame).

You have now set up the submenu for the Web section of the portfolio. The good news is that, with just a little work, this also can become the submenu for the Writing section as well.

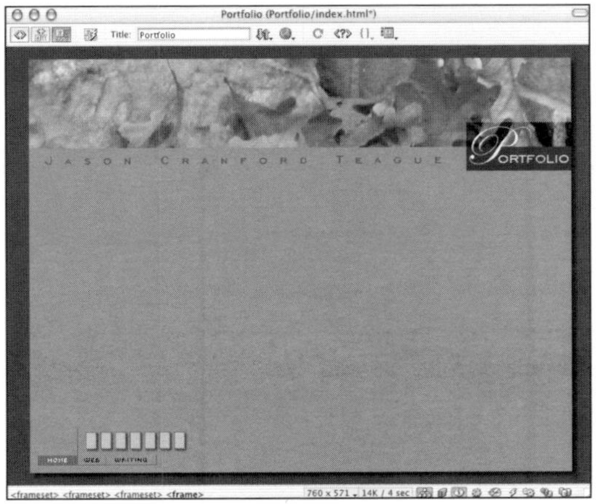

The Web submenu in place.

10 With the submenu frame selected, choose File>Save Frame As, navigate to the writing folder, and save the file there with the same name. You have just copied submenu.html, but the submenu for the Writing section needs to be slightly different:

Click the spacer GIF and change its width (using the Properties panel) to 97 pixels.

The Writing section has only five pages, so delete the first two pages (actually, delete pages 6 and 7 because they are in reverse order). To delete them, simply click the graphics and press Delete.

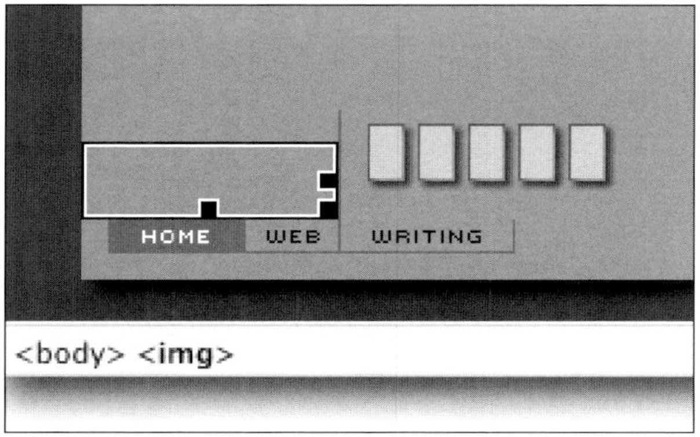

For the Writing menu, change the size of the spacer GIF to **97** pixels and delete the first two pages.

Note: Dreamweaver may have changed the links in the submenu saved in writing so that they point back to the web folder. If this happens, click each page graphic in the submenu and delete . . . web/ from the link. You also will need to do this in the Behaviors panel to the onLoad event. Double-click the event, and change the URL.

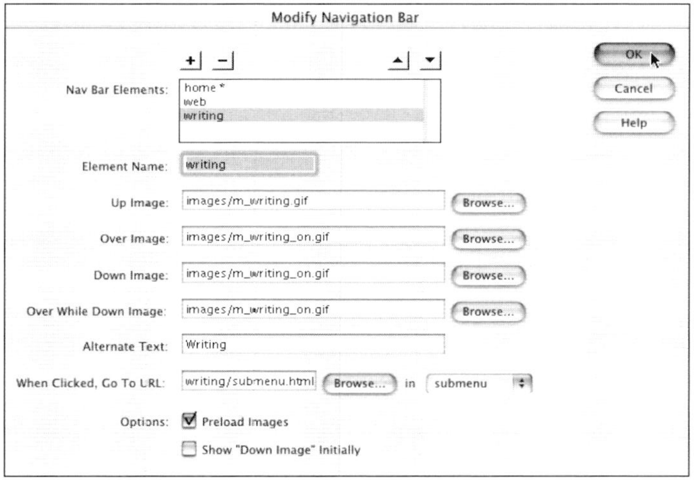

The Modify Navigation Bar dialog showing the writing option.

11 The final step is to change the source for the submenu frame back to home/submenu.html. To do that, select the submenu frame, and change the source in the Properties panel.

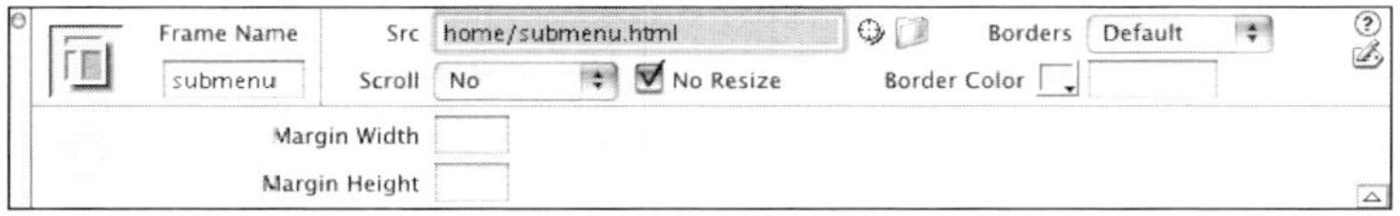

Change the source of the submenu frame back to home/submenu.html.

You can add only one navigation bar per web page. If you select the Navigation Bar option a second time, Dreamweaver alerts you that you can have only one at a time, but the program allows you to edit the current Navigation Bar on that page. Here you can add additional topics to the menu or add additional pages to the submenu. The only things you will not be able to change here is the navigation bar's orientation (horizontal or vertical) and whether the bar should use tables for layout.

Note: Most modern browsers include an annoying feature for links when they are clicked. They place a dotted line box around a link that has just been clicked, which persists until another link is clicked. This can tend to play havoc with a well thought-out web design, especially if you are using frames, as we are here. One simple solution to this is to place the following code in the <body> tag of your web page:

```
onmousedown="blur()"
```

This immediately deselects the link after it is clicked. However, if there are any form fields on the page, it also deselects them before they can be typed in, so instead of adding the code to the <body> tag, you would have to add it to each link individually.

Preparing a Content Page Template

You will be reusing the presentation page style a lot throughout the site, depending on how many items you have to show in your portfolio. It's silly to re-create the page for each and every instance, so we will set up a simple template that specifies the columns and editable items on the page. Then, when you want to create new display pages in the portfolio, you can simply use this template as the starting point.

1 Open the page index.html, and click in the content frame to open the content.html document. Immediately save the file as a template by choosing File>Save Frame as Template. In the Save As Template dialog box, make sure the Portfolio site is selected and type **coverPage** in the Save As field; then click Save.

2 Click the Draw Layer tool, and draw two layers on the page:

- **LeftColumn:** This column will contain the image for that page of the portfolio, so make sure there is enough horizontal space for it to fit. Set the left position to **35** pixels, top position to **10** pixels, and width and height to **300** pixels.
- **RightColumn**: This column will display the information about the work or project presented in the left column. Set the top position to **10** pixels, the left position to **375** pixels, and width and height to **300** pixels.

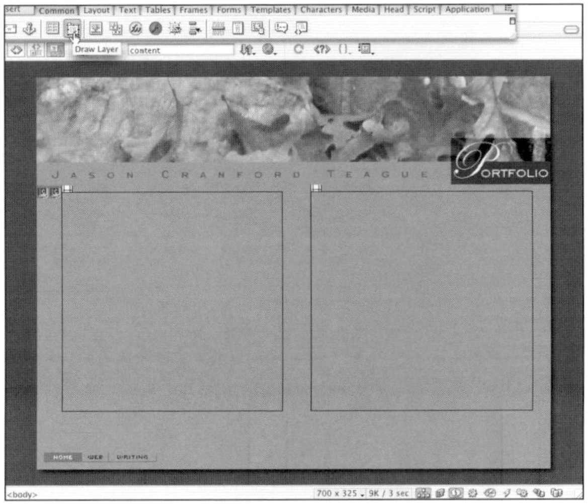

Use the Draw Layer tool to create two columns.

3 In each layer, insert an editable region by placing your cursor inside the layer and choosing Insert>Template Objects>Editable Region. Name the editable region in the left layer Title and the editable region in the right layer Other.

4 Save the template (File>Save) and then save it as a template again (File>Save Frame as Template), but this time name the template pageXX(web). Now you will create the template for pages in the Web part of the portfolio.

5 Select the editable region in the left column, and rename it Portfolio Image. Delete the editable region in the right column (Other) by right-clicking the region (Ctrl-click for Mac users) and selecting Remove tag <mmtamplate:editable>.

6 Add the web title graphics to the right column adding a carriage return after each one: st_title.gif, st_url.gif, st_client.gif, and st_comments.gif. All these graphics are in the images folder.

7 Under each title graphic and in the left column, insert an editable region (Insert>Template Objects>Editable Region) and give the region an appropriate name (perhaps the same name as the title above it).

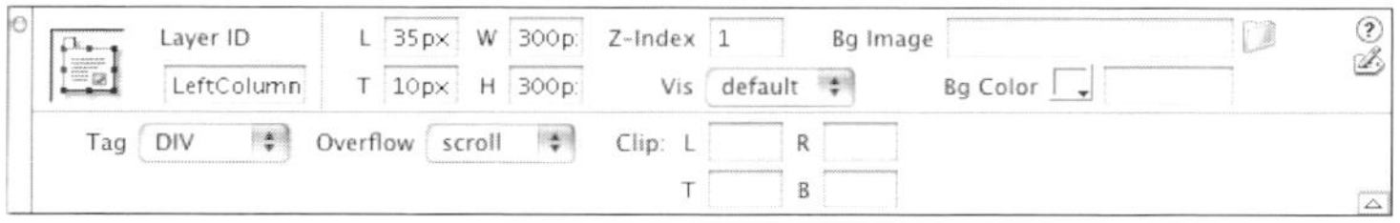

The easiest way to set the size, position, and other attributes of each layer is to use the Properties panel.

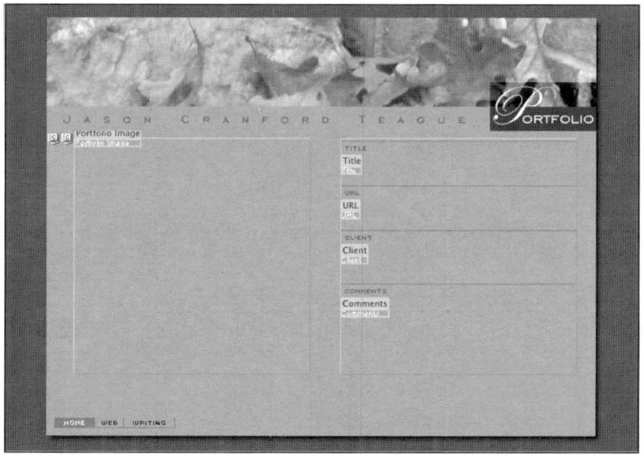

The Web template.

8 Save the Web template (File>Save Frame). Now, create the Writing template by resaving this file (File>Save Frame as Template), but this time name the template pageXX(writing). Now you need only to make a few changes to the Web template to create the Writing template:

- Delete the URL title and editable region.
- Change the Client title to Publisher by changing the graphic to st_publisher.gif, clicking the editable region, and changing its name in the Properties panel.
- Add a new editable region immediately under the Tile editable region called **Purchase**.

Save this template (File>Save Frame), and you now have the template ready to create pages in the writing section of your portfolio.

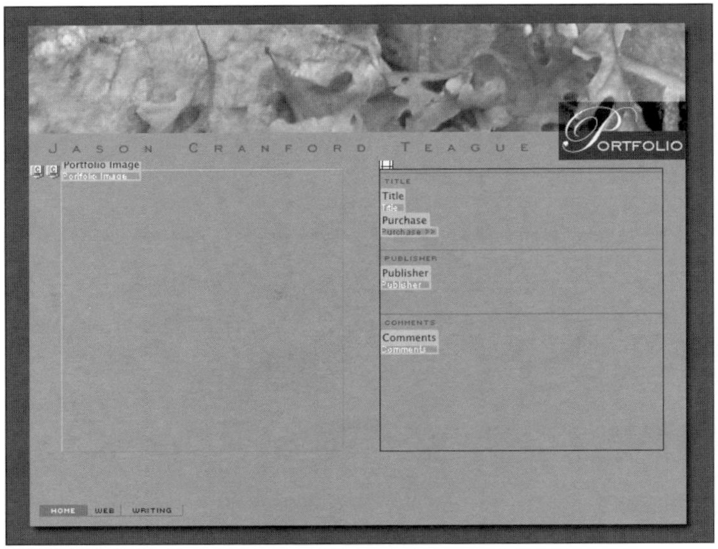

The Writing template.

ADDING PAGES TO THE PORTFOLIO

Everything is in place, and you are now ready to start building your portfolio presentation pages, using the template already constructed. Remember, though, that you do not necessarily want to present *everything* you have ever done in your portfolio—only your best work. Showing fewer high-quality projects is always preferable to a large number of inferior projects.

1 First you need to create the cover pages for each section. Open the Assets panel (Windows>Assets). Double-click the coverPage template. Add a brief bio in the left column and a photo in the right (I used images/me.jpg), and save this page as **cover.html** in the home folder using File>Save As (otherwise, a new template is created).

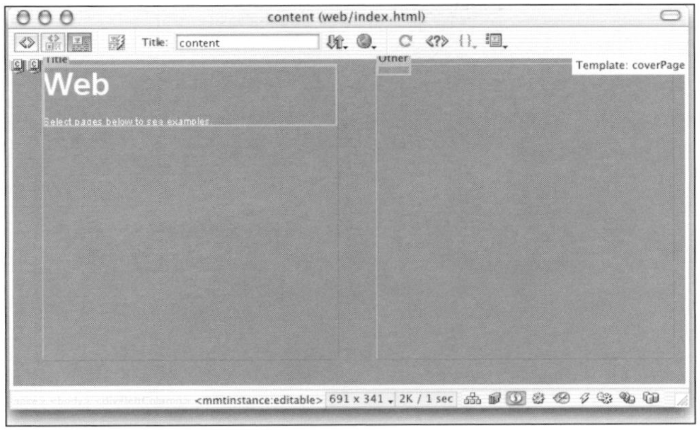

The home page template.

2 Create two more cover pages for the Web and Writing sections. Double-click the coverPage template, type the section name in the left column, and assign it an <H1> tag. Save these as **index.html** in their respective folders, using File>Save As (otherwise, a new template is created).

Note: Double-clicking a template in the Site Browser opens the template to be edited.

3 Now you are ready to set up the pages for the portfolio, starting with the pages in the Web section. Double-click the pageXX(web) template. In the new page opened from the template, add a portfolio image into the editable region in the left column. The images for the portfolio are in the portfolioImages folder in the images folder.

Now add some information in each item the remaining editable regions.

Save the file into the web folder as **page1.html**.

4 Repeat this for the remaining six items in the Web section of the portfolio, increasing the page number each time. Remember, however, that the menu will present the pages in reverse order, which means that the oldest item in the portfolio should be on page 1.

5 Repeat Steps 2 through 4 to create pages for the Writing section, using the writing template instead.

After you have completed making the portfolio pages, open index.html in your browser and take a look at your portfolio.

In this exercise, I showed you how to set up a portfolio using my own web sites and books as the content. You can now begin to experiment with putting your own work into the pages.

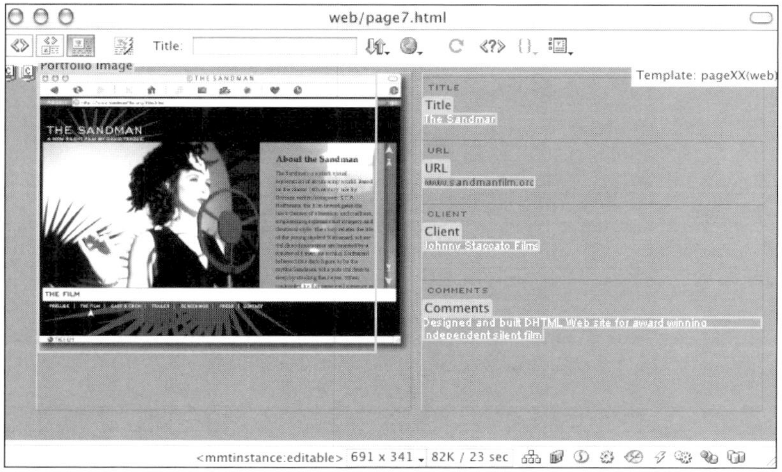

The home page with the portfolio pages added.

Modifications: Setting the Link Appearance

One modification you may want to make is to set the link colors for the portfolio pages. Currently, they will use the default browser colors, most likely blue and red, which does not look particularly good in this design. You can control link colors one of two ways with Dreamweaver: using HTML Styles or CSS. HTML styles would be difficult to apply to the site at this point, but you have already set up a style sheet in all of the files created from content.html (which includes all of the pages in the portfolio), so you can simply add a link style to that sheet.

CSS allows you to set four different link states:

- **link:** How the link should appear before being clicked.
- **visited:** How the link appears if it has already been followed.
- **hover:** How the link appears when the visitor places the mouse pointer over it.
- **active:** How the link appears while it is being clicked.

Note: I recommend selecting a color for unvisited links that highly contrasts with the background color for your page and also contrasts with the text color. Then, select a darker or lighter version of that color (depending on how light or dark the background color is) for that will still contrast with the background, but appear dimmer than the unvisited link color. "Brighter" unfollowed links will stand out more dramatically than the "dimmer" followed links.

1. In the Site panel, double-click content.html to open it.
2. Open the CSS panel (Window>CSS) and click the New CSS Style button to start a new style.
3. Choose Use CSS Selector, Define In: content.css and then select a:link from the selector drop-down.
4. In the CSS Style Definition dialog box, set the appearance for the link. For the portfolio, I chose simply to make the text black and bold, which contrasts with the gray background and clearly distinguishes the links from the white text. Click OK.
5. Repeat Steps 3 and 4 for the other link states, setting visited to light gray (#cccccc), hover to be red (#ff0000), and active to white (#ffffff).

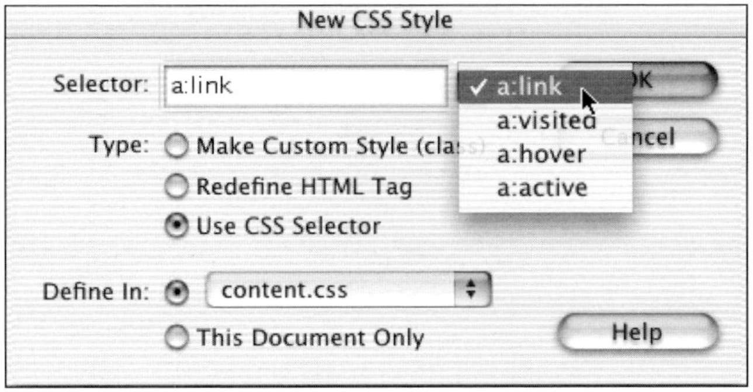

Select a link state to define.

LEADING THE WAY WITH "CRUMB TRAILS"

"Just remember, one of our patients is a cannibal. Try to guess which one. I think you'll be pleasantly surprised."

—DR. FOSTER, THE SIMPSONS, EPISODE 4F07

Hansel and Gretel Really Had Something

Hansel and Gretel left a trail of crumbs to help them find their way back to where they came from. We all know that story didn't end well, but it was a fairly ingenious solution to their navigation problems. Crumb Trails in web interfaces also have great advantages and some potential challenges. In this project, we explore some of the ways you can easily create Crumb Trails in Dreamweaver. Your site's visitors will eat them up!

Project 7

Leading the Way with "Crumb Trails"

by Zac Van Note

Before: This site's visitors have no immediate clue to tell them how they got to this particular page.

After: With a Crumb Trail, your visitors will be able to jump back instantly to a previously visited page.

It Works Like This

As the various projects in this book show you, navigation is a primary concern of web site designers. Getting visitors to your information is critical. Letting them easily retrace their steps to get back where they came from also can be a godsend.

Crumb trails have a lot in common with the browser's Back button. Unfortunately, you can't always trust that clicking Back will return you to the place you want to be. Clicking Back five or six times to find that elusive page is inconvenient. That's where crumb trails really shine. They don't take the place of your primary navigation, but they do provide a series of alternate routes, and give the user a better grasp of your site's structure.

You can create crumb trails many different ways, from manually coding each part to automatically generating parts with a database of pages and titles. In this project, we'll walk through one approach and see some alternative methods later.

You'll be using the Bread Crumbs command, created by Paul Davis of Kaosweaver.com, to help expedite and partially automate the process. This technique is best added on a new site where you have more control over the initial site setup. Reorganizing a large existing site to work well with this command could become very time-consuming. However, it is also possible that you already have a well-organized site that would lend itself well to the demands of this command.

Preparing to Work

The setup for this project is similar to those in the rest of the book. You'll copy a folder to your hard drive, start Dreamweaver, install an extension, and set up a new site, pointing to the folder you just copied.

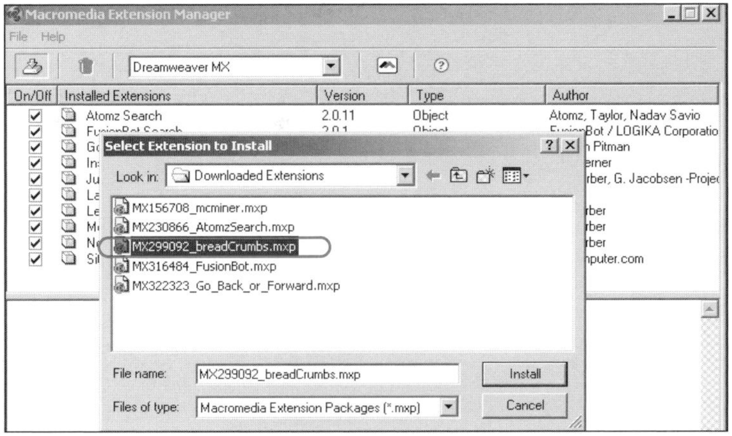

You can easily add extensions with the Extensions Manager, which you display by choosing Commands>Manage Extensions.

1 Install the Bread Crumbs command:

- Browse to the Extensions folder on the CD.
- Open the Commands subfolder.
- Double-click the file MX299092_bread Crumbs.mxp to install the command.

Note: The version of the Bread Crumbs command used to create and test this project is 1.4.2, currently available on the CD-ROM and at the Macromedia exchange. Check Paul Davis' site Kaosweaver.com for the latest revision. Because there sometimes are changes in functionality and stability, a newer version may not work exactly as described in this project.

2 Copy the project folder:

- Browse to the Projects folder on the CD.
- Copy the 07_bread_crumbs folder to a convenient location on your hard drive.

3 Define a new Dreamweaver site using 07_bread_crumbs as your local root folder.

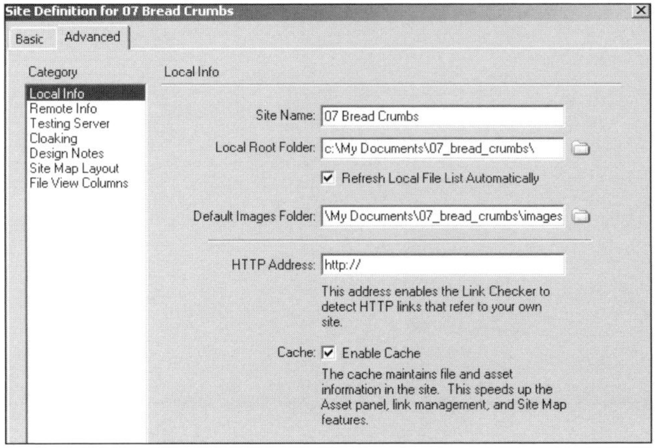

Set up your site with 07_bread_crumbs as your local root folder. A remote or testing server is not required, but is highly recommended.

Although you don't need to set up your site with remote or testing server information to work through this exercise, you should define a remote site before testing your final results. I would recommend that you take the time to set up a remote site now so you'll be ready when you get to the last step. For information on recommended hosting providers and setting up a site, see Project 8, "Creating a Customized Search Feature." To view the completed site, visit www.design-link.org/DreamweaverMX_Magic/07_bread_crumbs/.

Setting up a Site with Crumb Trails

Like any complex navigation scheme, you first need to decide whether crumb trails will benefit your site's users or just be another piece of clutter on the page. If your site has fewer than 10 total pages, the benefit of crumb trails is not as great. Once your site starts getting past that length (and it doesn't take long!), it's time to give them a try. Although there are many techniques you can use to create crumb trails, we are going to concentrate on one of the easier and most effective methods.

1 Open the site window and make sure you are looking at the local view of the new site you've created for this project. For now, we'll just be examining the site from here.

For the crumb trail to be useful, you need quite a few pages with at least a few levels of hierarchy. To expedite, I've already set up a skeleton site of 19 pages with three levels of hierarchy for demonstration purposes, but it is important to understand how and why I've done it this way.

For each level that you want to display in the crumb trail, you must create a folder and a default page. Normally, this default page will be named index.htm.

What this means is that you will have many folders and subfolders, with a file named index.htm in each folder. You may also choose to have a number of other files in a given folder, but only the presence of the default page in each folder will trigger a new crumb segment. Because the folder name is what displays as the element in the crumb trail, the folder name is more important than usual. It is common to use shortened names for folders, but that doesn't work well in this case because you want users to be able to understand the trail from the folder names you choose. Try to keep the folder name to one

Note: Structure is the name of the game here. If you're going to use a crumb trail, no matter how you implement it, you're going to have to consider the structure of your site. The Bread Crumbs command has some specific requirements to make it work, but other solutions will require just as much work up-front or later, as pages change.

The Bread Crumb command requires that you have an index.htm page in each subfolder of your site. Also, before crumbs can be automatically created, you'll need to create a subfolder for each potential crumb element and name it accordingly. For example, if you had navigated to Home>Products>Necklaces>Pearl Necklaces, you would need the following folders: Home, Products, Necklaces, Pearl Necklaces. You would need to have at least an index.htm file in each of these folders, although you can have additional files in each folder as well. The crumb trail will show the page title at the end of the crumb trail for each page that is *not* an index.htm page.

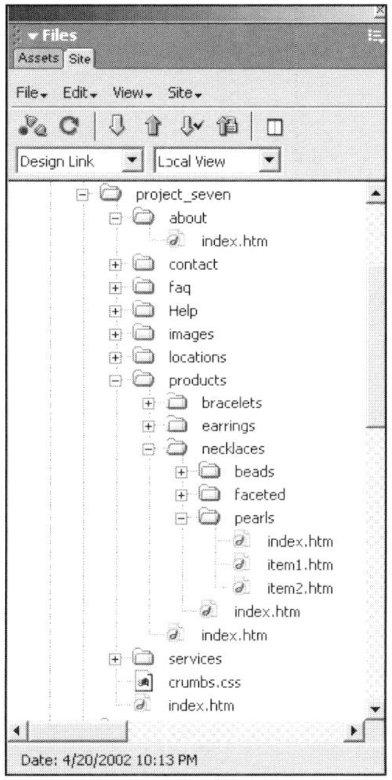

The hierarchy of the site is already set up, but pay attention to the structure and naming system. See the note in this section for more details on site structure.

word, but spell it out completely. If you need to use two words as the folder name, spell the words out and separate them with an underscore or hyphen as appropriate. If you don't do this, and include a space between words, various browsers will have difficulty resolving the folder names because of the space(s).

2 Open the index.htm file in the About folder. Notice that it does not have a page title. Assign the new page title **About Us**. Save and close the file.

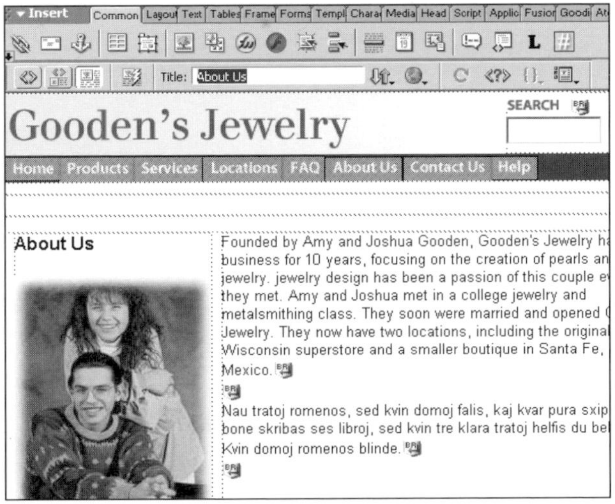

Giving a page title to each page is important. For the Bread Crumbs command to work properly, it needs an appropriate page title to tack onto the end of the crumb trail.

Tip: Assigning page titles is also just a good habit. They appear at the top of the browser window and they're often used by search engines to help index and/or list your site.

Using a brief and appropriate page title is extremely important because that's what the Bread Crumbs command will use to list the page. The directory names and structure dictate all but the last segment of the crumb trail. The page title is always the last segment.

Your page titles should be fairly concise. If they are all long, the crumb trail may exceed the space you've allotted. The Bread Crumbs command does have a provision to break the trail to a second line, but that generally is an awkward solution.

Leaving the Trail

Once you've set up the folder structure, creating the actual crumb trail is a piece of cake. Using the Bread Crumbs command, you'll enter a few settings to tell the command where to find your files and how you'd like them to display in the crumb trail. You'll be up and running minutes later.

1 Open the index.htm file in your root folder. Because this is the root of this site, it is automatically labeled Home on every page to come. For this reason, I've already left a crumb labeled Home without a link on this page. You also may choose to leave the crumb trail off your root page entirely.

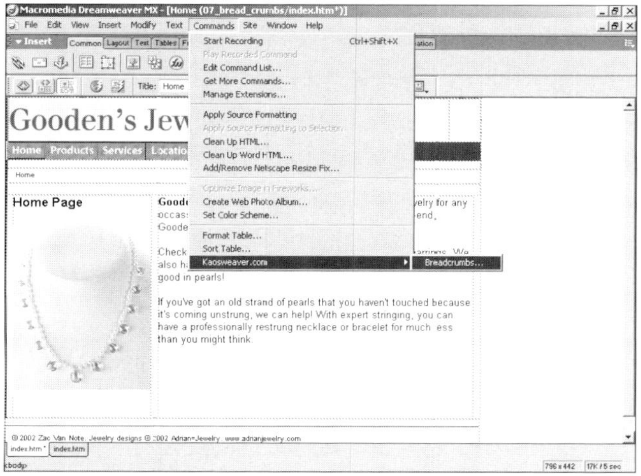

The home page (index.htm in your root folder) doesn't really have a crumb trail. I've added the text Home where the trail will be. You can choose to leave the title in the crumb trail area or leave it blank.

2 Now you can start at the top for the pages with a real crumb trail. Because most of the pages in the site are called index.htm, it's easy to get confused as to which page is which. You do have some basic content to go by and the path is listed at the top of your screen in Dreamweaver, but it can still be confusing. It's a good idea to save and close each page after you're done with it to avoid errors.

Open about > index.htm. You've already made sure it has an appropriate page title earlier.

3 Next you'll add a crumb trail.

- Click in the table cell in the middle, between the menu bar and the page title.
- As shown, choose Commands>Kaosweaver.com> Bread Crumbs. The Bread Crumbs interface pops up.

Select Commands> Bread Crumbs.

4 Now you can fill in the blanks in the Bread Crumbs dialog:

- For the Site Root Directory, you'll enter the path to your site. This is critical. If you don't enter the correct path, all of your crumb trails will stop working. Even worse, they may show links to non-existent files. The Bread Crumbs command is very specific in what it looks for in creating the crumb trail. When it doesn't find what it needs, the command starts to make guesses based on the path you entered.

  When I uploaded the site to my web server, the path was: www.design-link.org/DreamweaverMX_Magic/07_bread_crumbs/. For this project, you can just enter **07_bread_crumbs**. (See the sidebar, "Understanding the Site Root," for more information on finding the exact location of your root folder.)

- You need to fill out either Text Delimiter *or* Image Delimiter, not both. For now, let's stick with a text delimiter. This is the symbol that shows up between crumb segments. I used >>. Other options include a bullet, a single greater-than character (>), or a pipe bar (|), found by pressing Shift + \ (above the Enter key).

- Default Page is the name you've assigned to the base page in each subfolder. In our case, this is index.htm. If this is not set properly or you don't have an index.htm file as the base page in each folder, your trail won't work. Remember that depending on your own standards, the default page name could be different. Other variations may

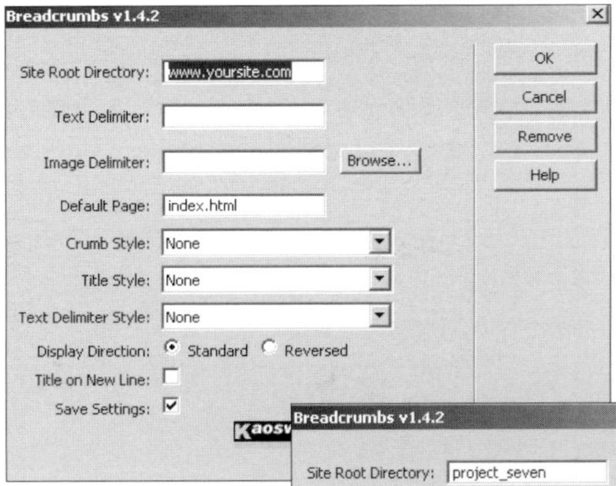

All the Bread Crumb command options are right here.

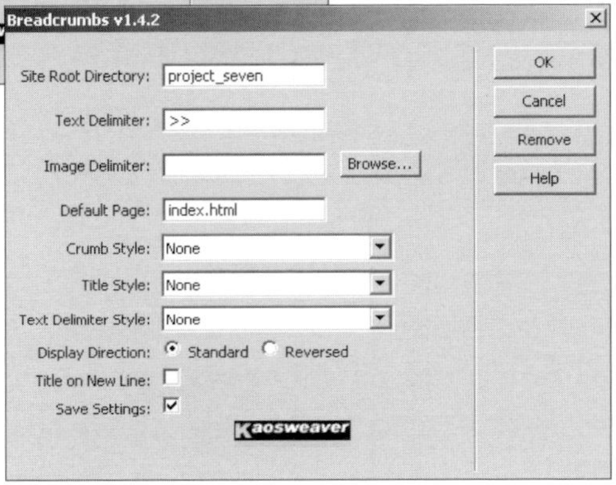

Input your values and click OK.

Note: For the most predictable results, always upload and test your files on a fully functioning web server. Because everything about crumb trails is relative to the Site Root Directory, you may not get the correct crumb trail when previewing your site in Dreamweaver. As long as you've set up your site structure as described, everything should work perfectly on the web.

include these: default.html, index.asp, index.html, index.cfm, home.htm, and so on. Just make sure that your pages are all labeled consistently so this command will work its magic.

- The next three fields are optional, but they should be used for most sites. You can assign CSS definitions to the Crumb Style (all but the last segment of the Crumb Trail), the Title Style (the last segment in the Trail), and the Text Delimiter Style (if you're not using an image). If you haven't already set up CSS definitions for these elements, the New Style and Edit Style buttons allow you to create and edit them on the spot. Once we finish creating this first Crumb Trail Without CSS, we'll look at how to include CSS in the next section.
- The Display Direction options put the crumb trail in chronological order (Standard) or reverse chronological order (Reversed). For this project, and for most uses, choose Standard.
- Title on New Line does just that—puts the title on a new line. Make sure that you've allowed room for this if you choose to use it. There's no reason to use it on this project, so you can leave the option unchecked.
- Save Settings will keep all of your entries available so that you can quickly add Bread Crumbs to additional pages. Unless you have some special reason, you should always leave this option checked.
- Click OK. You might get a notifier from DMX that the bread crumb elements won't be visible unless you turn on the invisible elements. Click OK in the warning box. Your Bread Crumb will show up as a little yellow script/shield icon (as long as you have your Invisible set to visible for Scripts in your Preferences settings; if you don't see the icon, click View>Visual Aids>Invisible Elements).
- Save your file.

After you've created your crumb trail, you'll see a small yellow shield/script icon marking its place. If you don't see it, check to see whether you've turned Scripts off in the Invisible Elements area of your Preferences (choose Edit>Preferences>Invisible Elements to find out).

Understanding the Site Root

Dreamweaver practically demands that you set up a site before you can start creating and linking pages. When you create a site, you're establishing a local root folder that will serve as the base for all of the pages in the site. There are two main kinds of links on a web page: relative and absolute. Absolute is easy; just spell out the entire path: www.design-link.org/DreamweaverMX_Magic/07_bread_crumbs.

Relative links can be a little trickier. Relative links are based on the relationship of a specific page and the page to which it is linked. Let's say you're working on Help/index.htm and you want to create a link to About/index.htm. Because the files are in different folders but on the same level, you need to "back out" of the current folder, go into the site root folder, and then move into the new folder. The link looks like ../About/index.htm. The two dots tell the browser to back out one folder to the site root folder and the rest of the path tells the browser exactly which folder and file to link to. In the 07_bread_crumbs files, some of the files are buried a few levels deep, so you'll see links like this: ../../../contact/index.htm.

The site root is important because it is the base that all relative links use to find other pages and images within your site. If the base of your site was www.design-link.org, finding it would be easy. Unfortunately, things can get confusing when your Dreamweaver site is really a sub-site (folder) inside a larger site. If you publish your 07_bread_crumbs folder to a live web server, chances are that you'll be tacking it onto an existing site. In this case, it is important to remember how you have defined your site in Dreamweaver. You may choose to have only one site defined with all of the sub-sites remaining as folders under the main site structure. Alternately, you could choose to make them all separate sites, pointing to the base folder for each sub-site.

It's critical for the Bread Crumb command to work correctly that you specify the appropriate Site Root Directory. This is the base from which all of your crumb trails will be built, whether it is the root folder of the entire site or just a folder within the site. In my case, I've uploaded the files to a live server at www.design-link.org/DreamweaverMX_Magic/07_bread_crumbs. As far as Bread Crumbs are concerned, I just need to enter 07_bread_crumbs for the Site Root Directory. In this way, whether I upload the file or test it on my local machine, it will give me the correct paths.

This could cause problems in some situations, however, as in cases where you have more than one folder with the same name anywhere in your site or you have different sets of crumb trails. If you do encounter problems using the short form noted above, you can always include the entire path for Site Root Directory (www.design-link.org/DreamweaverMX_Magic/07_bread_crumbs).

It's also important to note that previewing your page from Dreamweaver (F12) will give you different results from those you'll see if you open the file directly in the browser. To open a file in a browser, choose File>Open>Browse and then navigate to the file on your hard drive. The results of viewing the page on a web server and opening the file directly in the browser should be the same.

5 Now that you've gone through the steps to create the Bread Crumbs, you can start adding the crumb trails to each page using the Bread Crumbs command. Every other file already has an appropriate title, so you can concentrate on repeating only Steps 3 and 4.

Note: Once you've set up a Bread Crumb, you can go back and choose Commands>Kaosweaver.com>Bread Crumbs at any time and select Remove. This will remove the JavaScript it had placed in the Head and in the Body of your file. If you forget to click in the correct table cell before choosing the Bread Crumb command, you may have the script icon showing up in some inappropriate area of your page. The Remove option suddenly becomes very useful.

You might be tempted to use the Find and Replace command to add the Bread Crumbs to the entire site. Because the command places code in the Body and Head of the HTML and because there are a few levels of hierarchy, using Find and Replace will cause more problems than it will solve.

When you're done, view the site in your browser. If you do a preview from within Dreamweaver, the crumb trails may not display properly. It's best to upload your files to a web server or navigate to your pages in your browser by opening your browser, choosing File>Open, and then clicking Browse to find the index.htm page in the 07_bread_crumbs folder. Depending on how you chose to view your pages at this point, you may see the entire path of your local hard drive or you may see only the site's path.

Customize Your Crumb Trail with CSS

Cascading Style Sheets are a vital part of most web sites. From positioning to formatting, CSS gives you the control you need to make your pages cohesive and attractive. Applying CSS to your crumb trail is quite easy:

You can set up CSS definitions for your crumb trail elements using the standard tools available in Dreamweaver, or you can use the New Style and Edit Style buttons in the Bread Crumbs command. For more information on CSS, see Project 5, "Using CSS."

Before you begin assigning styles to your crumb trail elements, you need to define the styles. I have set up an external CSS file, crumbs.css, for you to use and modify. This file contains three styles: crumbs, title, and delimiters. To make these styles available, attach the stylesheet file to each document by choosing Text, CSS Styles, Attach Style Sheet. Click Browse and navigate to the 07_bread_crumbs base folder. Double-click crumbs.css. Make sure that Link is checked. Click OK. Make sure you do this on each page.

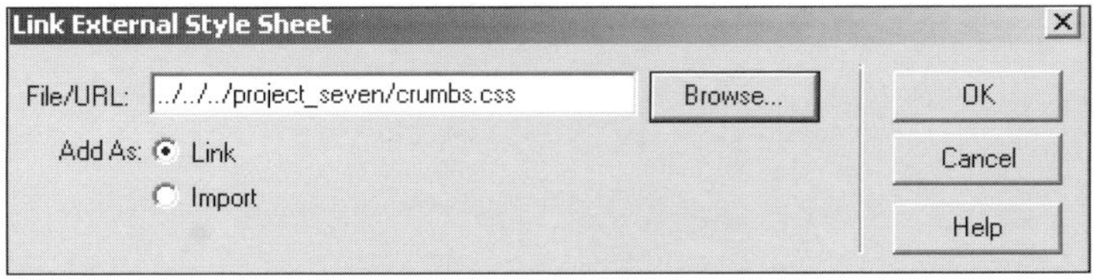

Attach the crumbs.css file to each page in your site. Then you're ready to add them to your pages.

Once you've set up the linked file, you can assign the corresponding CSS styles in the Bread Crumbs dialog box. You can assign CSS definitions to the Crumb Style (all but the last segment of the crumb trail), the Title Style (the last segment in the Trail), and the Text Delimiter Style (if you're not using an image). Just select from each of the three drop-down menus. If you imported my file, the choices should be fairly obvious.

Although this works great in Dreamweaver 4, I have to warn you that I haven't been able to apply styles through the dialog box in the last beta version of Dreamweaver MX. This problem may be resolved by the time you read this, so check the Dreamweaver Exchange or Kaosweaver.com for an update to this extension.

You can use a workaround if you are not able to assign the styles in the Bread Crumbs dialog box. Open any affected page in Split view and click the script/shield icon in Design view. Look at the highlighted HTML. You'll see None, None, None toward the end of the line. These values correspond to the three styles: Crumb Style, Title Style, and Text Delimiter Style, in that order. Just change the None values to crumbs, title, delimiters. This achieves the same effect and will work in any version of Dreamweaver. If you ever change the definitions of the CSS, the link will be maintained and your styles will be updated.

Apply styles within the Bread Crumbs extension in Dreamweaver MX may not work. If this happens, just edit the HTML to use your style sheets.

Spruce Up the Trail with Image Delimiters

Sometimes plain text delimiters like >> just don't fit with the style of your site. You can customize your delimiters by using any image. From a simple triangle to a round bullet to a spiral, the delimiters can be as fun or unobtrusive as you'd like.

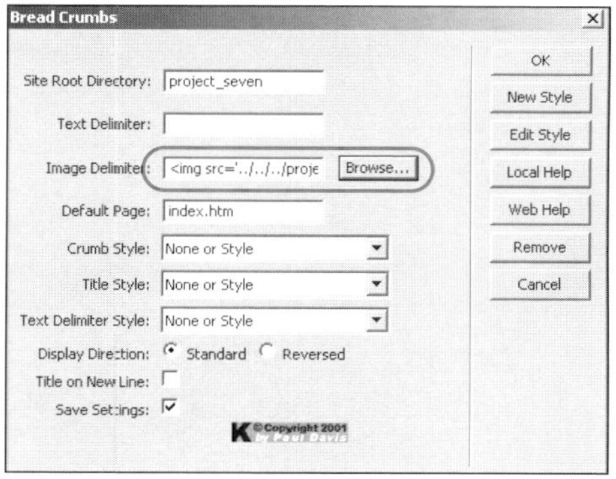

Select your image delimiters.

1. To replace your Text Delimiters with an Image Delimiter:
   - Click the script/shield icon to select the Bread Crumb placeholder.
   - Choose Commands>Bread Crumbs.
   - Clear the Text Delimiter field.
   - Click the Browse button and navigate to images/arrow.gif.
   - Click the file to select it and click OK.
2. When you preview your pages, the image of the arrow will appear between your crumb segments.

Note: If you didn't click the Bread Crumb placeholder (script/shield icon) before you chose Commands>Bread Crumbs, you may have actually created another crumb trail somewhere on your page. If this happens, the safest solution is to run the Bread Crumbs command and select Remove. This removes all occurrences of the Command. Then, just make sure you've clicked in the appropriate area before you create a new crumb trail.

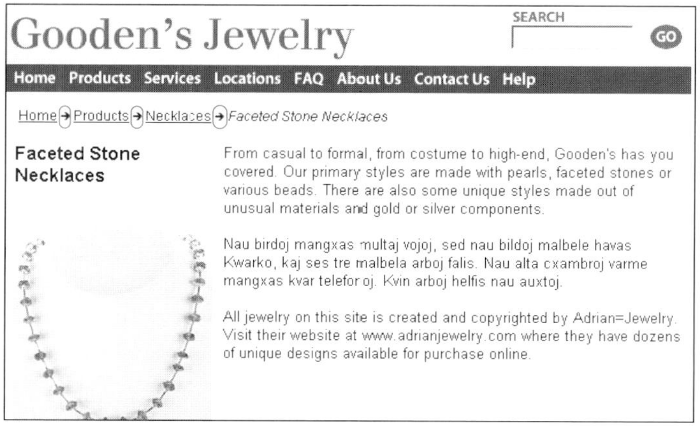

The final result using image delimiters.

Note: Because you are using an image, the path to that image is important and can potentially be broken. To ensure that you don't have any missing links to your Image Delimiter, make sure you click Browse on every page you add. If you've checked Save Settings in the Bread Crumbs interface, it's tempting to think that all of your settings are OK to apply to each page.

For many settings, this may be true, but not for the Image Delimiter. Even though the image will be the same, the path may not be. Avoid potential broken links by double-checking the path before you click OK.

Note: I've created a few extra images that can be used as Image Delimiters. Look in the images folder for arrow.gif, arrow2.gif, dot.gif, and dot2.gif. Of course, you can always create your own. Enjoy!

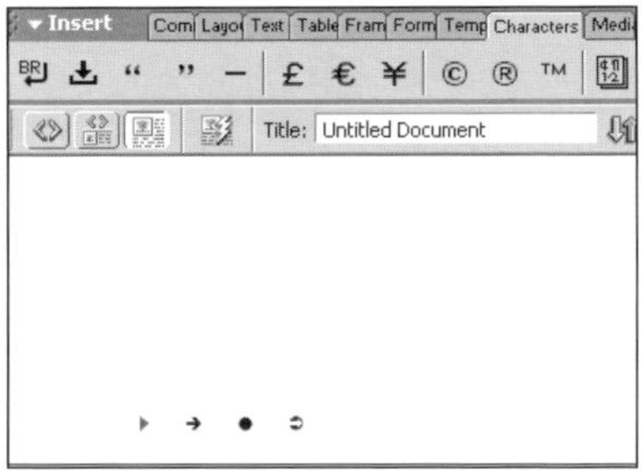

Some more Image Delimiters can be found in the images folder of 07_bread_crumbs.

Modifications

Crumb trails can be a great tool for your users, and the Bread Crumbs command can save you a lot of time manually changing text and links on countless pages. Depending on the size and structure of your site, however, this method could be cumbersome to implement. If you've tried this method and it's not flexible enough for your situation, you might consider the following:

- **Library Items and Templates.** To complete the project described in this section, you could have used a template with the Bread Crumbs command. If you're creating something like this from scratch, that's an excellent idea. Alternately, you might consider creating a series of Library items and/or Templates made up of standard HTML. For instance, you could create a crumb trail Library item for each crumb element. You could apply this library item to all of the pages that share the same crumb trail. This solution works especially well for existing sites that don't have a rigid structure. If your site changes frequently, though, this could become a nightmare to maintain.
- **Databases.** Dreamweaver MX brings the power of databases and application servers to the masses. See Project 11, " Building a Project Management Solution," and Project 12, "Database-Driven Username and Password Validation," for some hands-on exercises. Because there are so many variables, I can't recommend any one solution, but rest assured that there is a way to automate the creation of crumb trails using a database and your choice of App Servers. See the tip for some information about using ColdFusion or ASP to link your crumb trails to a database.

Tip: If you're interested in learning more about databases, work through Projects 11 and 12, and then hit the web. Here are a couple of crumb-related links to investigate:

ColdFusion:

http://hotwired.lycos.com/webmonkey/00/29/index3a.html?tw=programming

ASP:

http://www.asp101.com/articles/jason/yahoonavbar/default.asp
http://aspemporium.com/aspEmporium/examples/breadcrumbtrail_class.asp

- **Books.** You also can buy *Inside Dreamweaver* (New Riders) for a more in-depth look at how to integrate databases with Dreamweaver. The Macromedia and Microsoft web sites offer a wealth of information about ColdFusion and ASP, respectively.
- **Custom Scripts.** If you know some JavaScript, the Bread Crumbs command is actually fairly simple to modify. For example, you could make the underscores or hyphens in your folder names display as spaces, or you could capitalize all or some of the letters in your crumb trails.

  If you're not up on JavaScript yet, that's OK. Browsing through the Dreamweaver Exchange site frequently can net some amazing (and mostly free) tools. You also can suggest enhancements to Bread Crumbs creator, Paul Davis at Kaosweaver.com.

The bottom line is that crumb trails can be a valuable secondary mode of navigation. Many large sites, including Yahoo, Macromedia, and Webmonkey have noted this and use them throughout their sites. Now that you've given crumb trails a try, I'm sure you'll be using them as well.

"When you go in search of honey you must expect to be stung by bees."

—KENNETH KAUNDA, ZAMBIAN PRESIDENT

CREATING A CUSTOMIZED SEARCH FEATURE

Creating a Search Feature Without the Sting

Once your web site grows to more than a handful of pages, you'll discover that it gets harder and harder for your visitors to find the information they need. If they aren't already expecting your site to have a powerful search function, they soon will. This project explains how to implement a world-class site search that looks and feels like the rest of your site. Your viewers will find the information they need, you'll look like a hero, and you'll be done in under an hour!

Project 8

Creating a Customized Search Feature

by Zac Van Note

Before: Without a search feature, both you and your visitors miss a valuable tool.

After: With a Search feature, your visitors can find what they're looking for easily.

It Works Like This

Nothing is more frustrating for web users than not being able to find the information they're looking for. With the proliferation of sites on the Internet, most people know that the exact information they want is probably on a web page somewhere. But how do they find it? If you can help your site's visitors find the information they need with a minimum of clicks, you can make them very happy. And if the content on your site is unique, you've got a winning combination. We don't have time to cover your world-class content here (and that's always the biggest challenge). But we can solve the other half of the equation by showing you how to create a search feature your visitors will love.

Not too long ago, adding a search function to a site was very expensive and/or difficult to do. Along with the advent of friendly authoring tools like Dreamweaver came a surge of Application Service Providers (ASPs) that provide everything from automated search engine submissions to shopping cart services to supply chain management. Some of the providers offer very customized services and manage everything for you. Some have more of a "tools" approach, lending their software engineering expertise to you for little to no cost, hoping that you will come back for more or will help them stay in business by using affiliate programs of various kinds. So what does all this have to do with creating a site search function for your site?

Atomz, along with a handful of other companies, have created amazingly robust online applications that perform specialized tasks for your web site. For this project, we're most interested in Atomz, the company that created Atomz Search, a customizable site search service that automatically indexes your site (much like a "spider" in a traditional web search engine) and generates the results for your users.

Setting up this style of site search feature is fairly easy. After you choose a service provider (in this case, Atomz.com), you just set up your account, integrate some customized code into your pages, index your site, and start to see the magic. Once you have the site running, you can customize the look of the search pages and start to generate reports. After you customize the pages, you can let users perform a simple search or a more advanced search, just like the best search engines do. The best part is, for smaller sites, you get this service for free!

So what's the catch? Well, your users will see the Powered by Atomz logo on each search results page, but that's about it. Atomz is betting that after you try the free service, you'll want to join it as a corporate customer and pay the relatively low fees for more pages and more options. Not a bad bet, really. After you work through this project, I think you'll agree, this is the best feature you can add to your site in under an hour. As an added bonus, Atomz sends you a weekly report listing the most commonly searched-for words and phrases. This can help you keep in touch with customers' needs and help you make informed choices about updating your site's content, navigation, and structure.

If, after trying Atomz Search, you want to try another approach, you're in luck! We discuss several other approaches at the end of the project.

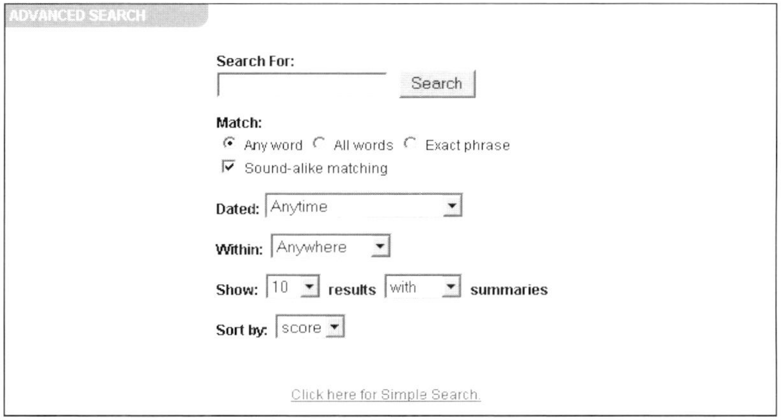

Your site search pages aren't limited to a wimpy simple search. With an advanced search, your visitors can search based on dates, complex combinations of words and phrases, and more.

AtomzSearch generates a weekly report that summarizes the most frequently searched-for words and phrases. You also can view the site reports at anytime and dig through the cumulative results. This can be invaluable information for what your site's users need most.

PREPARING TO WORK

The setup for this project is much like that in the rest of the book. You'll copy a folder to your hard drive, start Dreamweaver, install an extension, and set up a new site, pointing to the folder you just copied. The main difference is that you'll have to create a "live" site to make this feature work. This can just be a folder on an existing live site for now, or you can create a new account. See the section, "Setting up a 'Live' Site," later in this chapter for some inexpensive (and free) hosting providers that can get you up and running in minutes.

1 Install the Atomz Search command:

- Browse to the Extensions folder on the CD.
- Open the Commands subfolder.
- Double-click the file MX230866_Atomz Search.mxp to install the Atomz Search Command. (You also can find the latest updates to the extension at the Macromedia Exchange or directly from Atomz at http://center.atomz.com/dreamweaver/)

After you've successfully installed the extension, close Dreamweaver. Launch Dreamweaver again and check to see whether there is an Atomz tab on the Insert bar.

2 Copy the project folder:

- Browse to the Projects folder on the CD.
- Copy the Projects/08_search_engine folder to a convenient location on your hard drive.

3 You need to set up a site on a live server, which requires a hosting provider, if you don't already have one. (See the section, "Setting up a 'Live' Site," for information on a few providers I use.) If you try to work through this project without setting up a live site, you won't be able to index, customize, or search your pages. It really is mandatory that you have a live site for this project to function. If you already have a live site, you can just create a folder on that server.

Note: Because of the nature of this project, your site cannot be searched unless it is actually published on a web server with open access. An internal testing server will not get indexed because the web service can not find it. To see the project live on the web, go to http://www.design-link.org/DreamweaverMX_Magic/08_search_engine/.

4 Open the Site Definition wizard by choosing Site>New Site and clicking the Basic tab. Define a new Dreamweaver site using the 08_search_engine copy as your local root folder. Name your project **Project_eight** and choose not to use any server technology.

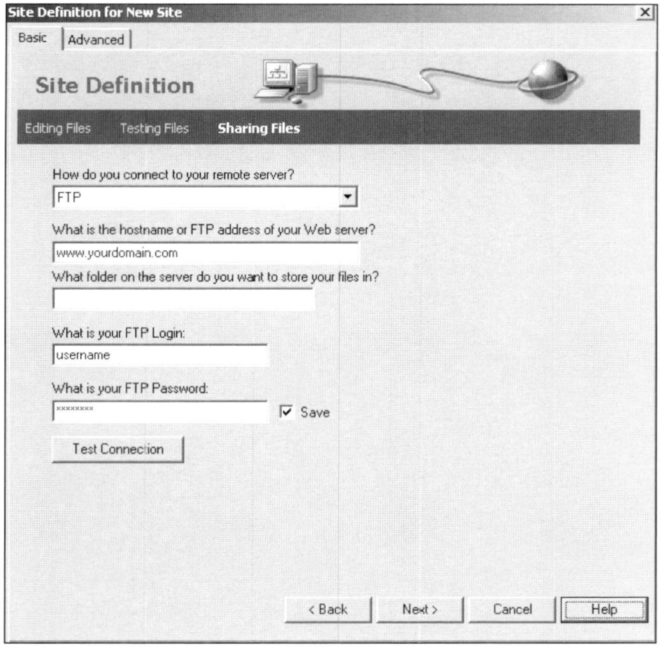

Site setup is easier than ever, thanks to the new Site Definition wizard.

5 Make sure that you set up the FTP connection for your site using the settings your hosting provider gives you. Specifically, you need the FTP host name (usually something like ftp.yourdomain.com or www.yourdomain.com); host directory (this often can be left blank if this is the root of your site, but it could also be a long path to your project folder, such as www/html/08_search_engine/); and your login/username and password.

If you are working behind a firewall, especially in a corporate environment, you may need to check the Use Passive FTP and/or Use Firewall options. After you have set everything according to your provider's specifications, test the connection and you're ready to go!

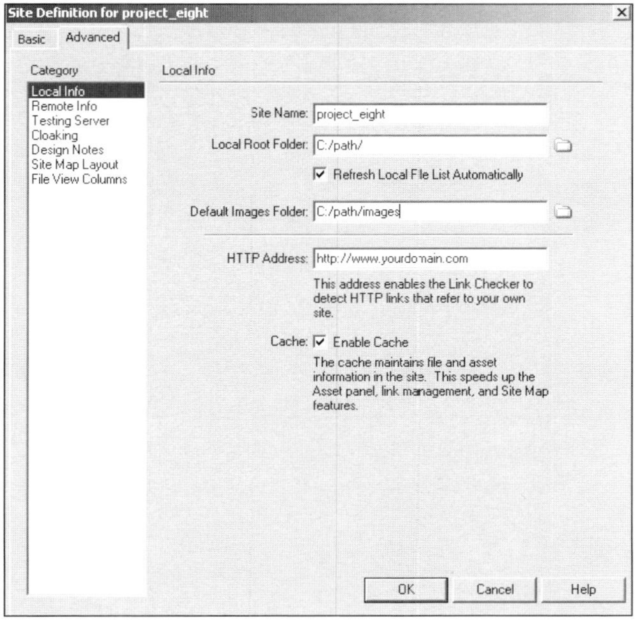

As in previous versions of Dreamweaver, you can use the Advanced Site Definition view to set up your site without the helpful prompts.

Setting Up Your Atomz Account

Before you set up your web pages, you'll need to create an Atomz account:

1 Open Dreamweaver. Open the index.htm file in your root folder.

2 The Atomz Search Extension you installed earlier can be found in its own tab on the Insert bar. Click the only button under that tab. A small window pops up.

3 Click Join. Your browser launches and take you to the Atomz web site, where you'll continue the registration:

- Enter your email address twice, once in each field. Click the Try Atomz button!, and you'll be sent a confirmation message.
- Check your email. Your password and additional instructions are in this message. Click the second link that says To confirm . . .
- Read the Service Agreement and click Agree. Next, you'll enter the required contact information. Click Next.
- Select Create New Account. Then, choose Atomz Search. Finally, click Atomz Express Search Account within the text describing the types of accounts. Read about the limitations and advantages of each plan.
- Now you'll answer several questions about your web site. You need to know your URL and roughly how many pages your site contains. Choose the free plan and click Add.
- After you submit that information, your account is created and you're ready to get back to Dreamweaver. If the Atomz Extension window is still open, close it for now. We'll get back to it soon.

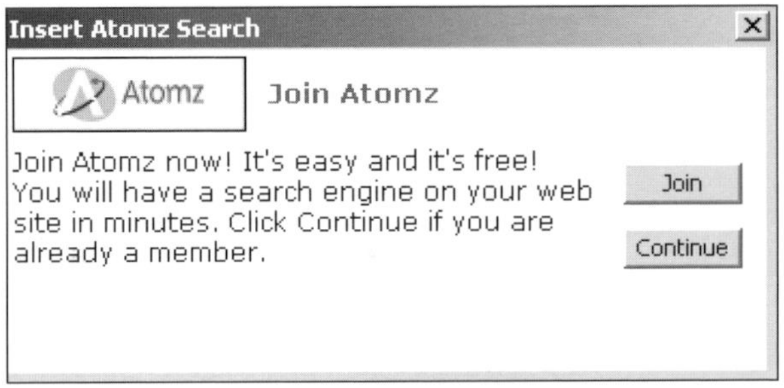

Click Join to create an Atomz Search account.

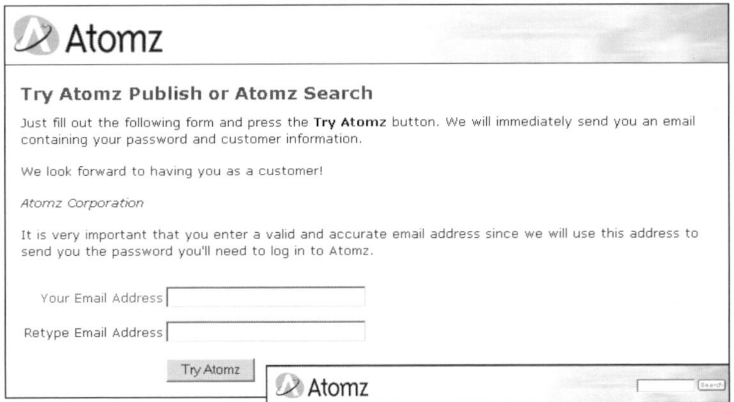

Atomz
Join Atomz
Join Atomz now! It's easy and it's free! You will have a search engine on your web site in minutes. Click Continue if you are already a member.
Web Site URL
Web Site Name
Web Site Category
Try Atomz Publish or Atomz Search
Just fill out the following form and press the Try Atomz button. We will immediately send you an email containing your password and customer information.
We look forward to having you as a customer!
Atomz Corporation
It is very important that you enter a valid and accurate email address since we will use this address to send you the password you'll need to log in to Atomz.
Your Email Address
Retype Email Address
Try Atomz

Enter your email address and Atomz will immediately send a confirmation message to that address.

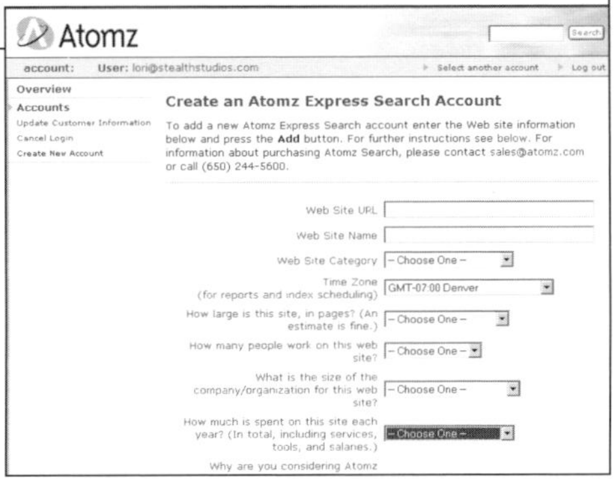

Creating an account is very simple. Just answer a few basic questions about yourself and your web site. Because web sites are updated frequently, it is possible that this screen and other Atomz.com screens will look a little different by the time you try this exercise.

Creating the Web Site

In this project, you're going to add the search functionality onto an existing framework. Basically, the same site you used for Project 7, "Leading the Way with Crumb Trails," is used here. Hopefully this will help you focus on the issue at hand and not on the structure of the site. Because there are many pages used in Project 7, that project makes a good candidate for a site search. All the pages are setup as a skeleton of the complete site with placeholder images and text. There's even a search form pre-built on each page.

You can create a search form many different ways. For now, we're going to concentrate on a simple site search, so let's back up and see how the form was built.

1 Open any page in your new 08_search_engine site *except* for index.htm in the root folder. The images for the navigation structure were created and sliced in Fireworks. Because Fireworks auto-named the resulting GIF files and created the table, the file names are cryptic. For now, concern yourself only with the two last cells in the first row of the table. They contain the Search graphic, a text input field, and a GO graphic that will serve as the submit button. These cells are surrounded by an HTML form tag, which makes it possible to capture and process the search request.

Note: The size and position of the graphics and form fields required some tweaking after the original importing from Fireworks. Also, because of the differences in the way browsers display form fields, you'll need to experiment with your settings to make the form look acceptable in all major browsers. As a general rule, test it in Netscape first. If the form fits and looks OK there, it should fit fine—Internet Explorer's forms are always more compact.

2 Now open index.htm in the root folder. Notice that the cells for the Search function are blank. You'll be putting it all together in the next few steps. First, to ensure predictable alignment, highlight both cells, and select Horz: Left and Vert: Top in the Cell Properties bar.

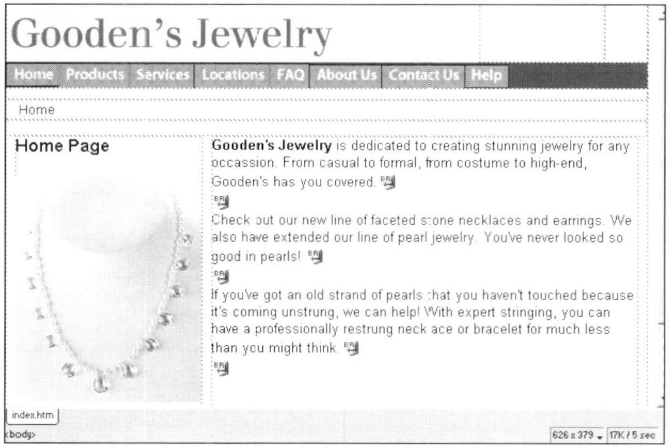

The index.htm (root folder) file is missing the search form. We'll build a new one from scratch.

3 Now you set up the form tags:

- Click in the first empty cell. Insert a blank form by selecting Insert>Form.
- Open the split view so you can dig into the HTML.
- Click inside the form area in Design view and look above in the HTML view. You should see the opening form tag.
- Highlight the <form> tag and move it *before* the preceding <td> tag.
- Edit the line to read: **<form method="get" action="http://search.atomz.com/search/">**
- Click in the second empty cell. Notice where the cursor moves in the HTML view. Select the closing form tag </form> and move it *after* the </td> tag of the second empty cell. It's very important that you get the tag after the second cell, or you'll have some strange alignment and Dreamweaver may add a second </form> tag in the next steps.

4 Next, you need to place the Search graphic. Insert in the first empty cell the file goodmans1_r1_c5.gif from the Images folder. Insert a line break
 (press Shift+Enter or Shift+Return) after the graphic.

5 Next, insert a Text Input field immediately below the graphic by choosing Insert>Form Objects>Text Field. In the Property inspector, set the field values to TextField Name: **"sp-q"**, Char Width: **"14"**, as follows:

```
<input name="sp-q" type="text" size="14">
```

It's very important that you set the name to "sp-q" or the search won't function.

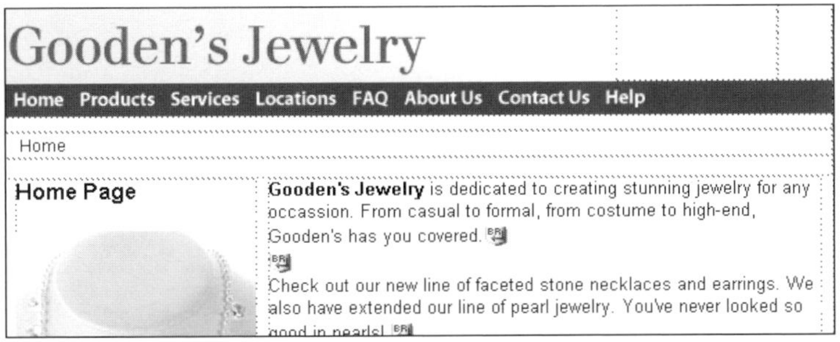

Placing the blank form tag is not enough. We need to edit the HTML to move the location of the form tags.

Note: Dreamweaver will automatically place a set of </form> tags around any new text field. This can give your form elements (and elements surrounding them) strange gaps and alignment. Pay close attention, especially when you are aligning graphics and form elements.

Note: If you have turned on any of the accessibility options in Dreamweaver's Preferences, many of these screen shots and options will appear different. Instead of the options shown here, you will see options specialized for making your form accessible to disabled users.

6 In the empty cell on the right, you need to insert an image field. Using Insert>FormObjects>Image Field, insert the file goodmans1_r1_c6.gif from the Images folder.

Again, it is very important that you insert the field as an Image Field and not as a standard image. This will allow it to act like a submit button for this form.

7 Save the file and preview it in a browser. The page should look like the other page you previewed earlier. The rest of the pages are already setup to this point for this project. Save the page.

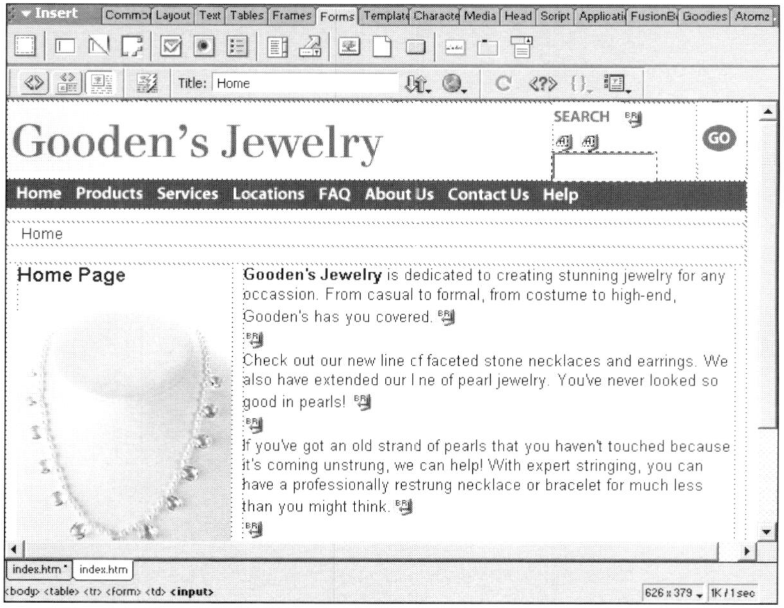

When you're finished, your form should look like this.

Making the Search Come to Life

Now you have set up your Atomz Search account and created the search field. There's still one element missing from your HTML: a form-based link to your account on Atomz.com. This is necessary so that users will see *your* site's index.

1 Now you're going to create a dummy Search button and plug the code it generates into your site.

- Create a new document in Dreamweaver. Choose File>New>Basic Page>HTML. Click Create to build the page.
- Open the Insert>Atomz tab. Click the Atomz Search object. Click Continue.
- Enter your email address and password. You only have to do this once if you leave the Save my login information box checked in the next dialog box.

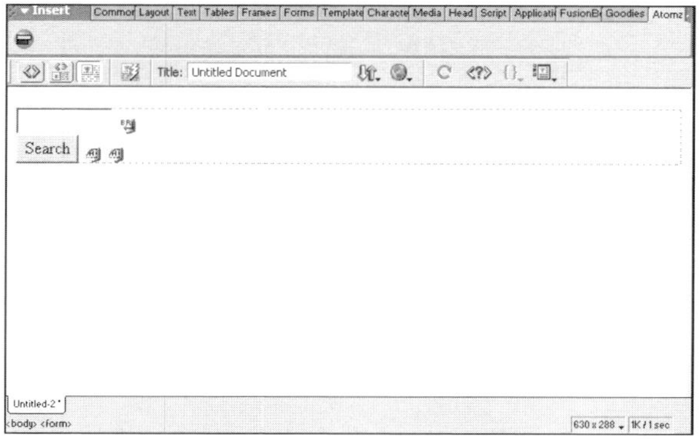

The Atomz Search Extension creates a generic search form.

- The extension connects you to the Atomz server and lists some options. Because you've only set up one account, you don't have a choice there. However, after you're finished with this project, you can create many accounts for various sites using just one login. For now, do not check the Use advanced search form option.
- Click OK. A new Search field and a submit button are generated for you. You could use this generic button as-is, but we're going for a custom look.
- Open the Split view to see the HTML behind the scenes. Take note of the </form> tag. The tag is the same as the one you edited earlier.
- On the next line, notice the name="xxx" value. This should read "sp-q", just like you added earlier.
- Next, find the two lines of hidden form tags. You'll be adding these between the form tags on all of the pages of the site. These codes are unique to your site, so it's critical that you copy these correctly.
- Note the five lines starting with the text field tag and ending with the two hidden tags. Remove the <br> tag and the Submit tag. Change the textfield line to read:

```
<input name="sp-q" type="text" size="14">
```

- You should have the following text left (your sp-a value will be different than the one shown here):

```
<input name="sp-q" type="text" size="14">
<input type=hidden name="sp-a"
➥value="sp9001d008">
<input type=hidden name="sp-f" value=
➥"iso-8859-1">
```

Note: As an alternative to using the AtomzSearch Extension to generate a search page, you can log in to Atomz.com, click the HTML link on the left, and get the appropriate snippets for your simple or advanced search pages.

```
<form method="get" action="http://search.atomz.com/search/">

  <input size=15 name="sp-q">
  <br>
  <input type=submit value="Search">
  <input type=hidden name="sp-a" value="sp9001d088">
  <input type=hidden name="sp-f" value="iso-8859-1">
</form>
```

The form tag is always the same for an Atomz Search page. We have already changed our form to reflect the appropriate action.

```
    <form name="sp-q" method="post" action="">
      <td align="left" valign="top"> <img name="goodmans1_r1_c5" src=
"images/goodmans1_r1_c5.gif" width="56" height="18" border="0"><br>
        <input type=hidden name="sp-a" value="sp9001d088">
      <input type=hidden name="sp-f" value="iso-8859-1">
      <input name="sp-q" type="text" size="14"> </td>
      <td colspan="2" align="left" valign="top"> <input name="imageField" type="image" src=
"images/goodmans1_r1_c6.gif" width="40" height="51" border="0">
      </td>
    </form>
```

We will use the special HTML codes the Extension generated here. Just copy and paste them into the index.htm page in your root folder.

Highlight these three lines of code and copy them. Choose Edit>Find and Replace.

- In this dialog box, set the following:

  Find In: **Entire Current Local Site**

  Search For: **Source Code**

  Replace With: **Paste your three lines of HTML**

  Don't close the Find and Replace box yet.

- Open the index.htm file you were working on in the last stage of this project. In Code view, highlight only the line with your textfield tag (not the hidden tags) and copy it.

```
<input name="sp-q" type="text" size="14">
```

- Back in the Find and Replace dialog box, in the box next to Source Code, paste this one line of HTML. Click Replace All. This action updates every page in the site with your unique hidden tags. If you are warned that the operation cannot be undone, click OK. This is necessary because each account generates unique login information. Not to mention, if you haven't used Find and Replace in Dreamweaver, you're missing one of its most powerful features!

2 Now that you've fixed the HTML in all your pages, upload the entire site to your live server. If you still don't have a live server, please skip ahead and read the section, "Setting up a 'Live' Site," for some ideas on resources you can investigate.

3 You can view your pages on the live site, but the search feature won't work yet. You have one important step to complete before you get to see some amazing results.

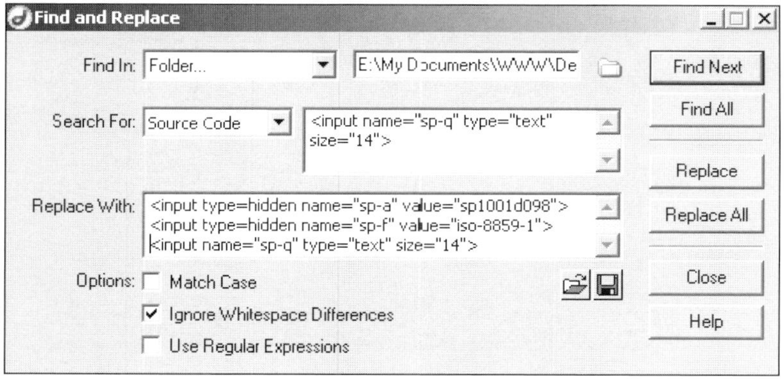

Use the Find and Replace command to update all the pages in your site with your unique hidden field information.

Indexing and Testing Your Site

A search engine can't return any results unless it has "crawled," or indexed, your site. Basically, this is a database of information about your site's contents, including all the text, alt tags, and even the text contents of standard formats like Acrobat PDF. Large search engines are usually automated, and Atomz Search can be as well. When you first create your account, no index is created and the search feature doesn't work yet.

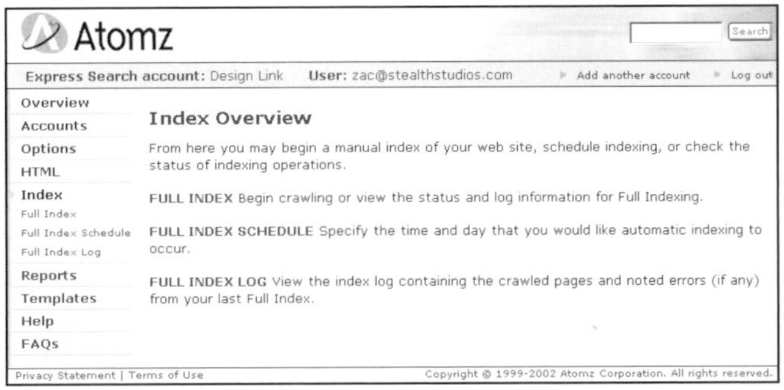

Select Full Index from the Index options screen

1 Generating your first site index and setting up a weekly time for automatic updates is really a simple matter, though. Read on:

- If you're not still logged on to the Atomz.com web site, go to www.atomz.com, click the Customer Login button, and enter your account login and password. Click the Index menu item on the left.
- On the right side, click Full Index. This opens a page with some information, options, and an Index Now button. It's a good idea to click the Clear index cache and Count all pages options. Then just click Index Now.
- A countdown graphic appears. When the count-down gets to 0, it displays "Click here now." Click it to view the index status. Because this site is small, it shouldn't take long to index. When you're done indexing, a listing will show the number of pages in the site and the number of words indexed.
- Now you're done creating the initial index.

Select the Clear index cache and Count all pages check-boxes; then click Index Now.

2 Open your browser and view your site. If you've followed everything up to this point, your search should be working. Try searching for these words and phrases: *Bracelets*, *Gold Earring*, *Silver*. The search results page will not look exactly like your site at this point. You can leave it like this if you choose, but you'll see how to customize the look in a bit.

Note: There are many possible reasons why a page or group of pages cannot be indexed. If you get a message that some pages weren't processed during the indexing process, you can always go back out to Index>Full Index Log to view all the results of your last index. This can help you troubleshoot a number of problems, including dead links and incorrect security settings on files and folders.

AUTOMATING INDEX UPDATES

Before we move on to the next major step, let's take a minute to set up a day and time of each week to perform an automated index update. The best time is usually in the very early morning hours. Depending on your site's traffic, that may not always be the case, especially if you have an international user base. See the tip at the right for more suggestions.

1 If you're not still logged on to the Atomz.com web site, go to www.atomz.com, click the Customer Login button, and enter your account login and password. Click Full Index Schedule.

- Select a time and a day of the week for the update and click Schedule Updates. From now on, at that day and time every week, a fresh index will be generated automatically. You can go back and change this option at any time.

If your host doesn't provide reports or the quality of the reports isn't very good, here are a couple of site statistics services you can employ for little or no cost. The best bet is to first see what your host provides because they may already have a good system.

Extreme Tracking (www.extremetracking.com) offers a free service (although you're supposed to put their logo on each tracked page) and an enhanced "invisible" tracker for $5 per month. This service gives you all the information you could hope for in a low-cost site tracker.

There are many other solutions, including SuperStats (www.superstats.com/service_options.html), but they usually cost more than others and don't necessarily give you any more information.

With any of these services, you will know with some certainty when your visitors are hitting your site, and you'll be able to make informed decisions about many things, including when to index your site.

184

Full Index Schedule

Overview
Accounts
Options
HTML
Index
Full Index
Full Index Schedule
Full Index Log
Reports
Templates
Help
FAQs

Select the time and day that you would like the Atomz Search robot to crawl and update your site index, then press the "Schedule Updates" button. Be aware that web servers often go down for maintenance in the middle of the night. If your server is one of these and you schedule your indexing during down time, this will prevent your automatic index from occurring. Be sure to select a time of day when your web server is available. The time you select is the local time for your configured time zone. Visit the Update Search Account Profile page under Accounts to check or change your configured time zone.

3 AM

○ No Automatic Updates
○ Sunday
○ Monday
● Tuesday
○ Wednesday
○ Thursday
○ Friday
○ Saturday

[Schedule Updates]

Privacy Statement | Terms of Use Copyright © 1999-2002 Atomz Corporation. All rights reserved.

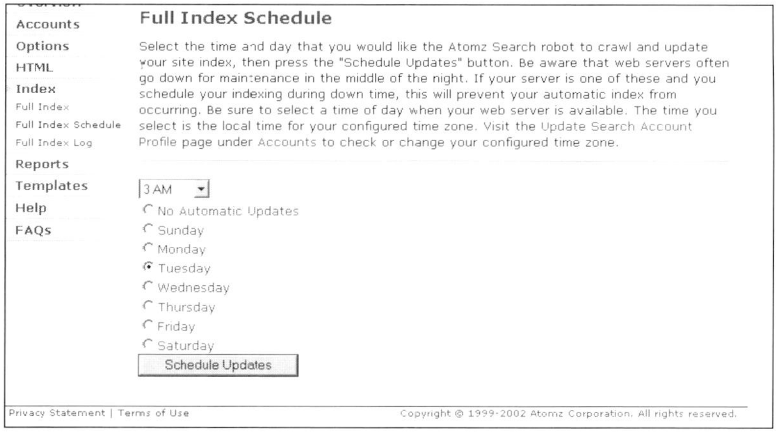

Select a day and time that your site will be re-indexed automatically each week.

Tip: Tracking the days, times, and pages your visitors view the most is very useful information. Knowing what kind of computers and browsers they use is also helpful. You can gather all of this information and more from your site's visitors very easily. In fact, you may already have this information on your server and not even know it. The process of gathering the information varies from server to server and hosting providers are all over the place on how much statistical information they provide. Some provide none, while others provide very detailed reports.

Customizing the Search to Match Your Site

One of the most powerful features of Atomz Search, and one that is incredible for a free service, is the sheer customizability it offers. In this section, we're going to look specifically at how to make the search results pages match the rest of the site's look and navigation, but you can customize much more than that. In the "Modifications" section at the end of the project, there are some tips on even more ways to customize your site search.

Tip: Although the simple search function is what most people will use, you can create an advanced search at any time by adding a link on each page or only on your search results page.

The easiest method is to create an advanced search page using the AtomzSearch object. Just select the Advanced Search option. You can then customize the search form and the results pages.

Atomz uses a special markup within its search results HTML. Be careful not to delete vital parts of that coding or your searches won't function.

1 Open any page in the site. Choose File>Save As and save the file as **search_results.htm** in your root folder.

2 Next, highlight the three cells in the center of the page with the placeholder image and text.

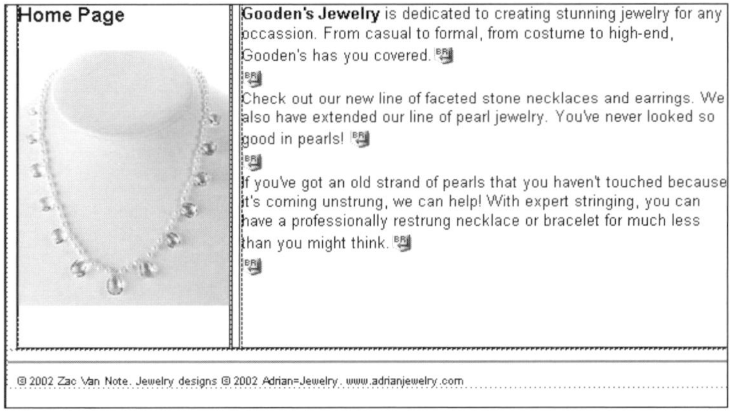

Highlight the three cells in the center of the page with the placeholder image and text.

3 Merge the cells together (choose Modify>Table>Merge Cells) and then delete the content in the new cell. Type **Results go here**.

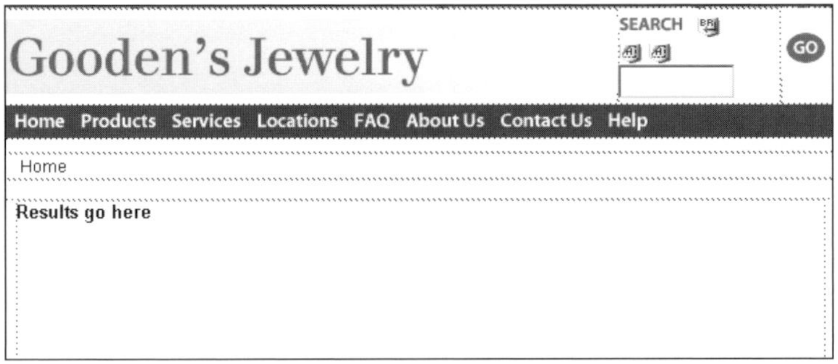

Merge the cells, delete the content, and type **Results go here**.

4 Next, you need to create a base tag so that all of your graphics files can be located from the remote Atomz server. Just below the <HTML> tag on your page, add the following tag:

```
<base href="http://www.yourdomain.com/path/">
```

Replace the path here with your site information. This is important because otherwise, all of your image links will be broken or you'd have to manually change each path on the page.

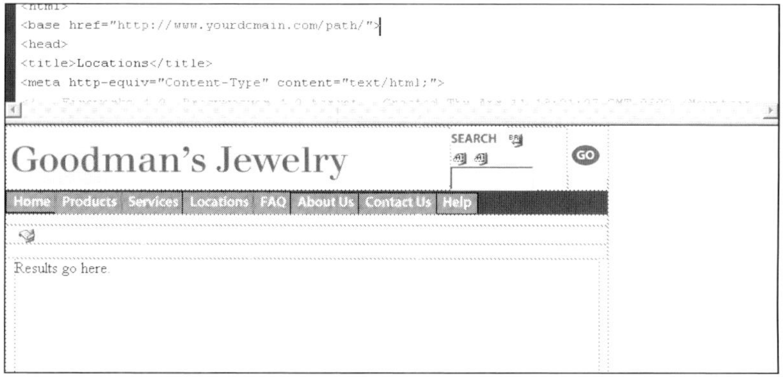

Add a base tag below the <HTML> tag.

5 Open your browser and log in to your Atomz account. Click Templates. On the far right, select Template Recipe. In the middle of the page is a scrolling text box with a long bunch of code. Select all the text, and then copy it.

6 Go back to Dreamweaver and highlight the text "Results go here," which you created in Step 2. In Code view, paste the code you should still have on the clipboard to replace this text.

7 Save the file. In HTML view, select all and choose Edit>Copy.

8 Open your browser to your Atomz account. Click Templates. On the far right, select Template Editor.

9 In the Edit tab, select all the text currently in the long text box and delete it. Click in the HTML view of Dreamweaver. Select all by choosing Edit>Select All. Choose Edit>Copy. Paste your HTML from Dreamweaver into the Edit window in your browser.

In the Edit window, change your <title> tag to something like **Search Results Page**.

Tip: Using Cascading Style Sheets (CSS) to style your text is always a good idea. You get much more control over the look and placement of your text. If you use CSS on your site and want your Atomz Search page to be customized to use your styles, you'll need to keep a couple of things in mind. First, due to the nature of this type of service, linking to a large file is somewhat cumbersome. Also, for whatever reason, I've noticed that linking CSS files to custom templates produces erratic results.

So, to stay worry-free, I suggest embedding your CSS definitions (or an appropriate subset) right into your custom template. See Project 5, "Giving Your Pages Some Style," for more information on creating CSS definitions for only one document.

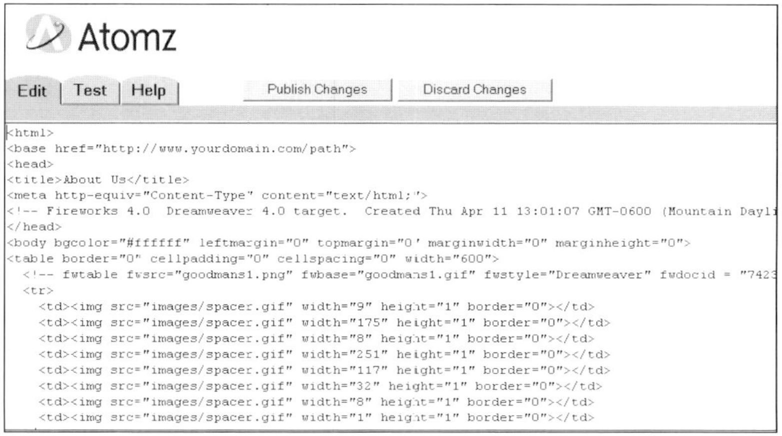

Paste your HTML from Dreamweaver into the Edit window.

10 Click the Test tab. Type a search word, like Gold and see what kind of results you get. You should get several entries.

11 If everything seems to be working properly, go back to your browser and click Publish Changes. Then click to confirm this choice.

12 Go out to the live site and double-check that everything is working properly.

Your site search is now up and running, and you have customized it to work seamlessly with the rest of the site.

Tip: Frames are the Jekyl-and-Hyde of the HTML world. While previewing the search results for your page, you've probably noticed that the results pages are actually hosted by the Atomz server, so an Atomz.com URL shows up for those pages. Although most users won't even notice this, it could cause unnecessary worries. To alleviate this, you can launch your search results pages in a frame. You can create a one-frame frameset for this purpose. This leaves your base web address (http://www.yourdomain.com) in the URL bar, even when the page goes out to Atomz.

Unfortunately, frames also can cause some linking problems (both within your site and from outside). Atomz has a partial solution to this frame problem. If you are using frames in your site and you're having problems with search results linking to the proper documents, log in to Atomz.com and click Options>Frames. You can alter the target for all search results.

Tip: Although it's not always necessary to get your pages to display in every browser, I recommend that you enclose your JavaScript section in the Head of your document with HTML comment tags: <!-- comment--> In some situations, the Atomz template editor page will not work unless you've put the JavaScript section inside the HTML comment tags. These tags should already exist on all pages for this project, but they may not be there for other custom code you apply to your pages.

Creating Reports on Your Visitors' Searches

In addition to all of the direct benefits searches offer to your site visitors, Atomz Search also can be a powerful agent of change. By default, Atomz Search sends you a weekly report listing the top searches for your site. From this information, you can draw a number of conclusions. First, you get a clear picture of what your customers are searching for. This could lead to content or navigation changes that make the most demanded information more accessible. You also can track patterns over time. For instance, with seasonal changes, you may see people searching for different things. As major news or economic changes occur, you can respond quickly.

Get a clear picture of what users are looking for on your site.

1 To generate more reports on demand:

- Log in to Atomz.com. Click the Reports link on the left.
- Select a Report from the drop-down list. Some examples include: Top phrases today and yesterday or Top words this month and last month.
- After you're done testing your site, you may want to click Reset Reports. Be careful not to click this later, however, because it will clear all entries and you'll lose that valuable customer information.

2 If you find the reporting especially valuable, you should consider upgrading to the Atomz' premium plans, which give you even more flexibility.

Modifications

You can modify your search features in many different ways. Atomz Search makes it possible to customize your search form and the search results pages. Because you can make the page look essentially like anything you want, you simply can't get any more flexible than this. Here are some additional ways to customize your Atomz Search features:

- Create lists of words to exclude from your site's search index. Go to Options>Excluded Words. Indexing words such as "a," "the," or other common words make your visitors' search results less useful. For this reason, exclude these common words by adding them to this list.

- Add URL entry points and/or URL masks to specify additional parts of a site that may not be directly linked, or intentionally leave portions of your site out of the site indexing. Go to Options>URL Entrypoint or Options>URL Masks.

- Create an advanced search page on your site. Give users the option of searching in a more refined way from the beginning. The easiest way to add this feature is to use the Atomz Search extension and turn on the Advanced Search option.

- Also, see the tips throughout this project for using CSS and Frames.

Although adding a search feature is a great idea for medium-sized sites, it's absolutely imperative for large sites. Especially if you're creating sites for large corporations, there is an expectation that your sites will have search capabilities. Luckily, the Dreamweaver community has several top-notch ways to make it happen. Although I'm sold on Atomz.com and its easy-to-use and easy-to-customize business model, other viable alternative services are available.

- **SiteMiner.** This is not a free service, but it does have a range of offerings, including a search feature. For mid- to large-size sites, this is another solution that's available as an extension from the Dreamweaver Exchange.

Options
Relevance
Words & Languages
Excluded Words
Frames
Synonyms
Collections
URL Entrypoints
URL Masks
Passwords
Content Types
HTML
Index
Reports
Templates
Help
FAQs

The Options tab is where you change many of the options associated with your **Rio Grande J** search account.

Indexing Options

RELEVANCE Control the relevance Atomz Search attributes to sections of your web pages, including your page content, title, meta tags, image alt text and URL.

WORDS & LANGUAGES Control how words on your Web site are indexed including case sensitivity, numbers, sound-alike matching, word endings and character sets for specific languages.

EXCLUDED WORDS Specify words you do not want indexed on your Web site.

Searching Options

FRAMES Change how the search results interact with frames that may be present on your site.

Crawling Options

URL ENTRYPOINTS Specify other U site may be entered in addition to y address.

URL MASKS Specify URL masks whic portions of the site you do not want you specifically want crawled but no

PASSWORDS If some portion of you passwords, enter them here so we o portion.

CONTENT TYPES Specify which con Documents, **Flash Movies, MP3 M** will be crawled and indexed for this default, only HTML and text files wil

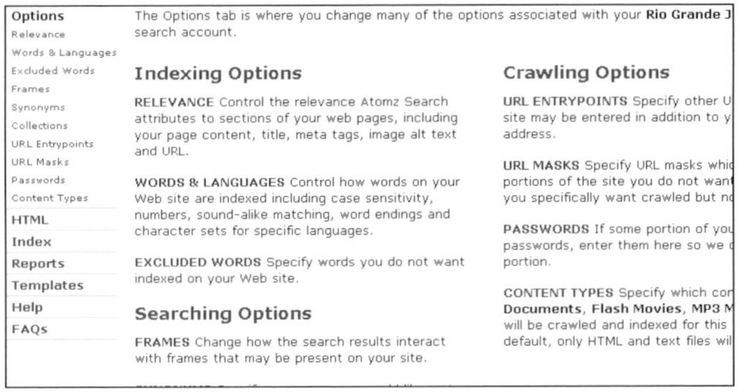

Atomz Search gives you a wealth of options to customize your site search.

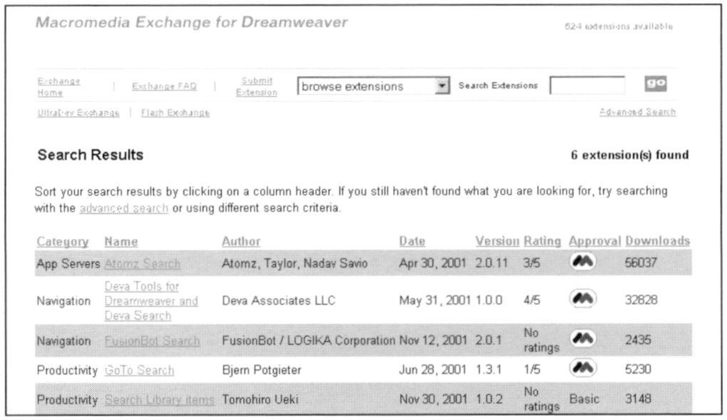

The Dreamweaver Exchange (http://exchange.macromedia. com) has a number of downloadable extensions to create search pages.

- **FusionBot.** This is a free service, much like Atomz.com. There's even an extension available from the Dreamweaver Exchange. It isn't nearly as slick and easy-to-use as Atomz, but it looks promising.
- **DevaSearch** (www.devahelp.com). This is not a free utility, but it offers some unique features. You can download a demo from the Dreamweaver Exchange. This utility has many of the same features as Atomz, but it's also portable, meaning that you can put it on a CD-ROM as well as the web.
- **Verity** (www.verity.com) **and Inktomi** (www.inktomi.com) are two vendors for heavy-duty enterprise-level search functionality. Their services also extend far beyond a basic site search. They can help automate a number of business processes as well. Prepare for sticker shock, because you'll lay down a big chunk of change for these high-end services. For most sites, these offerings are overkill. For a large organization, though, you might want to skip over Atomz and investigate one of these companies' industrial-strength solutions.

The bottom line is that no matter how you make it happen, a site search makes all of your information readily accessible. Dreamweaver and Atomz help make this complex task almost pleasant. Your site's users may already expect you to have this functionality. Now you can be the hero and still leave by 5:00!

Tip: For links to these search engine tools and much more, point your browser to www.design-link.org.

SETTING UP A "LIVE" SITE

Web site hosting providers seem to be a dime a dozen these days, but finding a *reliable* one at a good price can sometimes be a challenge.

Literally thousands of providers are out there, but many of them are fly-by-nights or a guy with a few computers in his garage. For an updated list of inexpensive and full-service hosting providers I recommend, visit my site at www.design-link.org. Though I can't guarantee these providers won't go belly up, I can steer you to those with a strong history of service and reliability.

Here's a listing of some hosting providers that I use:

- **Catalog.com.** This is a provider that will truly *host* your site for free, if you pay them $35 annually to maintain your domain name (www.yourdomain.com). If you want a domain name, you're going to have to pay someone $15 to $35 a year anyway. Altogether, this works out to less than $3.50 per month total cost! You can add on a long list of optional services for additional fees. This is one of the most reliable providers I've used at any cost.
- **ArisHost.com.** This provider offers the same basic deal as Catalog.com, but they haven't been around as long. Their deal is $30 annually to maintain your domain, and the hosting is free. You can add some optional services for a fee. Another bonus is that they will transfer your existing domain for free. This is great because most services, including Catalog.com, will charge up to $100 to transfer your domain. ArisHost just asks that you pay the $30, which pays to switch your domain and tacks on another year of domain registration.
- **Hypermart.com.** This is another provider that will host your site for free. If you don't mind not having your own domain, it costs you nothing, but they will put rotating ads on your site. You can upgrade to ad-free services for as little as $10 per month and get a site with a domain name for an additional fee. Hypermart is an excellent option, especially if you just want to test the waters for free.

All the providers listed above run Unix-based servers running Apache, which is fine for most sites. If you have special needs, like ASP or ColdFusion, you may want to look elsewhere. Catalog.com offers more expensive plans with advanced features. Intermedia.net and Hosting.com both offer a full range of plans, from Windows 2000 Servers for ASP to ColdFusion support.

Note: Finding a hosting provider for your web site should be easy, with the thousands of players available. Finding a reliable one at a decent price can be a challenge. On www.design-link.org, I maintain a list of the sites I recommend. I've used them for clients or I've received positive testimonials from colleagues.

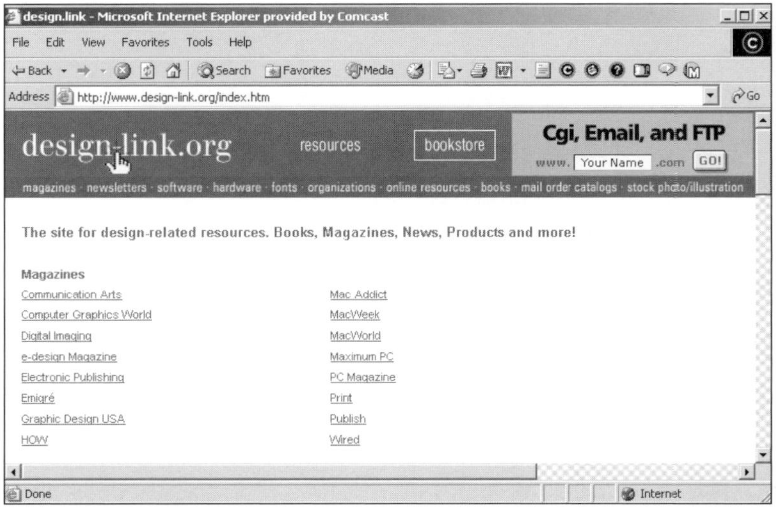

"It is good to have an end to journey toward; but it is the journey that matters, in the end."

—URSULA K. LE GUIN

POP-UP MENU AND MORE: ADDING SCRIPTS TO YOUR PAGES

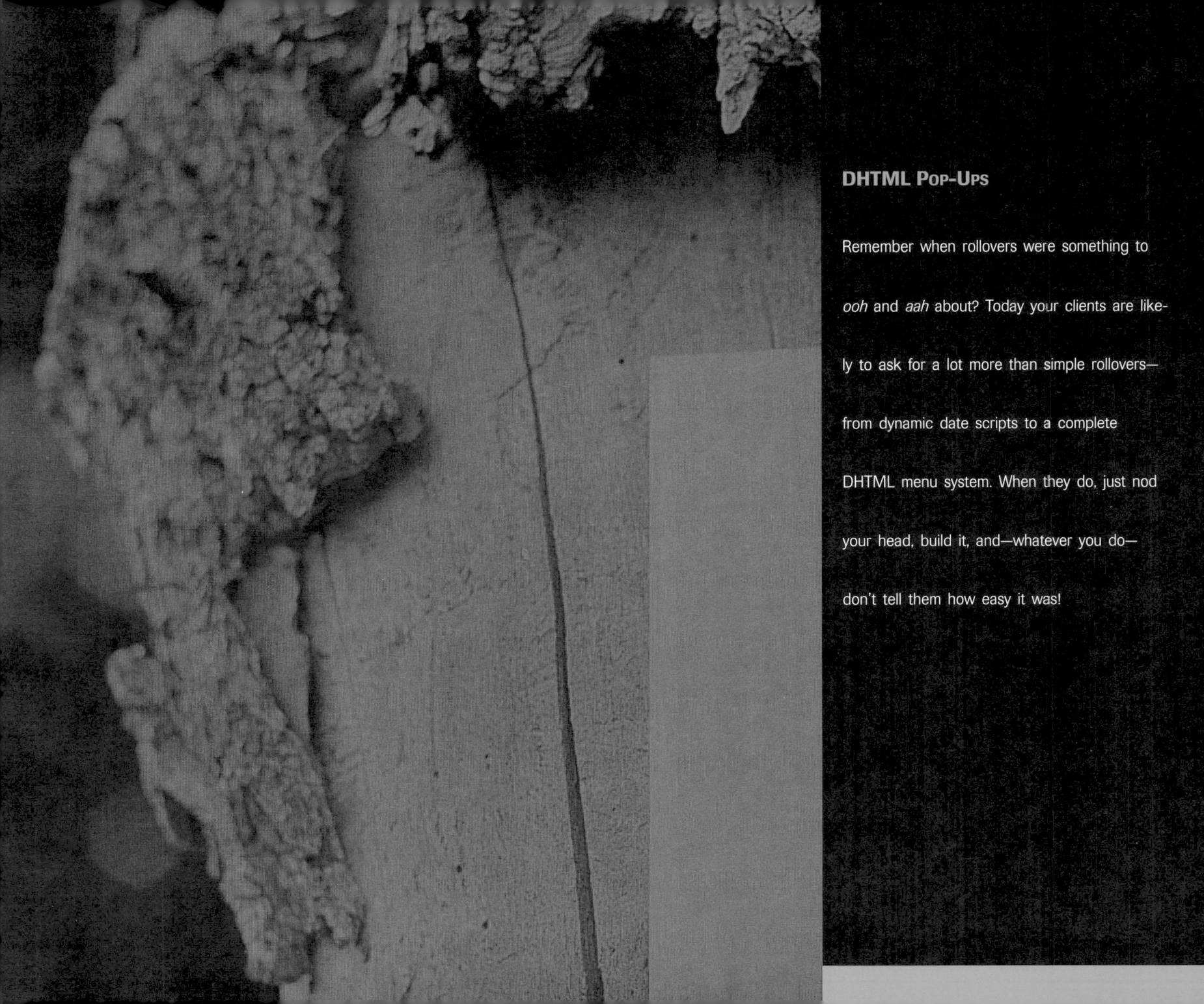

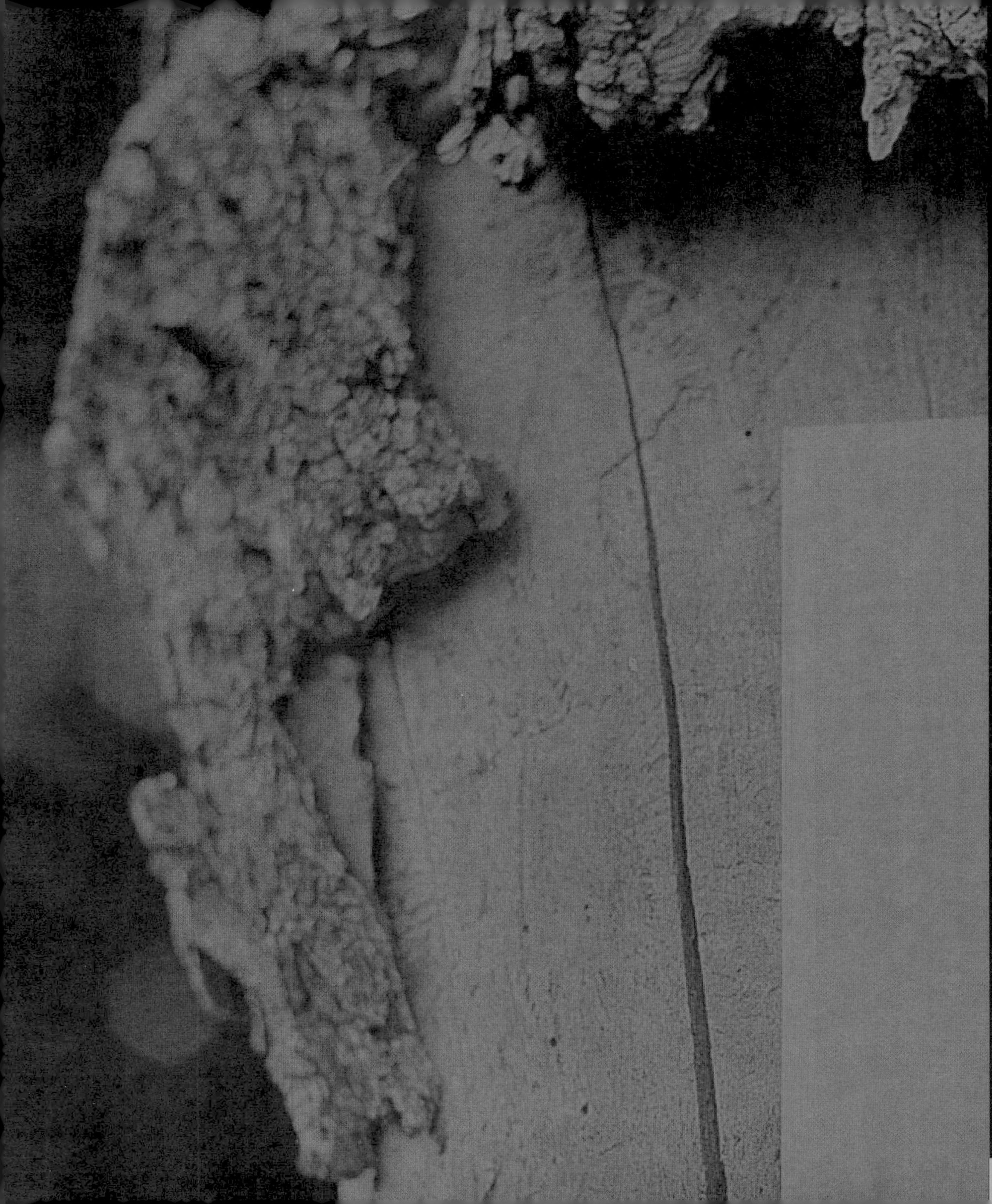

DHTML Pop-Ups

Remember when rollovers were something to *ooh* and *aah* about? Today your clients are likely to ask for a lot more than simple rollovers—from dynamic date scripts to a complete DHTML menu system. When they do, just nod your head, build it, and—whatever you do—don't tell them how easy it was!

Project 9

Pop-Up Menu and More: Adding Scripts to Your Pages

by Donna Casey and Joyce J. Evans

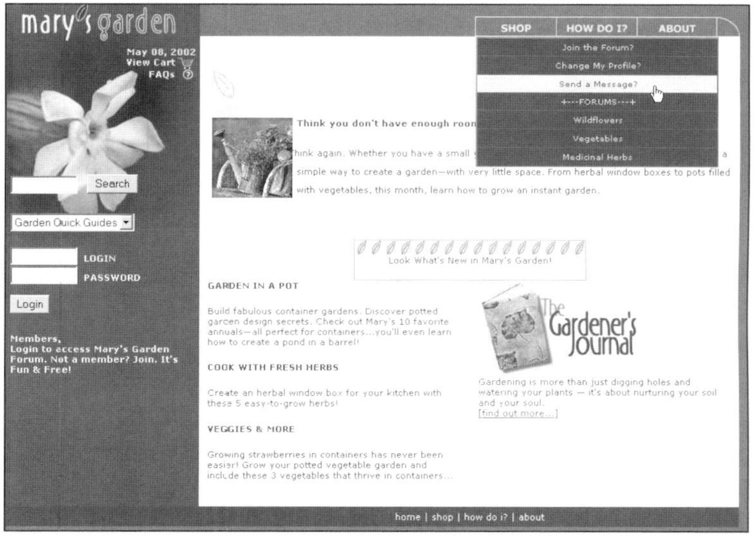

It Works Like This

Dreamweaver behaviors are the stuff of legends, and Macromedia has certainly struck a homerun with the Show Pop-Up Menu behavior. A fully configurable, dynamically positioned DHTML menu system is just a few clicks away—and you don't even have to install an extension! (Not that we don't love and use extensions every chance we get.)

In this project, you'll build one of these nifty menus with a few simple steps and explore options for more complex versions. This behavior overcomes the problem most DHTML menus have: They cannot dynamically reposition themselves when the trigger button is positioned relatively in the document. This script, native in both Macromedia Fireworks MX and in Dreamweaver MX, is a real treat!

But that's not all—we'll also show you a couple of custom scripts you can use in your own projects; an external Dynamic Date script and a very simple inline script that will let you randomly set an image's src attribute from a folder of graphics.

Preparing to Work

This should be old hat by now: you're going to copy the Projects/09_popups folder to your hard drive, start Dreamweaver, and define a site based on the project_start folder. Preview the finished project samples before you start to explore what's possible. Be sure to refresh (reload) your browser window a few times to see the random-image script in action.

1 Set up a Dreamweaver site.

- Locate the Project 9 folder (in the 09_popups folder) on the Magic CD.
- Copy the folder to a convenient location on your hard drive.

2 Define a site.

- Choose Site>New Site.
- Give the site a name, we used **Popup** and **Scripts**.
- Navigate to the Project 9\project_start folder.
- Select it.

You don't need to do anything else in this dialog box so you can close it.

Note: If you placed the new Project 9 folders into the Project 5 directory, you can use the site you defined for Project 5.

3 Double-click index.htm to open the page.

If your files are locked, refer to Project 3, "Dream Templates," for instructions on unlocking them.

Note: If you worked through Project 5, "Giving Your Pages Some Style," you can use the files from that project and just add the Scripts and Flowerimages folders from Project 5 into the Product 9 directory (it won't hurt anything).

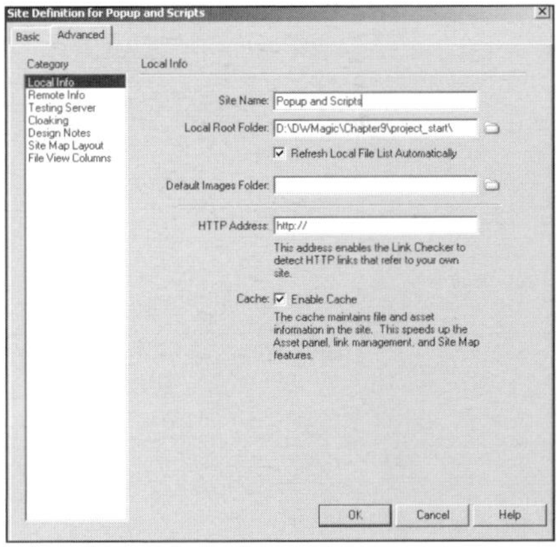

The Site Definition for this project's root folder.

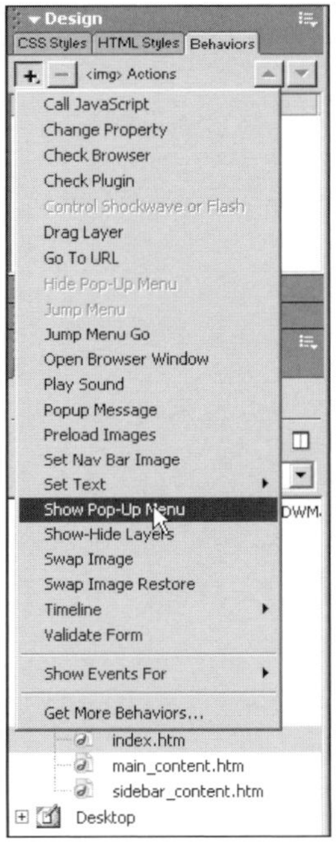

The Behaviors panel with the Show Pop-Up Menu behavior selected.

ADD SHOW POP-UP MENU BEHAVIOR

This page has three main navigation buttons in the top-right section of the page. For this project, you'll add a menu to each, setting it to pop down directly beneath the buttons. Of course, you can build as complex a menu system as you'd like, using the behavior and several modifications that are suggested at the end of this chapter.

1 Select the Shop button.

2 Apply the Show Pop-Up Menu behavior.

- Click the panel extender arrow in the Design panel and activate the Behaviors panel.
- Click the plus sign (+) and choose Show Pop-Up Menu. The Show Pop-Up Menu dialog box opens.

See? We told you it was easy! (Just kidding—there's more to come.)

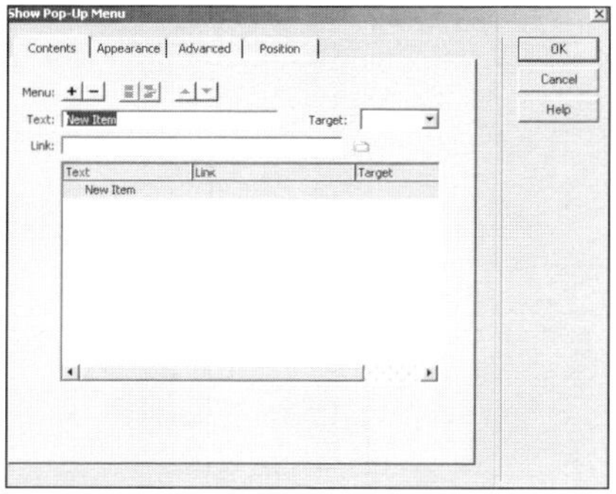

The Show Pop-Up Menu dialog box.

About Show Pop-Up Menu

Show Pop-Up Menu supports dynamic positioning, meaning that you can place the triggering buttons or links in a table cell that aligns them relatively to the page. However, if your menu is right-aligned (as is this project's) you cannot use a third-level flyout because it would appear off the document!

Planning is the key to successful pop-up menus. But using the Show Pop-Up Menu behavior makes creating and editing menus a piece of cake.

Create the Shop Button Menu

Now you need to work through the four screens that help you build a submenu. Every menu you build has code that is added to an mm_menu.js document that is generated when you make your first menu. Because the file is external, most of the code is downloaded only once and remains in cache.

1 Configure the menu items in the Contents panel.

- Highlight the New Item text in the Text box and type **Garden Tools**.
- In the Link box, type a null link of #.

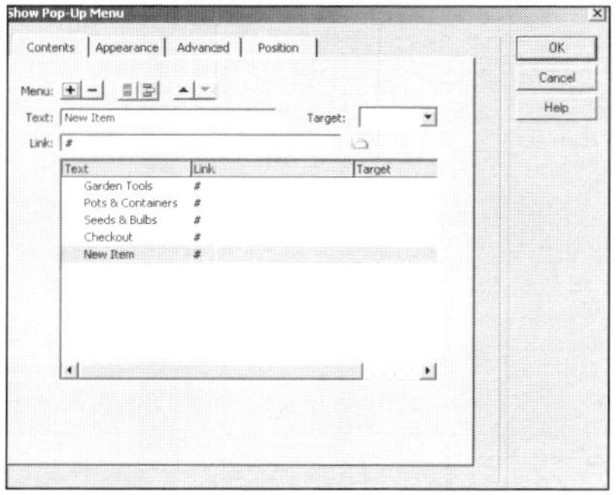

The Contents tab of the Show Pop-Up Menu dialog box with the menu items added.

- Press the (+) Add button to enter the item.

  The item is added and then New Item # appears in the Text field and in the Text box.

- Add the following selection options, highlighting and replacing the text and then clicking the (+) Add button to enter each new item. Use a null link (#) for the URL field in each:

  Pots & Containers

  Seeds & Bulbs

  Checkout

Note: You can link each page as you build the menu item by clicking the Browse button to find the correct page within a site, or you can put a null link (#) in place and either return when you have pages or edit the links in the head of the document. If your menu lives in a framed site, you can use the Target pull-down menu to select the correct target frame.

2 Click the Appearance panel.

3 Set the menu type to Vertical Menu.

4 Set the Font options.

Font: **Verdana, Arial, Helvetica, sans-serif**

Size: **10**

Style: **Normal** (Don't select anything)

Align: **Left**

Submenu Items

Although you can't use submenus because of the right alignment in this project, you'll need to know how to add them eventually. You add a submenu item the same way you add a menu item. The difference is that after you click the plus (+) sign, you select the menu item and click the Indent Item icon. After adding a few submenu items, if you want to return to a main menu item, you select it and click the Outdent item. As the names imply, the submenu items are indented and the main menu items are not.

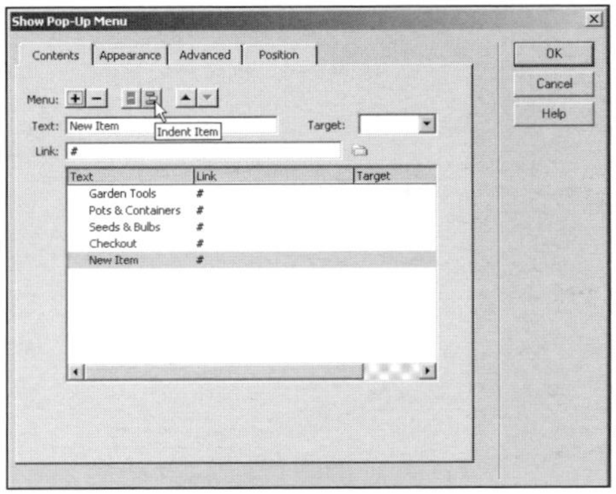

The Indent button is used to indent a submenu item.

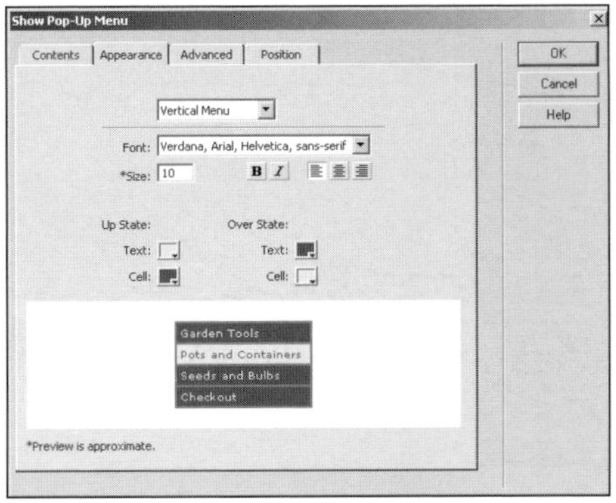

The appearance of the menu is set.

5 Set the background and text colors for the Up and Over States of the menu items. When you mouse-over the color swatches, the Hex numbers appear.

Up State Text: **#99FF66** (bright green)

Up State Cell: **#660099** (purple)

Over State Text: **#660099**

Over State Cell: **#99FF66**

Note: A quick way to select these colors is to sample them from the Up State color boxes. These are just reverse colors of what is used in the Up State.

The preview is approximate. Because you can set these options in any order, you can easily return to adjust the settings at any time.

6 Click the Advanced tab to configure additional options for the menu table and table cells.

Set Cell Width to **298 Pixels** by clicking the down-arrow and selecting Pixels and typing the value.

Leave Cell Height **Automatic**.

Set Cell Padding to **3**.

Set Cell Spacing to **0**.

Leave Text Indent and Delay at **Default**.

Show Pop-Up Borders.

Set Border Width to **1**.

Set Border Color to **#669900** (green).

Set both Shadow and Highlight to Default Color: None. To do this, select the red square with a line through it to the right of the Hex number field.

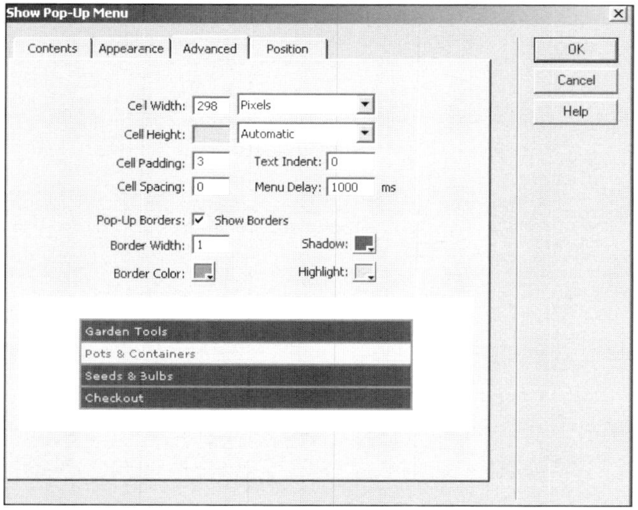

Setting the Cell Width, Padding, Border, and Shadow settings in the Advanced panel.

7 Click the Position tab.

The Position tab allows you to set the location of the menu relative to the trigger button. Clicking any button calculates coordinates from the Top, Left (0,0) point of the button. You can enter your own values to "tweak" the menu all you'd like.

8 Set the coordinates for the Shop button to the following:

X:**1** (to line up with the Shop button)

Y:**25** (the height of the button)

- Leave the Hide Menu onMouseOut Event option checked by default.
- Click OK.

The menu has been configured to be as wide as all three buttons. It aligns directly below all the buttons and the text is left-aligned. The width you set, 298px, is 2px narrower than the sum of all three buttons to accommodate the 1px border around the menu table. This keeps the menu lined up correctly with the buttons.

9 Create the How Do I? menu pop-up using the values given and matching the example shown. Refer to the steps for the first button if you get stuck.

- Select the How Do I? button and add the Pop-Up Menu behavior.

Note: The positioning values are determined by the size of the buttons. For this project, you have three 100px buttons for a total of 300px. The width of the menu is set at 298 to compensate for the 1px border on each side. The -99 value for the second button is derived from the fact that it is 100px from the edge, minus the 1px border. The third button is 200px from the left edge minus a 1px border.

Note: When you click the second button from the left, the proper location of the button should be listed. If it doesn't match the numbers given previously, change them to the ones supplied.

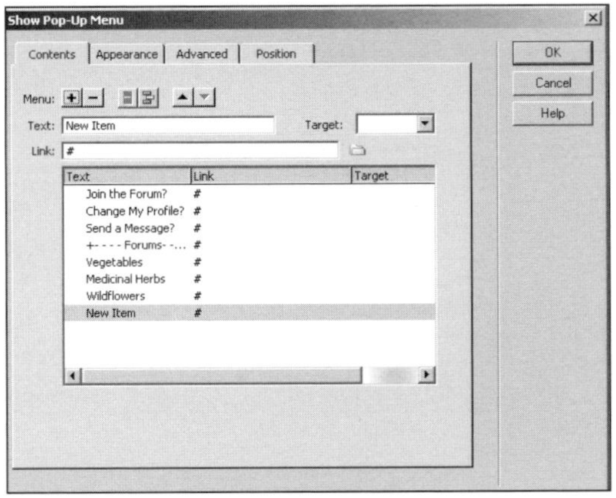

The menu items added for the HOW DO I? button.

- Add the following content with null links:

  Join the Forum?

  Change My Profile?

  Send a Message?

  +- - - - Forums- - - - + (Use the plus (+) sign and the dash key for the surrounding effect.)

  Vegetables

  Medicinal Herbs

  Wildflowers

Note: This particular menu setup doesn't support a flyout level 3 menu because it is right-aligned.

- Set the Appearance options to match the Shop button, but center align the text.

  It may appear that your most-recently used settings are already set, but be careful—only some are. The Width, Shadow, and Highlight have not been entered.

- Set the Advanced options to match the Shop button. Set the Positioning values as follows:

  X:**-99** (to line up with the Shop button)

  Y:**25** (the height of the button)

  The menu will align along the left edge of the Shop button and extend to the right edge of the About button.

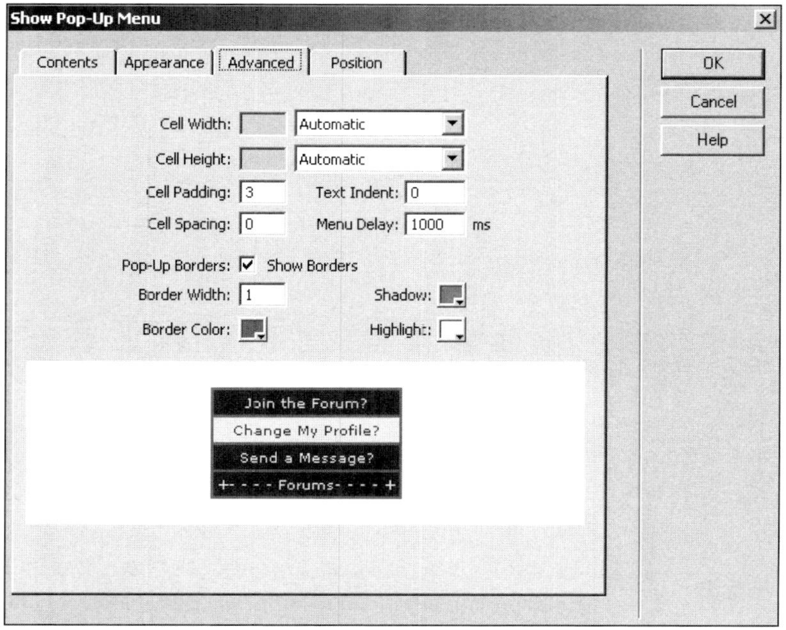

The text is now centered on this menu.

10 Create the last menu for the About button.

- Add the following content with null links:

  Mary's Garden

  Our Policies

  Contact Us

  What's New?

- Set the Appearance.
- Match the other buttons, but make this menu Align: Right.
- Skip to Positioning and set these values:

  X:**-199**

  Y:**25**

11 Click OK and save the document. Preview the file in your target browsers.

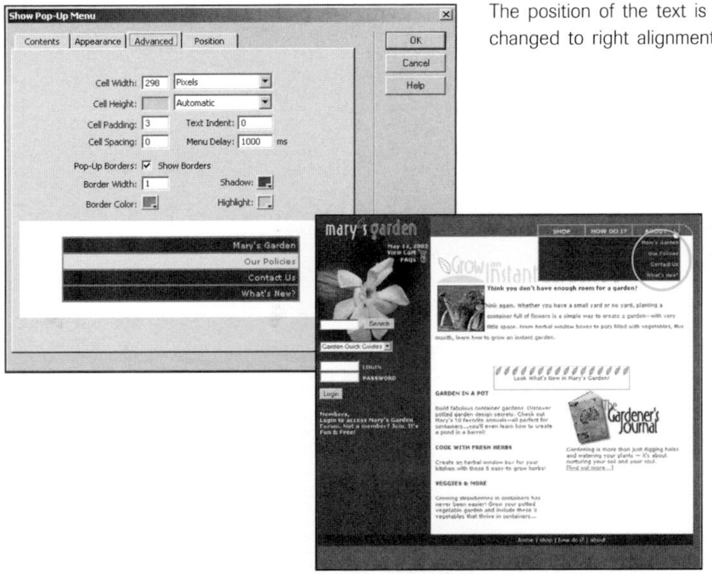

The position of the text is changed to right alignment.

Editing the Show Pop-Up Menu Behavior

Editing a menu is as easy as clicking a button! Just select the trigger button or link, go to the Behaviors panel, and double-click the Show Pop-Up Menu behavior. Don't add another behavior—just edit the existing one.

The mm_menu.js file serves the entire site. When you create additional menus in other pages, regardless of folder/page relationships, the code for the menu is stored in the mm_menu.js file. The only exception is the specific array information, such as the menu labels, links, and other settings particular to each menu. These are contained in the head of the page and in the HREF of the triggering button or link.

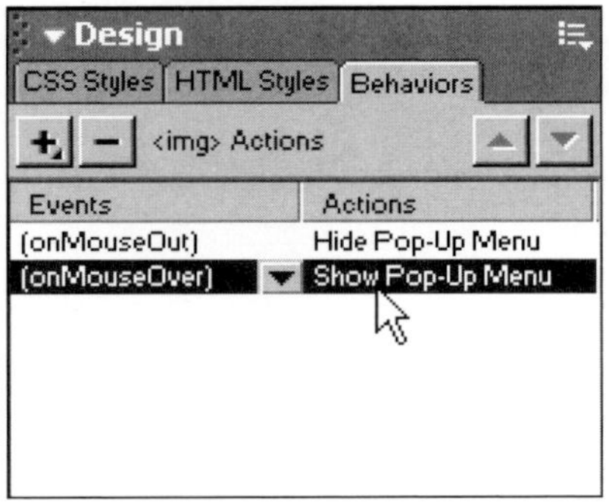

The Behaviors panel shows the added behaviors and the Show Pop-Up Menu behavior that you double-click to edit the menu.

Adding a Dynamic Date Script

Just for fun, we thought we'd give you our tried-and-trusted dynamic date script—the one we wrote on January 1, 2000, of course! (Remember Y2K?) This is an external file that you can easily place into your pages using the Insert button in the Assets panel. The script is set to use a custom CSS class named .date, so don't forget to add a style of that name to your stylesheets in your own web site's pages if you use this date script. (For the purpose of this project, the stylesheets include a specified .date class).

1 Set the location for the Date script.

- Choose Window>Others>Layers to call up the Layers panel.
- Select lyrSidebar.
- Place your cursor in the space above the View Cart icon.

2 Open the Assets panel and Insert the datescript.js file.

- Press F11 to call up the Assets panel.
- Click the Script icon.
- Highlight datescript.js.
- Click the Insert button.

The date will not display within Dreamweaver, but it will show up when you preview. You can see an Invisibles icon if you enable that feature, save the document, and preview in a browser.

You can edit the script if you understand JavaScript. We suggest you make a backup copy first, of course!

To edit the script, simply highlight it in Assets/Scripts and click the Edit Asset button.

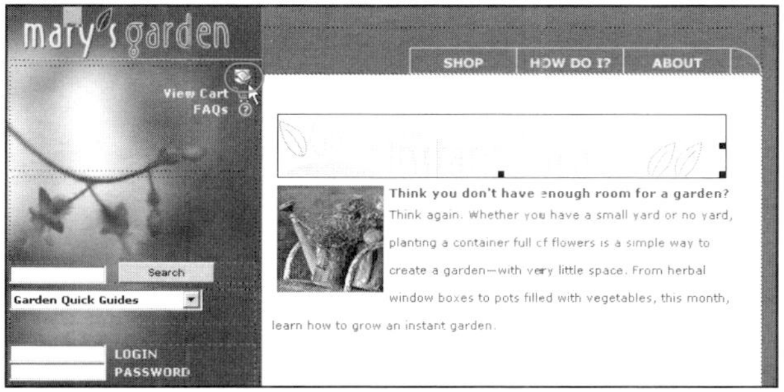

The anchor for the datescript.

The datescript as it appears in Internet Explorer 5.5.

Adding the Inline Random Image Script

This script is a fun way to jazz up your designs and show more images with less time loading. The script doesn't preload any images and you can have as many different images as you'd like.

This script is designed to set the image src randomly. This is done by using JavaScript to round off a random number between the value of 1 and the total number of images in your folder. You have to set the script to use the graphic's document reference name (value) and tell the script the path to the folder of similar images. Each image is named the same, except that a number is appended just before the file format extension. You also tell the script how many images are in the folder.

The main limitation to this script is that it is custom, which means that Dreamweaver will not update the script from a template or when you move a page about. Keep that in mind if you find that your images don't show up. Let's give it a shot.

This is a representation of the flower images used with the random image script.

1 Find the correct location for the script.

- Open the Layers panel and select lyrFlower.
- Select the flower image.
- Give the image a reference name using the Property inspector. Name it **sidepic**.
- Press the right-arrow key to move past the image code.

2 Get the code into Clipboard memory.

- From the Scripts folder in your site files, select and open Random.txt.
- Copy the code and close the text document.

Warning: This script *must* appear after the referenced image to work in all browsers. If you build your image in a layer, place the script after the image in that layer. If you build the script in a table cell, place the script after the image in the cell.

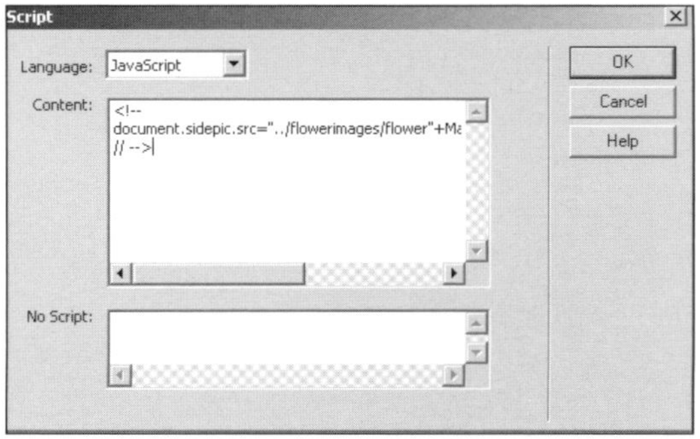

The Random.txt is pasted into the Script dialog box.

3 Add the code to the page.

- Choose Insert>Script Objects>Script.
- Select JavaScript from the Script Type menu in the Script dialog.
- Paste the code and click OK.

4 Edit the Dreamweaver code.

5 Save your page and preview it in your browser. Refresh several times to see the script in action.

```
<script language="JavaScript" type="text/JavaScript">
<!--
```

The highlighted type to be deleted.

Editing this Script for Your Designs

This is an easy-to-modify script. Just replace key parts of the script with information appropriate to your design. Here are the things you might need to modify:

```
<script language="JavaScript"
type="text/javascript">
<!--
document.sidepic.src="flowerimages/flower"+Math.
round(Math.random()*6+.5)+".jpg";
//-->
</script>
```

You might need to change the image reference name, as in document.imagename.src. The reference name tells the browser which page element to use. This example uses the name sidepic. You can use any name that follows the typical conventions required by JavaScript.

You also might change the folder to image path, as in flowerimages/flower. This path is minus the file format extension because that is added at the end of the appended image number.

The script function is another item you may change. Basically, this script rounds off a randomly chosen number by multiplying 1 times the number of images in the folder (a value you set) and then adding the value .5 to force the need for rounding.

The file format extension is another item you may change. Obviously, this is a value you supply based on your image type. All images must use the same value.

Some other tidbits of information about this script: All images must be the same width and height if you supply that value in the HTML code. When numbering your images, start by appending the file's name with 1. If you like the image set in the HTML code, duplicate it as one of the numbered images or you won't see it, or set the HTML src to one of the numbered images in the first place.

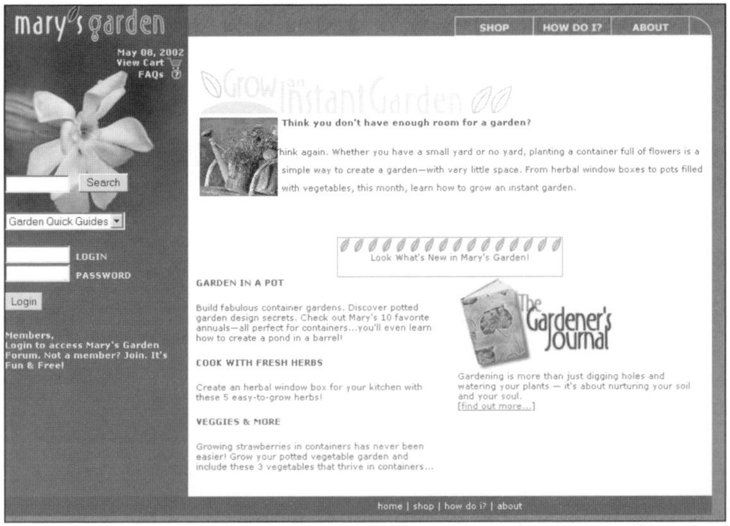

A different flower is displayed when the browser is refreshed or when the site is accessed another time.

Modifications

Try building a completely different pop-up menu or even creating your own buttons to replace the ones in this project.

Of course, you can use this layout with any imagery, so find some images and build your own set of randomly changing graphics. The flower images used here were developed in Fireworks, of course, and you can find them in the design files for this project. Vector masking was used to blend the edges of the image into the background color of the table cell.

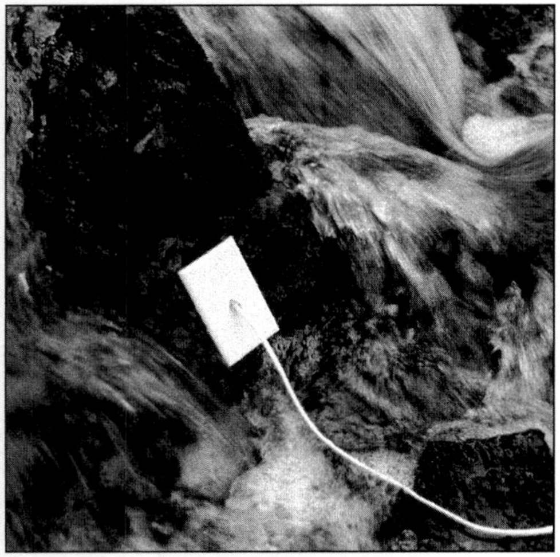

"Love is just a word until someone you meet gives it a proper meaning."

—UNKNOWN

CONTENT MANAGEMENT SYSTEM

Dynamic Updating with a Content Management System

Ever wonder how those web sites you visit for current news and happenings manage to update so quickly? That is exactly what you will be achieving at the end of this project. This project shows you how to create an effective content management system, which you can use to single-handedly create, update, and maintain a very dynamic site. You do all this using the immense capabilities Macromedia has bundled into Dreamweaver MX and integrating it with some of the best database technologies available to us today.

Project 10

Content Management System

by Alwyn Joy and Shailesh K L

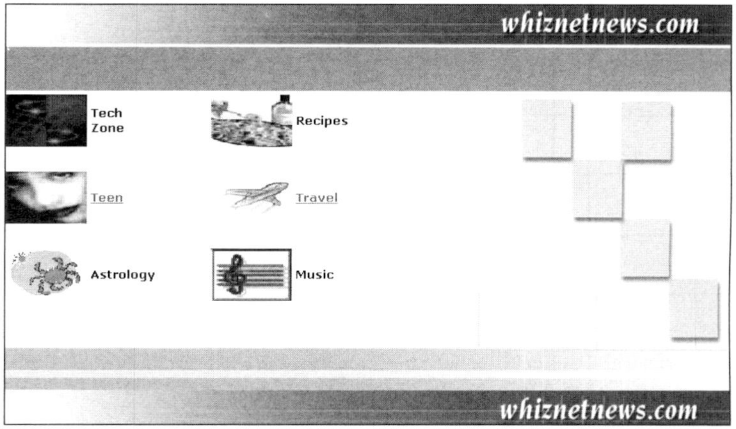

The Idea Behind a Content Management System

A content management system (CMS) primarily helps you separate the processes of designing and maintaining a site. Normally, as content on a web site is added, we keep making additional web pages. When you use a CMS, not only does it negate the need for additional pages for additional content, but it also helps you maintain the entire web site and its various elements from a central unit.

Following are some of the benefits of using a CMS:

- A CMS does not require the person in charge to know much about HTML or coding. The people who have access to the system have only to enter the content in the relevant fields and select the type of action they want to carry out using that content. The menu-driven system definitely is easier to understand when compared to achieving the same results by coding each individual page.
- A CMS reduces the need for creating and updating the different pages each time new content needs to be added.
- The appropriate use of templates can further improve content delivery. The same content can be delivered in a pre-customized format in different layouts to different users.

It Works Like This

This content management system uses Dreamweaver MX with technologies such as Microsoft's Active Server Pages (ASP) and a back-end Microsoft Access database. The concept here is to create a system in which the data stored in the backend can be delivered easily to the user's browser. In addition, by using the CMS, any user with the appropriate permission will be able to dynamically add, modify, and delete data from the backend in real-time, which means any data updated in the database would be visible to the end user immediately. This makes this type of system preferable for sites with rapidly changing content.

By the end of this chapter, you will create and understand the basic structure of the CMS, create user logins, and learn how to build pages that allow the user to add, modify, and delete data stored in the database. This may sound like a huge task, but this chapter has been divided into different sections that explain each of the core elements of a CMS. We have lots to do, so let's get straight into it.

PREPARING TO WORK

In addition to Dreamweaver MX, this project requires some understanding of Microsoft Access, ASP, and basic SQL commands. Although we have taken care to explain the important aspects at each step, there is one preliminary setup task that you are going to need to do. To make sure that you can follow along with the exercises, be sure that you have a web server installed that is capable of serving ASP pages, such as IIS or Personal Web Server. Once your web server software is installed and you are sure it is properly serving ASP pages, you're ready to go.

1 Begin by copying the entire chapter_10 folder from the Projects/10_cms folder on the accompanying CD to the root of your local web server. For example, if you are using Personal Web Server or IIS on Windows, copy the folder to C:\Inetpub\WWWRoot. For other web servers, you can make a virtual directory in your web server with the name CMS that will point to the folder chapter_10 you just copied.

2 Take a quick look at the folder you just copied to your web server root and you'll notice that there are two subfolders named workingfiles and Final Files. The working files are the files you will be using to complete each module. Each of these pages include the forms that will serve as the foundation for each module. The Final Files subfolder includes samples of what the pages should look like when each module is done, just in case you need to compare code.

Making a Site for the CMS

After configuring your system and copying the files, you need to define a Dreamweaver site that allows you to manage the CMS files.

1 Open Dreamweaver and click the Site sub-panel in the Files panel. Then click the Site menu and select New Site.

If you don't see the Site panel, you can also choose Site>New Site from the menu bar.

2 In the Site Definition dialog box, click the Advanced tab, and select Local Info in the Categories column on the left.

3 Type CMS as the Site Name and set the local root folder as the chapter_10 folder you copied into your local web server. If you are using IIS or PWS, the path would be C:\Inetpub\wwwroot\chapter_10\workingfiles.

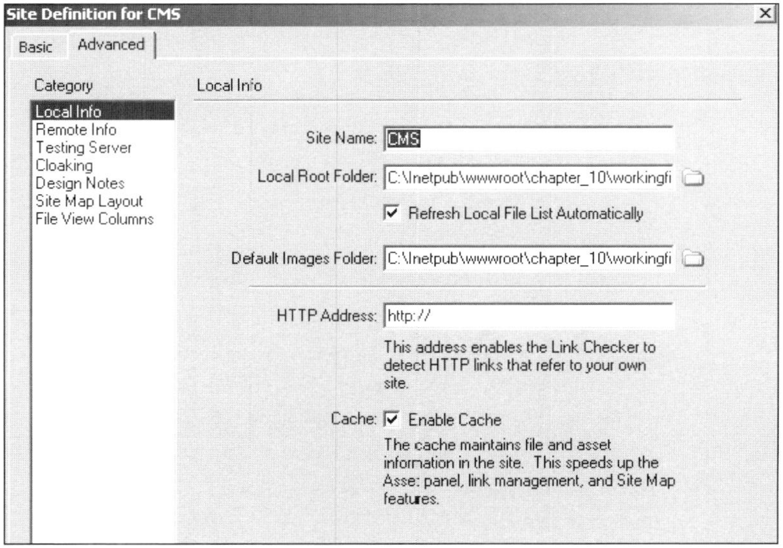

Use the Site Definition dialog box to configure the new site.

4 In the Default Images Folder field, enter the location of the images folder for your site: C:\Inetpub\wwwroot\chapter_10\workingfiles\10_images\.

5 For the HTTP address, type http://localhost/chapter_10/workingfiles.

6 In the Category panel, select Testing Server and choose ASP VBScript as your server model. In the Access drop-down list, select Local Network and notice that Dreamweaver MX automatically fills the rest of the related fields.

7 Click OK to complete the site setup. Notice that Dreamweaver MX creates the site and automatically maps the directory and sub–folder structure.

That's it. The site is defined and you are ready to proceed to the next stage: the database.

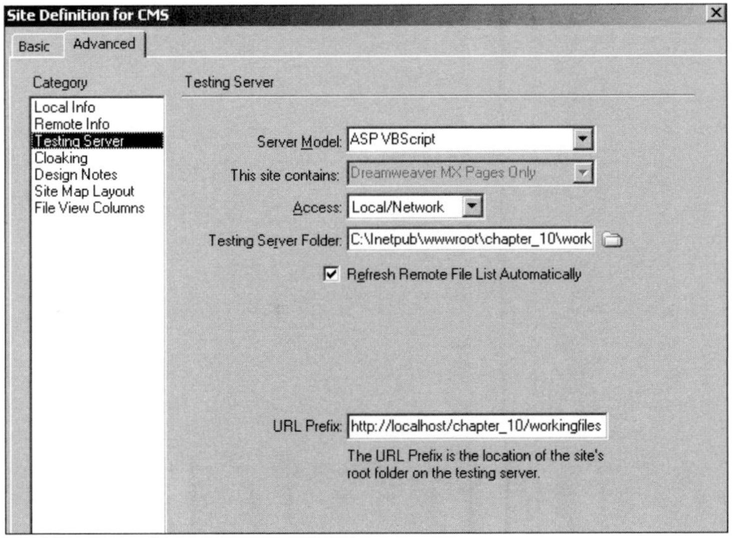

Configure the server model and select the testing server folders.

Understanding the Database

There's a wide variety of databases available today. The database you choose for your application depends on the needs of your web site, its functionality, and its requirements. Two of the most powerful databases are Microsoft SQL Server and Oracle, but their cost and complexity makes them unsuitable candidates for demonstration purposes. Instead, for this project we will use Microsoft Access, which is simple to use, readily available, and doesn't require the installation of any additional software.

1 Start Dreamweaver. Create a new page by clicking File>New. In the New Document window, click the General tab and select Dynamic Page from the Category list and ASP VBScript from the Dynamic Page list. Save the new file as 10_index1.asp in the 10_cmsmanage folder within workingfiles folder.

Note: You can find the 10_cms.mdb database for this project in the chapter_10/workingfiles/10_database folder that you copied to your web root. For those of you who have Microsoft Access and know how to use it, you can open the database and see the various tables and their fields. For those of you who do not have Access, you need not worry, because Dreamweaver MX allows you to make a live connection to the database and see all the different database elements without having to have Access installed. In the following steps, you learn how to do this.

2 In the Application panel, choose the Databases subpanel, which Dreamweaver uses to provide a direct connection to the database while you're building your application.

You also can display the Databases panel by choosing Window>Databases from the menu bar.

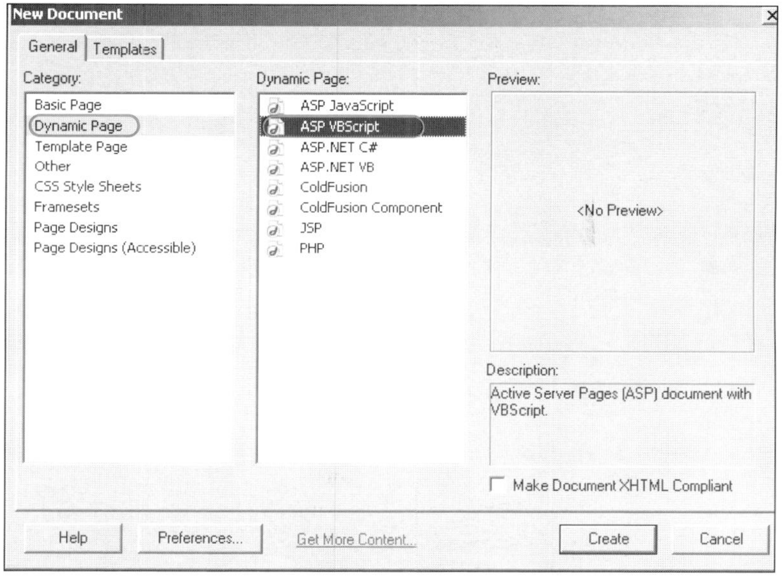

Create a dynamic page that uses ASP and VBScript.

3 In the Databases panel, click the plus (+) button and select Custom Connection String.

A connection string combines all the information your web application needs to connect to the database. Dreamweaver MX inserts this string into your page's server-side scripts for later processing by your application server.

4 In the Custom Connection String dialog box, type **dbconn** as the Connection Name.

This is name of the connection you would be using to establish a connection between the database and your page. Keep in mind that you can use any name for the connection name.

5 In the Connection String field, type **Provider=Microsoft.Jet.OLEDB.4.0; Data Source=C:\Inetpub\wwwroot\chapter_10\workingfiles\10_database\10_cms.mdb;**.

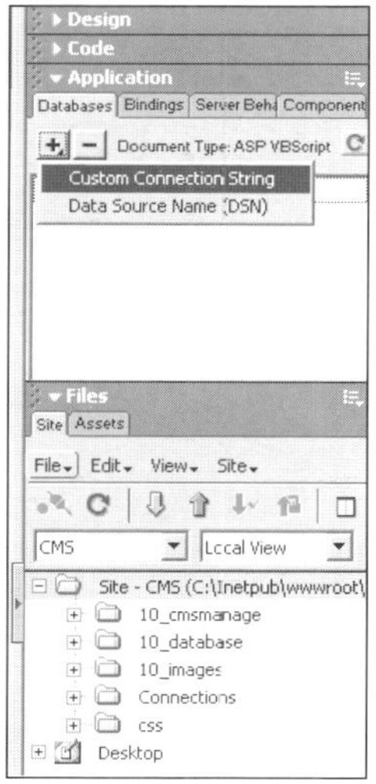

Build a custom connection string to connect to your database.

Note: Here's the breakdown of the code:

```
Provider=Microsoft.Jet.OLEDB.4.0
```

This indicates that the database being used is Microsoft Access, version 2000. The provider string changes depending on the version and type of database being used. For example, if the database was SQL, this string would be:

```
Provider=SQLOLEDB;
```

Or, if Oracle was the database:

```
Provider=OraOLEDB;
Data Source=C:\Inetpub\wwwroot\chapter_10\10_
➥database\10_cms.mdb;
```

Here we specify the exact location of the database; that is, 10_cms.mdb in the system. This will have to be adjusted according to the actual path where you have stored/extracted the files. If you have followed the instructions as provided in the initial steps, the above string should work perfectly.

6 Finally, choose to have Dreamweaver MX connect Using Driver on This Machine and click the Test button.

If you entered the correct connection string, you will get a message stating that the connection was established successfully. If you get an error, check to be sure that you typed the connection string exactly as shown. Note also that this connection string relies on the database being located in the C:\Inetpub\wwwroot\chapter_10\workingfiles\10_database\ directory. If your database is located elsewhere, you will need to make the adjustment.

7 Click OK to save your connection string.

8 If you open the Site window (choose Site>Site Files from the menu bar) and look in the workingfiles folder, you will notice a new folder named Connections. Dreamweaver MX created this folder to store the connection information used by the files in your Dreamweaver MX site. This folder should now contain a single file with the same name you gave to the connection earlier in the exercise.

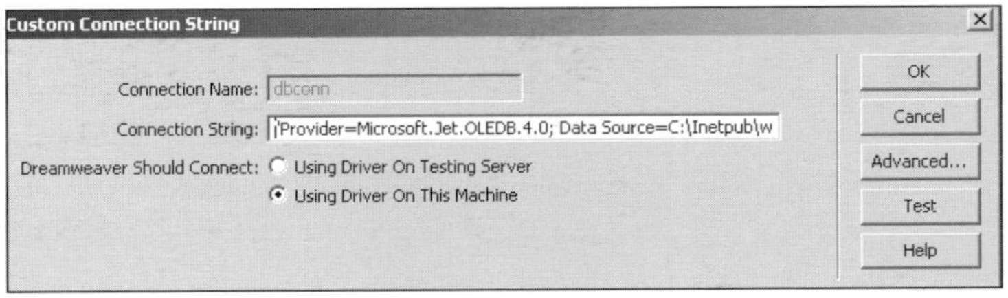

Set up your connection string using the correct syntax.

9 If you close the Site window and look at the Databases panel, you will now notice a new element called dbconn. In the Databases panel, click the plus (+) sign next to dbconn to expand the tree which will reveal various elements of the database.

The Role of the Database in the Content Management System

In a content management system, the database is the central location where all the information is stored. Because any information that the end user is going to see is derived from the database, it serves as the core for the entire system. Not only does the database provide an efficient way to store, edit, and retrieve the content data, it also eliminates the need for creating multiple pages for individual content.

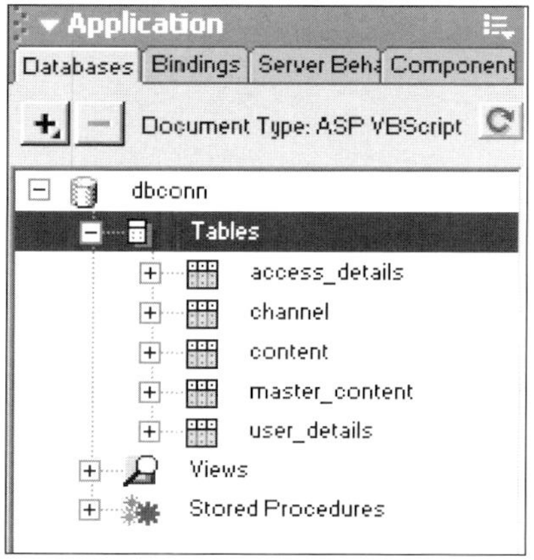

You can view the database components using the Databases panel.

For this project, we have created a database with five tables: access_detail, channel, content, master_content, and user_details. The figure to the right shows the database with its different tables.

Creating and naming the table forms are just the first steps. We need to create individual sub-elements within each table—namely, fields—to store the relevant data. We've already created the necessary tables and fields, but let's take a look at the individual components of each of the tables.

- **Channel Table.** The web site we are creating contains data designed for varied viewers; hence, it will have different topics to be covered such as teens, sports, horoscope, and so on. We have arranged these individual topics into "channels," which constitute the channel table.
- **Content Table.** As the name indicates, the content table is for storing the content for the various channels on the site.
- **Master_Content Table.** The master_content table is used for placing and organizing the content for searching and displaying the content to web site visitors.

Note: The database consists of elements called *tables.* A table can be defined as a collection of related data. For example, the content table contains a unique ID for each piece of content, the content itself, and the date the content was entered. Tables use the fields to organize each individual entry in the table, and these are called *records* (or sometimes, *rows*). To help you along, we have already entered some basic information in the database.

- **User_details Table.** This table is meant for the administrators of the site. Using this table, we can validate the different groups of users with relevant permission to log on to the management system and modify the contents of the database.
- **Access_details Table.** Closely related to the user_details table, the access_details table keeps track of the user(s) who is currently logged in to the system and the permissions he or she has on any channels.

Now you have used a specific set of fields for each table where the master_content table is related to the channel table by using the common field channel_id to identify which content belongs to which specific channel from the channel table. This is what is known as a *relational database*. As you develop your own web applications, you will need to determine what tables are necessary for your project and what relational structures are needed to form relationships between those tables.

Designing the Authentication Page

Usually, a content management administration console will require user authentication, because not everyone should have permission to access and modify the database. This section of the project takes you through the creation of the Management Login Console.

Using this console, the administrator or the persons with appropriate permissions can log into the system to make the required changes to the system. When I say *changes*, I mean adding new channels and/or new users, deleting users, adding content, and so on. For the sake of this project, however, we already have defined a user with relevant access permissions. The username is alwyn and has administrator rights, and the password is admin.

1 Close the 10_index1.asp page you created earlier and open the 10_index.asp page already present in the 10_cmsmanage folder of your site.

This page is similar to the page you just made, except that it already contains the form elements for the User Authentication page. The form has been named userauthenticate and the two text fields have been named uname and pwd, respectively. (We have skipped the step-by-step description of creating the elements because we are sure that you have done it a number of times already.)

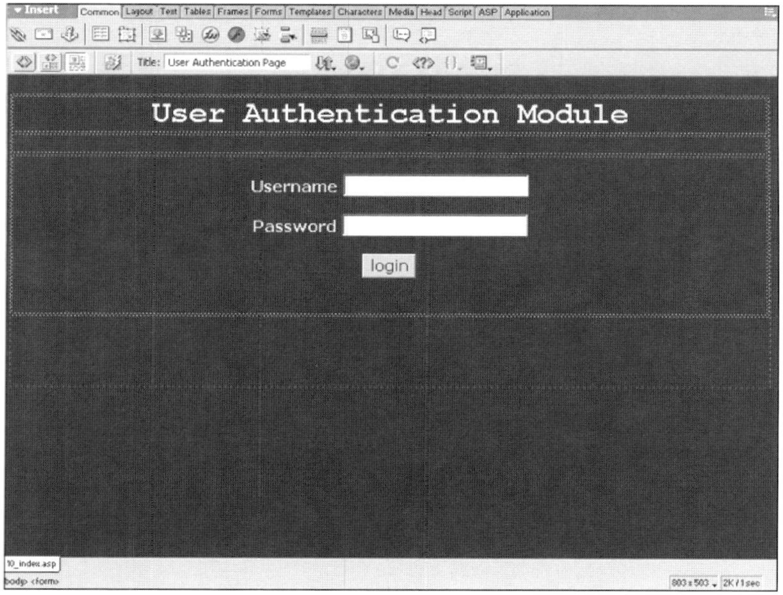

The index page is the beginning for your site.

2 Choose the Server Behaviors Panel and click the plus (+) sign. From the menu, select User Authentication>Log In User.

3 In the Log In User dialog box notice that the field for Get Input From Form is automatically set to userauthenticate, which is the name of the form included in your page. Remember that the Username and Password textfields in the form have been named as uname and pwd, so you need to select uname as the Username Field and pwd as the Password Field.

4 Now in the Validate Using Connection area, select dbconn as the connection method.

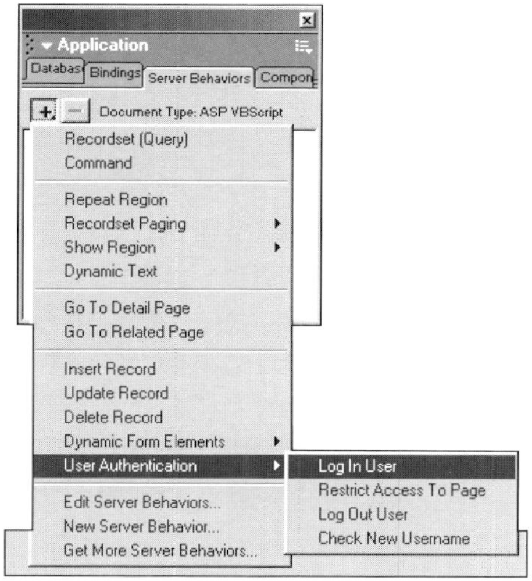

The Log In User server behavior allows you to authenticate visitors.

5 Select the following values for the rest of the fields:

Table: **user_details**

Username Column: **username**

Password Column: **upassword**

If Login succeeds, Go To: **10_adminmanage.asp**

If Login Fails, Go To: **10_index.asp**

Restrict Access Based On: **Username and password**

The 10_adminmanage.asp page is the default page the administrator is taken to once he or she successfully logs in. This page allows the administrator to manage the various elements of the system.

6 Click OK and your authentication page is ready in a jiffy. Hasn't Dreamweaver made it simple? Imagine hand-coding this much code!

7 Save and close the file in Dreamweaver and test the 10_index.asp file by opening your web browser and typing **http://localhost/chapter_10/workingfiles/10_cmsmanage/10_index.asp**. For testing purposes, enter the username **alwyn** and password **admin**. If you have followed the steps correctly, you will have a perfectly working module.

This finishes the login page for the CMS. For this project, we have already created a user who is the administrator and has complete unlimited access to the different components of the web site. Because the authentication is successful, the next step is to create the page that users will be taken to once they have logged on successfully. This happens to be the Administrator Management Module, which we will look at in detail in the following section.

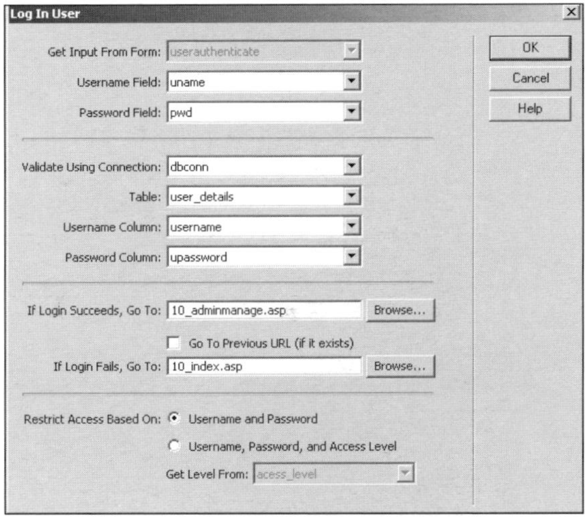

Set up the Log In User server behavior like this.

Warning: Sometimes when working with databases, Dreamweaver MX opens the database exclusively and does not allow any other program to access it at the same time. This could lead to problems if you are testing the page you created while Dreamweaver MX is open. This problem can be bypassed only by exiting Dreamweaver so that it releases the database for use. If you run into problems previewing your pages, try shutting down Dreamweaver MX and see whether that resolves the issue.

The Administrator Management Module

Once successful login has occurred, users should be automatically transferred to the administrator module, which allows them to manage the whole system.

To restrict unauthorized visitors from simply typing the direct URL to the administrator module, we can use Dreamweaver MX's Restrict Access To Page server behavior. This server behavior looks to see whether users have previously logged in and grants them access if they have. If not, users are redirected to a page that allows them to log in. This also keeps administrators from bookmarking the page. Let's see how we can achieve this for our project.

1 In Dreamweaver MX, open the 10_adminmanage.asp file located in the 10_cmsmanage subfolder of your site.

2 Choose the Application panel and go to the Server Behaviors sub-panel. Click the plus (+) sign and select User Authentication>Restrict Access To Page.

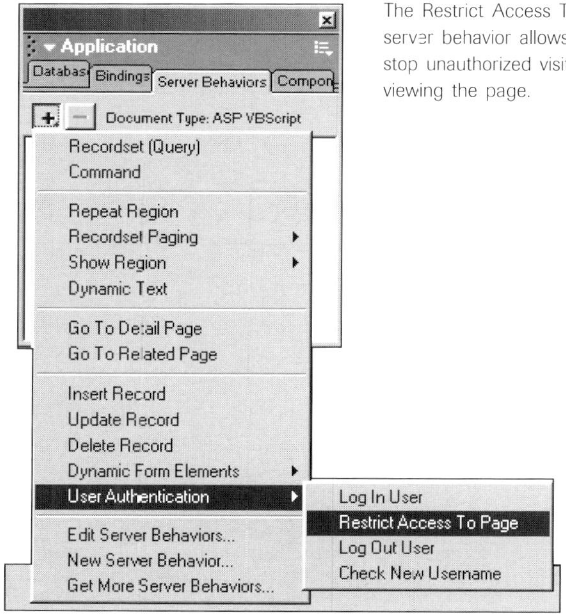

The Restrict Access To Page server behavior allows you to stop unauthorized visitors from viewing the page.

3 In the Restrict Access To Page dialog box, select the restrictions to be based on Username and Password, and select 10_index.asp as the page to display if the user is denied access. This gives the user the opportunity to log in.

4 Click OK and save the page.

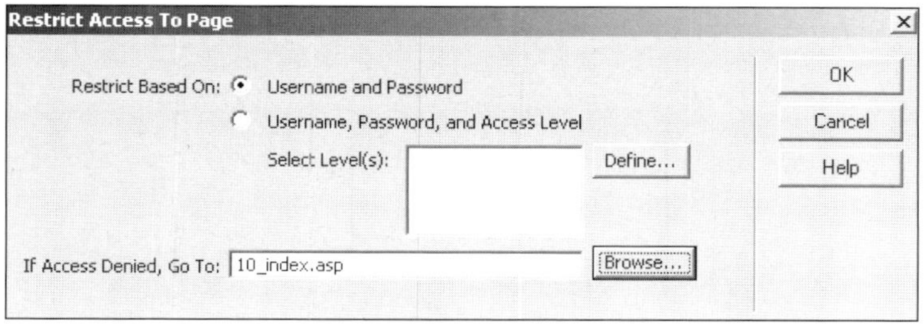

Configure the Restrict Access To Page server behavior like this.

5 To ensure that the server behavior is functioning, open your web browser and go to **http://localhost/chapter_10/workingfiles/10_cmsmanage/10_adminmanage.asp**.

If you have followed all the steps accurately, you are denied access to the 10_adminmanage.asp page and the server redirects you to the 10_index.asp page to log in.

6 Next you need to offer the user the opportunity to log out. In the 10_adminmanage.asp page, place your insertion point at the bottom of the page. On the Server Behaviors panel, click the plus (+) sign and select User Authentication>Log Out User.

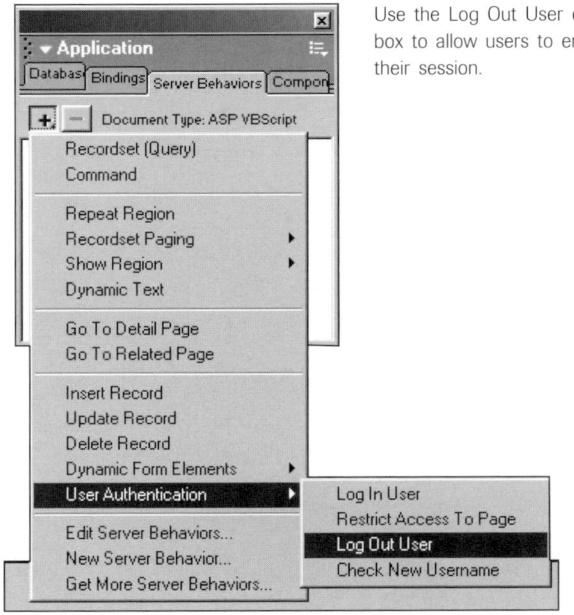

Use the Log Out User dialog box to allow users to end their session.

7 In the Log Out User dialog box, select the Link Clicked option for Log Out When and leave the Create New Link: "Log Out" as the selection in the selection box. You want Dreamweaver MX to build a new link called Log Out so that users have the option to log out when they want.

8 In the When Done, Go To field, type **10_index.asp** as the page where users are taken when they log out of the system. Click OK and notice that a Log Out link has been added to your page.

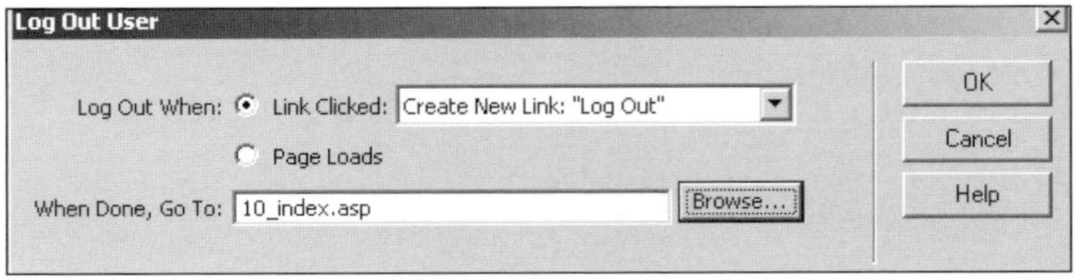

Configure the Log User Out server behavior like this.

9 This takes care of the unauthorized access situations for the 10_adminmanage. asp page. Similarly, you can incorporate access restrictions in the other files of this project. Save the page.

For the sake of this project, we have already incorporated three separate sections (Channel, Content, and User) into the database, and data has already been entered into the relevant sections. The Administrator Management Module provides the administrator with options to edit and modify data related to this field. In a real-life scenario, the number of such sections would be numerous—and so would the administrator's options for editing them. Because the basic functionality of updating and managing the database remains same, we will look at one such example, taking the channel section into consideration.

Designing the Channel Management Module: Retrieving Information from a Database

The Channel Management Module allows the administrator to create, modify, and delete channels present in the system. In this project, channels play the role of different sections on any web site—be it sports, current affairs, personals, and so on. We have already added a few channels to the table. Now we will use the CMS to add a fresh channel to the system and see whether the changes are reflected. This section will give you a clear understanding of how data is added, modified, and retrieved from the database using pure Dreamweaver MX elements and capabilities.

1 Log into your management module by opening your web browser and typing **http://localhost/chapter_10/workingfiles/10_cmsmanage/10_index.asp** as your URL. Login using the username **alwyn** and the password **admin**.

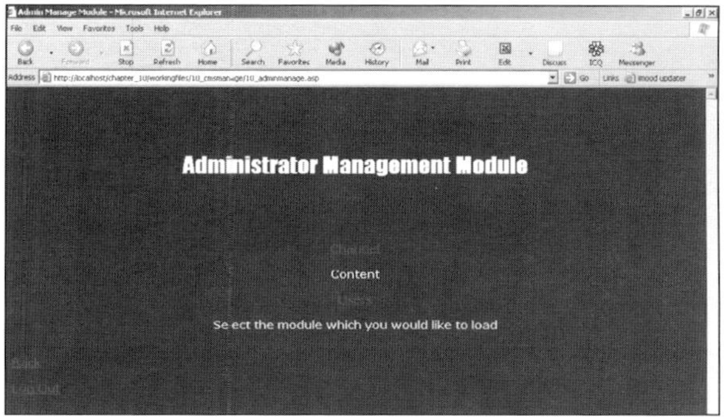

The Administrator Management Module allows authenticated users to manage the site content.

After you have logged in as the administrator, a page appears on the right; namely, the 10_adminmanage.asp page. This is the main page that allows authenticated users to manage the content shown on the site. One of the links on this page is the Channel link. The rest of this exercise shows you how to build the channel page to which this links.

2 Switch back to Dreamweaver MX and open the page named 10_channel.asp from the 10_cmsmanage folder.

3 Select the Bindings panel and click the plus (+) sign. From the menu, choose Recordset (Query).

4 In the field for the Recordset Name, type **showchn**. In the Connection drop-down list, select **dbconn**. Because this page is going to be used to view and edit contents of the channel table, set the Table field to **channel**.

5 For the Columns field, click the Selected radio button and choose channel_id, channel_name, and description. Leave the Filter set to None for this page, and in the Sort field, select channel_id to display the channels sorted by the channel_ids and in Ascending order.

The figure to the right shows you how the window should look with all the fields entered.

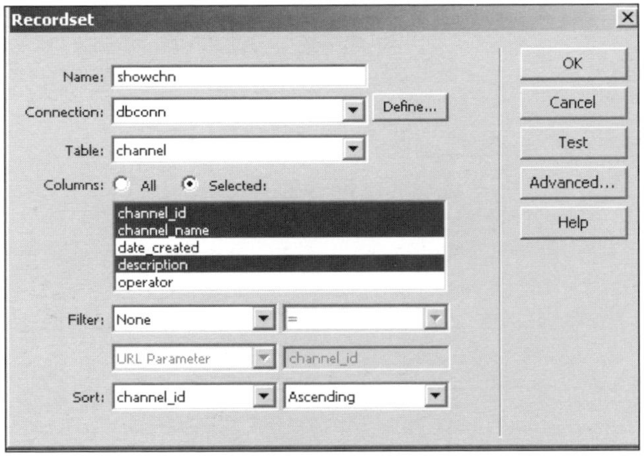

Create a Recordset that looks like this.

6 Click OK and the Recordset is created. The name you gave it is displayed in brackets in the Bindings panel.

The Recordset is used to retrieve data, but how do you display the data retrieved by the recordset in your page? To accomplish this, Dreamweaver MX provides the Dynamic Text server behavior, which helps you display database content on the page.

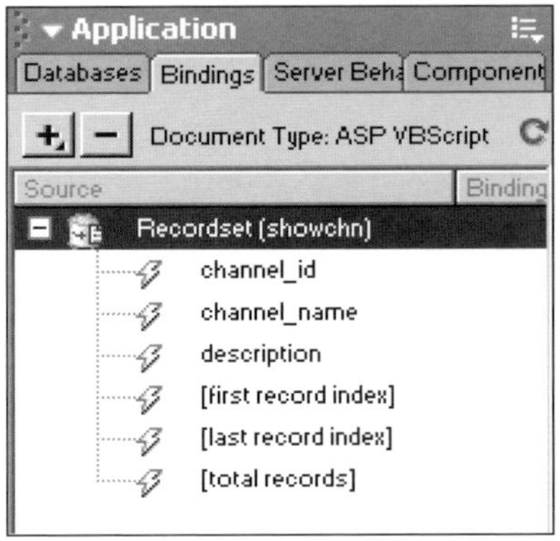

The Bindings panel displays the new Recordset.

7 Select the Server Behaviors panel and click the plus (+) sign. From the menu, select Dynamic Text.

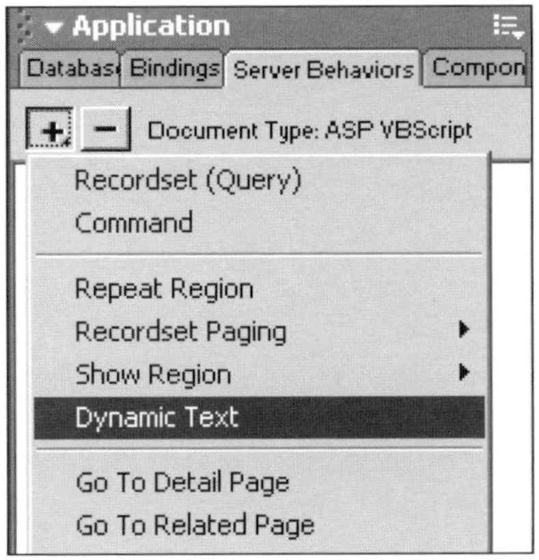

The Dynamic Text server behavior allows you to add database-driven text to our pages.

8 In the Dynamic Text dialog box, click the plus (+) sign to expand the Recordset. From here, select the channel_name field and click OK. Notice that Dreamweaver MX adds a dynamic text field to the page automatically.

9 Press the right-arrow key on your keyboard to move the insertion point to the right of the new dynamic text and then press the spacebar. This gives you some space between the dynamic elements.

10 Using the Dynamic Text server behavior, add the description field to your page.

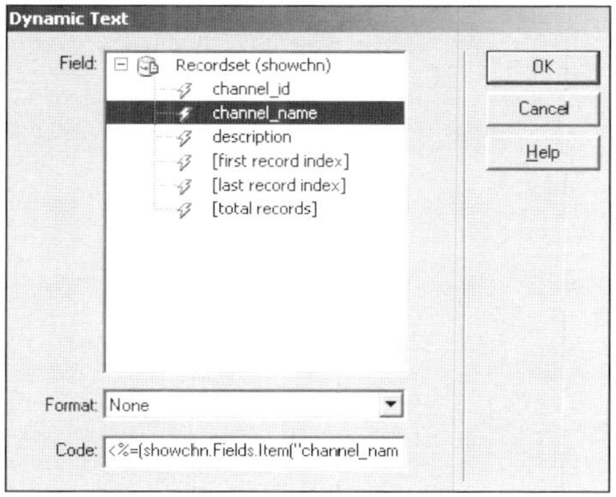

Add the Channel Name dynamic text to the page.

11 With the description dynamic text highlighted, click the plus (+) sign in the Server Behaviors panel and choose Go To Detail Page.

12 In the Go To Detail Page dialog box, notice that most of fields have been automatically selected. In the Detail Page field, select the 10_channeldet.asp page from the current folder Click OK. The link you just created takes the administrator to a page that displays the details of the particular channel.

13 Again, press the right-arrow key and the spacebar to separate the dynamic elements. Type the words **Modify This Channel** and then highlight the text.

14 Click the plus (+) sign on the Server Behaviors panel and select the Go To Detail Page server behavior.

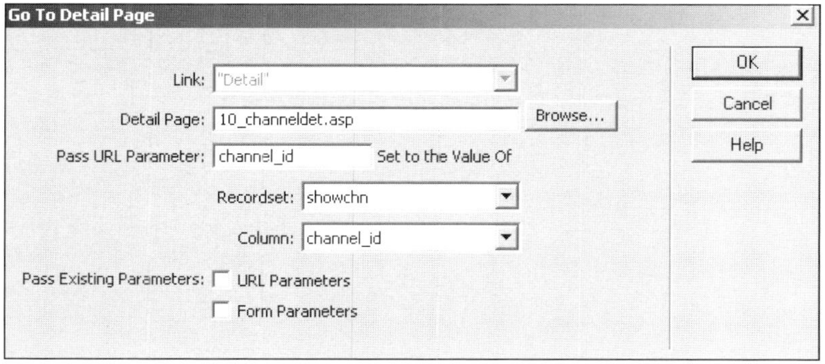

The Go To Detail Page server behavior allows you to build a dynamic link to a detail page.

15 In the Go To Detail Page dialog box, select the 10_modifychannel.asp page as the detail page. Leave all the other default values as they are and click OK. The link you just created takes administrators to a page that allows them to modify the details of a particular channel.

16 Once again, press the right-arrow key and the space-bar. Type the text **Delete This Channel** and then highlight it.

17 Click the plus (+) sign on the Server Behaviors panel and select Go To Detail Page. In the Go To Detail Page dialog box, choose 10_deletechannel.asp as the detail page and click OK. This link takes administrators to a page that allows them to delete a particular channel.

18 One last time, press the right-arrow key so that your insertion point is at the end of the line where you added the new elements. Press the Enter key. If you don't do this, the Repeat Region server behavior discussed next will not behave correctly.

The next step is to use the Repeat Region server behavior to display multiple records from a recordset within a page. Any dynamic data selection can be turned into a repeated region.

Note: Are you wondering why we didn't just create these links using the traditional method? Using the method described here makes life easier because it generates the links dynamically. The values of the particular channel link being clicked are generated and passed at run-time, meaning that you won't have to create the links for each and every channel.

19 Select the dynamic text (that is, channel_name and description) along with the three links you created (Detail, Modify This Channel, and Delete Channel). Click the plus plus (+) sign on the Server Behaviors panel and choose Repeat Region from the menu.

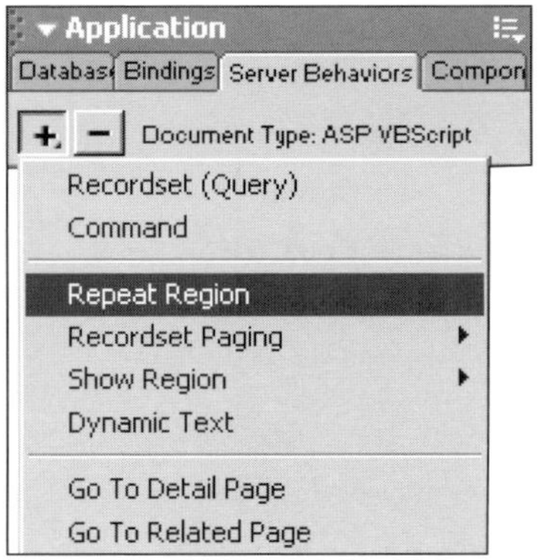

Use the Repeat Region server behavior to display all the data stored in the recordset.

20 In the Repeat Region dialog box, choose the showchn recordset and choose to display all the records. We are selecting all records because we have very few records in the database. In a real-world scenario, you should select 10 or 15 records at the max so that you don't tie up the server.

21 Click OK and you will see that the entire segment has now been marked with a Repeat Region indicator.

22 Save the page. In your browser, test the page by clicking the Channel link in the Administrator Management Module page. After you click the link, you should be able to view the Channel Management Module and see the various channels in the database. In addition, you now have links to view the channel detail, edit the channel, and delete the channel. Notice that the Repeat Region server behavior is showing all the channels in the datbase.

In the Channel Management Module, do you see an additional link called Add Channel that is just a plain hyperlink? This link takes you to a new page called 10_addchannel.asp where you can add new channels to the database. You will be looking at this later in the chapter, but take note that the link exists.

Next you go on to create the Detail Page, which is the first dynamic link you created on this page. The Details page allows you to see all the relevant information about a specific record.

23 In Dreamweaver MX, open the 10_channeldet.asp page. Notice that only a back button appears at the bottom, which will take you back to the previous page.

Choose the Bindings panel and click the plus (+) sign and select Recordset (Query). This is a different type of recordset than the ones you created previously because you have to obtain information from two different tables instead of one.

Name the recordset **channeldet**, the Connection **dbconn**, the Table source **channel**, and the check the Selected option because you want only the channel_name, date_created, and description fields from the channel table to be displayed. We will use the Filter feature to distinguish and retrieve information about only the specific channel referred to in the previous page and not all the channels at once. This is done by selecting the fields as shown here:

Channel_id: **=**

URL Parameter: **channel_id**

Here you are telling the recordset to retrieve information for only that channel whose channel_id has been specified in the URL from the previous page. After this is done, click the Advanced button.

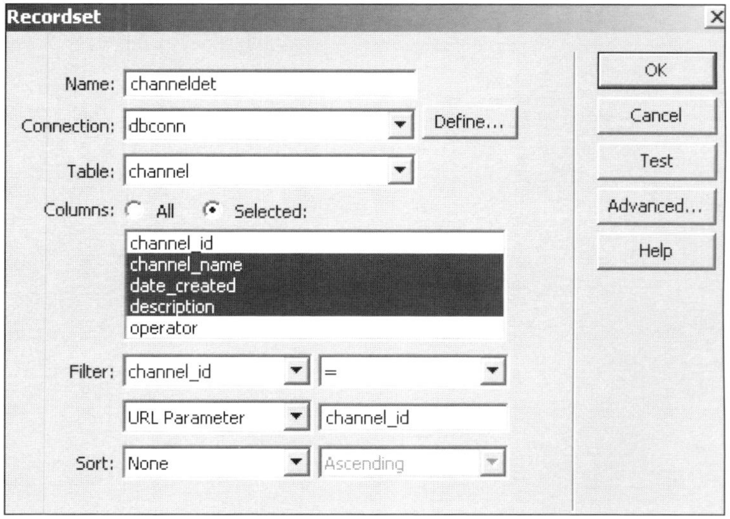

Configure your new recordset to look like this.

24 Once you are working in Advanced mode, go to the Database Items section at the bottom of the window and click the plus (+) sign to the left of Tables. Then repeat the same for user_details to view the different fields of that table. Now select the username field from the list and click Select under Add to SQL. You select username from the user_details table because you want to display the name of the user who is in charge of a specific channel and not just his user_id.

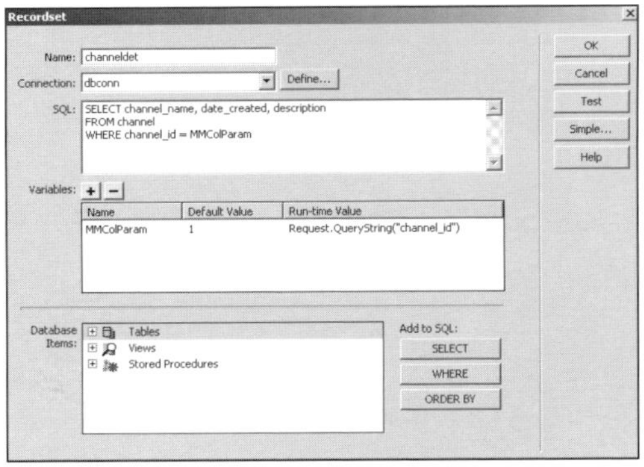

Use the advanced recordset view to add custom SQL statements to your recordset.

25 To get the proper username from the user_details table, you need to check the user_id against something. This is done by comparing the user_id with the operator details present in the channel table. To do this, click the plus (+) sign on the left of channel table and select operator from the list. Then click the Where button. Now go to the SQL section and enter = to the right of operator. The code in the SQL section should look like the code you see here.

```
SELECT channel_name, date_created, description, username
FROM channel, user_details
WHERE channel_id = MMColParam AND operator=
```

26 Now, click the plus sign next to the user_details table below and select user_id from the list. Then click the Where button to compare operator with user_id, and your code should look like the code to the right.

```
SELECT channel_name, date_created, description, username
FROM channel, user_details
WHERE channel_id = MMColParam AND operator=user_id
```

27 You are almost finished except for one part. Both the channel and user_details tables contain a common field called date_created, which can lead to an error because when the script executes, it won't know where to get the info. Should the details come from channel or user_details? To solve this, you will specify in the query itself that you want to get the date_created info from the channel table by entering channel.date_created in place of date_created. Your code should look like the code to the right.

```
SELECT channel_name, channel.date_created, description, username
FROM channel, user_details
WHERE channel_id = MMColParam AND operator= user_id
```

28 Now click the Test button, and if you have followed everything correctly, you will get the details of the first channel (that is, Teen). Click OK to close the Test and click OK to save your recordset.

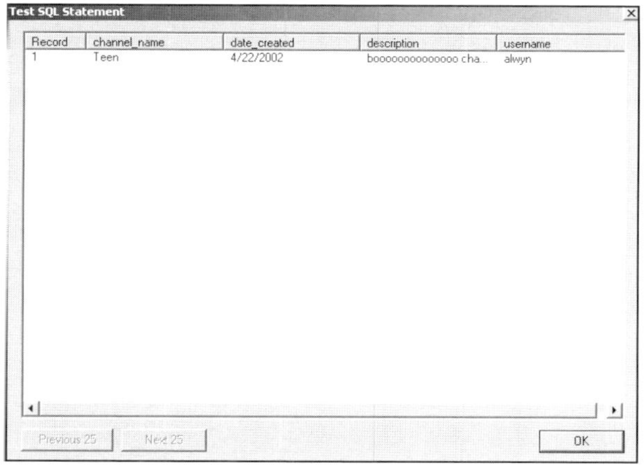

The results of testing our custom SQL statement.

29 Next you need to display the contents of the recordset in your page. What better way is there to display dynamic data than using the Dynamic Text option? You know where to find this option because you worked through this in the previous module. In the Dynamic Text dialog box, select channel_name, date_created, description, and username, one after the other.

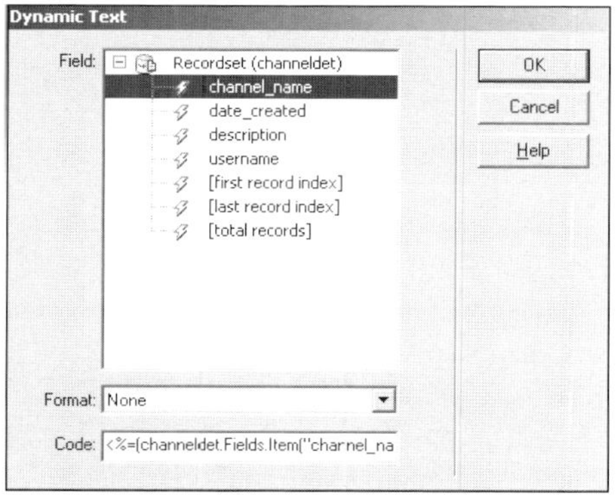

Add the dynamic text to your page.

30 You then will notice that all the fields are displayed in the Server Behaviors panel. Now you can save the file and test it in your browser.

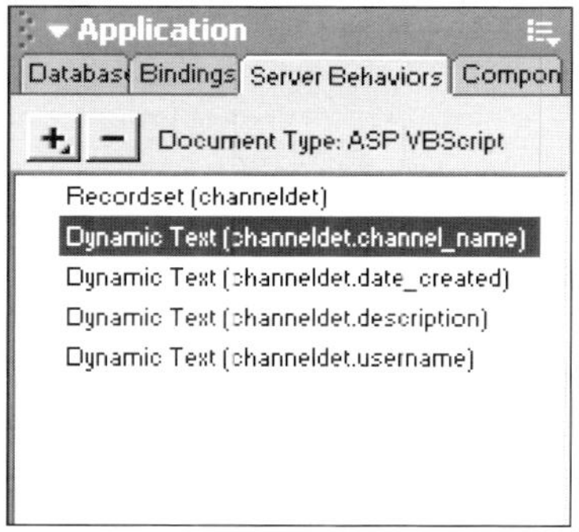

The Server Behaviors panel displays the dynamic text placeholders currently added to the page.

If you have followed each step correctly, your page should look similar to the 10_channeldet.asp file in the Final Files folder. The look is different once again, but because of the formatting done in the regular manner, the details and functionality remain the same.

Well, that brings us to the end of this section. And by now you have learned how to retrieve and display data from the tables, single or multiple, in a database.

Designing the Channel Management Module: Updating Information in a Database

This section deals with changing the existing content of a database. If you click Modify This Channel in the Channel Management Module, you are taken to a page that lets you modify the contents of a particular channel. So what are you waiting for? Read on.

1 In Dreamweaver MX, open the file named 10_modifychannel.asp from the working files folder.

2 Next, select the Bindings panel and create a new recordset. In the Recordset dialog box, go to Simple view and name the recordset showchannelinfo, set the Connection to dbconn, the Table as channel, Columns as All, and the Filter as follows:

Channel_id: =

URL Parameter: **channel_id**

Leave Sort as None. Click OK and the recordset is created and displayed in the Bindings panel.

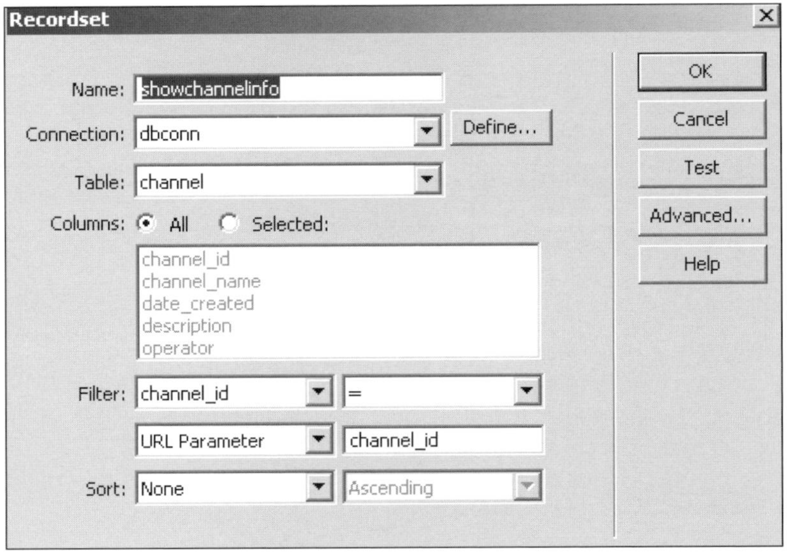

Build a reccrdset that filters by channel_id.

3 Create an additional recordset and enter the name for the recordset as listuser, the Connection as dbconn, the Table as user_details, and then check the Selected radio button because you only want user_id and username fields from the user_details table to be displayed. Select the user_id to be sorted in Ascending order. Click OK and the recordset is created and displayed in the Bindings panel.

On this page, you are using two recordsets because you have an option called Channel Operator on the page which can be modified to change the operator responsible for the particular channel. Because this data corresponds to the user_details table of the database, you use two recordsets to achieve the goal of modification.

4 Now select the text box beside the Channel Name on the page. In the Property inspector, notice that an Init Val slot and an icon like a lightning bolt appear. Click it. You will see the Dynamic Data dialog box similar to the one you saw in the previous section. Click the plus (+) sign next to the showchannelinfo recordset and select the channel name.

5 Click OK and you will see that the dynamic binding is applied to the text field. Follow the same steps for the description box, but be sure to select description as the source field for the text field.

6 The Operator drop-down list is slightly different. Select the drop-down form element and click the Dynamic button on the Property inspector. In this case, select listuser for the Options from Recordset field, which happens to be the name of the recordset created earlier. Select user_id for Values and username for the Labels, and once again click the lightning bolt icon next to Select Value Equal To at the bottom of this window. From the pop-up window that opens, select operator under the showchannelinfo recordset. Click OK to close the Dynamic Data dialog box.

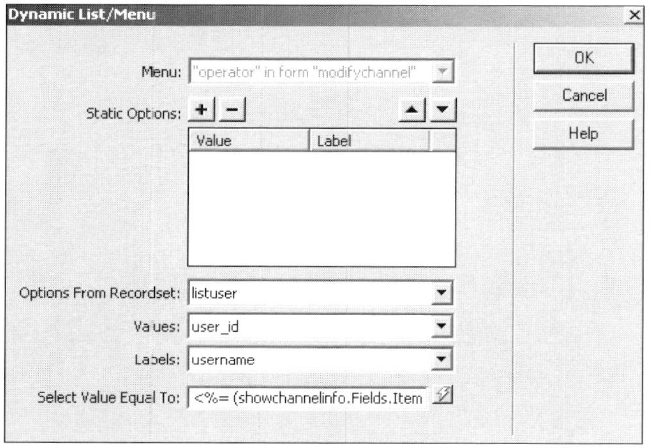

The Dynamic List/Menu dialog box allows you to build database-driven lists and menus.

7 Click OK again to close the Dynamic List/Menu dialog box.

8 Click the plus (+) sign on the Server Behaviors panel and select Update Record. In the Update Record dialog box, select the values as shown here:

Connection: **dbconn**

Table to Update: **Channel**

Select Record From: **showchannelinfo**

Unique Key Column: **channel_id**

After Updating Go To: **10_channel.asp**

Get Values From: **modifychannel**

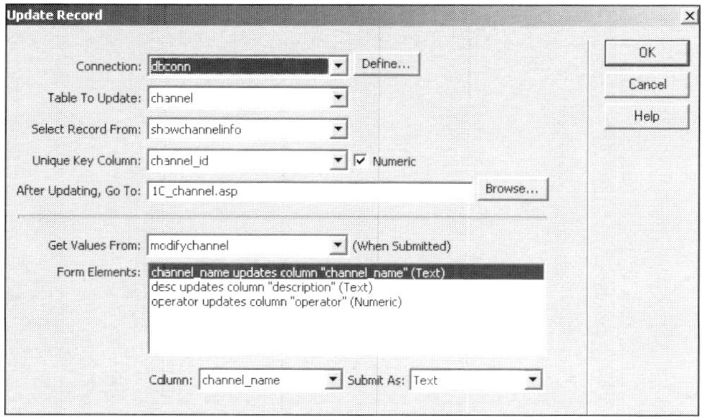

The Update Record server behavior allows you to add forms to your pages that enable you to edit the data stored in the database.

9 Click OK to close the Update Record dialog box and save the page.

You can now test this page by switching to your browser and clicking the Modify Channel link in the Channel Management Module. For each channel in the database, you should be able to update the information. That's it—you will notice that everything is working perfectly and the changes you made are updated in the database. You are taken back to the 10_channel.asp page, which you created earlier, and the changes are reflected immediately as they should be.

As this section comes to an end, you now know how existing content in any database can be modified using pure Dreamweaver MX capabilities. And have you stopped yet to think that you have written hardly one line of code?

Warning: When testing the update module, you might encounter an error that says the operation must use an updateable query. This is caused by incorrect privileges on your database when using Windows NT, 2000, or XP. If you are faced with this error, use Windows Explorer to browse to the folder where your database is located and make sure that your InetUSR account has read/write privileges to everything in that folder. For more details, check out the technote at http://www.macromedia.com/support/ultradev/ts/documents/80004005update.htm.

Designing the Channel Management Module: Deleting Information from a Database

Now that you know how to modify the data that is stored in the database, it would probably be a good idea to build a page that allows you to remove unwanted data. As with the modification page, you can easily accomplish this task using Dreamweaver MX server behaviors.

1 Open the file 10_deletechannel.asp from the working files folder in Dreamweaver MX.

2 You then will see that a form named deletechannel has been created and contains a button called Yes, which is used to submit the request to delete the selected channel.

3 Now let's go into the Bindings panel and build a new recordset. In the Recordset dialog box, enter the name for the recordset as delchannel, set the Connection as dbconn, the Table as channel, Columns as All, and the Filter set as follows:

Channel_id: **=**

URL Parameter: **channel_id**

Leave Sort as None. Click OK and the recordset is created and displayed in the Bindings panel.

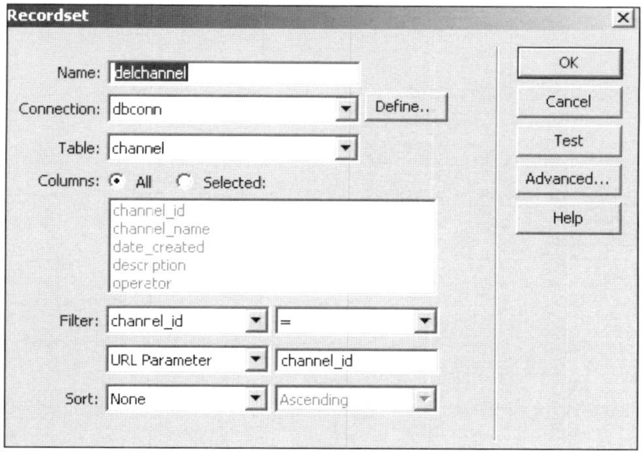

Build a new recordset to use with the Delete Record server behavior.

4 Select the Server Behaviors panel and click the plus (+) sign. From the menu, choose Delete Record. In the Delete Record dialog box, set the values as shown here:

Connection: **dbconn**

Delete from Table: **Channel**

Select Record From: **delchannel**

Unique Key Column: **channel_id**

Delete By Submitting: **deletechannel**

After Deleting Go To: **10_channel.asp**

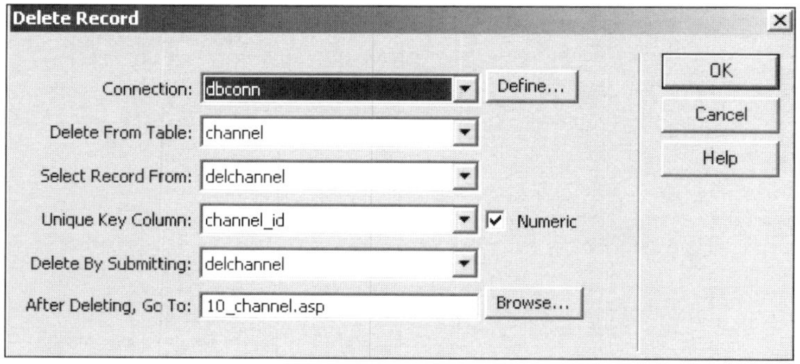

The Delete Record server behavior allows you to remove data from the database.

5 Click OK to close the Delete Record dialog box and the server behavior is added to the Server Behaviors panel.

6 Finally save the page and test it by switching to your browser and clicking the Delete Channel link for any channel in the Channel Management Module.

That's it—the module is working perfectly and the channel you had selected has been deleted from the database. You are taken back to the 10_channel.asp page.

DESIGNING THE CHANNEL MANAGEMENT MODULE: INSERTING INFORMATION INTO A DATABASE

Now that you know how to edit and delete data stored in the database, the last step is to create a page that allows you to add brand new data. In this section, you create a page that adds a brand new channel to the database. Using similar steps, you can experiment with adding other elements such as new users, new content, and so on.

1 Open 10_addchannel.asp in Dreamweaver MX, which you can find in the working files folder under chapter_10.

We already have created the form for you. The form has been named addchannel.

There are two text boxes named channel_name and desc. It also has a list menu named operator. When using a database as a content source for a dynamic web page, you must first create a recordset in which to store the retrieved data. This is exactly what you will be doing here.

2 Select the Bindings panel and click the plus (+) sign and select Recordset (Query) from the menu.

3 In the Recordset dialog box, type **listuser** as the name for the new recordset. Next in the Connection, select the connection name, which is dbconn. This is the same connection to the database which you created in the initial steps of this chapter. Set the Table field to user_details. For the columns field, click the selected radio button and choose user_id and username. The Filter remains sets to None for this page, and in the Sort field, select user_id in Ascending order.

4 Click OK to save the recordset and you will notice that a new entry for your recordset has been added to the Bindings panel.

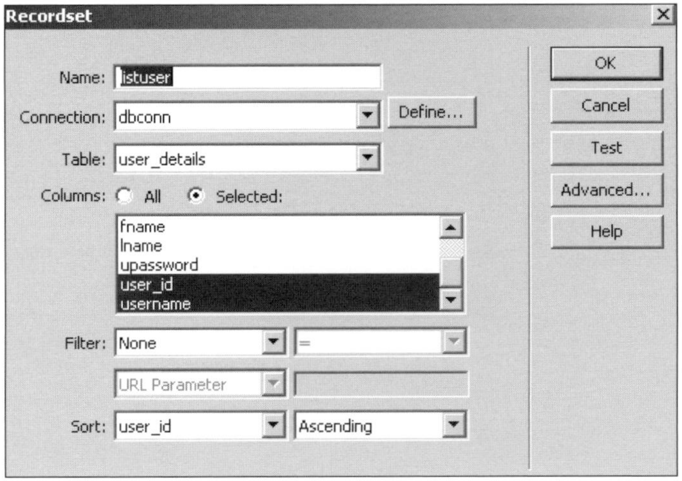

Add a recordset to the page that looks like this.

5 Select the Operator drop-down list from the form and in the Property inspector, click the lightning bolt icon dynamic button. In the Dynamic List/Menu dialog box, select listuser for the Options From Recordset. Select user_id for Values and username for Labels. Click OK.

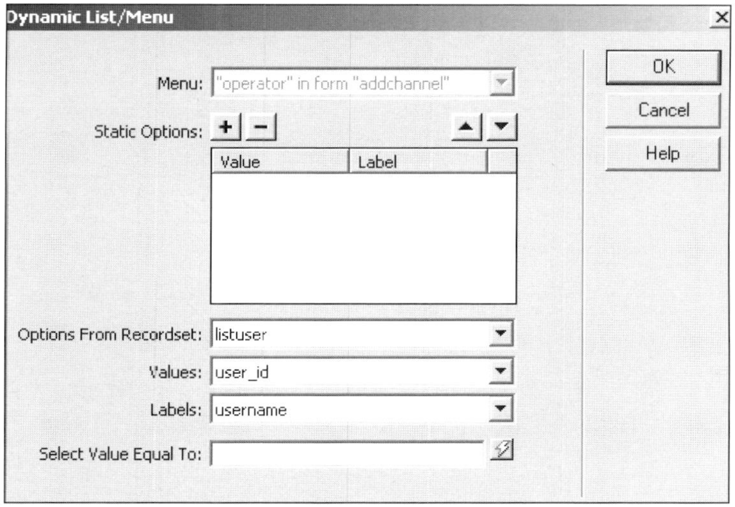

The Dynamic List/Menu dialog box allows you to configure the drop-down list.

6 Switch to the Server Behaviors panel and click the plus (+) sign and select Insert Record from the menu. In the Insert Record dialog box, select the values as shown here:

Connection: **dbconn**

Insert Into Table: **Channel**

After Inserting Go To: **10_channel.asp**

Get Values From: **addchannel**

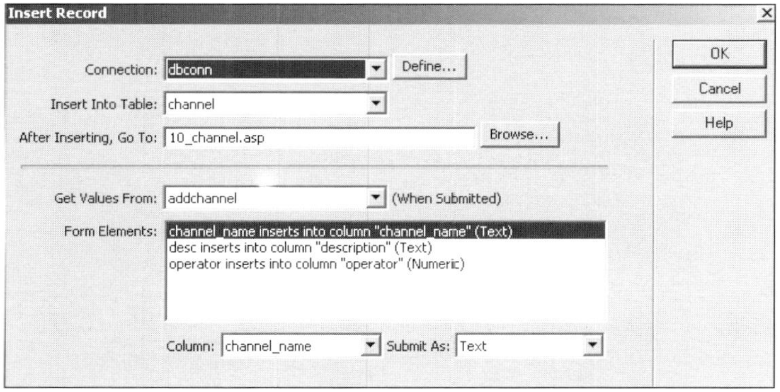

The Insert Record dialog box allows you to add forms to your pages so you can add content to the database.

Note: If you use description as the text area name, Dreamweaver would automatically set this correctly by performing a smart match, where it matches the form element name with the recordset element names and displays the result.

7 In the dialog box, notice that there is another box called Form Elements. Select the second row in Form Elements and from the Column field, select description as the corresponding value. Click OK.

8 Save the file and test it by switching to your browser and clicking the Add Channel link in the Channel Management Module. You should find that you can now create a new channel based on the data entered in the form.

That brings us to the conclusion the chapter. In the preceding sections, you have learned about each of the intricate elements that make any content management system. You have gone through a step-by-step process of learning about User Login, Restrict Access, Log Out, Inserting, Retrieving, Updating/Modifying and deletion of data from a database, using Server Behavior, Recordset, and Dynamic Text features of Dreamweaver.

Modifications

The CMS has so many features that we could include several more projects and several more pages. But here are some thoughts about modifications you could implement that would really enhance the overall system.

A Search Capability: Now you have used templates to display data picked up from the database. But you have only a few pages here; the actual CMS would be designed to support a vast amount of data. In a large system, if users have to go through page after page to reach the data they want, wouldn't that be restricting and primitive? Especially when you have a database and each channel/content has its own set of related keywords. That's where a search module for users would be a boon—they can simply enter the relevant keywords, click Search, and view the relevant search details in a neatly formatted form.

When I say *search* it does not mean that this facility is limited to the end user. The administrator also will find a search within the management module very useful. In a system in which administrators must manage hundreds of channels and content, wouldn't it be easier if they could find what they need by using a set of keywords?

Well, now it's up to you to experiment with this project and see what you end up creating. Again, this is just one suggestion. For hardcore Dreamweaver MX users who want to test out all the immense new features, the sky is the limit.

Final Wrap Up

Although there are many topics I would like to have covered in detail, time and space limitations prevent me from doing just that. CMS is a huge system and what I have covered here provides you with a starting point to explore the vast depths of this powerful system. As a user of Dreamweaver MX, I suggest that you not limit yourself to the design capabilities of this package, but also use the immense programming and integration capabilities to bring the best out. It may be difficult in the beginning with so many new features, but the best things in life never come easy. I hope that I have managed to open a small-yet-useful path toward understanding a Content Management System; maybe if there is a sequel to this chapter in later versions, I can implement a complete-in-all-aspects CMS. Last but not least, a word of gratitude to Shailesh K L, for his contribution to this project. Without his help, this project would not have been possible.

"It was not a project to build a computer only. It was a project to build a computer, to learn how to use it and then to solve some problems."

—MAURICE V. WILKES

BUILDING A PROJECT MANAGEMENT SOLUTION

Web-Based Project Management

Whenever a project involves more than two people, project managers seek tools that can assist them in the management of the entire project. Whether it is tracking the progress of the project, assigning tasks to participants, or simply communicating within the workgroup, any technology that streamlines the project management process is very valuable. Looking at the technologies available to project leaders, it is easy to see that the web is one the most effective tools for delivering high-impact solutions. Communication via email, sharing of schedules, and task management allows groups to share work and communicate at a level that would boggle the minds of project leaders 25 years ago.

So if other project managers are using the web to streamline the process, it seems logical that you, too, could do the same for your projects. Right? Fortunately, the answer is "Right!" Using Dreamweaver MX, you can develop a project management module that allows you to assign tasks and monitor the progress of each element of your project. This chapter introduces you to the tools you can use to establish the basics for a project management system that allows users to see which projects they are working on and allows a project manager to control the flow of work.

Project 11

Building a Project Management Solution

by Matthew David
with contributions by Sean Nicholson

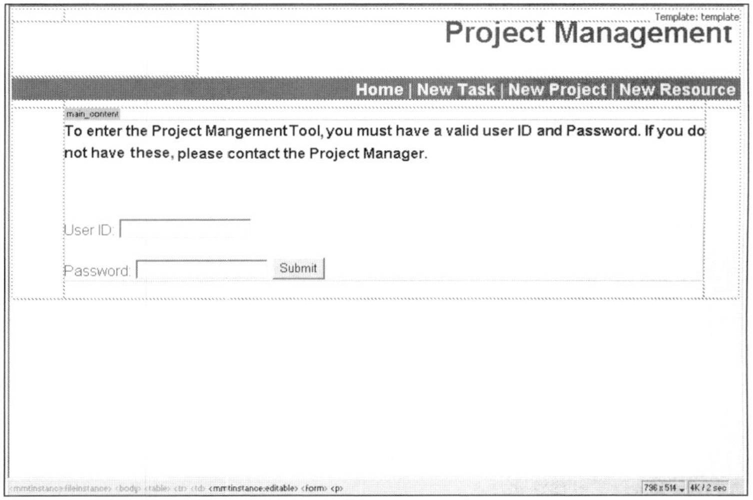

It Works Like This

In this project, you will be developing a dynamic web site that allows you to manage projects. The server model we will be using is Macromedia's ColdFusion MX. ColdFusion MX is a radical enhancement over previous versions of this server solution. If you have not used it before and are skeptical about its efficiency, capability to track bugs, and ability to leverage a broad range of server solutions, you should be impressed with it by the end of this project.

ColdFusion MX works with your traditional web server application to enable you to serve pages that go beyond static pages. Using ColdFusion, you can develop pages that communicate with a backend database and build dynamic pages based on the information stored in the database. In the project management system, this allows you to build pages that display the details about projects, telling who is assigned to them, and showing their current stage of development. Why is this a better way? It works better because no one has to build an individual static HTML page for each module of the project. Instead, you can build a single template page that is suitable for the various aspects of the project and ask ColdFusion MX to communicate with the database to fill in the appropriate information.

Sound difficult? Sound confusing? As you will see in this chapter, with Dreamweaver MX and ColdFusion MX, it's a snap!

Preparing to Work

Before we get started, you need to make sure that the technology is in place to allow for the development of your pages. The requirements include a single Microsoft Access database, your web server software, the ColdFusion Server application, and, of course, the pages developed in Dreamweaver MX.

You will need to use the Access database on the CD for this chapter. The database is called projects.mdb. The database will be the core on which you build the site. In addition, because the Project Management Solution will be built using ColdFusion, you need to have ColdFusion installed on your computer or have access to a web server that is running ColdFusion before proceeding.

Before we start, it also would be a good idea to ensure that your web server application is functioning properly. For this exercise, you can use IIS or Apache, depending on your workstation's operating system, but make sure that they are capable of serving up simple HTML files. After you have that component functioning properly, download and install the ColdFusion MX application. It is a relatively simple application to install and can be downloaded for free from Macromedia's web site.

Tip: You will need to be running Windows NT4-SP6a/2000/XP Professional, Linux, or UNIX to run ColdFusion.

Once you have the two server applications up and running, you can turn your focus to the fun part of developing dynamic pages in Dreamweaver MX! During the course of this project, you will complete the following actions:

- Create ColdFusion-driven forms.
- Use server bindings to create recordsets using custom SQL statements.
- Use application objects to build forms dynamically.
- Control authentication with server behaviors.

As you can see, there is a lot to do. So, let's get cracking.

Establishing the Site

When building any dynamic application, it is crucial that you get all the correct tools working together. For this site to work, we need to balance ColdFusion, a web server, the database, and the local and production environments. Because you have already established that your web server is functioning properly, let's ensure that your ColdFusion server is working as well.

1 First, you need to verify that ColdFusion has been installed and is processing pages. A quick way to do this is to run a ColdFusion formatted document on your server. From the Projects/11_project_management folder on the accompanying CD, locate the file called testfile.cfm located in the 11_project_management_finishedfiles folder. Preview the file in your web browser. What you will see when you run this file is a calendar that is created dynamically. If you do not see the calendar, you may not have ColdFusion correctly configured. Check that the Remote Server Settings are correct and that ColdFusion is running.

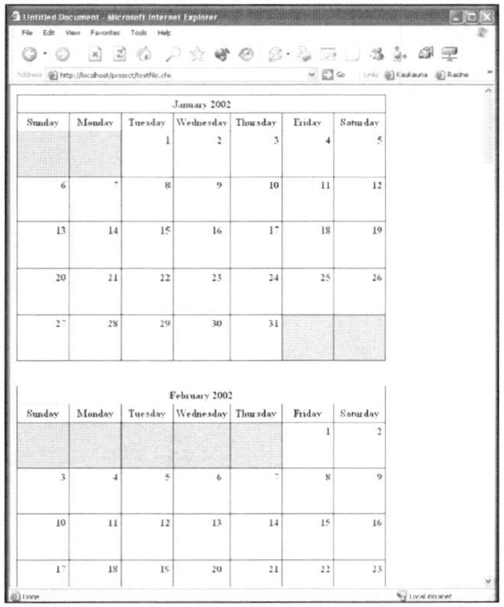

The test file is used to determine whether ColdFusion is correctly installed.

2 When you are sure ColdFusion is functioning, create a new folder called **projects** on your web server. In this project, I use Microsoft's IIS server, but you can use Apache or WebSphere. ColdFusion also can be installed as its own HTTP Server and Application Server.

Tip: For IIS, create a folder called projects in the wwwroot folder. The path to your new folder should be c:\inetpub\wwwroot\projects. If, however, you are using Apache, Netscape Enterprise Server, and WebSphere, create a folder called projects in the htdocs directory. If you are using the default settings in these applications, the path to your new folder would be c:\htdocs\projects. If you are using a remote server rather than your workstation, you may want to work with your web administrator to make sure that the folders are established correctly.

3 Now that you have a working folder, copy all the files and folders from the Projects/11_project_management_workingfiles folder on the accompanying CD to the new projects folder in your web root.

4 Once the files and folders are in the proper location, open Dreamweaver MX and define a new Dreamweaver site. To do this, choose Site>New Site from the menu bar. Apply the following formatting to the Local Info category:

Site Name: **Project Management**

Local Root Folder: This should be the path to the images folder located in your projects folder.

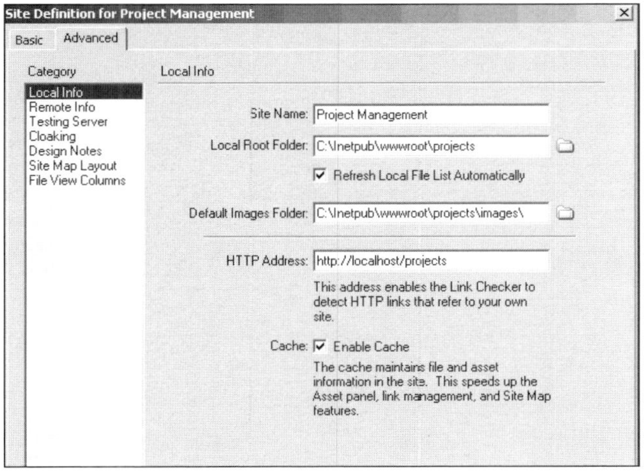

The local site information.

Default Image Folder: Path to the images folder you recently created.

HTTP Address: **http://localhost/projects**

5 In the Site Definition dialog box, select the Testing Server category. This is where you establish which server version you will be using. Configure the server with the following settings and then click OK:

Server Model: **ColdFusion**

This Site Contains: **Dreamweaver MX Pages Only**

Access: **Local/Network**

Testing Server Folder: **c:\inetpub\wwwroot\projects**

URL Prefix: **http://localhost/projects**

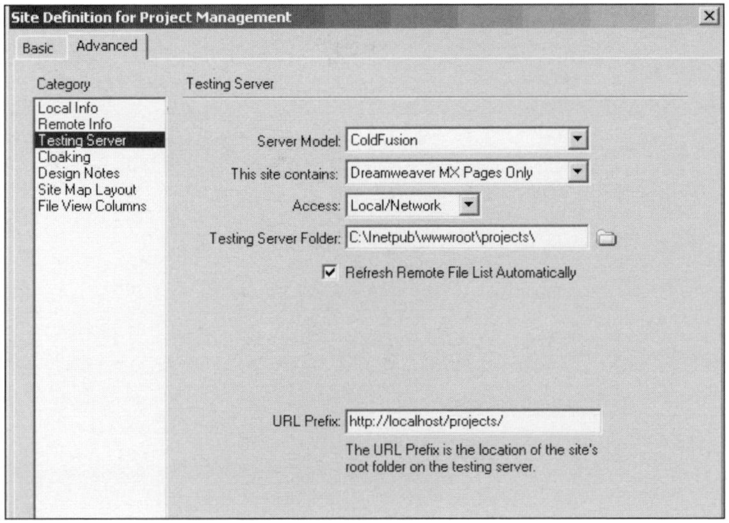

The Testing Server settings determine which application server you will be using.

Note: Because you have a web server application and ColdFusion MX installed on your local workstation, you do not need to have a remote server. In some instances, however, you may be setting up a production server on a different machine. In this case, you will need to make sure that your site connects to that remote server (either through your network or FTP).

Now you have your Dreamweaver MX site set up and ready. The next step is to configure the server to connect with the projects.mdb database.

Making the Connection

Any database-driven web application must have a connection with a database because this connection is what feeds the customized content to the site. You can set up this connection a number of ways, but with ColdFusion MX, the easiest way is by using ODBC drivers, also referred to as *Open Database Connectivity drivers*.

Note: When you install Dreamweaver MX, you will be asked to install a tool called Microsoft's MDAC. The MDAC (Microsoft Data Access Components) is a set of tools that allows you to connect to database content.

There are several different components. The one we are interested in is the ODBC component.

If you do not have MDAC installed, Dreamweaver MX will not install.

If you are not sure whether you have the correct level of MDAC installed, go to Microsoft's MDAC Site (http://www.microsoft.com/data/download.htm). The site has a component checker tool that will run a test of your computer and tell you which version of MDAC you have installed.

1 The first thing you need to do is to set up the database connection as a DSN (data source name) in ColdFusion. To do this, you will need access to the ColdFusion Administration console. This tool could be accessed differently on each computer; however, it is generally set up at the following location: http://localhost/cfide/administrator/datasources/index.cfm. You also can access the Administrator by selecting Start>Program Files>Macromedia ColdFusion MX>Administrator.

2 When accessing the Administration Console, you will be asked to provide the administrator password you established when setting up ColdFusion MX. Be sure to have it handy before you try to log in.

3 Once you are logged into the Administration Console, click the Data Sources link.

4 You can manually connect a path to a database through the Data Source manager; however, you will use the Add New Data Source tool. Type the name **Project** in the Data Source Name field and choose Microsoft Access from the drop-down list. Click the Add button.

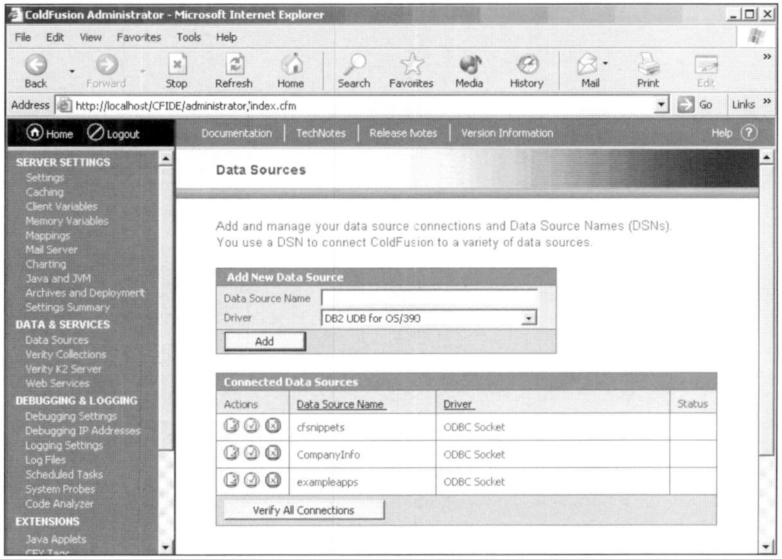

ColdFusion manages all of its data connections through the Data Sources service.

5 In the Microsoft Access Data Source dialog box, click the Browse Server button for the Database File field. Navigate to where projects.mdb is located in the database subdirectory for your Projects site. Select the database and click the Apply button.

Click Submit to create the DSN.

Log out of the Administration Console and close your browser.

Now that you have established an ODBC connection to your database and in the ColdFusion administrator, you need to take a final step to build a connection that allows Dreamweaver MX to access the database.

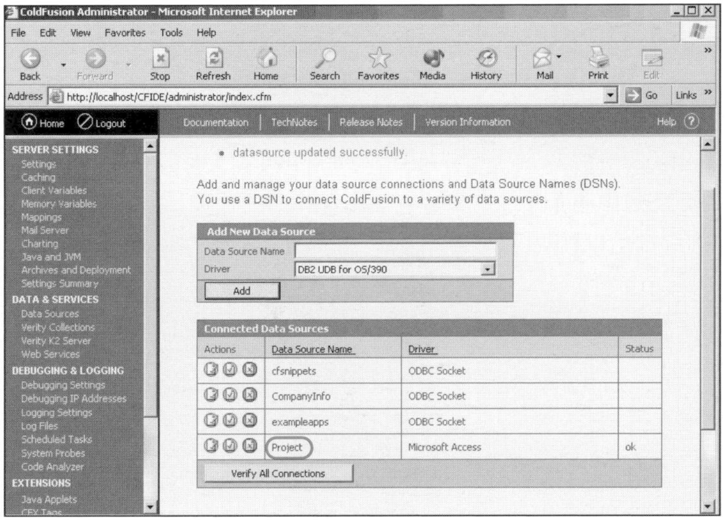

The new DSN called Project is added to the list of DSNs.

6 Open Dreamweaver MX. Make sure that the Project Management site opens. If a different site opens, you can move back to the Project Management site through the Site window. To access the Site window, choose Site>Site Files from the menu bar. From the Site drop-down list in the Site window, choose Project Management. You will now be working in the Projects Management site. Close the Site window to return to the layout view of Dreamweaver MX.

7 Open the Bindings Panel by choosing Window> Bindings. A series of steps needs to be taken in order to ensure that a connection to the database is present. When a checkmark is visible next to each step, it indicates that the step has been correctly configured. Because we are using ColdFusion, question 4 is "Specify the RDS login for your ColdFusion server." Because an RDS login has not been previously established, there is no checkmark next to the step and the words *RDS login* are underlined.

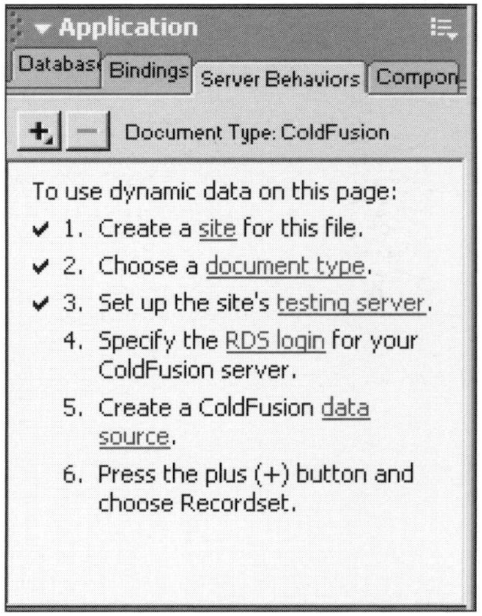

The Bindings panel allows you to ensure that all the necessary steps have been taken to build dynamic pages.

8 Click the link to establish an RDS login and type the password you have established for accessing your ColdFusion server. Click OK. By entering your password, you now have given Dreamweaver the ability to access your database and add content to your ColdFusion pages. Because you have created your DSN using the ColdFusion console, Dreamweaver MX also places a checkmark next to "Create a ColdFusion data source."

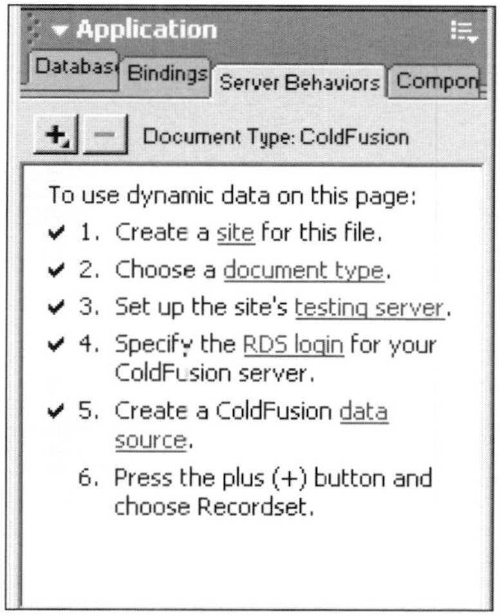

Now that all the steps have been fulfilled, you are ready to begin building database driven pages.

Establishing the Site Structure

Let's begin by setting up the navigation architecture for your new site.

1 Open the Site window by choosing Site>Site Files from the menu bar and add the following folders to your site by right-clicking on the Project Management folder and selecting New Folder from the menu:

Admin

Client

Projects

Resources

Style

Tasks

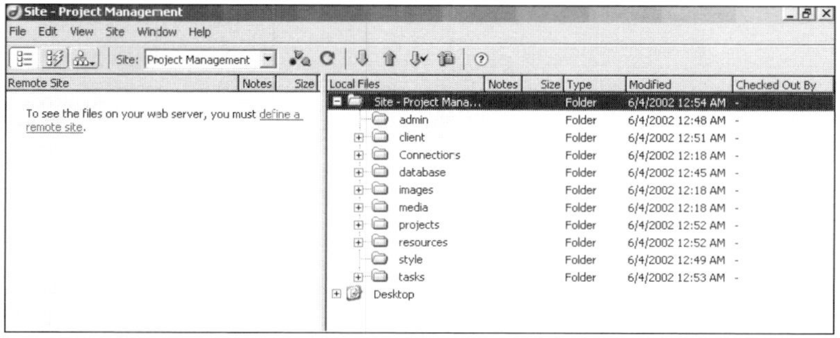

The new site structure allows you to manage and edit your files easily within one window.

2 The next step is to create the blank pages that you will use in the project management system. Some web developers like to create new pages as they need them, but I prefer to create blank placeholders for each page so that I can continually monitor the site structure I have established. To create the placeholders, right-click the Client folder and choose New File from the menu.

details.cfm

edit_client.cfm

index.cfm

new_client.cfm

3 Right-click the Projects folder and add the following files:

details.cfm

edit_project.cfm

index.cfm

new_project.cfm

4 Right-click the Resources folder and add the following files:

details.cfm

edit_resource.cfm

index.cfm

new_resource.cfm

5 Right-click the Tasks folder and add the following files:

details.cfm

edit_tasks.cfm

index.cfm

new_tasks.cfm

6 Right-click the Site-Project Management folder (the top-level folder) and add the following files:

index.cfm

personalized.cfm

validation.cfm

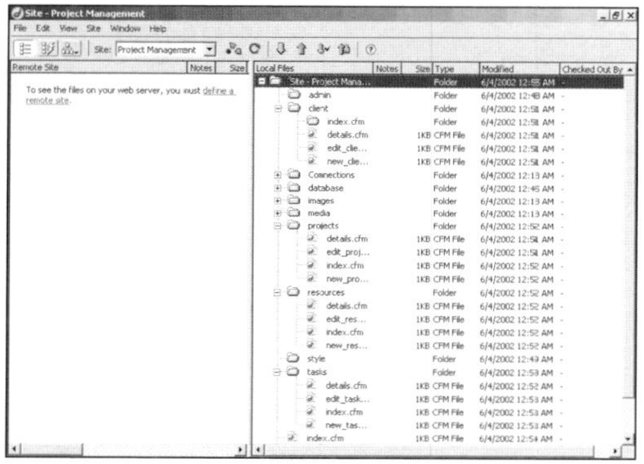

The site structure is in place with placeholders for each page.

ADDING NEW CLIENTS

Any project that is created must have started with a client requesting that the project be done. This may be an internal client, such as a department head or manager, or an external client, such as a customer. Either way, you need to be able to retain information about that person or department so that you can understand who you are doing the work for and how to contact them.

The files you added to the Clients folder will be the foundation for your forms.

1 Open the file called new_client.cfm. You need to add a simple form to the page that allows you to post a new client's information to the database.

2 The quickest way in Dreamweaver to add a form that interacts with a database is to use one of Dreamweaver's built-in Application Objects. Place your insertion point in the page and select Insert>Application Objects>Record Insertion Form.

3 From the Data Source drop-down list, choose Project.

4 From the Table drop-down list, choose Customers. Notice that the Form fields below change to reflect the fields in the Customers table.

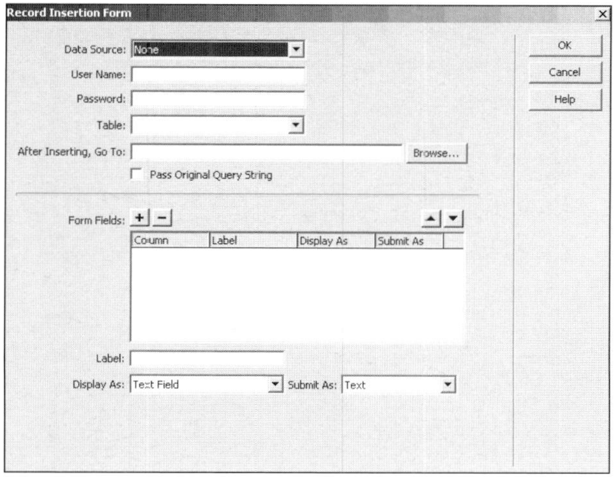

The Record Insertion Form is used to add new records to a table in a database.

5 For the After Inserting, Go To field, type index.cfm. This is the home page for the Client section.

6 You want to accept the form fields as they are, with a few exceptions:

- Select CustomerID and choose the minus (–) button in the top-left corner to remove the field. We remove this because the field is an autonumber field in the Access database and customers will automatically be given a unique ID from the database.
- Select each field and add spaces between the words in the Label field.
- Select the Notes field and change Display As to Text Area. This will give you more space for notes instead of just a single line.

7 Click OK. The form will be automatically generated on the page. Press F12 to preview. You can use this form to add a new record. When you have done this, you will be sent to index.cfm. Save the page.

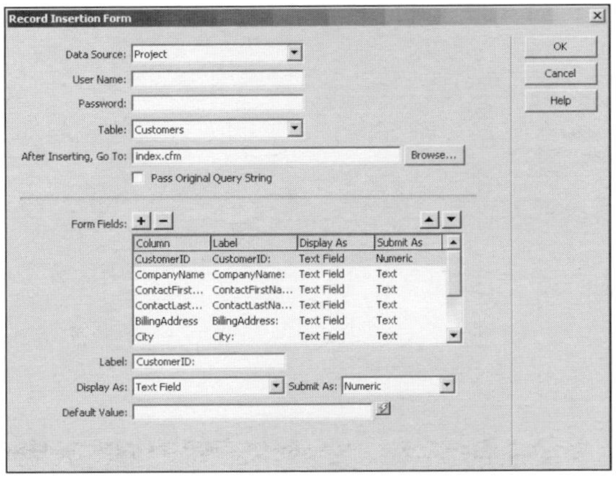

After a record has been added, you can choose to redirect the user to a different page.

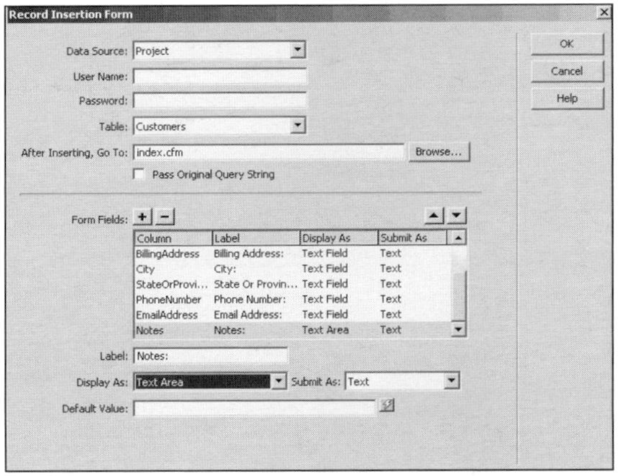

Each field element can be changed with the Record Insertion Form. Here the Text field is changed to a Text Area field.

This new form gives you the ability to add new client information to your database. Before you do that, however, let's look at building a reference page that shows you information about clients after it is entered.

Client Home Page

Again, you want to use Dreamweaver's Application Objects to construct pages as quickly as possible. In this case, you want to create a single page that lists all of the clients you have entered into the database and an additional page that displays all of the details about each client. Later, you also will add a list of all open projects owned by that client.

1 Open the index.cfm file located in the Clients folder.

You want to be able to list all the clients on the page. To do this, you are going to use the Master/Details Application Object. For this Object to work, you must first create a recordset that points to the clients. Think of a recordset as a snapshot of specific data located in the database. At this time, you want to see your clients and their relevant information.

2 To create a recordset, open the Bindings panel by choosing Window>Bindings. Click the plus (+) sign and choose Recordset (Query) from the menu.

3 In the Recordset dialog box, name the Recordset **rsClients**.

4 For the Data Source field, select Project and notice that you can now choose a table. Choose Customers as the Table and click OK.

5 Now that a recordset is available, you can build your master and details pages. From the menu bar, choose Insert>Application Objects>Master Detail Page Set.

The Insert Master/Detail Page Set dialog box has two main panels. The top panel allows you to configure how the current page (also known as the *master* page) will look. The lower panel configures how the details page will look.

6 For the Master Page Fields, remove every entry except CompanyName, ContactFirstName, and ContactLastName.

7 From the Link To Detail From drop-down, choose CompanyName. This provides you with a specific field that acts as a link to the details page. Use CustomerID as the unique key to link and move to the correct record on the details page.

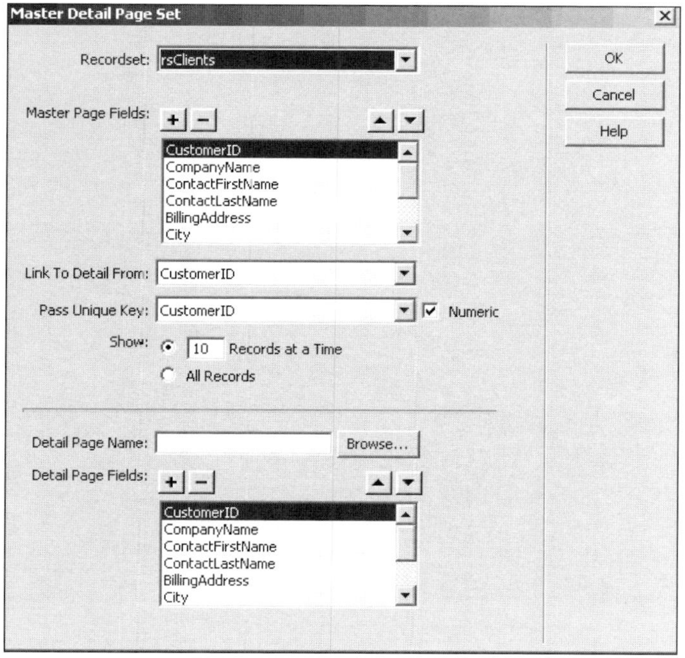

The Master Detail Page Set object is a quick way to insert a lot of information into a site.

8 Choose to show only 10 records on a page at a time. This will allow you to see 10 clients on a screen at once. Navigation buttons or links will later allow you to see more clients if you have more than 10.

9 You need to know which page will be used to show the details for the client. Press the Browse button for Detail Page Name and locate details.cfm in the Clients folder. Highlight details.cfm and click OK.

10 Finally, choose which fields you want to see on the details page. Keep all the fields. Click OK. Dreamweaver now builds two pages: a master and a details page.

11 In the index.cfm page, you need to add a link to the New Client page so that you can add a new client. The easiest way is by using a plain, old-fashioned link. Place the insertion point at the bottom of your page and press the Enter key twice. On the new line, type the words **New Client** and use the Link field in the Property inspector to link to the new_client.cfm.

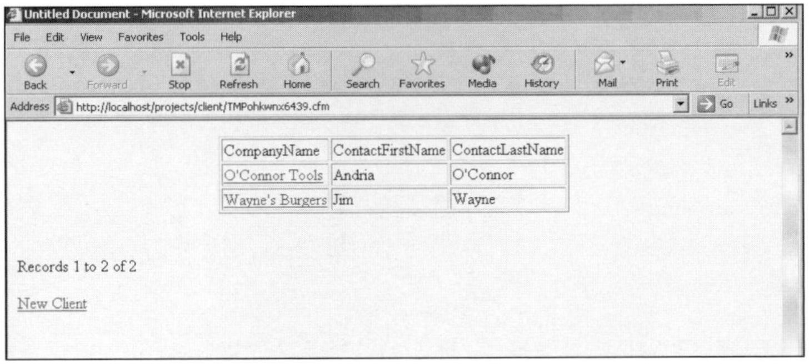

A preview of the master pages shows dynamic data retrieved from the database.

12 Preview this page in your browser by pressing the F12 key. If you have less than 10 records in the table, you will see that the navigation buttons are missing. Actually, they are hidden. Dreamweaver inserts a script to hide these buttons if there are not enough records for them to be needed. If you have more than 10 records, you will see the buttons appear.

13 Save all your pages. Press F12 and, once again, preview index.cfm. You should see some clients listed on your screen. Selecting the company name takes you to a page with greater detail. Back on the index.cfm page, you can select a link that will allow you to add a new client. When you do so, you will be sent back to the index.cfm page, where you can see the new client listing.

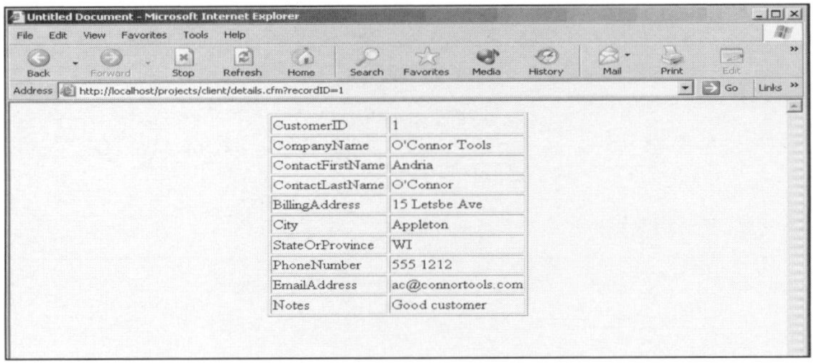

Here is the details page for the Master Details Object.

OK, the pages do not currently have flair and pizzazz, but the functionality is there. The good looks can come later. Next you need to build a page that allows you to update the information stored for each client. Once again, you can do this very easily using Dreamweaver's built-in functionality.

EDITING A CLIENT'S INFORMATION

The final function this section of the site needs is the capability to update client information already stored in the database. In many ways, this is not too different from creating a new form with the Record Insertion Form object.

1 Open the edit_client.cfm page. You are going to use a Record Update Form to complete this section. To do this, you first need a recordset. Click the plus (+) symbol on the Bindings panel and choose Recordset (Query) from the menu. Name the new recordset **rsCustomers** and choose the Project data source. Select the Customers table and for a Filter, choose CustomerID. Leave the rest of the default values for the filter. Click OK.

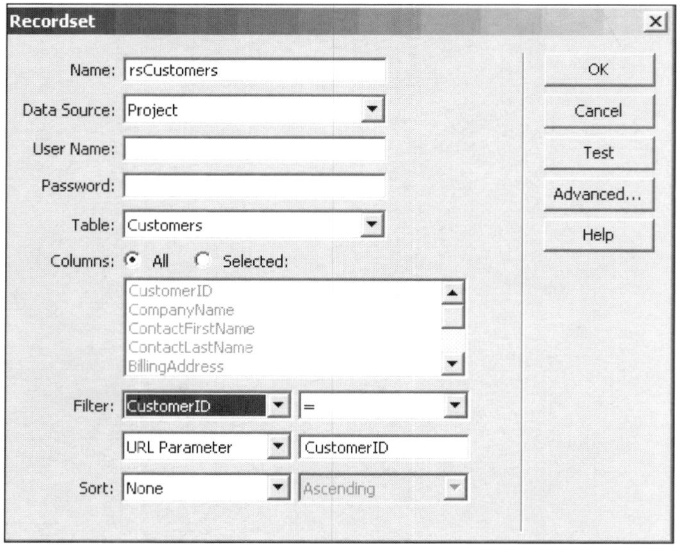

The rsCustomers recordset allows you to use the Record Update Form.

2 Place the insertion point in your page and choose Insert>Application Objects>Record Update Form from the menu bar.

3 In the Record Update Form dialog box, choose Project for the data source. Select Customers as the Table to update and choose rsCustomers as the record form. The unique key should be set to CustomerID.

4 In the After Updating, Go To field, type **index.cfm**.

5 For the Form Fields, leave all entries except the CustomerID field. To remove the CustomerID field, select it from the list, and click the minus (–) button.

6 Click OK and save your work.

That's it. With the completion of this page, you now know how to build pages for your Client section that allows you to view information stored in the database, add new clients, and edit their information.

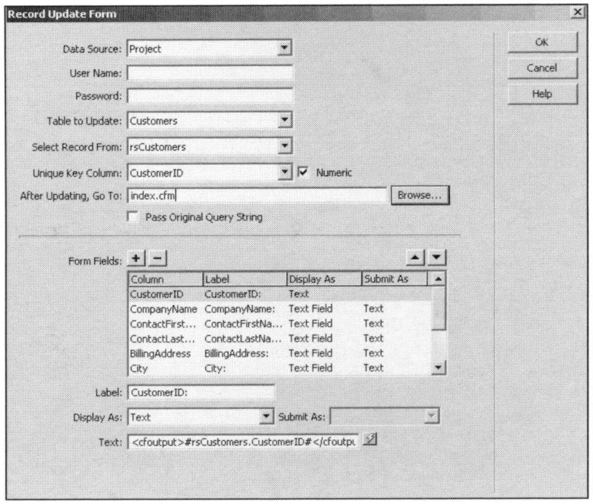

The Record Insertion Form manages in one step all the actions needed to update a record in the Clients Table.

Creating a New Resource

In the previous section, you created a series of pages that allow you to quickly build the Client section of the site. There still are three more main sections of the site: Resources, Projects, and Tasks.

Each section is divided into the four subsections that allow you see all the records and edit, delete, and modify a record. As you have probably noticed, this reflects the way in which the Client section is created. What you have here is the foundation for many applications you will build. At some point, you will need to add, delete, and modify records in your database, whether they are for a project tracking application or for some other application.

As you will see in this exercise, tracking the way your resources are managed follows this layout as well.

You need to begin by creating the home page and details page that allows you to view all the resources you have for your site.

Note: An employee is listed as a resource in this application. The reason for this is that employee time can be tracked in a way similar to capital resources like conference rooms and rented equipment. For instance, just as specialized camera equipment can be rented by the client for a specific time period, the time spent by an employee working on a project can be tracked as well.

1 Open the index.cfm page in the Resource folder.
This will be your home page for this section.

2 Let's start by building Master/Details pages for the resources section. Begin by building a recordset in the index.cfm page by clicking the plus (+) sign on the Bindings panel and clicking Recordset (Query).

3 Name the new recordset **rsResource**. The data source should be set to Project and the table you want to link with is Employees. Leave all other options at their defaults. Click OK.

4 From the menu bar, select Insert>Application Objects>Master Detail Page Set. Choose to have the following records appear on the master page:

FirstName

LastName

EmailName

WorkPhone

Skills

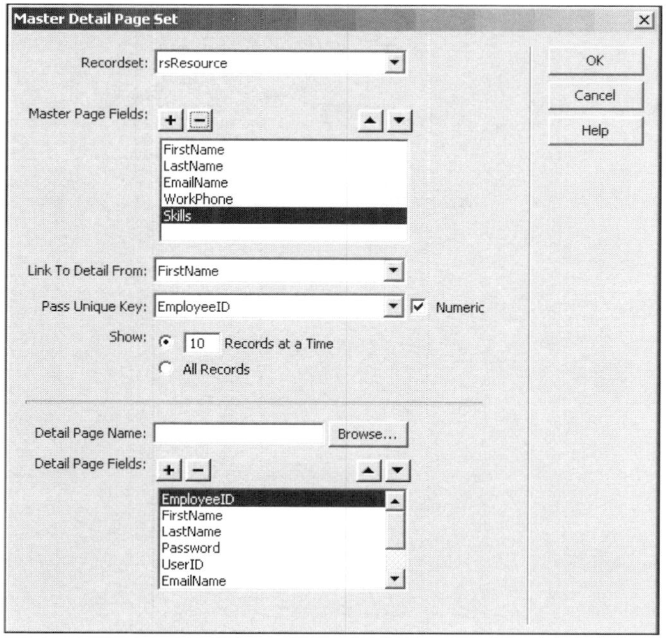

Select the appropriate fields to be included in the master page for the Employees section.

5 Select LastName to be the link from this page to the details page and choose EmployeeID as the unique key. Finally, select details.cfm in the Resources folder as the details page. All records, with the exception of EmployeeID, should appear on the details page. Click OK and Dreamweaver MX adds the appropriate data to your pages.

The pages are now generated by Dreamweaver MX. The next steps for creating new and update forms are similar to the new and update forms created in the Clients folder.

6 Open the file new_resource.cfm.

7 Place the insertion point in the page and choose Insert>Application Objects>Record Insertion Form from the menu bar.

8 Choose Project as the data source.

9 Select Employees as the table that will be updated.

10 Choose index.cfm as the page you will be redirected to when you have inserted a record correctly.

11 From the Form Fields, remove EmployeeID by selecting that field name and clicking the minus (–) button. The Access database has been set up to automatically generate an Employee ID and add it to the record.

12 Select the defaults for all the records with the exception of Skills. This form element should be changed to Text Area. Click OK.

13 Save both pages. Test the form by viewing it in your web browser and adding a new record.

Now, you need to modify this process to allow us to modify all of the records.

14 Open edit_resource.cfm. Add a recordset by clicking the plus (+) sign on the Bindings panel and choose Recordset (Query). Name the Recordset **rsResource**. Select the Project data source and choose the Employees table. Leave other options at their defaults. Click OK.

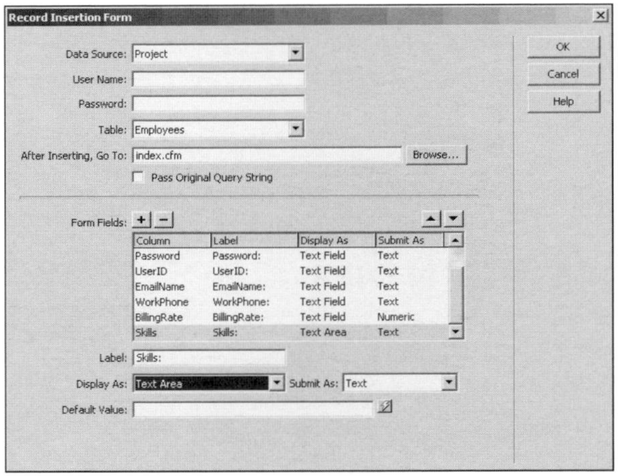

A new resource can be quickly added with the Record Insertion Form.

Naming Conventions

As you have seen throughout this chapter, I have been keeping to a number of conventions as I add content. For instance, all recordsets begin with rs and all connections begin with conn. Using conventions consistently like this helps you follow the changes you make to your code.

Other conventions I have used include placing an underscore between file names that would be two or more words in length. Very few web servers understand a space in a name, so using an underscore character in place of a space keeps you code more universal. This also makes it easy to read the name of the file.

15 Place the insertion point in the page and select Insert>Application Objects>Record Update Form from the menu bar. Choose Project as the data source and select Employees as the table to be updated. Choose rsResource as your recordset, set the unique key to EmployeeID, and in the After Updating, Go To field, type **index.cfm**. Remove EmployeeID from your list of form fields and change the Display As field to Text Area for Skills. Click OK.

You now have a complete section. As you can see, there is a lot of double duty here with the previous section, but Dreamweaver makes the process very simple.

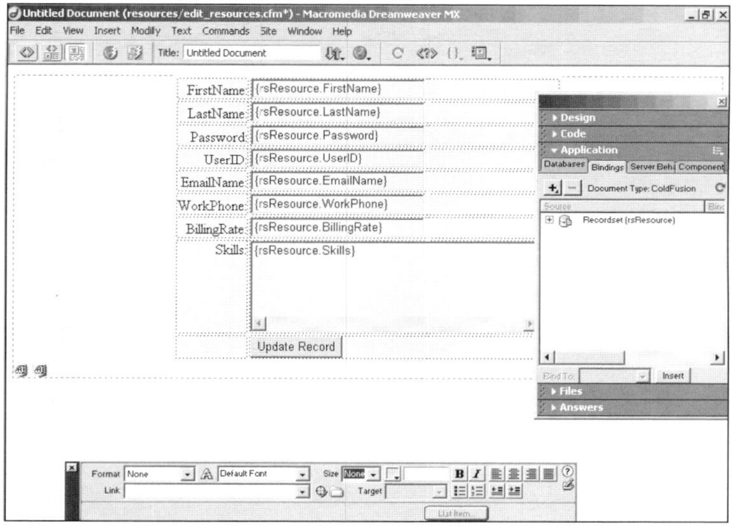

The Record Update Form application object creates the objects necessary for you to update the information stored in the database.

Adding a New Resource and Other Odds and Ends

As you might imagine, adding new content to a database and creating a Master/Detail page is similar for each section of the site. There are some slight differences, however. Here is a breakdown of how each section is defined:

The steps for creating a new resource are identical to those for creating a new client. You will notice that the resource also has room for a User ID and Password. Later, you will use these fields to validate that users are who they say they are when accessing the site.

The Tasks and Projects sections also are similar. Use the Record Insertion Form Object to build your forms rapidly. Each section also allows for the information stored in the tables to be edited. I'll leave it up to you to follow the same steps outlined earlier to create all the pages you need for both the Tasks and Projects section. Don't forget to add a link from the index page.

Setting Up the Master/Details Pages

The Master/Details pages for each section (Resource, Project, and Task) are identical. The only difference is that you will need to create a recordset to point to the correct table in the Projects database. For instance, the Resource recordset needs to point to the Employee table, the Projects recordset needs to point to the Projects table, and the Tasks recordset needs to point to the Tasks table.

Once you have this all squared away, you should be set to go with the Master/Details page. Remember that the Master page should have only highlight information. If you have a lot of records, you do not want to bombard your users with rows of information.

Personalizing the Experience

Up to this point, you have created the administrative files for the site. These files allow for actions to be created and executed. Now you need to turn your attention to the people actually using this tool and think about how it can be personalized for their experience.

This will be achieved through the use of the login and authentication tools built into Dreamweaver. Once users have successfully entered their username and password, a personalized page listing all of their Projects and Tasks will be displayed.

1 Open the index.cfm page located in the top level directory. This page should currently be blank. You want this page to be a login page that will authenticate users against their passwords and user IDs.

2 Insert a form in your page by selecting Insert>Form from the menu bar. In the Property inspector, type **validation.cfm** in the Target field and select Post as the Method. Next, place the insertion point inside the form and insert a new table on the page. Make the table three rows and two columns.

3 In the left column, type **User ID:** in the top row and **Password:** in the middle row.

4 Place the insertion point in the upper-right field and choose Insert>Form Objects>Text Field from the menu bar. Name the new text field **userid** in the Property inspector.

5 Add an additional text field in the middle-right field and name it **password**. In the Property inspector, set the Type to **Password**.

6 In the remaining bottom-right cell, insert a button form object and label it **Submit**.

7 This page now contains the form that allows users to login. Save the page.

8 Open the validation.cfm page located in the root of the projects folder. Build a recordset by selecting the Server Behaviors panel and clicking the plus (+) sign. Choose Recordset (Query) from the menu.

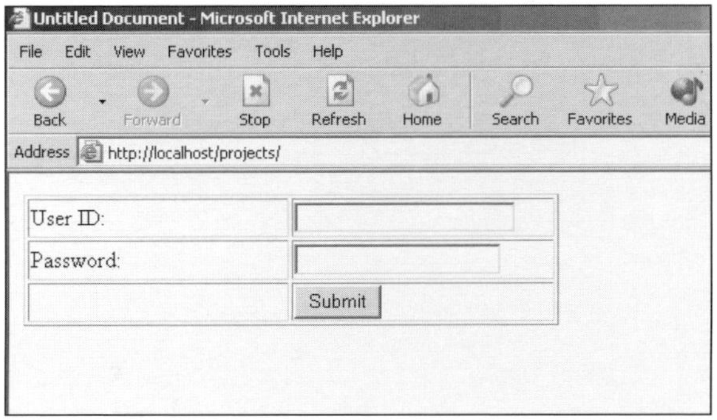

The login page has been created.

9 In the Recordset dialog box, name the recordset **rsLogin** and choose Prcject as the data source. Switch to the advanced mode. In the SQL box, type the following SQL query:

```
SELECT UserID,Password, EmployeeID FROM
Employees WHERE UserID='#FORM.userid#' AND
Password='#FORM.password#'
```

This query simply compares the username/password combination with all the records in the database to see whether there is a match.

10 Click OK to save the recordset.

11 Place the insertion point in the page and type **We're sorry; your password could not be validated. Click here to try again.** Highlight the Click here text and link it to index.cfm.

12 Press the Enter key twice. On the new line, type **Thank you for logging in. Click here to view your projects.** This time, highlight the Click here text and click the folder icon next to the Link field in the Property inspector. In the Select File dialog box, highlight the personalized.cfm page and click the Parameters button.

13 In the Parameters dialog box, type **EmployeeID** as the parameter name and then place your cursor in the blank space under the Value column. You should now see the lightning bolt icon that symbolizes dynamic data. Click the icon.

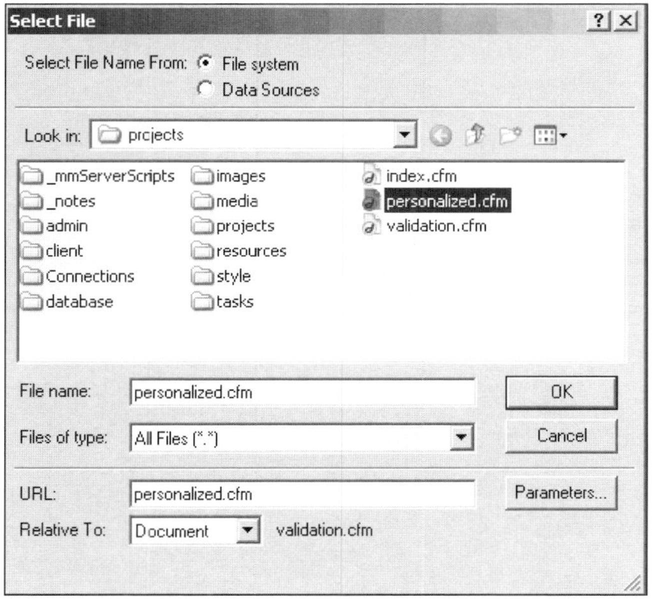

The Select File dialog box allows you to build custom links.

14 In the Dynamic Data dialog box, expand the recordset and select the EmployeeID data binding. Click OK.

15 Click OK to close the Parameters dialog box and click OK again to close the Choose File dialog box.

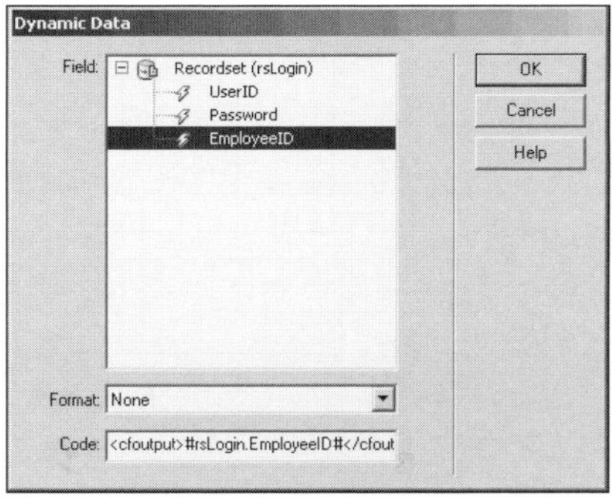

The login page has been created.

16 Now you need to ensure that only one of your confirmation messages is displayed depending on whether the login was successful. To do this, you will use two of Dreamweaver's server behaviors. Highlight the first sentence of text and click the plus (+) sign on the Server Behaviors panel. From the menu, choose Show Region>If Recordset Is Empty. In the dialog box, choose the rsLogin recordset and click OK.

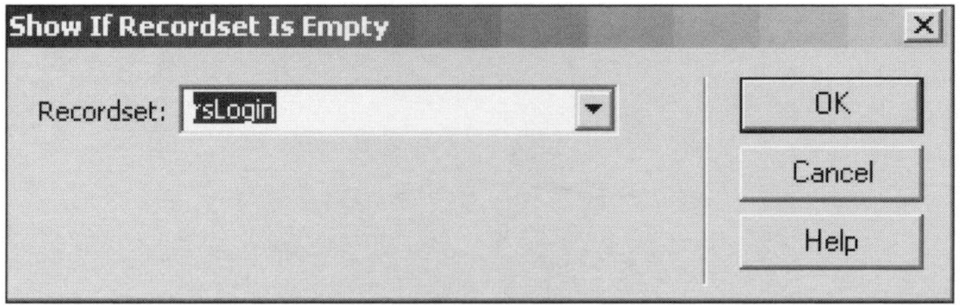

You want to show only the first line of text if the rsLogin recordset is empty.

17 Now highlight the second line of text, click the plus (+) sign on the Server Behaviors panel, and choose Show Region>If Recordset Is Not Empty. Again, choose the rsLogin recordset in the dialog box and click OK.

18 Save the page.

This is all you need to do to validate a user. When the user logs in successfully, a session variable is stored which allows the visitor to travel between protected pages without adding his or her username and password each time a page is opened. In addition, now that the server knows who you are, this information can be used to personalize pages to your settings throughout the site.

On the Personalized page, you will want to list all of the projects and tasks the user is actively involved with. You need to personalize the page so that the user knows that the information is correct.

19 Open the personalized.cfm page from the top level folder. Because you passed the employee ID to this page, you can now build a recordset that retrieves only the project associated with this user. To do this, build a new recordset and name it **rsProjects**. Switch to simple mode if you are not already there.

20 In the Recordset dialog box, choose the Project data source and set the Filter so that EmployeeID is URL Parameter EmployeeID. Click OK.

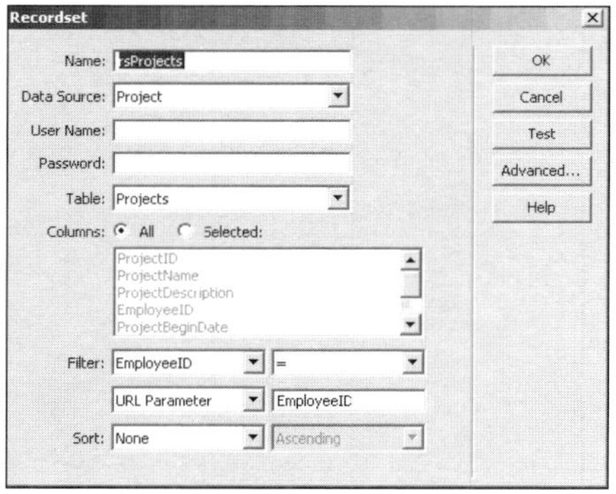

Build a new recordset that filters by EmployeeID.

21 Place the insertion point in the page and type **Your projects are:** and press Enter.

22 Switch to the Bindings panel and expand the rsProjects recordset. Click the ProjectName binding and drag it onto the page.

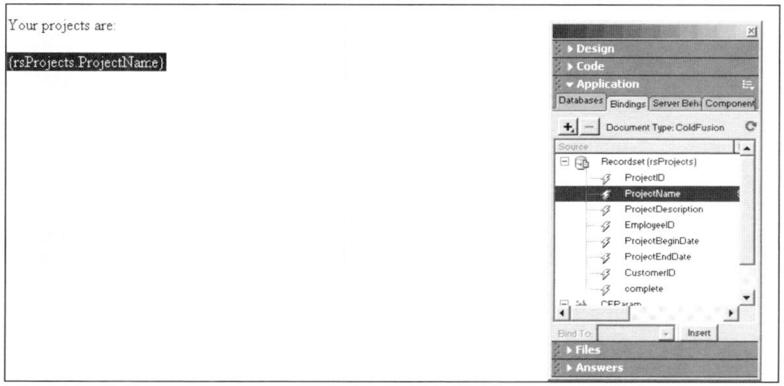

Add the dynamic text to your page by dragging it from the Bindings panel.

23 Highlight the new dynamic text and switch to the Server Behaviors panel. Click the plus (+) sign and select Repeat Region from the menu. Choose to repeat the region for all records in the rsProjects recordset and click OK.

24 Press the right-arrow key on your keyboard and press Enter.

25 Type **You have no projects**. Highlight this text and click the plus (+) sign on the Server Behaviors panel. Choose Show Region>If Recordset Is Empty from the menu. Without this server behavior, someone who visited this page who had no projects would receive an ugly error stating that the recordset is empty. This step saves people the fear of thinking they messed something up.

26 Save the page and test it by opening your browser and typing **http://localhost/project/** as the URL. You should now be presented with the opportunity to enter a username and password. Enter the username **wsleep** and the password **ballet**. Click Submit.

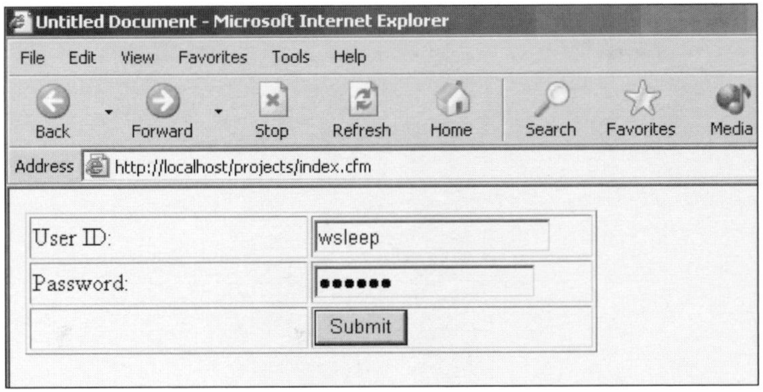

Log into the system.

27 Because you entered a valid username and password, you were granted access to the site. Click the link to view your projects and notice that there are two projects associated with this username. Keep in mind that you could have added as much or as little content to the page as you wanted. By adding only the project title, this section demonstrated how to add some content quickly.

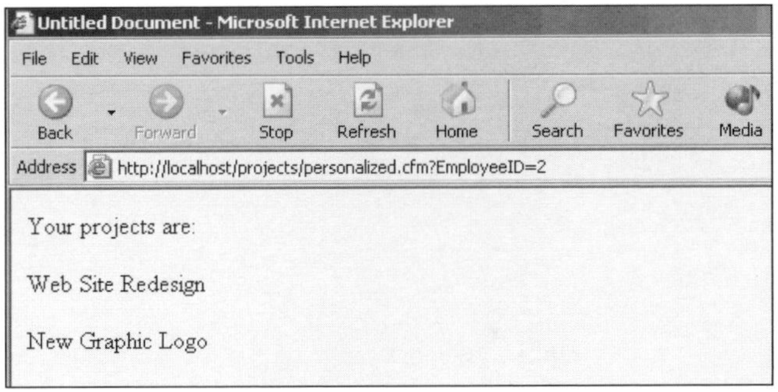

The username you used has two projects associated with it.

Modifications

Through this chapter, you have been able to build and execute a web-based project management solution using only Dreamweaver MX as the development tool. A great benefit of the application being web-based is that it is relatively easy to extend the tool to add new features.

One set of tools you may want to add is a section on reports. Currently a lot of information is being captured and passed around the system. This information is being accessed only at a high level; that is, users can come in and see which tasks they are working on and to which projects those tasks apply. A section on reports can give a more rounded appreciation for the work being completed. Simple reports can compare project hours, list projects that successfully hit their targets, and show which projects over-extended their budgets (both in time and cost).

As you build the current application with ColdFusion, you can leverage ColdFusion's integration with Flash. Both ColdFusion and Flash can be written with ActionScript (the programming language for Flash). With this advantage, you can now build stateless client/server-based solutions over the web. The combination is safe, fast, and light on your network, something that cannot be said for Java or ActiveX controls. Flash can be used to build richer and more intuitive reporting and interface tools.

All the techniques in this chapter have been built on a platform configured for ColdFusion. However, Dreamweaver is a smart tool. You could have easily been building for ASP, ASP.Net, JSP, or PHP and your database could just as easily be MySQL, MS-SQL, Postgres SQL instead of Access. Your situation will vary depending on your hosting provider's service offerings. Dreamweaver only cares in the set up. From there onward, you can use many of the same tools (the Server Behaviors, the Binding panel, and Application Objects) with the same degree of control. It is this ability to allow a user to exchange tools swiftly that makes Dreamweaver the most powerful tool a web designer can choose.

DATABASE-DRIVEN USERNAME AND PASSWORD VALIDATION

"Treat your password like your toothbrush. Don't let anybody else use it, and get a new one every six months ..."

—CLIFFORD STOLL, AUTHOR OF *CUCKOO'S EGG: TRACKING A SPY THROUGH THE MAZE OF COMPUTER ESPIONAGE*

Restricting Web Page Access Using Usernames and Passwords

Allowing your web site visitors to create and maintain personal usernames and passwords can have a wide variety of uses. As a web developer, you can restrict access to areas of your site, engage in e-commerce, or even allow visitors to customize the site to match their individual tastes.

Whatever your use, understanding how to develop and implement an application that allows visitors to log in and log out can open new doors for your site's functionality and increase the likelihood that your visitors will come back for return visits.

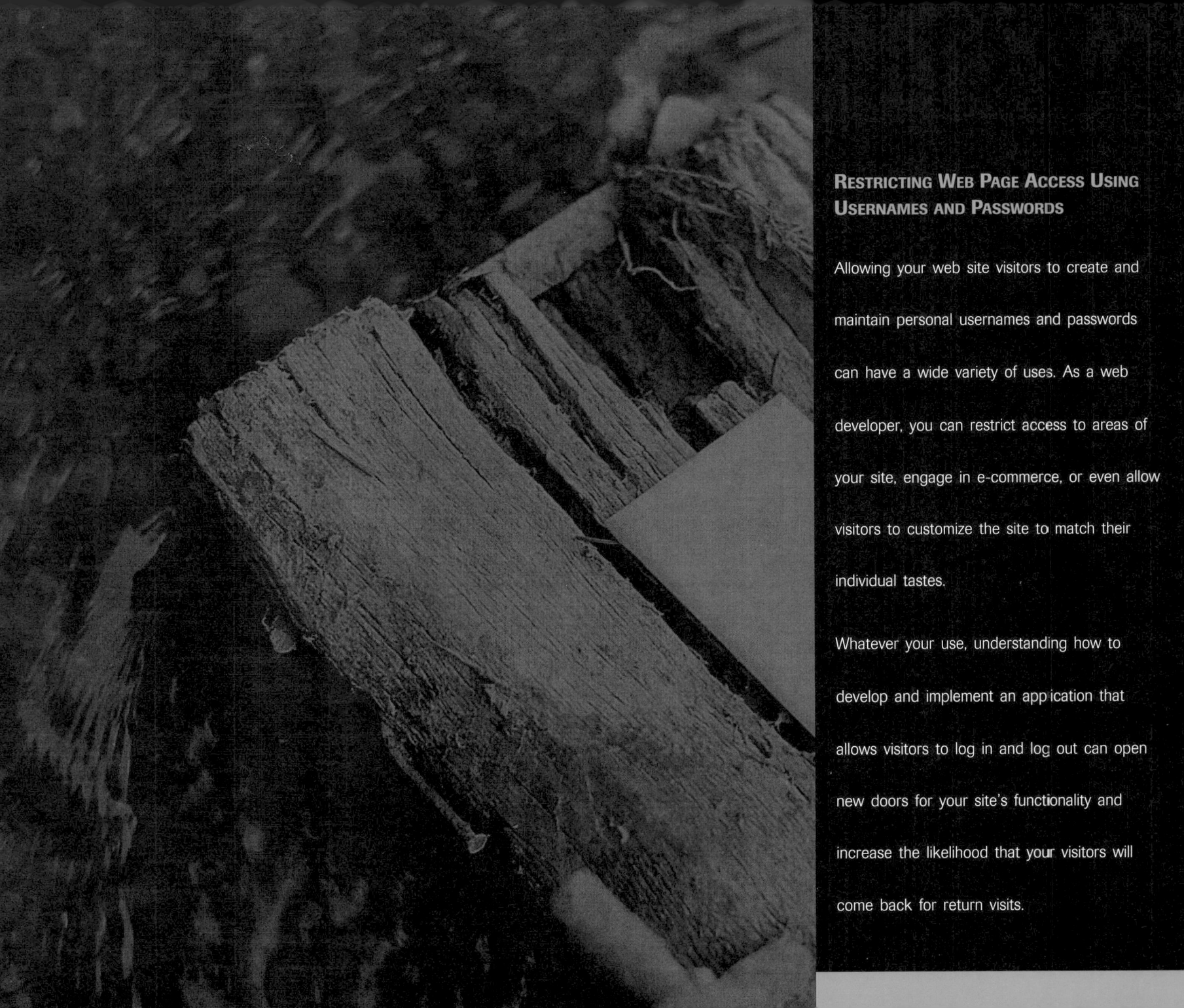

Project 12

Database-Driven Username and Password Validation

by Sean Nicholson

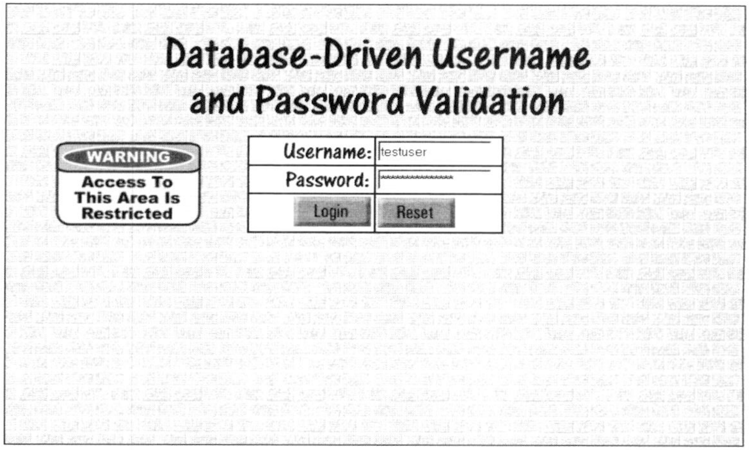

IT WORKS LIKE THIS

Building a database-driven username and password application is really one of those complicated-sounding processes that, thanks to Dreamweaver, is relatively simple. Basically, a visitor comes to your web site and enters a username and password into an HTML form. When they submit the form, the contents are passed to a second page that builds a recordset consisting of all the usernames and passwords stored in the database matching those that were submitted. If the username/password combination is present in the database, the visitor is presented with a confirmation message, a session variable is created on his or her machine, and the user is allowed to continue into the protected areas of the site. If, however, the username/password combination is not found in the database, the visitor is denied access to the protected areas of the site and is asked to re-enter the username and password or create an account.

But what if a clever visitor tries to circumvent the login process and just type the direct URL of a page within the site? A good username and password application anticipates this potential situation and includes security measures to prevent unauthorized access. Fortunately, Dreamweaver includes a server behavior that makes protecting pages from unauthorized visitors as simple as a few clicks of the mouse. Using these tools, you can easily build a page that checks to see whether the visitor has a valid session variable before the page is loaded. If a session variable does not exist on the user's machine, the user is automatically redirected to the login page.

The final element of a good username/password application gives the visitor the ability to log out from the site. Again, Dreamweaver allows us to create a link that, when clicked, destroys the session variable located on the user's machine. Without this variable, the user is unable to access the protected areas of the site without logging back on.

PREPARING TO WORK

Before we get down to business building the username and password validation application, it's important that your machine is configured properly to serve Active Server Pages (ASP). Although this project can also be done using ColdFusion (CFML), Java Server Pages (JSP), or PHP, we are going to use ASP for demonstration purposes here. For those of you working with JSP, CFML, or PHP, we include a discussion at the end of the chapter giving the modifications you can make so this application will work on these platforms.

Because this exercise uses Active Server Pages, you will need to have either Personal Web Server, Internet Information Server (Windows NT), or Internet Information Services (Windows 2000) installed on your machine. Users with Apache Web Server also can serve ASP pages as long as they have ChiliSoft! installed.

Note: If you are using Windows 9x or Windows NT, you can download the appropriate web server software from www.microsoft.com/ntserver/nts/downloads/recommended/NT4OptPk/default.asp. If you are using Windows 2000 or XP, you can install Internet Information Services by choosing Control Panel>Add/Remove Programs option. Mac users can use the Mac Personal Web Sharing Service included with OS8 or later.

Once you have the appropriate web server application installed and configured to serve ASP pages, you need to create a subfolder called username in the root directory of your web folder. If you are using PWS or IIS, the default root directory is c:\inetpub\wwwroot\, which means the path to your new folder will be c:\inetpub\wwwroot\username\.

Tip: If you are using Personal Web Server or IIS, there is no configuration needed to run ASP pages. Once you install the program or service, they are ready to go. If, however, you are using Apache and ChiliSoft! on a Mac, you will need to refer to your application's documentation for details on the configuration needed to run ASP.

The only other requirement for this project comes if you would like to build the database from the ground up. To do so, you need to have Microsoft Access installed on your workstation. Again, this exercise can be implemented using a variety of other database management systems, but Access is used in this project. If you don't have Access installed on your machine, you can still follow along with the process and copy the pre-built database from the CD-ROM to your local folder. Once the database is on your workstation, you can follow along and build the rest of the application.

Building the Database

The first step in building any database-driven application usually is developing the database—and this application is no exception. Luckily, the database required is very simple and takes only minutes to construct. Once completed, the database is placed in a folder in your web directory, which allows the ASP pages to interact with it.

Note: For this project, it's helpful to have Microsoft Access. If you don't have Access installed on your workstation, however, you can still follow along with these steps. The included images convey the concepts that you can apply to your database of choice.

1 Open Microsoft Access. Choose to create a Blank Access Database and click OK. Save the database as **username.mdb** in the recently created username folder in your web server application's root folder. If you used the default settings, the path to this database should now be c:\inetpub\wwwroot\username\username.mdb.

2 From the database manager, select Tables from the Objects bar. Choose to create a table in Design view.

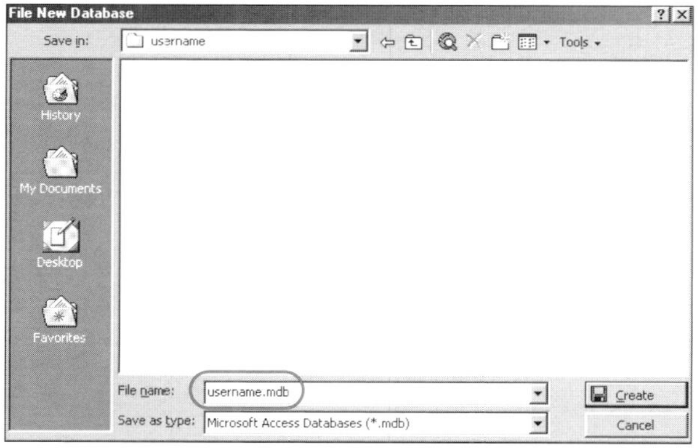

Save the new Access database to your username folder.

3 In the first row, type **Username** for the field name and select Text for the Data Type. In the Field Properties at the bottom of the page, set the Allow Zero Length field to Yes.

4 In the second row, type **Password** for the Field Name and select Text for the Data Type. In the Field Properties at the bottom of the page, set the Allow Zero Length field to Yes.

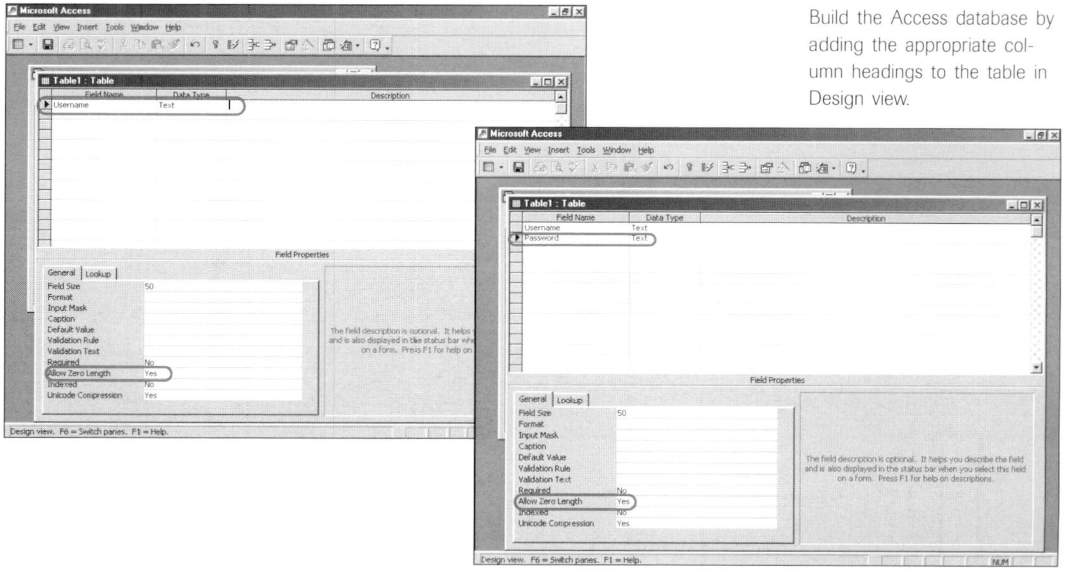

Build the Access database by adding the appropriate column headings to the table in Design view.

5 Close the table and save the table as **tbLogin**. When Access asks you whether would like a primary key created, choose Yes.

> **Note:** If you are using Windows NT or Windows 2000, it is very important that you set the permissions on the folder containing your database to read/write for the IUSR account. If this account does not have read/write access, your applications will be unable to update the database and your ASP pages may not load at all. For complete details, see the Microsoft Knowledge Base article at http://support.microsoft.com/default.aspx?scid=kb;EN-US;q175168.

6 Open the tbLogin table in Table view. In the first row, type **testuser** in the Username field and **testpassword** in the Password field.

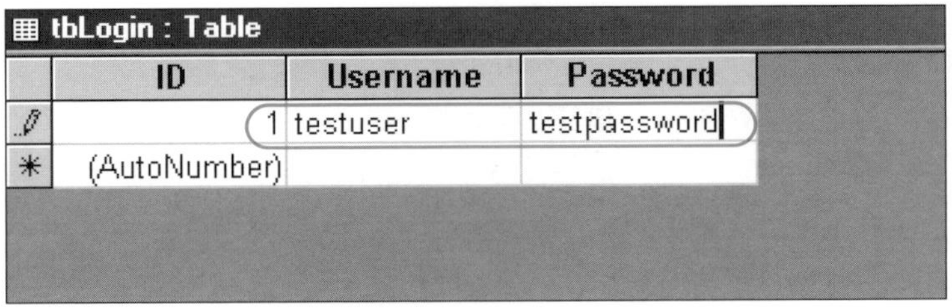

Add a record to the Access database in the Table view and save the file.

7 Save the file and close Microsoft Access.

> **Note:** If you don't have Microsoft Access installed on your workstation, you can find a copy of the database in the Project 12 folder on the CD-ROM that accompanies this book. Just copy and paste the database file into the wwwroot/username folder and you're on your way! The Project 12 folder also contains the completed pages created in this project. If you want to skip a section of the project, simply copy and paste the appropriate page to your username folder.

Defining the Dreamweaver Site

When you are building a database-driven application, setting up your Dreamweaver site is extremely important. Because Dreamweaver uses the concept of a site to group pages together by platform, an improperly configured site can quickly cause dynamic applications to break. Fortunately, Dreamweaver MX now includes a simple wizard that makes configuring a new site a snap. Although the basic site wizard is suitable for a vast majority of dynamic applications, it is important to familiarize yourself with the advanced options that arise when you are building a Dreamweaver site. To help you can familiarize yourself with some of these advanced features, this project uses the advanced method of establishing a site instead of the basic wizard.

1 Open Dreamweaver MX. Choose Site on the menu bar and select New Site.

2 In the Site Definition dialog box, set the following:

- Choose the Local Info category and type **Username** for the Site Name.
- Set the Local Root Folder to the username folder you created in your web folder's root directory (for example, c:\inetpub\wwwroot\username).
- In the HTTP Address field, type **http://localhost/username**.

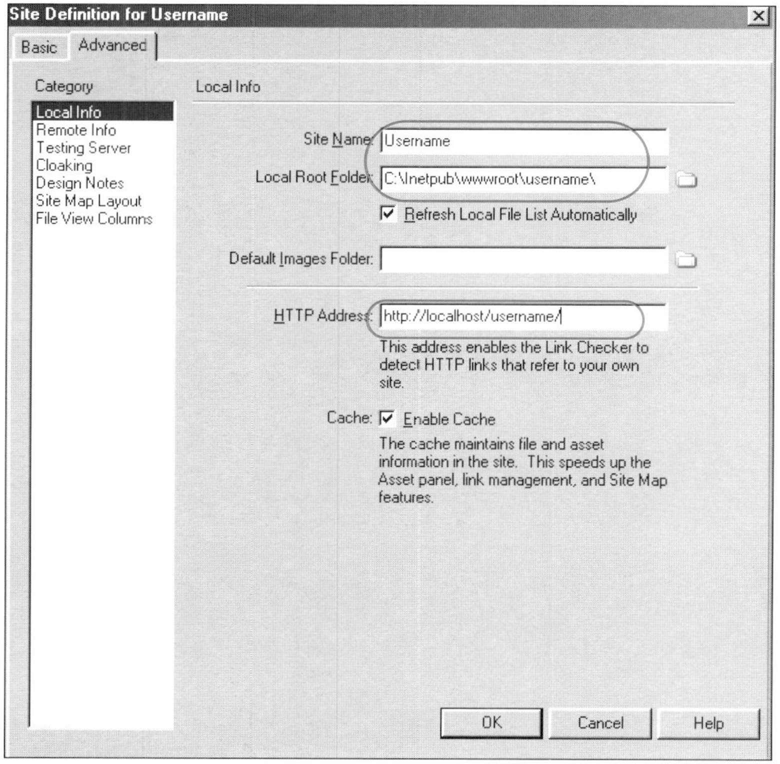

Configure the Local Info settings for your Dreamweaver site.

3 Click the Testing Server link in the Category panel and set the following:

- For the Server Model, choose ASP VBScript. Set the Access to Local/Network.
- In the Testing Server Folder, set the path to the Username folder you created.
- In the URL Prefix field, type **http://localhost/username/**.

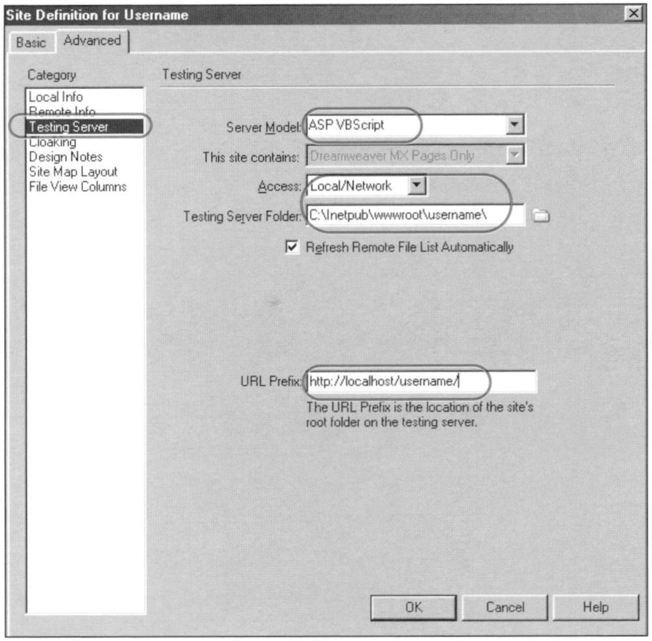

Choose the ASP VBScript server model and configure your testing server.

4 Click the Site Map Layout link in the Category panel and default.asp in the Home Page field. Click OK. When Dreamweaver asks whether you would like the default.asp page to be created, choose OK. When Dreamweaver asks whether an initial site cache should be created, click OK.

Note: If the Site window opens, close it so that you are looking at Page Layout view in Dreamweaver.

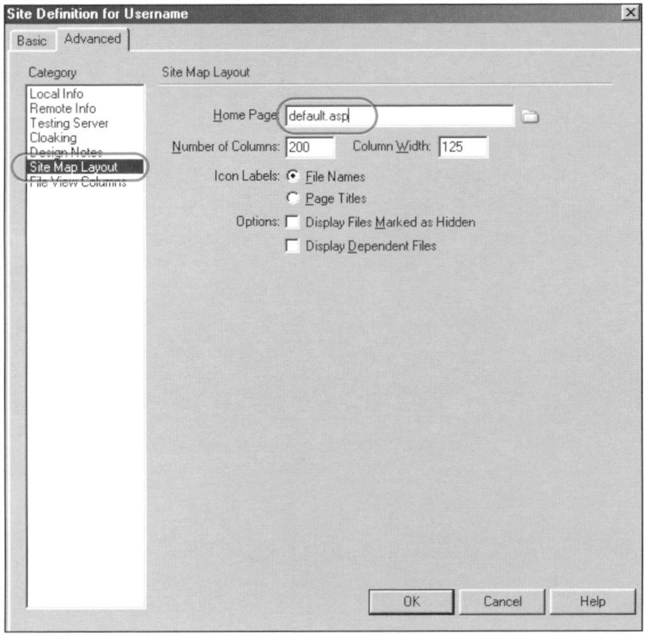

Set the home page for the new Dreamweaver site.

Creating a Login Page

The login page provides the first interaction your visitors will have with the username and password application. The login page for this project consists of a form, a table, two text fields, and two buttons. After the user types a username and password in the text fields, he or she can use the Submit button to transmit those values to the validation page or the Reset button to clear the form and return it to its original state.

1 From the menu bar, choose File>Open and open the default.asp page. With default.asp open, place the insertion point in the page and click the Align Center button on the Property inspector. Choose the Advanced tab.

2 Choose Insert>Form from the Dreamweaver menu bar.

3 With the cursor inside the form, type frmLogin in the Form Name field of the Property inspector. In the Action field, type validation.asp. Leave the Method dropdown as POST.

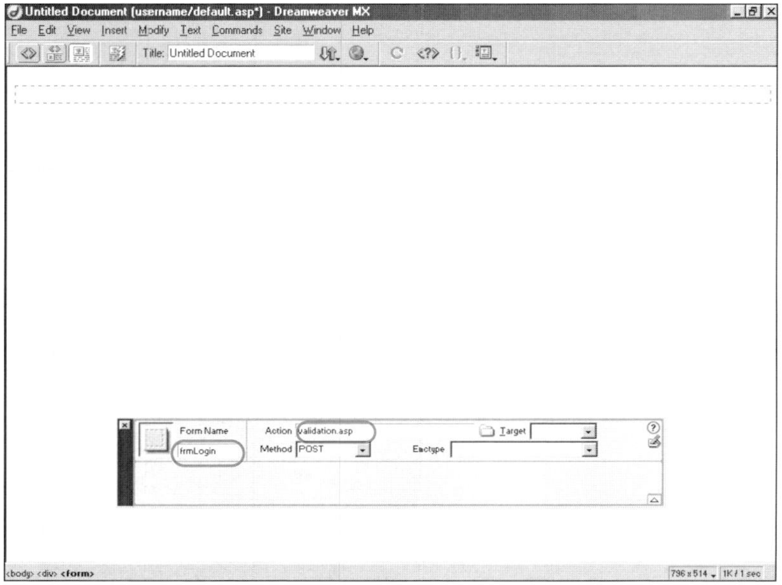

Add the form to your new page and set the form properties.

Note: The Method attribute of a form determines how the data will transmitted to the page or script designated in the Action field. Using the GET method (which is also the default method), the information in the form is submitted to the action page in the body of the submission. The POST method, on the other hand, submits the information by passing it to the next page in the URL.

4 From the menu bar, select Insert>Table. In the Insert Table dialog box, create a table that has three rows, two columns, and a width of 300 pixels. In addition, set the border, cell padding, and cell spacing to 1. Click OK. On the Property inspector, click the Align Center button. Save your file.

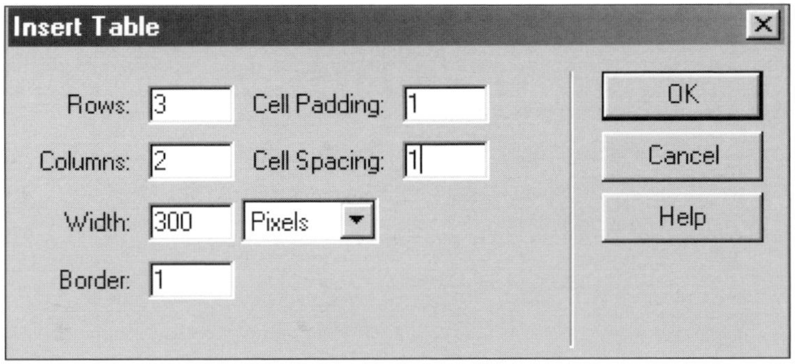

Add a new table to your default.asp page.

5 Select the cells in the left column by moving your cursor to the top of the left column. When the cursor changes to a down-arrow, click the mouse button.

6 On the Property inspector, click the Align Right button.

7 Select the right column and click the Align Left button on the Property inspector.

8 In the top-left cell of the table, type **Username:**. In the middle-left cell, type **Password:**.

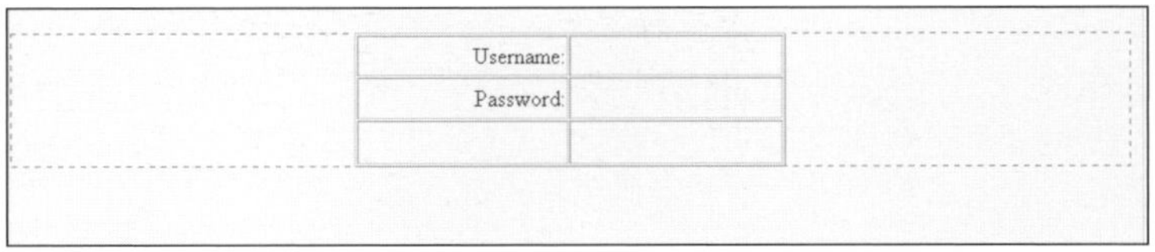

Add the Username and Password labels to the table.

9 Place the insertion point in the top-right cell and select Insert>Form Objects>Text Field from the menu bar. In the Property inspector, name the new text field **tfUsername**. If you have Dreamweaver's Form Accessibility features turned on, click OK to close the dialog box without making any changes.

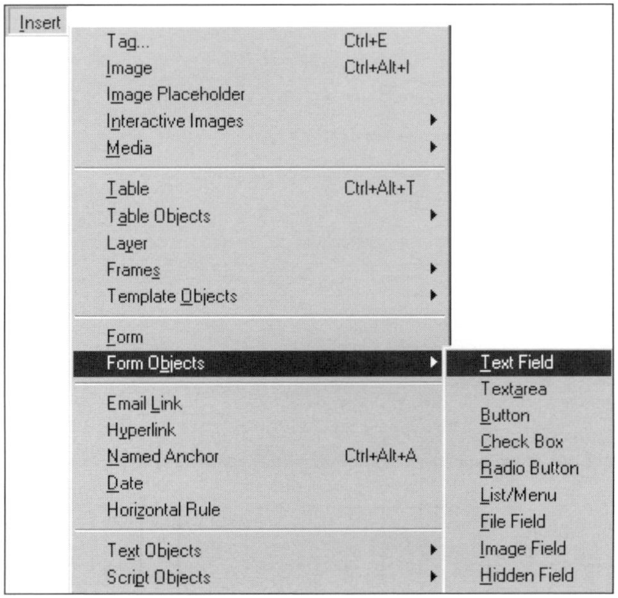

Insert a text field into the form.

10 Place the insertion point in the middle-right cell and select Insert>Form Objects>Text Field from the menu bar. In the Property inspector, name the new text field **tfPassword** and set the type as Password.

11 In the bottom-left cell, add a Submit button by selecting Insert>Form Objects>Button from the menu bar. Name the button **btSubmit** in the Property inspector. Be sure that the Form action is set to Submit Form.

12 In the bottom-right cell, add a Reset button by selecting Insert>Form Objects>Button from the menu bar. Name the button **btReset** in the Property inspector and choose the Reset Form action.

13 Save the page. Close the page, but do not exit Dreamweaver.

Tip: If you haven't already begun developing a coding style, it is a good idea to begin using naming conventions in your web applications. For instance, the tf placed before tfUsername allows anyone looking at the code for this page to identify this object as a text field. Adding identifiers such as these also helps you avoid using reserved words for your object names, which can cause problems in web applications.

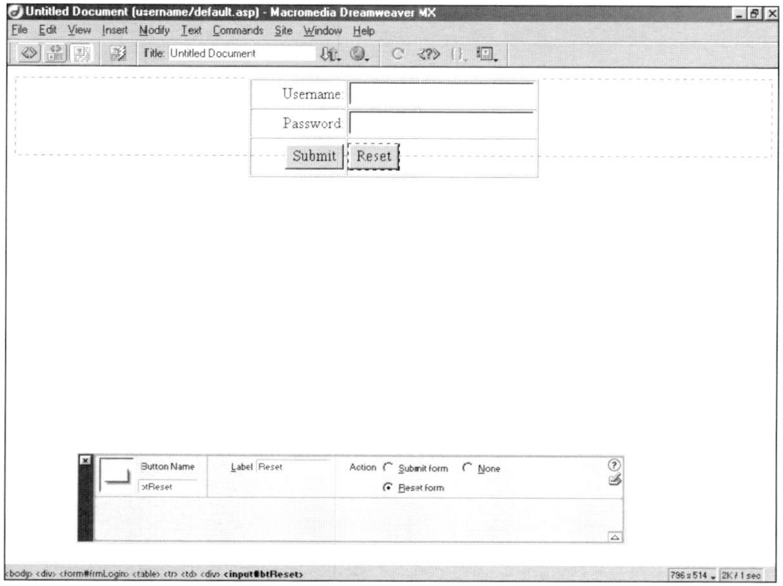

Add a Submit and a Reset button to your form.

Establishing a Database Connection

Before you can get your pages to "talk" to your database, you have to build a connection that tells each page where the database resides on the server and what kind of database it is. You have two options for building a database connection in Dreamweaver:

- You can use the ODBC Data Source Name (DSN) connection, which requires you to set up the ODBC driver on the server itself.
- You also can use the Custom Connection String (also known as the *DSN-less connection*). This DSN-less connection has a few advantages over the traditional DSN in that it doesn't require you to have any access to the server, and it actually performs better than the DSN when lots of users are accessing the data at the same time.

Regardless of which method you use, Dreamweaver makes it easy to set up your connection and test to ensure that everything is functioning properly. This project shows you how to configure a DSN-less connection.

1 Create a new page in Dreamweaver by choosing File>New from the menu bar. Choose to create a Dynamic Page using ASP VBScript and click Create. Save the page as **validation.asp**.

2 Choose Window>Server Behaviors from the menu bar. On the Server Behaviors panel, select the Databases tab and click the plus sign. Choose Custom Connection String from the drop-down menu.

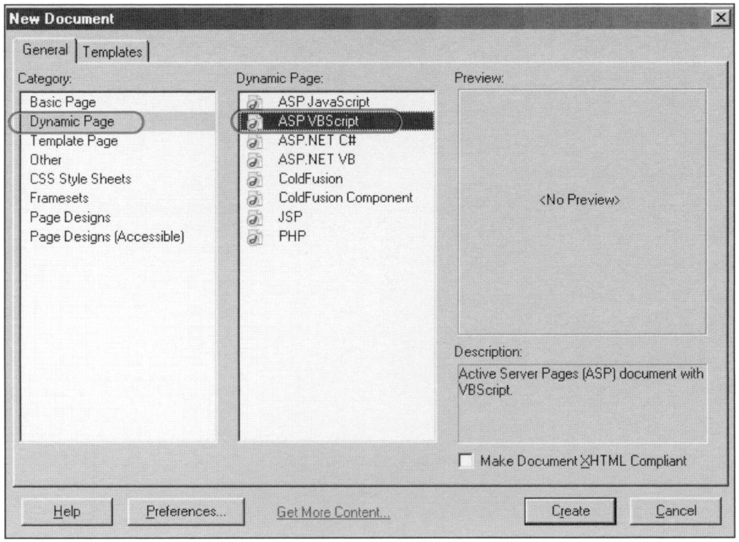

Create a new dynamic page that uses ASP VBScript.

3 In the Custom Connection String dialog box, type **connUsername** in the Connection Name field. In the Connection String field, type **"Driver={Microsoft Access Driver (*.mdb)};DBQ=c:\Inetpub\wwwroot\username\username.mdb"**.

Be sure that the path accurately reflects the path to the username.mdb database on your workstation. Be very careful when typing the string, because any error will cause the connection to fail.

5 Choose the Using Driver On This Machine radio button to indicate how Dreamweaver should connect to the database.

6 Click the Test button. You should receive a message that a connection was made successfully. If you receive an error message, check the syntax of your connection string very carefully.

7 Click OK. Dreamweaver places an icon for your new connection in the Server Behaviors panel.

Note: The custom connection you are creating in this project is often referred to as a *DSNless connection* because you do not have to build an ODBC Data Source Name on the server. Dreamweaver also allows you to easily build connections using an ODBC DSN.

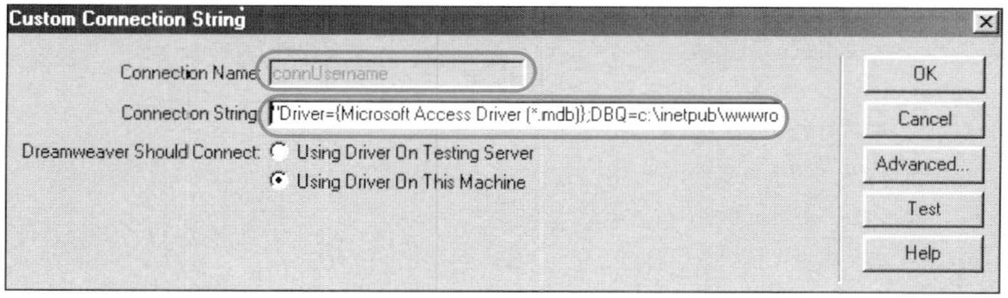

Build the Custom Connection String.

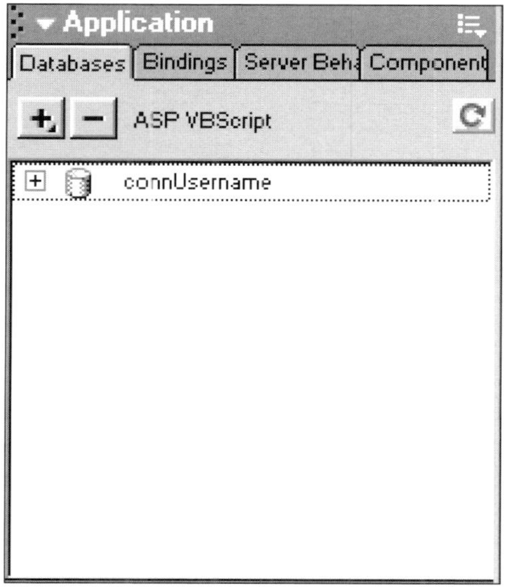

Dreamweaver adds an icon indicating that a connection to the database has been made.

BUILDING THE RECORDSET

Once a connection has been successfully created and tested, you're ready to begin building pages that communicate with the database. Because ASP pages do not speak the same "language" as database applications, you need to figure out a way to allow your pages to search and manipulate the contents of the database. To do this, you use a Structured Query Language (SQL) query to "ask" the database about its content. Based on the answer the database gives, your pages then can populate a recordset that holds all the results. Just think of the SQL query as the request you make to the database (like "Show me records that match this specific username/password combination") and the recordset is the container that actually holds the results of your request (like "Here are all the records that match that username/password combination").

Dreamweaver has a built-in Recordset (Query) server behavior that makes creating a recordset relatively easy. For basic database requests, the server behavior has a simple mode that allows you to select a table and the fields you would like to see. From this simple mode, you can even limit the results based on a single variable and can then sort the returned results.

For queries that require more tailored results, the server behavior also includes an Advanced mode, which allows you to develop powerful SQL queries to obtain very specific results from the database. Because your username and password application requires that you compare both the username and the password, you need to use the Advanced mode when building your recordset. The recordset for this application takes the username and password that were passed from the login form and checks to see whether that specific combination matches any records in the database. If there is a match, the username and password are stored in the recordset.

1 In the validation.asp page, select the Server Behaviors panel by either choosing Window>Server Behaviors or by clicking the Server Behaviors tab if the panel is already open.

2 Create a new recordset for the page by clicking the plus sign on the Server Behaviors panel and choosing Recordset (Query).

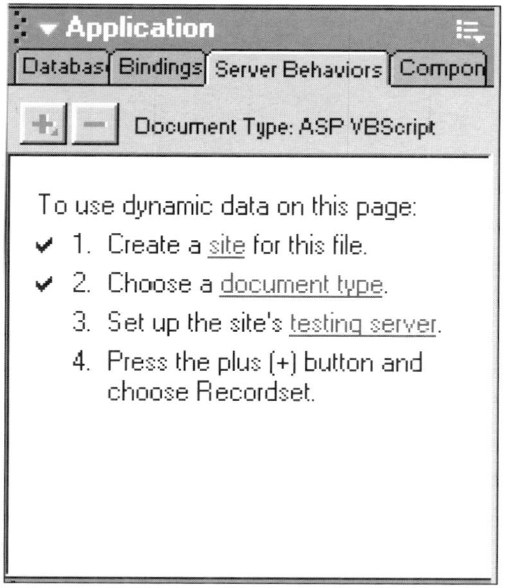

Dreamweaver's Server Behaviors panel.

3 In the Recordset dialog box, type **rsLogin** in the Name field and select the ConnUsername connection and the tbLogin table.

4 Click the Advanced button to switch to the advanced view of the Recordset dialog box.

5 In the Database Items panel, click the plus sign next to Tables. You should now see the tbLogin table. Click the plus sign next to tbLogin and you should see the three fields stored in the table.

6 Click the Username field and click the Select button. Notice that Dreamweaver adds an appropriate select statement in the SQL textfield. Click the Where button and notice that Dreamweaver expands the SQL statement.

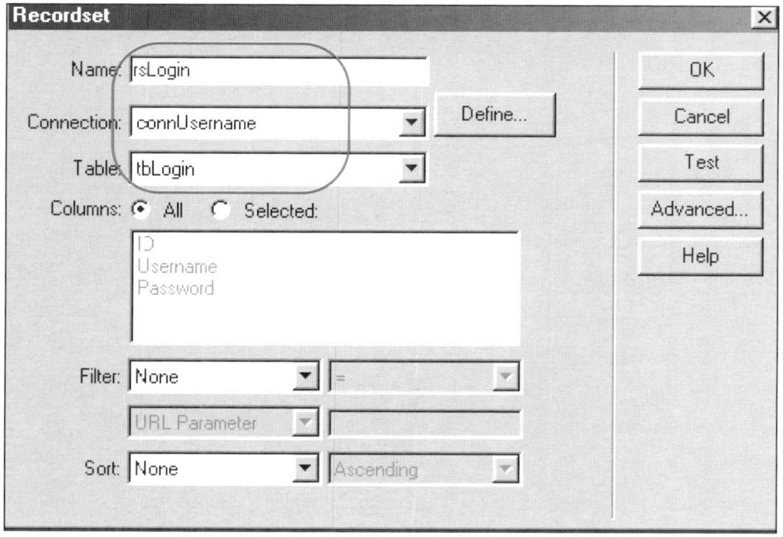

Name the recordset and choose a connection and a table.

7 Click the Password field and click the Select button. Click the Where button.

8 Place the insertion point in the SQL text field after the WHERE Username statement and type ='varUsername' (don't forget the apostrophes).

9 Move the insertion point to a point after the AND Password statement and type ='varPassword' (don't forget the apostrophes).

Warning: When creating your own custom SQL queries, be very careful with your syntax. Forgetting to type a single quote or misspelling a variable name can cause your entire application to fail.

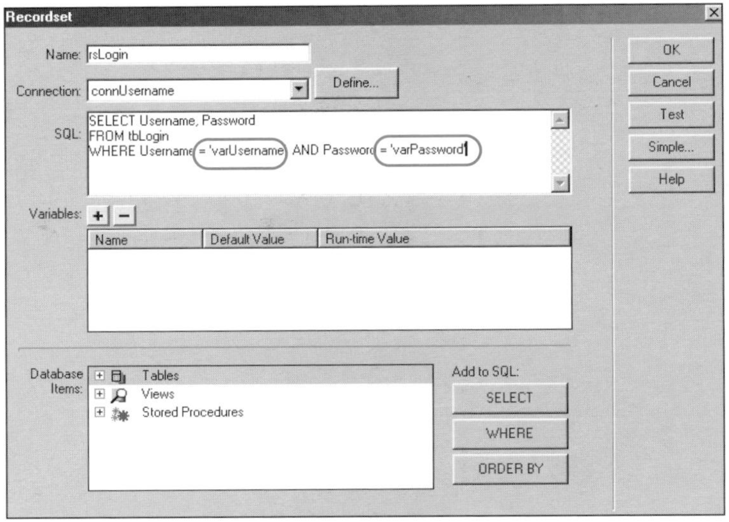

Complete the custom SQL statement with the appropriate SELECT, FROM, and WHERE statements.

10 Click the plus sign for the Variables field and place the insertion point in the Name field. Type **varUsername**. Press Tab. In the Default Value field type 0 and press Tab. In the Run-time Value field, type **Request.Form("tfUsername")**.

11 Click the plus sign for the Variables field and place the insertion point in the Name field. Type **varPassword**. Press Tab. In the Default Value field, type 0 and press Tab. In the Run-time Value field, type **Request.Form("tfPassword")**. Click OK. Dreamweaver adds an icon to the Server Behaviors panel indicating that a recordset has been created.

12 Save the page and leave it open because you will be using it in the next section.

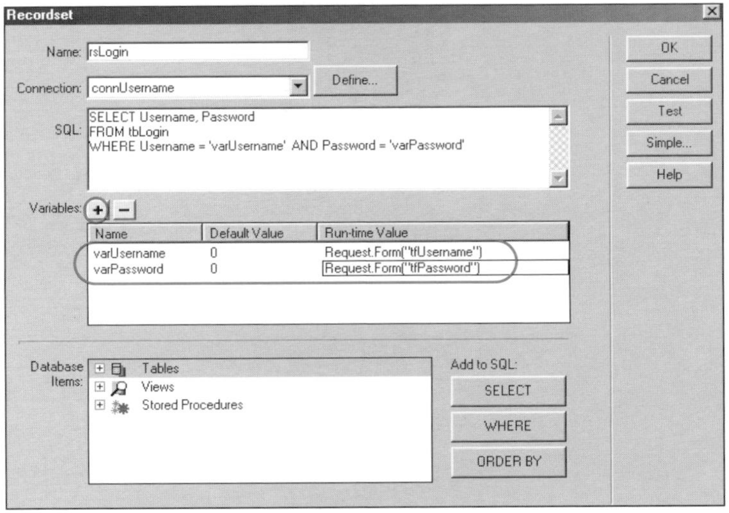

Create the variables that store information submitted on the login form.

Creating the Validation Page

Now that the recordset is complete, you need to build a page that looks at the contents of the recordset and displays an appropriate response. For instance, if the recordset is empty, it means that the supplied username and password did not match any of the records in the database. This means that either the user does not have a valid username and password or he or she typed it wrong. In either case, you want the page to display a message indicating that the username and password are not valid. You can then offer the visitor an opportunity to try again. If, however, there is a record in the recordset, this means that the username/password combination matched a record in the database and the user can be successfully logged in.

Although this may sound like a complicated process, Dreamweaver makes the process very easy through the use of the Show Region server behaviors. With these behaviors, you can select an area of the page and apply one of the Show Region behaviors to indicate when the text should be visible.

1. In the validation.asp page, place the insertion point in the document and click the Align Center button on the Property inspector.
2. Type **You have been successfully logged on. Click here to add a user to the database.** Highlight the second sentence in this text and type **add_user.asp** in the Link field of the Property inspector. Press Enter.
3. Highlight all the text and click the plus sign on the Server Behaviors panel. From the drop-down menu, select Show Region/Show Region If Recordset Is Not Empty.
4. In the Show Region If Recordset Is Not Empty dialog box, select the rsLogin recordset and click OK. Dreamweaver adds a border around the text with a label that indicates that this text is displayed only if the recordset contains a valid record.

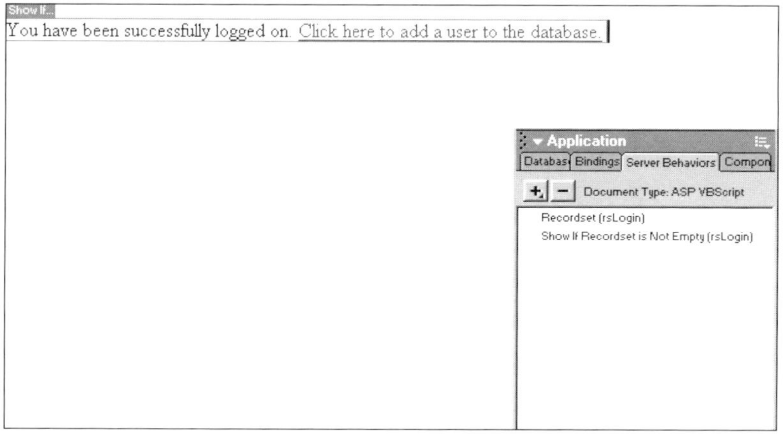

This text is displayed if the username and password match a record in the database.

5 On the line below the text, Press Enter and type **Your username or password is not valid. Click here to try again**. Press Enter.

6 Highlight the second sentence in this text and type **default.asp** in the Link field of the Property inspector.

7 Highlight this text and click the plus sign on the Server Behaviors panel. From the drop-down menu, select Show Region/Show Region If Recordset Is Empty.

8 In the Show Region If Recordset Is Empty dialog box, select the rsLogin recordset and click OK. Dreamweaver adds a border around the text with a label that indicates that this text is displayed if only the recordset contains no records.

9 In the validation.asp page, switch to Code view by clicking the Show Code View button on the toolbar.

10 Next, you need to create a session variable that allows the visitor to move from page to page without having to enter a username and password at each page. In your code, find the line that says <% If Not rsLogin.EOF Or Not rsLogin.BOF Then %> . Create a blank line after this code and add the following line of code on the new line: **<% Session("MM_Username") = Request("tfUsername") %>**.

11 Save the page. Close the page and leave Dreamweaver open.

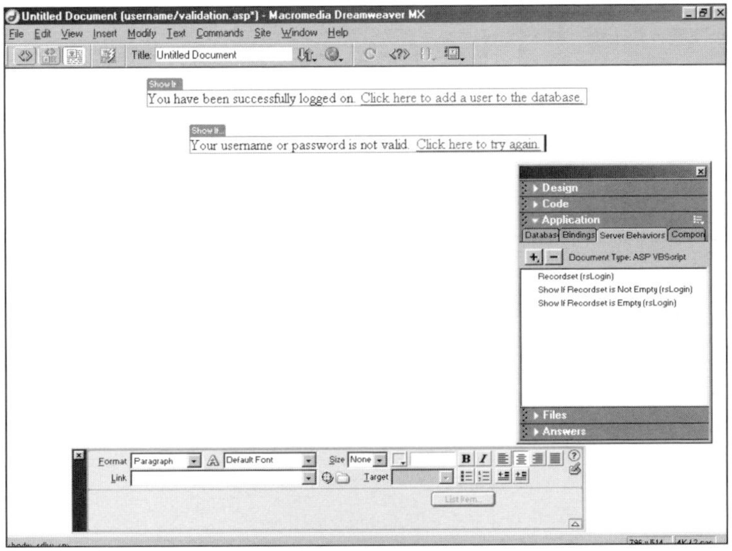

The second line of text is displayed if the submitted username and password are not found in the database.

```
37 <body>
38 <div align="center">
39   <p>
40     <% If Not rsLogin.EOF Or Not rsLogin.BOF Then %>
41     <% Session("MM_Username") = Request("tfUsername") %>
42     You have been successfully logged on. <a href="add_user.asp">Click here to
43     add a user to the database.</a>
44     <% End If ' end Not rsLogin.EOF Or NOT rsLogin.BOF %>
45   </p>
```

Add the code in line 41 to build a session variable.

Note: Dreamweaver does have a Log User In server behavior, but it does not create a session variable for the user. Because this session variable is what allows users to move throughout the site without having to type their usernames and passwords, it is often more useful to skip the server behavior and add the session variable by hand.

Restricting Access to a Page

Now that the application is capable of checking to see whether a user has a valid username and password, you need to ensure that a user cannot just skip the login process by typing the direct URL to a page without logging in first. To do this, you make use of the session variable created in the last section. When visitors successfully log in to the site, a small file called a "cookie" is placed on their computers. This file stores the visitors' usernames and the times they logged on. When users leave the site or log out, those cookies are destroyed. Because only validated users have the session cookie, you can easily build pages that check whether the cookie exists and, if it doesn't, you can keep that user from viewing pages without logging in.

To implement this restriction, you can use Dreamweaver's Restrict Access To Page server behavior. When it is applied to a page, the server behavior looks at the visitor's machine to see whether a valid cookie exists before it loads the page. If a cookie is present, the page is displayed. If, however, the cookie does not exist, the visitor is automatically redirected to a new page—in our case, the login page.

1. Create a new page by choosing File>New from the menu bar. Choose to create a dynamic page using ASP VBScript and click OK. Save the page as add_user.asp.
2. Place the insertion point in the page and click the Align Center button on the Property inspector.
3. Type This page is password protected. Since you have logged in, you can view it.
4. On the Server Behaviors panel, click the plus symbol and select User Authentication/Restrict Access To Page. In the Restrict Access To Page dialog box, choose to restrict access based on Username and Password. Click the Browse button, select the default.asp page, and click OK. Click OK to close the Restrict Access to Page dialog box.
5. Save the page. Close the page and keep Dreamweaver open.

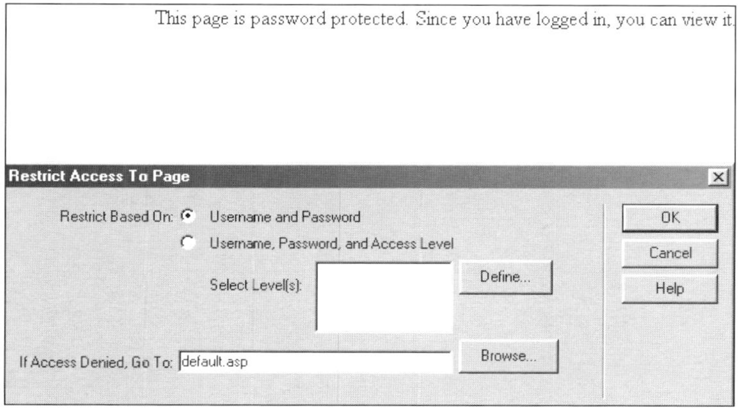

Protect the page using the Restrict Access To Page server behavior.

Adding Users to the Database

After a visitor's username and password are authenticated, you can offer the user the opportunity to search your database and add, remove, or edit information stored in the tables. In this section, you see how easy Dreamweaver makes it to add a new username and password to the database. Using Dreamweaver's built-in Record Insertion Form application object and a few clicks of the mouse, you can add the required form, form objects, and code to your page, which allows the user to add a new record.

1 Place the insertion point at the end of the text in the add_user.asp page and press Enter.

2 From the menu bar, choose Insert>Application Objects>Record Insertion Form.

- In the Record Insertion Form dialog box, choose the connUsername connection and the tbLogin table.
- In the After Inserting, Go To: field, type **user_added.asp**.
- Highlight the ID field in the Form Fields panel and click the minus button to remove it.
- Click OK. Dreamweaver adds a form and table to your page that includes text fields for adding a new username and password to the database.

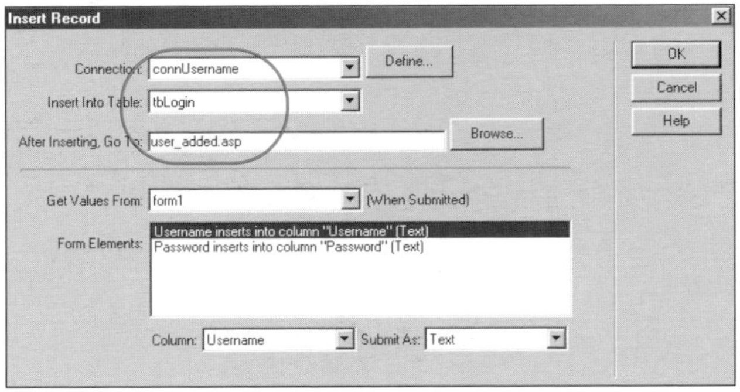

Use the Insert Record dialog box to build a form for adding new username/password combinations.

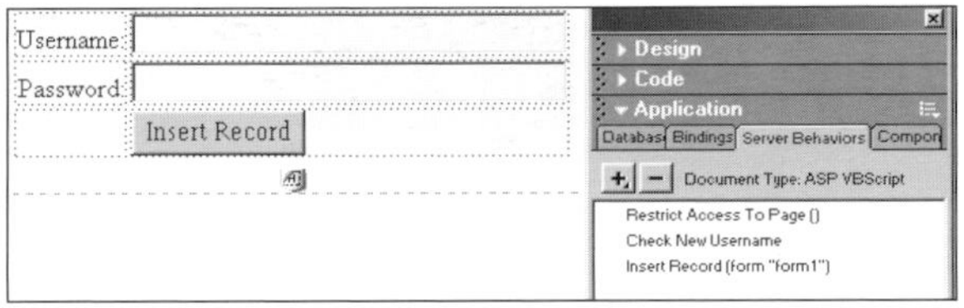

Dreamweaver has added a form for inserting new records into the database.

3 On the Server Behaviors panel, click the plus sign and choose User Authentication>Check New Username.

- In the Check New Username dialog box, Choose Username as the Username Field.
- In the If Already Exists, Go To: field, type **username_taken.asp**. Click OK.

4 Save the page and close it. Do not exit Dreamweaver.

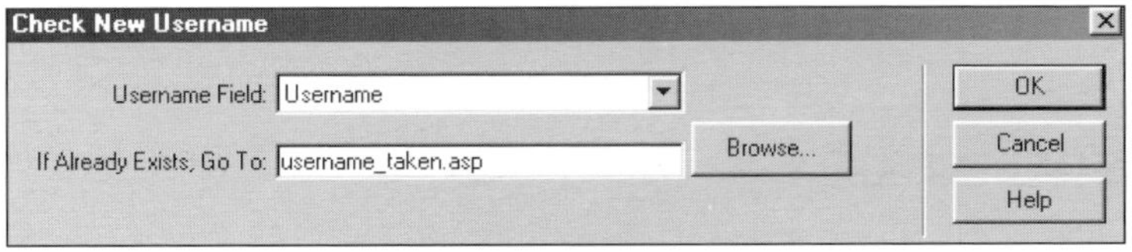

Use the Check New Username dialog box to ensure that the record does not already exist in the database.

Adding Confirmation Pages

When adding, removing, or deleting records from your database, it's always a good idea to develop pages that confirm that the requested action was performed. For instance, when the application finds that the visitor is trying to add to the database a username that already exists, a confirmation page warns him or her that the record was not added because it already exists. Likewise, when a new unique record is added to the database, the visitor is directed to a page that confirms that the operation was performed without problems.

1 Create a new dynamic page using ASP VBScript and save it as **username_taken.asp**.

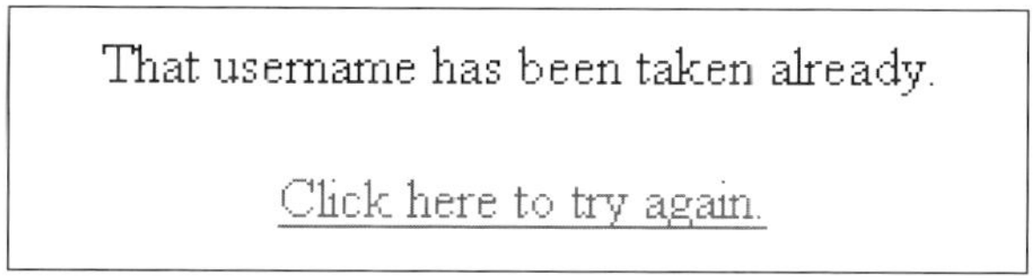
That username has been taken already.
Click here to try again.

Create a page that warns the user that the submitted username already exists in the database.

2 Place the insertion point in the page and click the Align Center button. Type **That Username has been taken already**. Press Enter.

3 Type **Click here to try again.** Highlight this text and type **add_user.asp** in the Link field of the Property inspector.

4 Save the page and close it. Do not exit Dreamweaver.

5 Create another new dynamic page using ASP VBScript and save it as **user_added.asp**.

6 Place the insertion point in the page and click the Align Center button on the Property inspector.

7 Type **This user has been successfully added**. Press Enter.

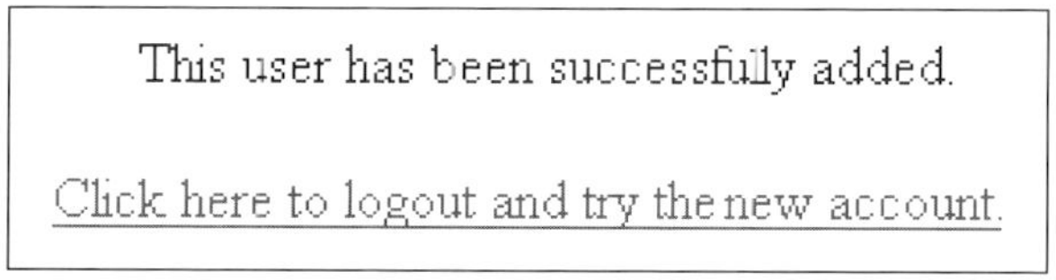
This user has been successfully added.
Click here to logout and try the new account.

Create a page that confirms that the record was successfully added to the database.

8 Type **Click here to logout and try the new account**. Highlight this text and type **logout.asp** in the Link field of the Property inspector.

9 Save the page. Close the page and keep Dreamweaver open.

Creating a Logout Page

The final step in developing the username/password application is to provide the visitor with the ability to log out. From the visitor's point of view, the user may just be clicking on a button or a link or simply closing the browser. From the application side, however, you need to create a page that removes the session cookie from the user's machine to ensure that the user cannot access the password protected sections of the site without logging on again.

To build this functionality, you create a logout page asking visitors to confirm that they want to log out, and then use Dreamweaver's Log User Out server behavior to build a link that, when clicked, destroys the session cookie.

1 Create a new dynamic page using ASP VBScript. Save the document as **logout.asp**.

2 Place the insertion point in the new page and click the Align Center button on the Property inspector.

3 Type **Click here to confirm that you wish to log out**. Press Enter.

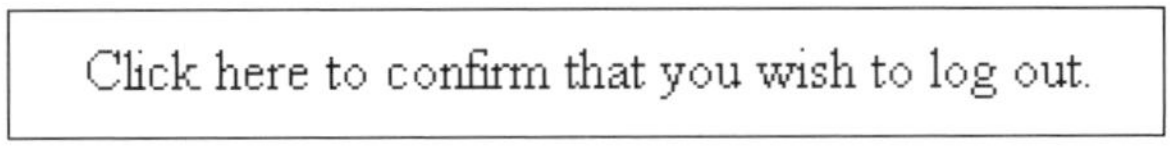

Create a page that confirms that the user wants to log out.

4 On the Server Behaviors panel, click the plus sign and select User Authentication/Log Out User.

5 In the Log Out User dialog box, select the Link Clicked option. Be sure that the Create new link "Log Out" option is selected in the drop-down list

6 In the When Done, Go To field, type **default.asp**. Click OK.

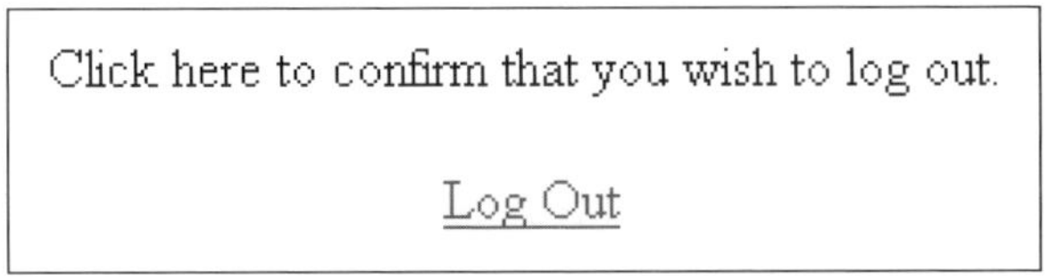

Build a link that, when clicked, logs the user out.

7 Switch to Code view in Dreamweaver and find the two lines of code that say:

```
Session.Contents.Remove("MM_Username")
Session.Contents.Remove("MM_UserAuthorization")
```

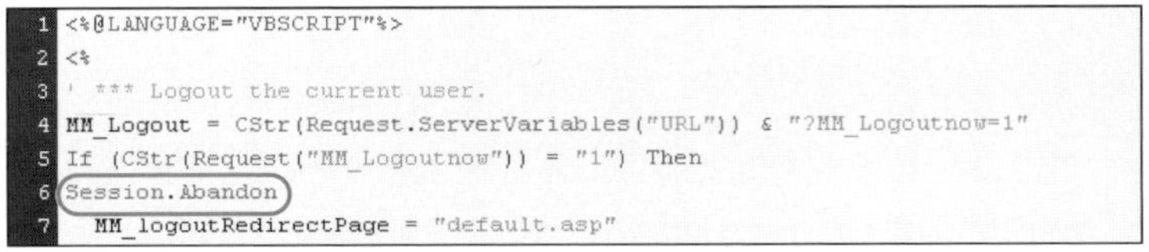

<%@LANGUAGE="VBSCRIPT"%>
<%
' *** Logout the current user.
MM_Logout = CStr(Request.ServerVariables("URL")) & "?MM_Logoutnow=1"
If (CStr(Request("MM_Logoutnow")) = "1") Then
Session.Abandon
MM_logoutRedirectPage = "default.asp"

Replace the Sessicn.Contents. Remove code with the Session.Abandon code.

8 Replace these two lines with a single line of code that says **Session.Abandon**.

Note: You may be wondering why I told you to remove the Session.Contents.Remove() code that Dreamweaver placed in the page. This change is merely one of personal preference. When I log users out, I want to know that all the data pertaining to their visit has been removed from their machine. I can do this quickly and with one line using the Session.Abandon code. If, instead, I choose to use the Sessions.Contents.Remove code, I have to be sure that each and every session variable I have created within the site is destroyed when the visitor leaves. This doesn't seem like that difficult of a task if I am using two variables, but imagine a complex site that uses 20 variables. With one line of code, I can perform the same function that would require 20 lines using the Session.Contents.Remove method.

9 Save the page.

Testing the Application

Before unleashing the new username/password application on the web, it's always a good idea to walk through and test every aspect of its functionality. In your tests, you need to ensure that:

- A visitor cannot access a protected page without first logging on.
- A visitor who submits a username/password combination that does not match a record in the database is denied access to the site.
- An authenticated visitor who tries to add a username/password combination that already exists in the database is warned and the record is not added.
- An authenticated visitor who adds a new, username/password combination is advised that the record was added successfully.
- Once a new username/password combination has been added to the database, it can be used to access the site.

1 Open Internet Explorer or Netscape and enter **http://localhost/username/add_user.asp** as the web address.

Notice that because you have not logged on using a valid username and password, you were automatically redirected to the login page. You can confirm this because the URL now displays http://localhost/username/default.asp?accessdenied=%2Fusername%2Fadd%5Fuser%2Easp, indicating that access was denied by the add_user.asp page.

2 In the login form, type abcdefg in the Username field and qwerty in the Password field. Click the Submit button.

Because the username and password that were entered do not match a valid record in the database, the validation page denies access to the site.

3 Click the link to try again and type testuser as the Username and testpassword as the Password. Press the Submit button.

Because the username/password combination exists in the database, access is granted. If you get an error message that says something about a volatile connection, you need to check the permissions on your database to ensure the IUSR account has read/write permissions.

4 Click the link to add a user to the database.

Because you have successfully logged in, you can now access this same page that previously denied you access.

5 In the Username field, type testuser and in the Password field, type testpassword.

6 Click the Submit button.

Because this username already exists in the database, the record is not added and you are redirected to a page letting you know that the record already exists.

7 Click the link to try again. This time, type user2 as the Username and password2 as the Password. Click Submit and notice that you are now directed to a confirmation page, letting you know that the record has been added.

8 Click the link to log out. On the logout page, confirm that you want to logout by clicking the link. After you confirm, your session is ended and you are redirected to the login page.

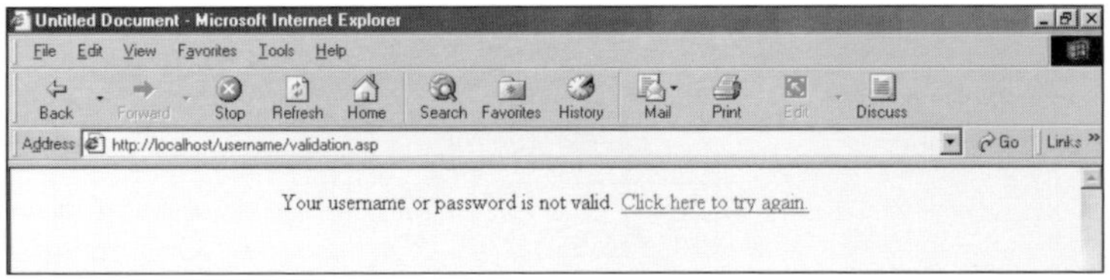

Because a valid username/password combination was not provided, access is denied.

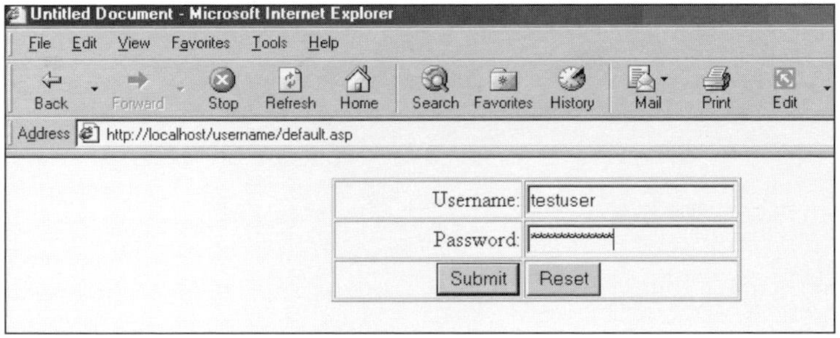

Log in using the username and password you added to the database when it was created.

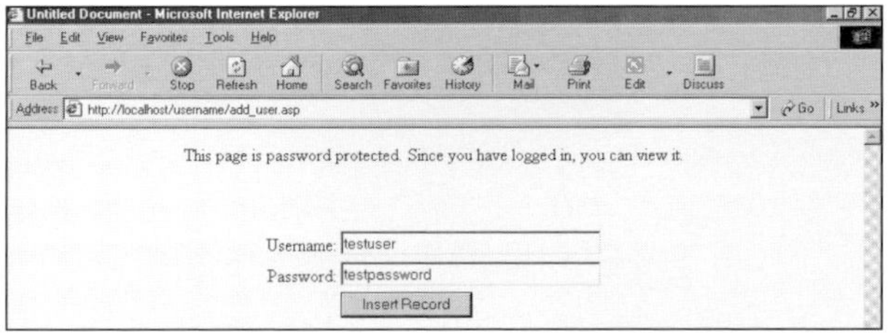

Test the Check New Username server behavior by typing a username and password that is already in the database.

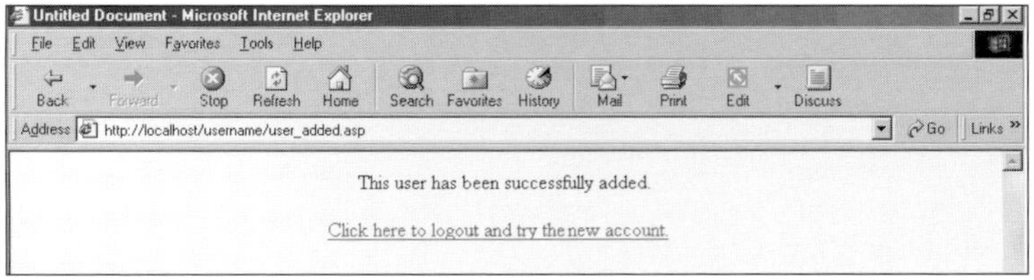

The username and password combination has been added to the database.

9 In the login form, type user2 for the Username and password2 as the Password. Click Submit and notice that this username/password combination is now valid because it has been added to the database.

10 Close your browser and Dreamweaver.

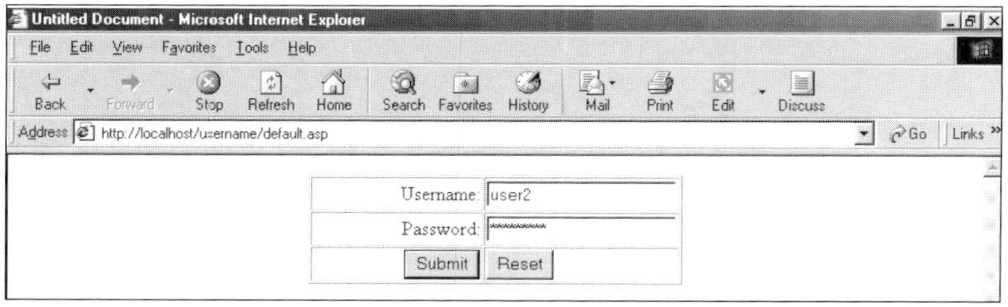

Test the new username and password to ensure that they are accepted.

Modifications

A database-driven username and password validation application such as this one can be a very handy tool regardless of the platform for which you are developing. For demonstration purposes, this project used Active Server Pages and an Access database. Dreamweaver, however, has the capability of producing code for a variety of platforms (including ASP, JSP, ColdFusion, and PHP) and databases (including Access, SQL Server, MySQL, Visual FoxPro, and Oracle). With a few modifications in the setup of your Dreamweaver site and database connection, you can easily follow the remainder of the steps in this chapter to develop a username/password application for your platform and database.

ColdFusion

If you are developing on the ColdFusion platform, the first modification you need to make is to install and configure the ColdFusion Server on your local workstation. Dreamweaver ships with a single-license version of ColdFusion Server, but you need a full version of the software to put your pages into production. After you install the server application, you need to configure an ODBC DSN for your database of choice. For details on setting up this DSN, check out Project 9.

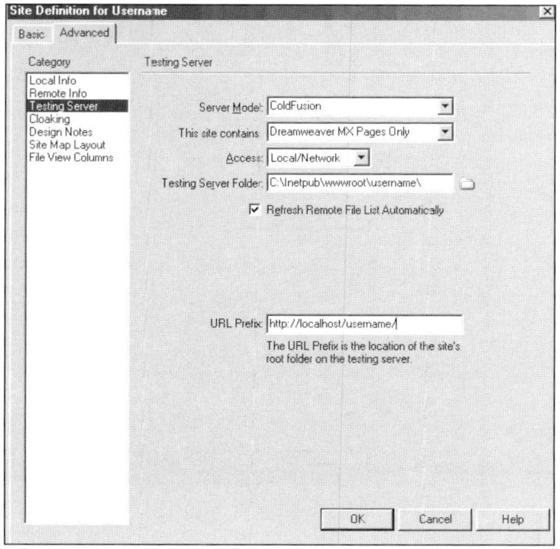

When configuring your Dreamweaver site, indicate that the site should use the ColdFusion server model.

The final modification you need to make when configuring Dreamweaver to code these pages in CFML is to indicate that your site will be a ColdFusion site. When you are setting up your site in the Testing Server category of the Site Definition dialog box, set the Server Model field to ColdFusion and indicate whether you will be using only Dreamweaver MX pages or a combination of MX and UltraDev 4 pages.

After you have configured your site, you can basically follow the steps given earlier to develop your application on the ColdFusion platform. Keep in mind, however, that all the pages developed should have a .cfm extension rather than the .asp extension used in this project.

JSP and PHP

Many of the changes that need to be made to configure a ColdFusion site also need to be made when using the JSP or PHP server model. If you are using JSP, you need to install a server application capable of serving Java Server Pages. Dreamweaver ships with a trial version of JRUN, a very popular JSP application. Those wanting to develop in PHP will need to install Apache web server, the PHP application, PERL, and a PHP-compatible database such as MySQL. After you install and configure that server software, you can either configure a JDBC DSN or an ODBC DSN.

Tip: For details on installing and configuring JRUN, check out the article at www.macromedia.com/support/ultradev/installation/installing_ jrun/installing_jrun06.html.

For details on configuring a Windows 9x workstation to serve PHP pages, check out the article at www.phpbuilder.com/columns/ boutwell19991212.php3.

If you choose to use an ODBC DSN, however, you will need to use the JDBC-ODBC Driver when establishing your database connection. This connection is relatively simple to set up and gives your JSP and PHP pages the ability to work with ODBC database such as Microsoft Access and SQL Server.

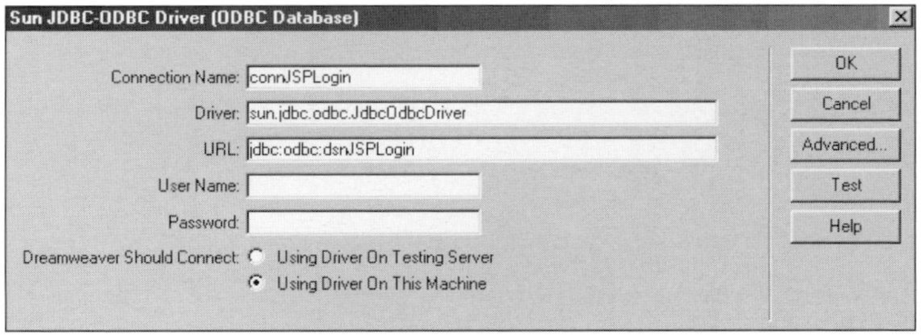

You can use the Sun JDBC-ODBC Driver to connect your JSP or PHP pages to an ODBC database such as Access.

The final step in modifying this project to work with JSP or PHP is to modify your Dreamweaver site to use the JSP or PHP platform. In the Testing Server category of the Site Definition dialog box, set the server model to JSP or PHP and you will be ready to build your pages.

Note: You can find out more information on JRun and ColdFusion Server on the Macromedia web site at www.macromedia.com. Information regarding Apache Web server can be found at the Apache Software Foundation site at www.apache.org and details on ChiliSoft! can be found at www.chilisoft.com.

NO NEED FOR FLASH

"Iron rusts from disuse; stagnant water loses its purity and in cold weather becomes frozen; even so does inaction sap the vigor of the mind."

—LEONARDO DA VINCI

No Need for Flash

"No Need for Flash" began as a joke between Graphic Designer Pierre Dausse and DHTML Developer Massimo Foti. After viewing web pages like the one you are about to create, people would comment that they liked the Flash. Massimo and Pierre—with very big smiles—would reply, "Flash? No thanks, we don't need it for this sort of thing."

Project 13

No Need for Flash

by Massimo Foti, Angela C. Buraglia, and Daniel Short

with special contributions from Pierre Dausse

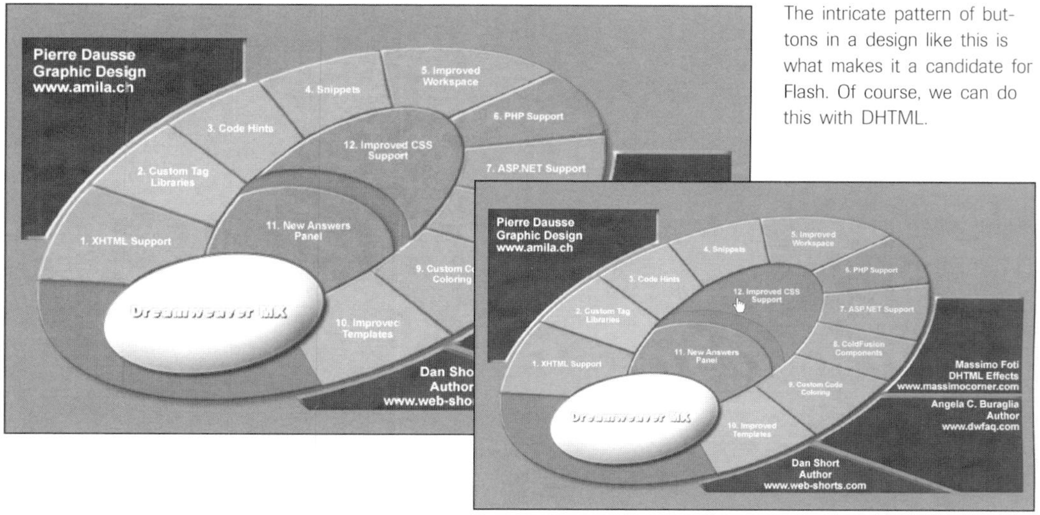

The intricate pattern of buttons in a design like this is what makes it a candidate for Flash. Of course, we can do this with DHTML.

As the user moves the mouse over each of the buttons, a layer is shown to give the impression that the button is being pressed.

It Works Like This

A design like the one in this project is often considered a candidate for Flash because of its complexity. The unusual shape of the layout graphic's buttons—and their position within the graphic—is what makes this project so special. Because the buttons are spread over the graphic in a non-linear fashion, it would be nearly impossible to create this layout using tables. Layers give you the flexibility to precisely place images in the desired position with very little code. In fact, the HTML (without JavaScript or images) is approximately 6K.

One very important thing to consider when creating this project is the file size of the images. The complete project is approximately 121K, including all images. Without images, the file (including JavaScript) is only 12K. That means you have well over 100K of images that must be downloaded for the page.

Note: Massimo asked Pierre for a gorgeous design—and he got it. Sometimes a larger file size is totally worthwhile.

With that in mind, you should be aware of your site's audience and know whether you can afford an overall size such as this. You certainly can create layouts of a smaller size to keep the weight of the page down when you develop projects derived from the concepts you will learn here.

Often when working with DHTML, people usually forget that the CSS z-index property allows them to take advantage of a third dimension. The CSS z-index property allows you to place a layer on various levels, which is known as *the stacking order*. The example in this project uses three different levels; you will be placing a background image in a layer on the lowest level, a transparent image in a layer that uses an image map on the highest level, and all the button image layers in-between as the middle level.

Note: The higher the z-index value, the closer to the top that the layer is in the stacking order.

The concept is simple, but powerful. The illusion of Flash occurs because it appears that the end user is interacting with the buttons themselves. In fact, they aren't really interacting with buttons at all, but with an image map. The transparent GIF is assigned an image map that uses the same exact hotspot shapes as each of the buttons. Because the image map precisely covers each button's shape, you get the feeling the mouse events occur when you mouse over and out of the buttons. Instead, the mouse events are applied to the map areas only. We told you it was simple!

Preparing to Work

Before we begin this project, the usual preparation is needed. All the files used in this project are found in the Projects/13_no_Flash folder on the Dreamweaver MX Magic CD.

1 Install two extensions—both are Behaviors:

- Launch the Extension Manager.
- Verify that Dreamweaver MX is chosen in the list menu.
- Choose File>Install Extension.
- Browse to the Extensions folder on the CD.
- Open the Behaviors subfolder.
- Choose the align_layer.mxp Behavior by Massimo Foti.

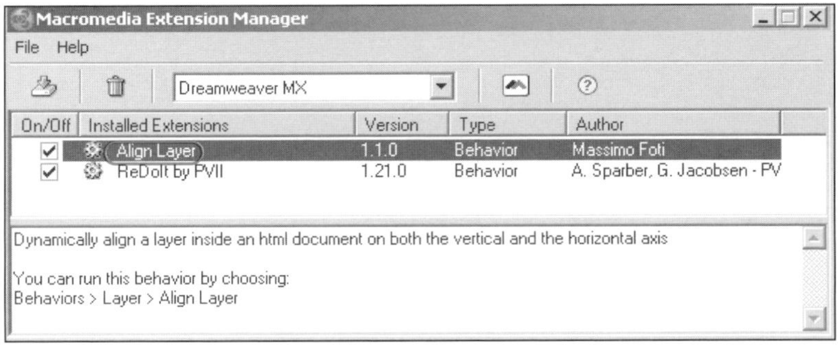

Be sure to install Align Layer by Massimo Foti and ReDoIt by PVII so that they are ready when you need them.

- Accept the license agreement and the installation confirmation.
- Repeat the same procedure to locate and install the P7ReDoIt.mxp by Project Seven Development.

2 Copy the necessary files for this project:

- Browse to the projects folder on the CD.
- Copy the project_thirteen folder to a location on your hard drive.

3 Define a new site using the project_thirteen hard drive copy as your site root.

4 If you don't already own Macromedia Fireworks MX, you should check out the free trial available in the Software folder on the accompanying CD. Fireworks version 4 also will work fine for this project. You will need it for its precise automated creation of image maps. If you choose not to use Fireworks, you'll either need to draw all image maps manually or try to use a similar feature in another graphics editor.

Browser Compatibility

"No Need for Flash" has been tested in the following browsers:

Microsoft Internet Explorer 5 (Windows and Macintosh)

Microsoft Internet Explorer 5.5 (Windows)

Microsoft Internet Explorer 6 (Windows)

Netscape 4.08 through 4.6 (Windows)

Netscape 4.5 (Macintosh)

Netscape 6 (Windows and Macintosh)

PREPARING THE IMAGES IN FIREWORKS

You have just a few steps to go through to get your images set up correctly for our mouseovers. Because the focus of the project is on the DHTML effects, we're going to cover these steps only briefly.

You'll need two layers for your buttons (one for the Up state, and one for the Over state). We've already provided the Up state buttons on their own layer in the 13_layout.png file in the project_thirteen/images/ folder on the CD. We'll use the Up state buttons to export one large JPEG image and the Over states to export individual slices for the mouseovers.

Note: When creating your own buttons, be sure to give each of your paths a meaningful name so that you can find them later. Notice how we've named all our vector paths.

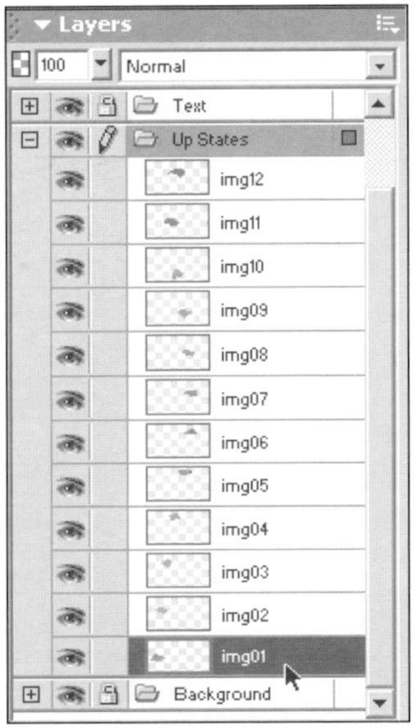

Give your layers and vector paths meaningful names from the start, so that it is easier to switch layers on and off later in the process.

CREATING THE BUTTON OVER STATES

In order to have a proper mouseover, you need to create a separate layer containing all the buttons for the mouseover. These will look slightly different than the Up state in order to give a visual indication to visitors that they've moved the mouse over a link.

Note: A finished PNG with each button's Over state, hotspot, and slice has been provided as 13_layout.png. You should work with 13_layout-start.png to complete all the steps on your own. You can refer to 13_layout.png to see that you have completed each step correctly.

1 Open 13_layout-start.png in Fireworks or your graphic editor.

2 Duplicate the layer containing your Up state buttons.

- Click the Up States layer to select it.
- Click the Options Menu icon in the upper right of the Layers panel and choose Duplicate Layer.
- When the Duplicate Layer dialog box appears, choose the After current layer option to put the Over state layer below the Up States layer; then click OK.
- Rename the new layer **Over States** by double-clicking on the new layer in the Layers panel and typing the new name.

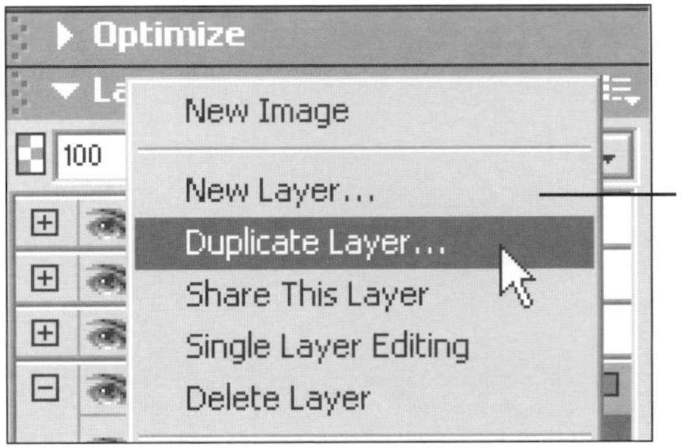

Duplicate the Up state images to create images quickly for the Over states. Be sure to choose After Current Layer.

3 You need to create a noticeable change in the Over state buttons so the user can see that something's happening.

- Select the entire Over States layer and, using the Opacity slider in the top-right corner of the Layers panel, change the opacity to 60%.
- Select each Over State button path and disable or remove all the effects by unchecking the Effects fields in the Property inspector.

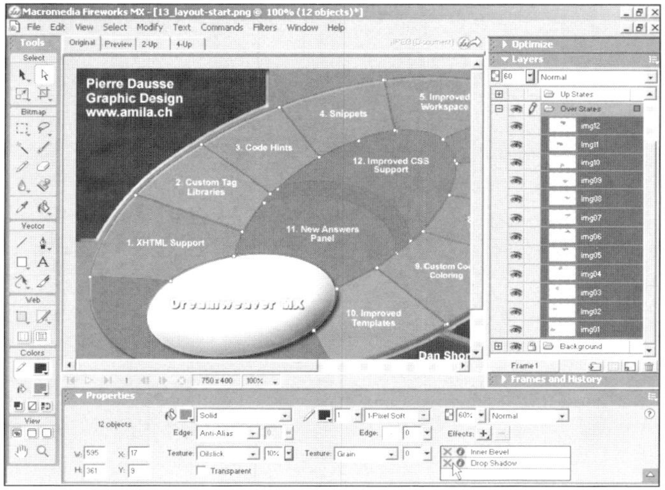

Change the opacity and remove effects to create Over states quickly.

Creating Hotspots and Exporting the HTML

Now you need to create your image map. Fireworks does all the work for you here, including creating all the hotspots and creating the HTML for the image map.

1 Once you have created all your buttons, make sure the Over State layer is hidden and the Up State layer is fully visible. To hide the Over State layer, click the eye icon next to the layer name.

2 Create a hotspot for each button. Shift-click each button path in the document so that all 12 buttons are selected.

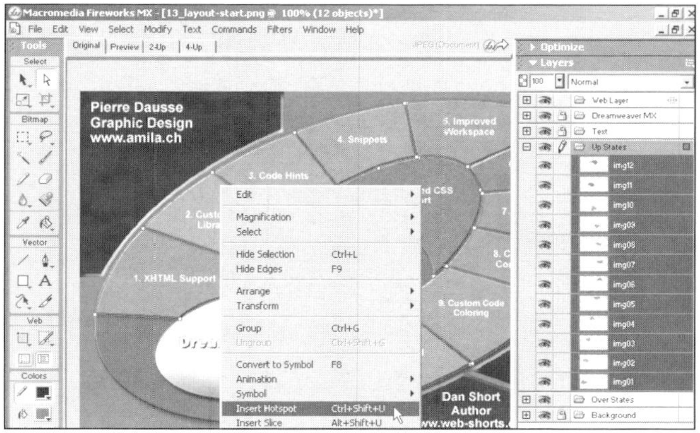

Select each path in the Up States layer, and add multiple hotspots to create the image map.

3 Right-click (Ctrl-click) any of the selected layers, and choose Insert Hotspot. You will be prompted that multiple items are selected and asked whether you'd like one hotspot or multiple. Choose Multiple.

Tip: Use the keyboard shortcut Ctrl-Shift-U (Cmd-Shift-U) to quickly add the hotspots.

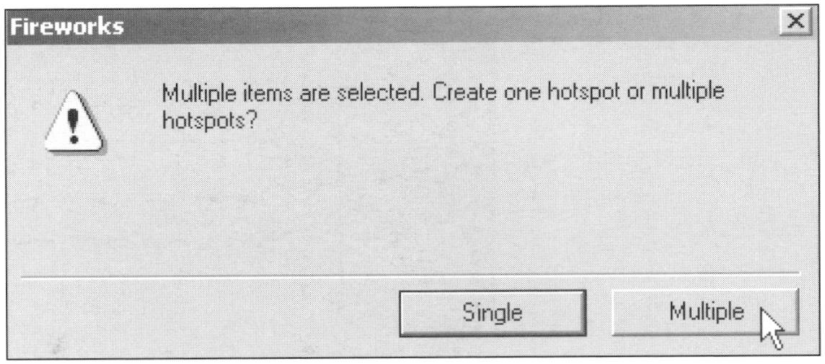

When prompted, choose Multiple to insert all the hotspots at one time.

4 When you're done, you should see a hotspot over each of the buttons. Now choose File>Export and export HTML and Images without any slices. This will give you an HTML page (imgMain.htm) with your full JPEG (imgMain.jpg) and an image map. Now you have exported to the images folder of your site. Once you start building your layers and adding DHTML, you'll change this JPEG to a transparent GIF (imgMap.gif).

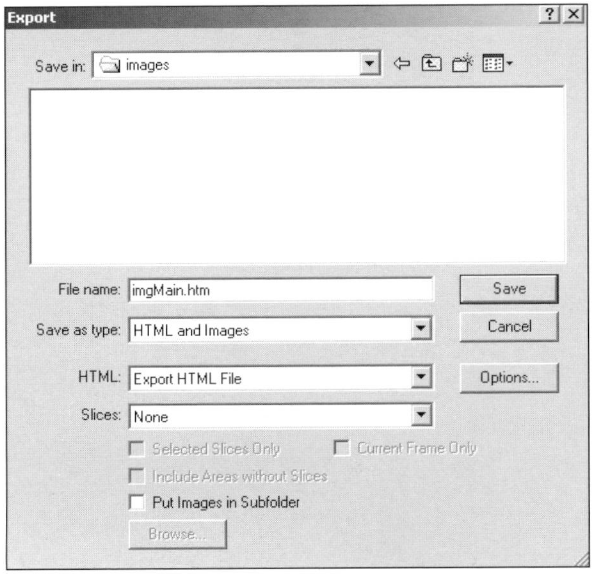

Export HTML and Images to save the layout graphic and image map for use later in the project.

Creating and Exporting Slices

Next, you need to create all your slices. These slices will be the mouseover images for each of the hotspots. You're going to have to follow a few tedious steps to get this part done, and you also need to take some notes while doing it. In this section, you need to get each button's Over image exported with the adjacent buttons in their Up state.

1 Hide all the hotspots by clicking the eye icon next to each hotspot in the Web Layer.

2 Hide the Up state for the one image you want to export and leave the rest of the Up state images showing. You're going to start with img01.

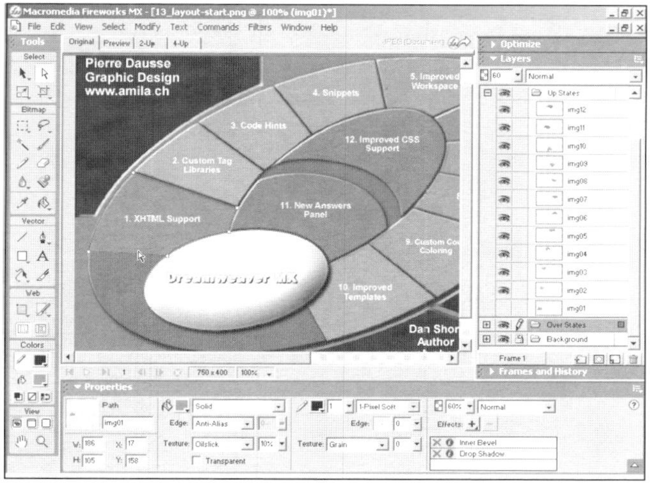

This image shows the Up state for img01 hidden, the x, y, height, and width of the slice, as well as the slice name.

3 Create a slice for the Over state.

- Click the path for the Over state, right-click and choose Insert Slice or press Alt-Shift-U (Ctrl-Shift-U) to create a slice that covers the entire path.
- Right-click the slice and choose Arrange>Bring to Front.
- Write down the width, height, x, and y coordinates for each slice as it's created. You will need these values later.

4 Click in the name field in the Property inspector (Window> Properties) and give the slice a meaningful name. In this example, the images will be named *img[number]*. So you'll name the first slice img01.

Note: We have already done all the exporting for you. This means that if you export to the same folder, you will be asked whether you'd like to overwrite the images. It is okay to do so—you can always get the images from the CD again if needed.

5 Right-click the slice and choose Export Selected Slice to the images folder in your site.

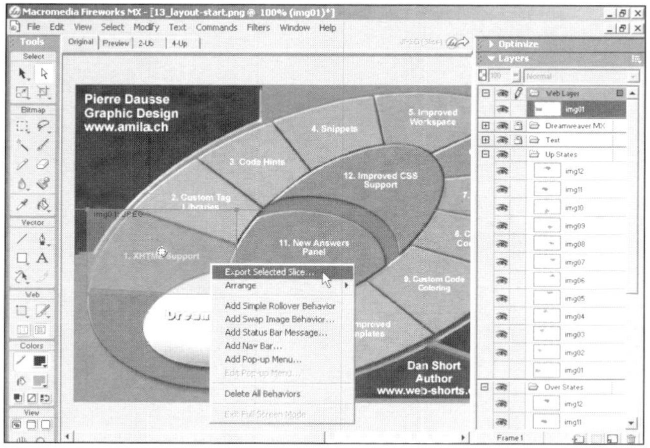

Right-click the slice and choose Export Selected Slice in order to export only the current slice.

Note: Make sure that the slice you want to export is at the very top or it will get chopped into pieces. To do this, right-click the slice and choose Arrange>Bring to Front or press Ctrl-Shift-Up Arrow (Cmd-Shift-Up Arrow on the Mac).

6 Repeat Steps 2 through 5 for each slice, hiding the Up state of the button you want to export while making sure that all adjacent buttons are showing the Up state.

Note: Remember that it is important that your JPEG images are all exported using the same optimization settings. If you choose different settings, you may experience color matching and blending issues that will destroy the overall effect you are trying to achieve.

7 Create a 40×40 slice of the solid gray background to use as the page background. Name it imgBackground and export it the same way you exported the rest of your slices.

Now you're ready to start putting the layers together in Dreamweaver.

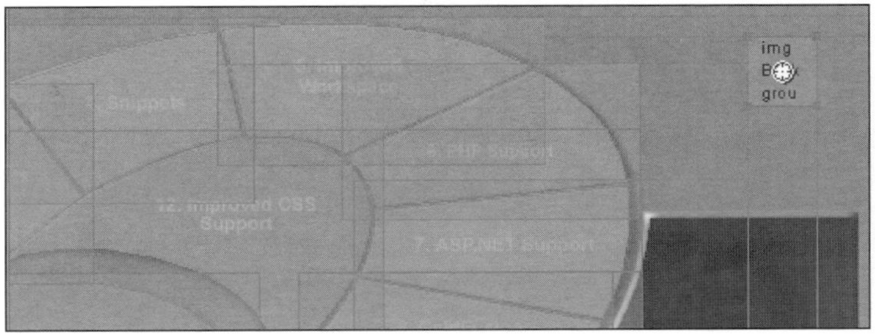

Make sure that you export a small patch of the background color—with the same export settings—to use as a background image on your page. Otherwise, you could run into color matching problems.

Creating the Layers in Dreamweaver

Adding the layers and their contents is very easy. Much of this part of the project is filled with repetitive tasks. After doing a task once, you will be able to go through and repeat them quickly.

Creating the Main Layer

The main layer is the foundation for the entire project. As described earlier, the main layer contains the layout graphic, the nested button layers and the map layer. In this case, a 750×400 pixel JPEG image is used as the design for the project. The JPEG format was chosen in order to preserve as much detail in the image as possible for the highest quality. Depending on the graphic you choose to use with this project, the GIF format may be suitable.

Tip: To keep things simple and intuitive, we've used a simple naming convention. Each image file is named with a prefix of img because images are contained in <img> tags. Likewise, the layers are all named with a prefix of div because the <div> tag is what makes a layer. Almost all images correspond to a layer in this project. For example, img01 would belong inside of div01 just as imgMain belongs inside of divMain. Later, when it comes time to use the extension, you'll see why having a simple naming convention is helpful.

To create the main layer, follow these steps:

1 Open the file named index.htm located in the Site panel.

We've chosen to use an HTML file for this project, but ASP, CFML, JSP, or PHP will do just fine. We're dealing only with HTML, JavaScript (through the use of an extension), and some very simple CSS. There is nothing special about this HTML file. This is an ordinary new document, which has been given a page title.

2 Use the Draw Layer object located in the Common category of the Insert bar to click and drag a layer onto the page. It doesn't matter what size it is or where it is positioned. You will be adjusting this in the next step.

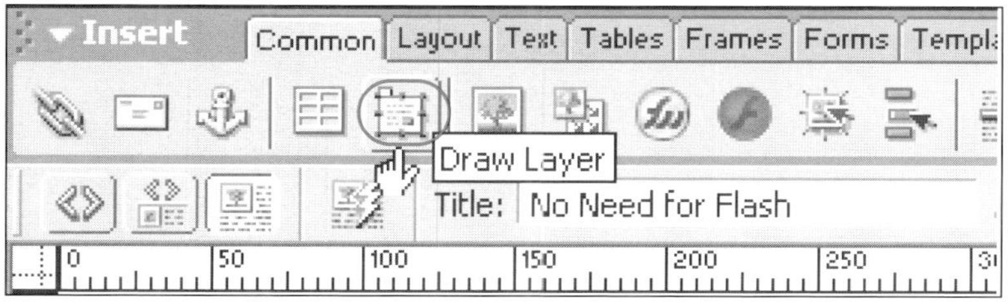

Use the Draw Layer object to draw layers quickly on the page. The layers can be adjusted later using the Property inspector.

A small yellow shield bearing the letter C may appear in the document. This is known as an "anchor point for layers." Though the anchor points can be a helpful visual aid, in this project they will become distracting as you add the button layers. Layers may appear as though they are not positioned the way they should be. To avoid this issue, disable the feature temporarily by choosing View>Visual Aids>Invisible Elements and verifying that there is not a checkmark beside Invisible Elements.

3 Select the layer, and set the following values in the Property inspector (Window> Properties):

Layer Id: **divMain**

L: **0px**

T: **0px**

W: **750px**

H: **400px**

z-index: **1**

visibility: **default**

All other fields should be left blank.

4 Click inside the newly created layer.

5 Locate imgMain.jpg in the Images category of the Assets panel. Drag the file into the layer or click the Insert button. You will notice that the image is sized the same as the divMain layer.

If you do not see the images in the Assets panel, try one or more of the following options:

- Make sure that the Site radio button, not Favorites, is selected.
- Choose the Refresh Site List icon.
- Right-click (Ctrl-click) inside the Site list area (below the preview area), and choose Recreate Site List.

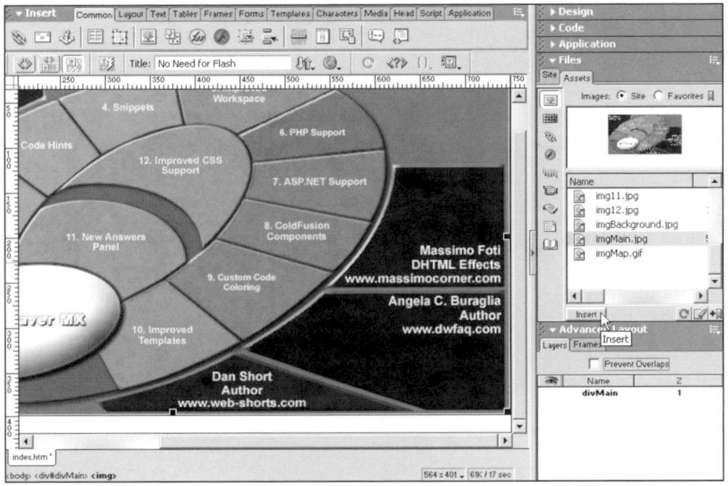

Once you've drawn the divMain layer and given it the proper size and z-index, you can quickly insert imgMain.jpg from the Assets panel.

Creating the Button Layers

Each button Down state has its own image that will be inserted into its own individual layer within divMain. Placing layers within other layers is known as "nesting." The divMain layer is the "parent" layer of the button layers, also known as "child" layers.

The button layers are nested inside of divMain so that they will always move along with their containing layer. This is great for those times when you want to center everything in the browser (as you'll be doing later) or simply move everything over a couple of pixels. To create the nested layers that will contain the button images, follow these steps:

Tip: It is good practice to save your work often. If you haven't done so already, choose File>Save. Save your document after completing the steps in each section.

1 Select the Drag Layer icon in the Common category of the Insert bar.

Tip: Ordinarily, to draw layers one after the next without having to click the Drag Layer icon between each layer, you need to use the keyboard shortcut Ctrl-click (Cmd-click) while dragging. In this situation, however, the layers need to be nested inside the divMain layer. We add the Alt (Option) key to the combo, Ctrl-Alt-click (Cmd-Option-click), so that multiple consecutive nested layers may be drawn.

2 In this step, you will be drawing multiple consecutive layers. Ctrl-Alt-click (Cmd-Option-click) and drag a small layer over each of the buttons' text in divMain. This will ensure that you do not inadvertently click in another button's layer, causing additional nesting. Begin at number 1 and go through to number 12. Do not worry about their size or placement at this time. You will adjust that later.

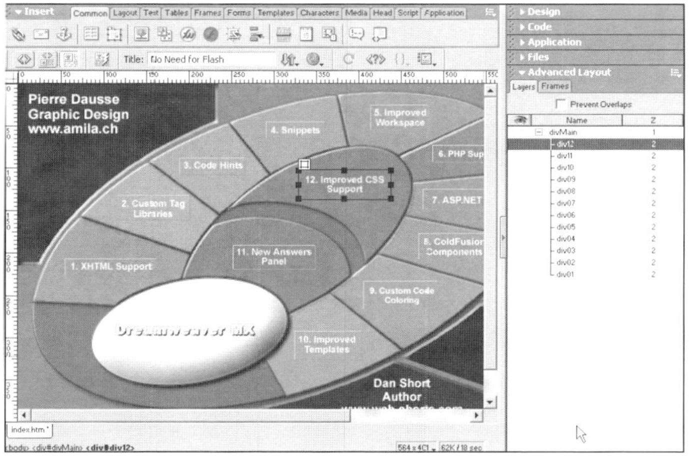

Draw a layer over the top of each button. Notice that they're now nested under divMain in the Layers panel.

3 Open the Layers panel by pressing F2. You will notice that divMain now has a plus symbol (right arrow) or a minus symbol (down arrow) to the left of it that can be clicked to expand and contract the list of nested layers.

4 With divMain expanded to show all the child layers, rename each of the 12 child layers according to the naming convention we are using for this project. Layer1 should be renamed to div01, Layer2 should be div02, and so on. To name the layer, double-click it in the Layers panel—so that it is highlighted and hence editable—or assign the Layer ID in layer Property inspector.

Note: When renaming the default layer names, you are setting the id attribute of the <div> tag. You are not setting the name attribute.

5 Set the z-index value to 2 for each of the nested button layers in the Property inspector.

Placing Images and Positioning

When you created the buttons in Fireworks, you were instructed to write down the x and y coordinates for each slice and the image's dimensions.

For each button layer, follow these steps:

1. Select the layer in the Layers panel.
2. Click inside the layer.
3. Select the corresponding image from the Assets panel, and then click Insert.
4. In the layer Property inspector, assign the width and height values of the image to the layer in the W and H fields, respectively.
5. Assign the X coordinate value to the L field in the Property inspector. This is the number of pixels from the left edge of divMain that the child layer should be positioned.
6. Assign the Y coordinate value to the T field in the Property inspector. This is the number of pixels from the top edge of divMain that the child layer should be positioned.

Note: Having the coordinates available in advance is a real time-saver. If you do not have the coordinates to enter, you can manually position each layer. You can drag the layer by first choosing the selection handle, and then clicking and dragging the layer to the proper position. Alternatively, you can move the layer by first selecting it, and then using the arrow keys for precise pixel-by-pixel movements.

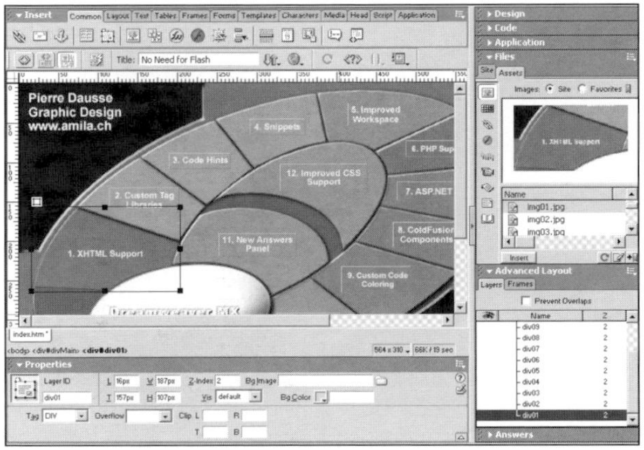

Insert the corresponding button image into each of the layers.

Note: If you do not have the sizes to enter, you can select the image and get the size values from the image Property inspector.

When you have completed these steps for the first child layer, the code should look like the following:

```
<div id="div01" style='position:absolute;
➥left:16px; top:157px; width:187px;
➥height:107px; z-index:2;"><img
➥src="images/gifs/img01.jpg" width="193"
➥height="113"></div>
```

Creating the Image Map Layer

The final layer is divMap, which also is nested within divMain. As you should recall, this layer is the topmost layer, which holds a transparent GIF with an image map of hotspot shapes that match the underlying buttons.

1. Select the Drag Layer icon in the Common category of the Insert bar.

2. Alt-click (Option-Click) and drag a small layer over divMain. This keyboard shortcut will allow you to draw a single nested layer. Do not click inside any of the button layers or this layer will be mistakenly nested within it. For this project, a safe area to draw the layer would be in the top left corner. Do not worry about the size or placement at this time. You will adjust that next.

3. In the layer Property inspector, set the values as shown:

   Layer Id: **divMap**

   L: **0px**

   T: **0px**

   W: **750px**

   H: **400px**

   z-index: **3**

   visibility: **default**

   All other fields should be left blank.

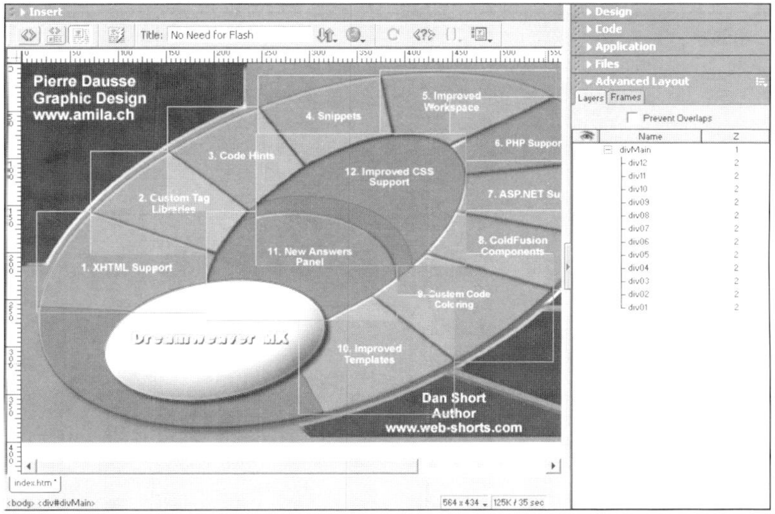

Having followed the same steps for each of the layers, your page should look like this.

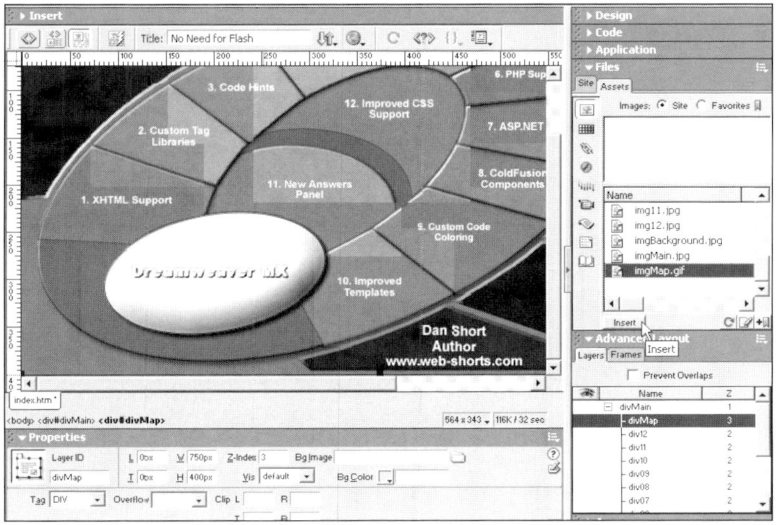

Prepare the divMap layer to hold a transparent GIF image (imgMap.gif) that will use an image map made of hotspots for each of the buttons.

4 The divMap layer will contain a transparent GIF image equal to the size of imgMain.jpg. Locate the transparent image named imgMap in the Assets panel, and insert the image into the layer.

5 Change the width and height values of the image to the same dimensions as the layout graphic. In this case, the layout graphic is 750×400 pixels.

ADDING THE IMAGE AND THE MAP

When creating your own version of "No Need for Flash," using the Fireworks generated image map will make this process incredibly easy. On the other hand, if you did not use Fireworks to create the image map, you'll need to carefully draw each hotspot in Dreamweaver. This can be a very tedious process—especially with complex shapes. To save you time, we have provided the Fireworks HTML file, imgMain.htm, that contains the image map for you.

Locate and then double-click imgMain.htm in the Site panel to open the file in Dreamweaver. You'll see that the imgMain.jpg we used earlier is in this file with a complete set of hotspots that complete the image map. All we really need here is the image map code.

1 While holding the Shift key, click each of the hotspots. You should have all 12 hotspots selected.

2 Choose Edit>Copy.

3 Switch back to the index.htm file.

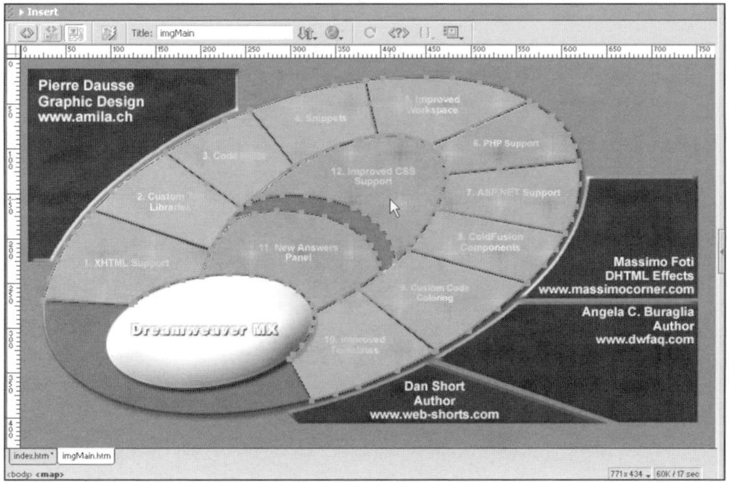

Select each of the hotspots exported from Fireworks by Shift-clicking on each one. Choose Edit>Copy to move the image map to your other file as described in Steps 3 through 5.

4 Click the imgMap.gif.

5 Choose Edit>Paste.

Voila! All of the hotspots are now applied to imgMap.gif and the divMap layer is complete. Feel free to close imgMain.htm; you won't need it anymore.

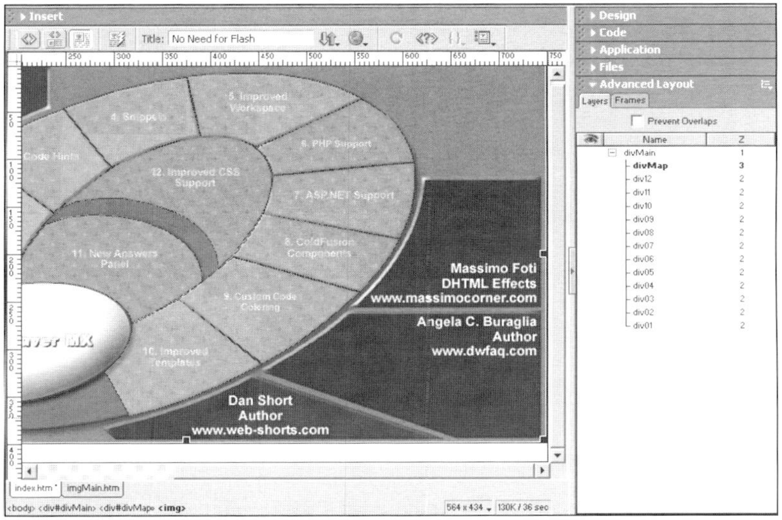

Once inside the working file (index.htm), select the transparent GIF (imgMap.gif in the divMap layer). Then choose Edit>Paste

Applying the Behaviors

Now that your layout is complete, it is time to add all the JavaScript you need to make things work. Don't panic—you won't be doing any hand coding at all. If you can push a few buttons (and obviously you *can* because you've gotten this far already), you can do this! All the JavaScript code needed to complete this project is inserted by way of third-party Dreamweaver extensions and the built-in Show-Hide Layers behavior.

Note: In order to complete these steps, you must be allowing events for 4.0 and later browsers. To verify this, click the Add (+) button on the Behaviors panel, choose Show Events For and make sure that 4.0 and Later Browsers is checked.

Aligning the Layout

We've decided that this layout would look best if it is centered horizontally and vertically in the browser. In order to achieve this effect, we must apply the Align Layers extension by Massimo Foti.

1 Choose the <body> tag in the lower left of the document window.

2 On the Behaviors panel (Window>Behaviors) click the Add (+) button and choose Layer>Align Layer from the pop-up menu.

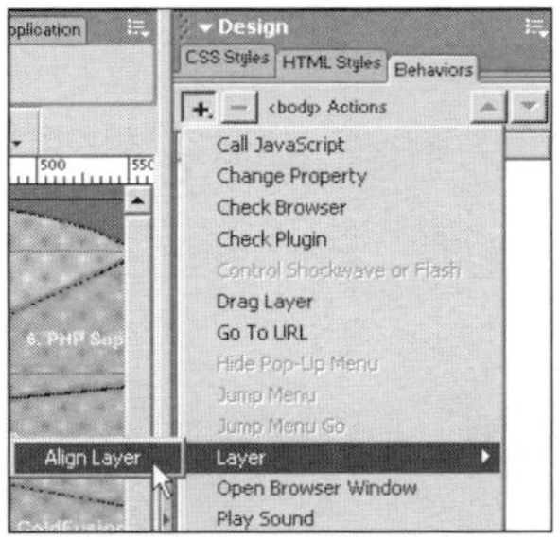

Choose the Align Layer option from the Layers submenu in the Behaviors panel.

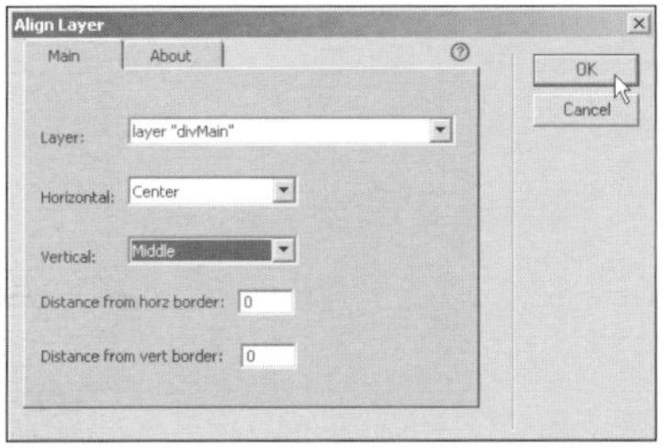

Use the Align Layer extension by Massimo Foti to center the divMain layer on the page.

3 In the dialog that appears, choose the following settings:

Layer: layer **"divMain"**

Horizontal: **Center**

Vertical: **Middle**

Distance from horz border: **0**

Distance from vert border: **0**

Tip: Click the question mark icon to go to the online demo of the extension in use.

4 Click OK. The event should appear as onLoad in the Behaviors panel.

5 Repeat Steps 1 through 3. Click OK and a second instance of the behavior will appear onLoad.

6 Change one of the two onLoad events to onResize.

To change a behavior's event:

- Click the behavior listed in the panel.
- Choose the arrow between the event and the action. A list of events will appear.
- Choose the appropriate event.

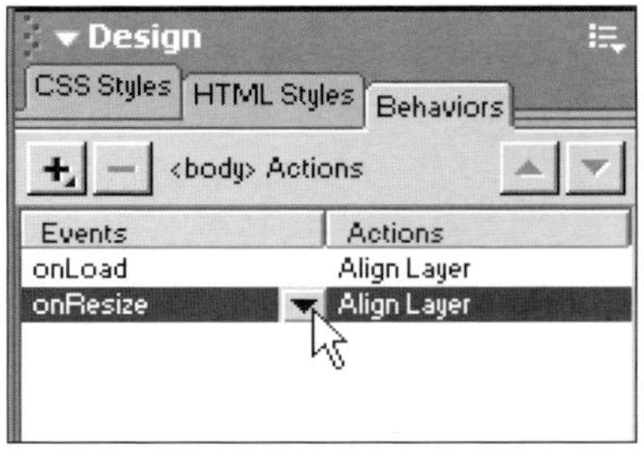

After applying the Align Layer behavior twice, you should have both an onLoad and onResize event listed in the Behaviors panel.

When the page loads, the layer and all of its contents will be snapped to the center of the browser. If the browser's size is changed, the snapping will occur again so that the layout is always in the desired position.

Showing and Hiding the Layers

Each button will need the Show-Hide Layers behavior applied twice. The first time will be set to show the button's Over state layer when the mouse moves over the hotspot. The second time the behavior is applied it will be set to hide the same layer. We'll leave the layers' visibility at default in the Property inspector (no eye icon beside it in the Layers panel) for now. We'll adjust the visibility a bit later.

Beginning with the hotspot that covers the first button for each of the hotspots, follow these steps:

1. Select the hotspot.
2. On the Behaviors panel, click the Add (+) button and choose Show-Hide Layers from the pop-up menu.

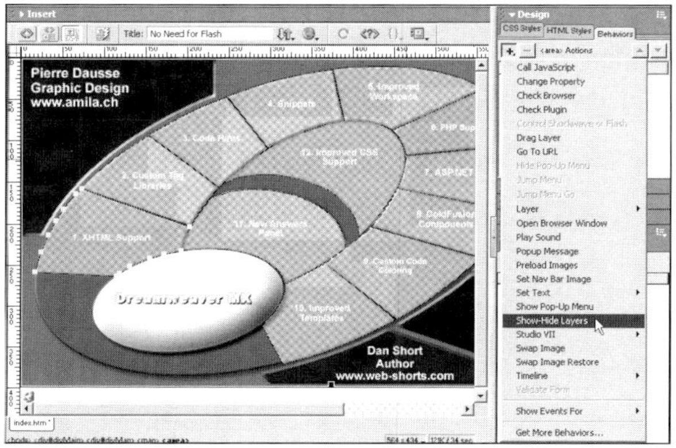

Select each hotspot and add a Show-Hide Layer behavior.

3. Select the layer that should be shown, then click the Show button. The layer will now be marked with (show) beside it.
4. Click OK.
5. Verify that the event listed in the Behaviors panel is listed as onMouseOver.
6. On the Behaviors panel, click the Add (+) button and choose Show-Hide Layers from the pop-up menu.
7. Select the same layer that was previously shown, and then click the Hide button. The layer will now be marked with (hide) beside it.

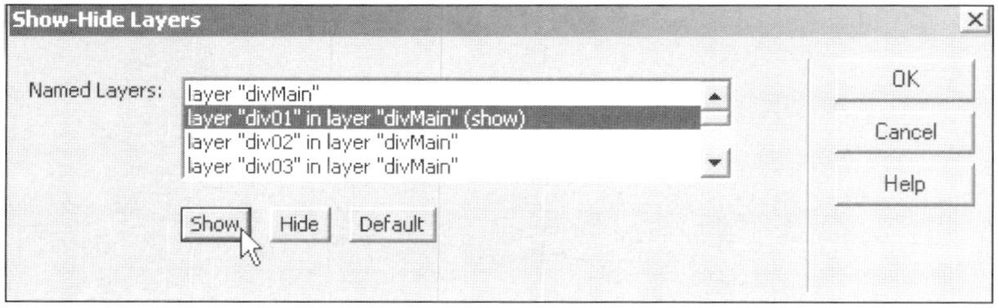

Choose the corresponding layer to show for each hotspot.

8 Select the second listed behavior in the panel—the one you just added. Change the event to onMouseOut in the Behaviors panel. You may notice that the event jumps above the onMouseOver event. This is normal, so don't worry about it.

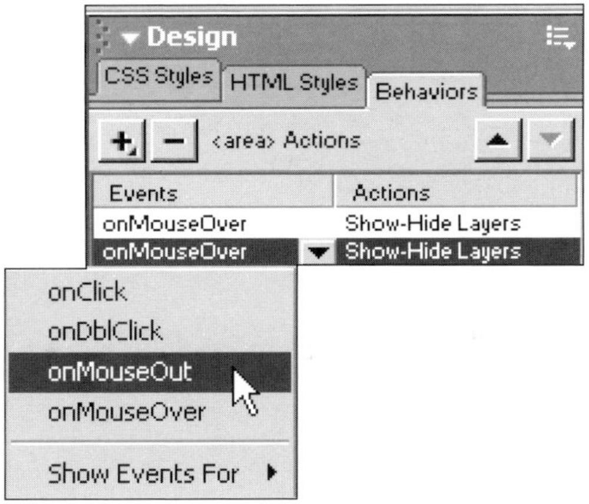

Change the second behavior—which hides the layer—to onMouseOut.

Tip: It is very easy to accidentally move a hotspot. Keep the History panel open as you follow the steps, and if you make a mistake, you'll see the step listed there so you can move back past it by moving the slider.

9 Repeat Steps 1 through 8 for each of the remaining hotspots. Remember to show/hide the proper layer for the hotspot and set the events for onMouseOver and onMouseOut accordingly.

Hiding Until the Page Loads

You have just one more thing to do with Show-Hide Layers. When the page is still loading, you don't want anything to show up in the browser. Like Flash, everything should appear only after it is loaded.

First, we hide all of the layers. The easiest way to do this is to click to the left of each layer listed in the Layers panel. Click until what appears to be a closed eye is shown to the left of each listed layer. Do this for all listed layers except the divMap layer that will be left at default (no icon).

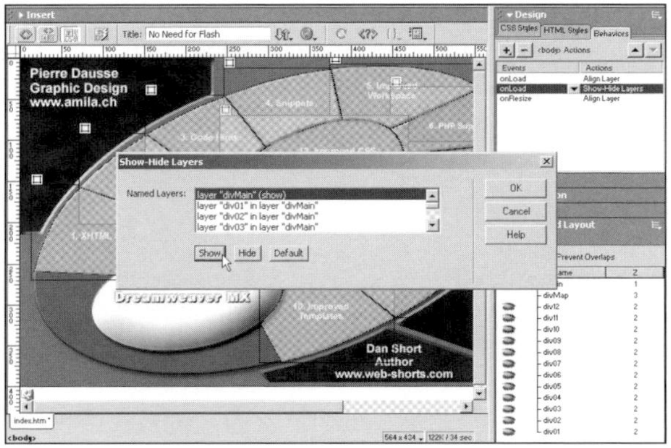

To give the impression of a fully loaded Flash movie, apply the Show-Hide Layer behavior to the <body> tag to show the divMain layer once the entire page has finished loading.

Similar to the steps you followed previously, perform these steps:

1. Choose the <body> tag in the lower left of the document window.
2. On the Behaviors panel, click the Add (+) button and choose Show-Hide Layers from the pop-up menu.
3. Select the divMain layer from the list. The layer will now be marked with (show) beside it.
4. Click OK.
5. The event listed in the Behaviors panel should be onLoad.

Dealing with Resized Browser Windows

Dreamweaver has a native command known as the Netscape Resize Fix. This command adds code to the page that will force Netscape 4.x to reload so that layers will be properly positioned if the browser is resized. If there is an onResize event called on the <body> tag, the Netscape Resize Fix will fail. We've already added an onResize event with the Align Layer behavior. Fortunately, there is a fix for this situation: ReDoIt by PVII.

> **Note:** The Netscape Resize Fix must already be inserted for ReDoIt to be enabled. Choose Commands>Add/Remove Netscape Resize Fix. If you see a button labeled Add, click it. If you see a button labeled Remove, click Cancel.

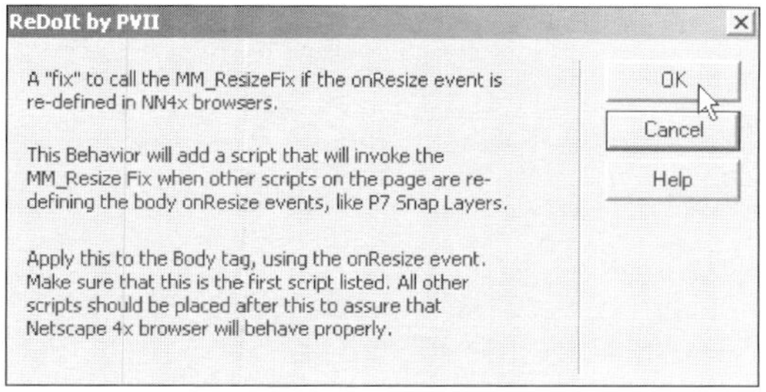

Add the Project VII ReDoIt extension to the <body> tag to get past a bug that occurs in Netscape 4.x when a page has more than one onResize event.

To add the Project Seven ReDoIt extension, follow these steps:

1. Because the layers were set to hidden, the border should not be showing at this time. Click anywhere inside the document window. However if the layer is showing for some reason, be sure to click anywhere outside the divMain layer in the document.
2. Before applying the behavior, verify that Behavior panel indicates <body> Action to the right of the Remove (–) button.
3. On the Behaviors panel, click the Add (+) button. Choose Studio VII from the pop-up menu and select ReDoIt by PVII in the submenu.
4. When the dialog appears, all you need to do is click OK. The behavior will show up with the other ones we applied earlier. The event is automatically set to onResize.

Note: Clicking the <body> tag in the Tag Selector may not work in this instance. Be sure to click in the document—but not inside the divMain layer. Otherwise, the extension will be dimmed—and hence unavailable—in the Behaviors panel.

The ReDoIt action should occur before all other onResize events, as mentioned in the dialog box you saw when you applied the extension. Follow these simple steps to ensure that it is the first onResize event fired.

1. Select the ReDoIt action listed in the Behaviors panel.
2. Click the Move Up arrow to move the Behavior upward in the list. You may move it all the way to the top of the list if you like, but as long as it is above the other onResize event, that is all that matters.

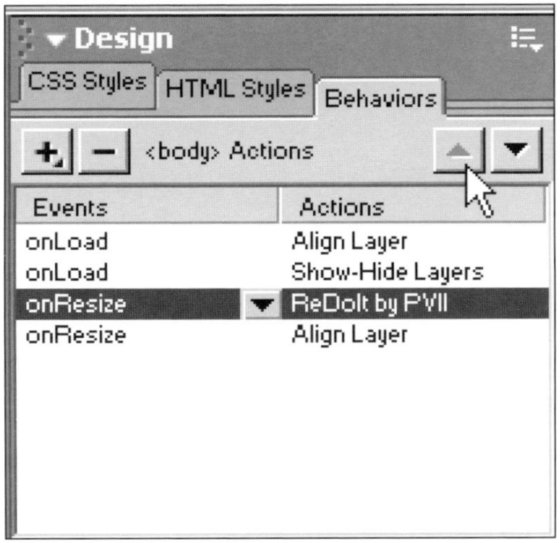

Make sure that the ReDoIt behavior appears before the Align Layer behavior; making ReDoIt the first onResize event listed.

A Little Bit of CSS

By now, you've probably previewed your work to see what you've achieved. You'll see that you have a great layout but it is sitting in the middle of a white page in the browser. We'll take care of that in these final steps:

Note: Color values, though sampled from the image, may not always match the graphic in the browser. To avoid this issue it is best that you use an image as a background that is a clipping of the original graphic and exported using the exact same optimization settings. We've chosen to use CSS rather than attributes of the <body> tag, in view of the fact that CSS is the recommended standard by the W3C.

1 Temporarily turn on the visibility of the divMain layer so that you will be able to sample a color from it. If you happen to know the background color value, you can skip this step.

2 If the CSS Styles panel is not already available, choose Window>CSS Styles.

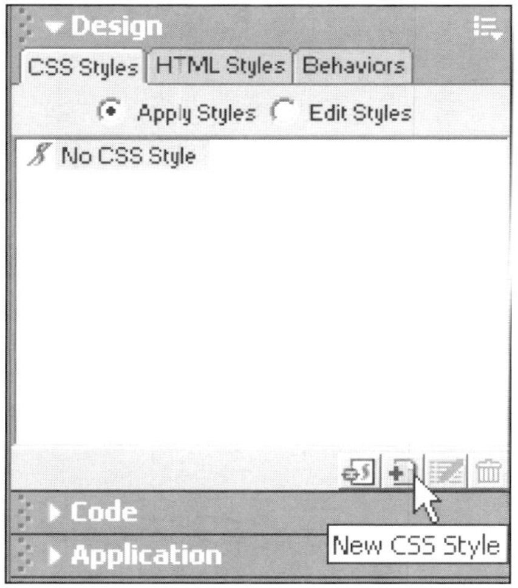

Click the New CSS Style button to add new styles to your page.

3 Select the New CSS Styles button near the bottom of the panel.

4 Select the following options in the New CSS Styles dialog that appears:

Tag: body

Type: Redefine HTML tag

Define In: This Document Only

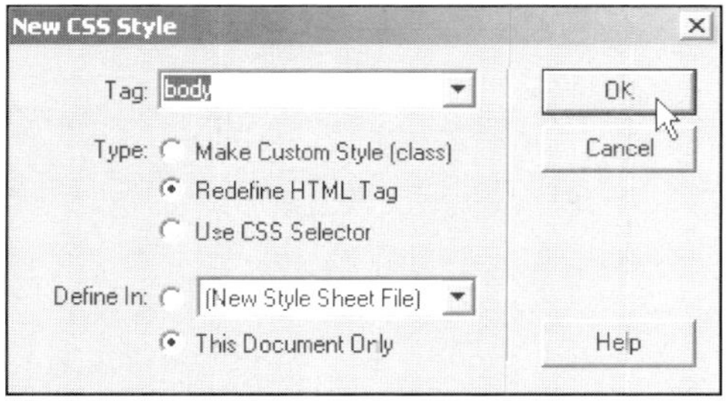

Redefine the <body> tag and click OK to open the Style Definition dialog box.

5 Click OK. In the CSS style definition for body dialog box, click Background in the category listing on the left.

6 Enter the background color as #676767 or sample the gray color using the color picker that appears if you click the color swatch.

7 In the background image field, enter the path to the imgBackground.jpg provided, or use the Browse button to locate it.

8 When you are done, click OK. The style definition should look like this in Code view:

```
body {
     background-color: #676767;
     background-image:
     ➥url(images/imgBackground.jpg);
}
```

9 Unless you skipped Step 1, return the visibility of divMain to hidden.

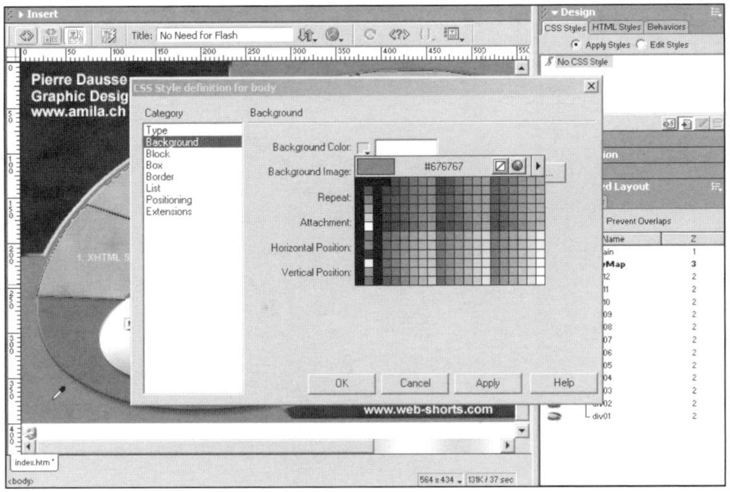

Use the color picker to sample the gray background of the layout graphic so that the page background will match our jpg.

The background color is used so that while the image loads, the background is still a closely matched color to the layout.

Modifications

Feel free to explore additional possibilities with this example once you have completed the project. For example, you could make the layers each appear to be pressed once consecutively—by using Timelines when the page is loaded.

We have provided an example of this concept in the project folder named modification.htm. Preview it in the Browser to see the effect, and then examine the Timeline that was added. Imagine creating a puzzle with pieces that are revealed with each click. With a little creativity, you will surely come up with many possibilities.

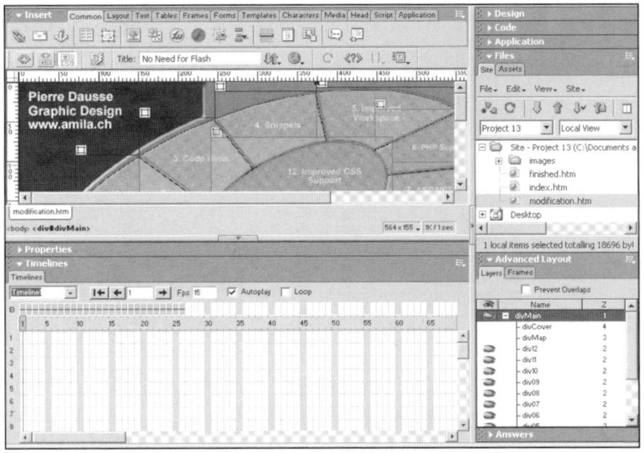

One option for modification is to involve the use of Timelines in the project

"The important thing is this:

to be able at any moment to sacrifice

who we are for what we could become."

—CHARLES DUBOIS

APPENDIX
WHAT'S ON THE CD-ROM

The accompanying CD-ROM is packed with all sorts of exercise files and products to help you work with this book and with Macromedia Dreamweaver MX. The following sections contain detailed descriptions of the CD's contents.

For more information about the use of this CD, please review the ReadMe.txt file in the root directory. This file includes important disclaimer information, as well as information about installation, system requirements, troubleshooting, and technical support.

Technical Support Issues: If you have any difficulties with this CD, you can access our web site at www.newriders.com.

Loading the CD Files

To load the files from the CD, insert the disc into your CD-ROM drive. If autoplay is enabled on your machine, the CD-ROM setup program starts automatically the first time you insert the disc. You can copy the files to your hard drive or use them right off the disc.

Note: This CD-ROM uses long and mixed-case filenames, requiring the use of a protected mode CD-ROM driver.

Exercise Files

This CD contains all the files you'll need to complete the exercises in *Dreamweaver MX Magic*. These files can be found in the root directory's Projects folder. To use these files, you need to copy the individual projects to your hard drive, and you are prompted to do so at the beginning of each exercise.

Third-Party Programs

This CD also contains several third-party programs and demos from leading industry companies. These programs have been carefully selected to help you strengthen your professional skills in Dreamweaver MX.

Please note that some of the programs included on this CD-ROM are shareware, "try-before-you-buy" software. Please support these independent vendors by purchasing or registering any shareware software that you use for more than 30 days. Check with the documentation provided with the software to find out where and how to register the product.

Software Folder

To save you time downloading from the Internet, we've included copies of the following demo software for you:

- Macromedia Dreamweaver MX demo
- Macromedia Fireworks MX demo
- Macromedia ColdFusion MX demo

You might want to try the new version of Dreamweaver because it's used throughout each of the book's projects; however, only some of the projects integrate Fireworks and ColdFusion.

Extensions Folder

Several of the projects in this book require the use of Dreamweaver extensions. You will find these in the Extensions folder. Please see the individual projects for installation requirements.

Read This Before Opening the Software

By opening the CD package, you agree to be bound by the following agreement:

You may not copy or redistribute the entire CD-ROM as a whole. Copying and redistribution of individual software programs on the CD-ROM is governed by terms set by individual copyright holders.

The installer, code, images, actions, and brushes from the authors are copyrighted by the publisher and the authors.

This software is sold as-is, without warranty of any kind, either expressed or implied, including but not limited to the implied warranties of merchantability and fitness for a particular purpose. Neither the publisher nor its dealers or distributors assumes any liability for any alleged or actual damages arising from the use of this program. (Some states do not allow for the exclusion of implied warranties, so the exclusion may not apply to you.)

INDEX

Symbols

A

B

C

D

G-H

I

J-L

M

Q-R

S

HOW TO CONTACT US

VISIT OUR WEB SITE

WWW.NEWRIDERS.COM

On our web site, you'll find information about our other books, authors, tables of contents, and book errata. You will also find information about book registration and how to purchase our books, both domestically and internationally.

EMAIL US

Contact us at: **nrfeedback@newriders.com**

- If you have comments or questions about this book
- To report errors that you have found in this book
- If you have a book proposal to submit or are interested in writing for New Riders
- If you are an expert in a computer topic or technology and are interested in being a technical editor who reviews manuscripts for technical accuracy

Contact us at: **nreducation@newriders.com**

- If you are an instructor from an educational institution who wants to preview New Riders books for classroom use. Email should include your name, title, school, department, address, phone number, office days/hours, text in use, and enrollment, along with your request for desk/examination copies and/or additional information.

Contact us at: **nrmedia@newriders.com**

- If you are a member of the media who is interested in reviewing copies of New Riders books. Send your name, mailing address, and email address, along with the name of the publication or web site you work for.

BULK PURCHASES/CORPORATE SALES

The publisher offers discounts on this book when ordered in quantity for bulk purchases and special sales. For sales within the U.S., please contact: Corporate and Government Sales (800) 382-3419 or **corpsales@pearsontechgroup.com**. Outside of the U.S., please contact: International Sales (317) 581-3793 or **international@pearsontechgroup.com**.

WRITE TO US

New Riders Publishing
201 W. 103rd St.
Indianapolis, IN 46290-1097

CALL/FAX US

Toll-free (800) 571-5840
If outside U.S. (317) 581-3500
Ask for New Riders
FAX: (317) 581-4663

New Riders

WWW.NEWRIDERS.COM

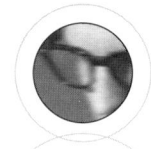

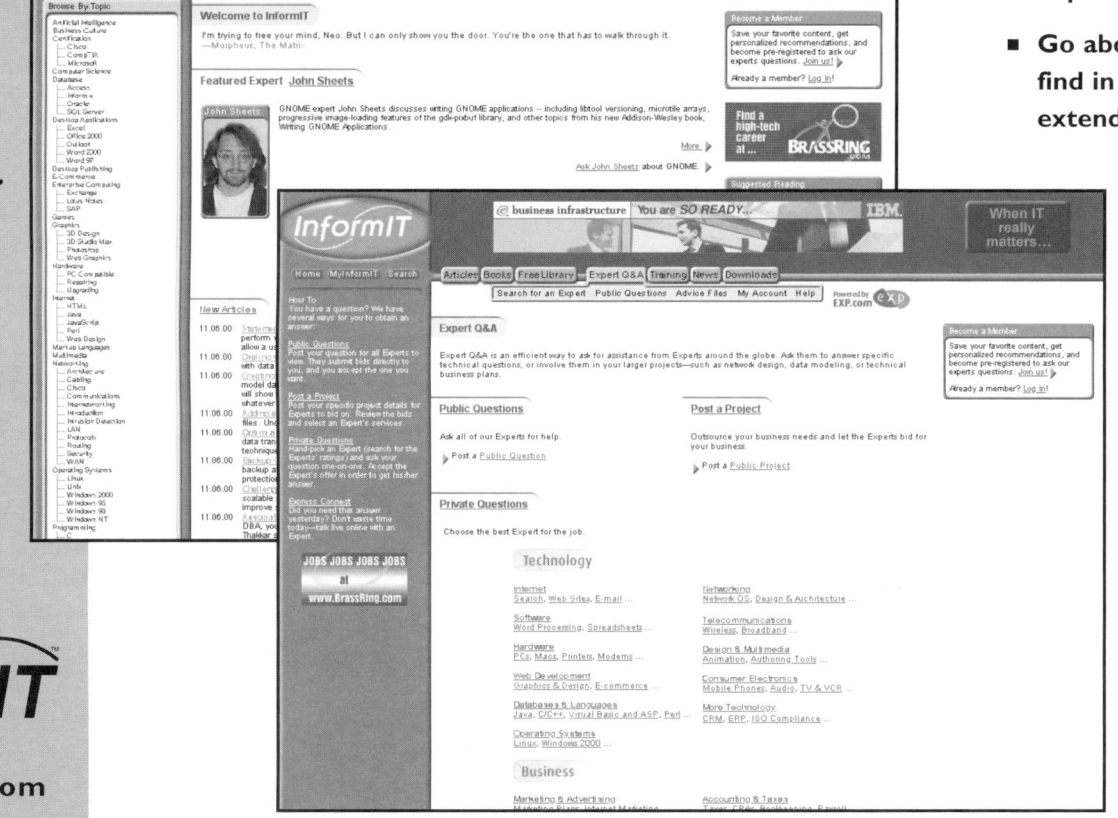

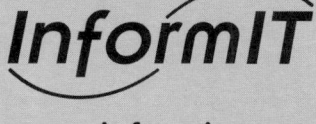